MARKETING MANAGEMENT

A FINANCE EMPHASIS

(Fourth Edition - thoroughly revised)

MARKETING MANAGEMENT

A FINANCE EMPHASIS

(Fourth Edition - thoroughly revised)

B.K. CHATTERJEE

JAICO PUBLISHING HOUSE

Ahmedabad Bangalore Bhopal Chennai
Delhi Hyderabad Kolkata Lucknow Mumbai

Published by Jaico Publishing House
A-2 Jash Chambers, 7-A Sir Phirozshah Mehta Road
Fort, Mumbai - 400 001
jaicopub@jaicobooks.com
www.jaicobooks.com

MARKETING MANAGEMENT: A FINANCE EMPHASIS
ISBN 81-7224-654-4

First Jaico Impression: 1989
11th Jaico Impression: 2012

Printed by
Pashupati Printers, Delhi

To

My Uncles

Late S K Chattakhandi

Late P K Chattakhandi

who have been my beacon lights

PREFACE

The continuous and growing popularity of this book is a matter of satisfaction. Since the print copies of its third edition have nearly exhausted, this fourth edition is published. Even though this does not introduce too many major changes, this edition contains some qualitative improvements:

- One of the Chapters i.e. Chapter 20 (Evaluation of Distribution) has been thoroughly revised and rewritten.
- Two important topics have been added, which are:
  Financial Evaluation of Brand (in chapter 11) and
  Life Cycle Costing (in chapter 13).
- Correction of several data entry / printing errors that had inadvertently crept in, in the third edition.

I have recently conducted two Management Development Programmes at the Indian Institute of Management Calcutta on the theme of this book, using of course a bit different title namely, "Marketing Finance Interface". I have been regularly offering this subject also as an optional course in Marketing to the post-graduate students of the Institute, The conceptual discussions and illustrations in the book are consistently well received by the discerning students and corporate executives. The experience gained through such recent involvements has been made use of in introducing some qualitative changes in this revision of the book, I trust the readers also will notice and like these value additions.

Apart from my academic and professional friends and colleagues mentioned in the note of Acknowledgement in the third edition, I have to mention here the name of Prof. Sunil Shah, one of my bright ex-students and now a Financial Consultant & Visiting Faculty, IIM Calcutta for assisting me in revising this book.

— B K Chatterjee

PREFACE (3RD EDITION)

Way back in 1982, when the 'Marketing Management : A Finance Emphasis' was first published with the stated objective of integrating finance and marketing functions in an enterprise, the need for such integration or interface was just emerging in the Indian industrial management. Naturally the book was received well by the practising marketing executives as well as the academic community including the business schools all over the country.

Over these years, the book — considered to be a pioneering work in responsible quarters — has gone for multiple reprints, which is an indication of its popularity and usefulness. For the last couple of years we have been seriously thinking of bringing out a thoroughly revised edition of the book, incorporating in the process the latest developments in the field. Despite our best intentions, however, this could not been done so far. Better late than never — we have at last been able to present to our discerning readers and patrons this handy volume, after restructuring and revising the entire contents of its earlier versions.

It may not be out of place to mention here some of the important changes underlying this revision :

i) The chapter that have been thoroughly rewritten are:
   - Marketing Management - An Overview,
   - Long-range Planning, rechristened as 'Corporate Planning and Marketing'
   - Planning the Marketing Organisation
   - Marginal Costing & Break Even Analysis
   - Investment Decisions
   - The entire Section VI comprising Marketing Control

ii) The chapters deleted are :
   - Marketing Arithmetic and Indirect Taxes
   - Profit Planning
   - Product Pruning Decisions

   (since the relevant materials under these have been included in different other chapters elsewhere.)

PREFACE

iii) The new chapters added are :
Marketing Audit
Receivables Management

Apart from these major changes, the contents of the other chapters have also been reviewed and revised.

Here is an extract from the Preface of the first edition of the book, since the observations continue to remain valid :

> This book is neither exclusively on Marketing Management nor on Financial Management & Management Accounting. Yet it covers almost all the important and modern concepts in Marketing Management and also most of those principles, tenets, tools and techniques in Financial Management & Management Accounting which have some relevance to marketing operations. What the book tries, therefore, is an integration between the principles and concepts of Marketing Management and the tools and techniques of Financial Management & Management Accounting. Therefore, the book could have been titled in various other ways say, <u>Marketing, Finance, Marketing Finance and Evaluation, Marketing Finance Interface, Marketing Control, Marketing MIS and Control etc.</u> And each of these titles would have been perhaps equally relevant as the present one in indicating the nature and purpose of this book.

Finally, we have brought to bear upon this revised edition our years of experience in the industry, as management consultants and as visiting faculty to some of the leading management institutes like Jamnalal Bajaj Institute / Mumbai, University of Calcutta and Indian Institute of Management, Calcutta. We believe this has contributed towards substantial 'value addition' of the treatise.

ACKNOWLEDGEMENTS

Our acknowledgements are due to the large number of marketing executives in our client-organisations who have interacted with us in course of consultancy work with them, executives who have attended our Management Development Programmes in marketing and allied fields and our MBA students who have attended our classes on this subject. It is indeed these persons who have stimulated our thought-process underlying this work. Though unnamed, they cannot remain unsung and unhonoured.

Our grateful thanks are due to, besides numerous other friends and colleagues :

Prof. S K Chakraborty (Management Centre for Human Values, Indian Institute of Management, Calcutta) who is a friend, philosopher and guide and a continuous source of inspiration.

Our good friends in the teaching fraternity viz. Prof. (Dr.) P Chattopadhyay (Burdwan university), Prof. (Dr.) Bhabatosh Banerjee, (Calcutta University), Prof. Vinod Javeri (Institute of Modern Management, Calcutta) and Dr. Anand Patkar (Jamnalal Bajaj Institute, Mumbai and a Management Consultant).

My debts are due to my late father, mother, wife Supriya and son Tathagata who have been my never-failing sources of inspiration.

Mumbai
March 1998

B K Chatterjee

LIST OF ILLUSTRATIONS (I), TABLES (T), DIAGRAMS (D) & CASES(C)

CONTENTS

SECTION III
MARKETING PLANNING 122-175

SECTION IV
MARKETING DECISION 180-268

SECTION V
MARKETING PERFORMANCE EVALUATION 269-347

SECTION I

GENERAL INTRODUCTION

This first section of the book comprising three chapters is devoted to clearing the ground. Chapter 1 attempts to present in an encapsulated form the principles and concepts of Marketing Management. Similarly, Chapter 2 gives a bird's-eye view of all the basic principles and concepts of Accounting and Finance. Chapter 3 presents the underlying theme of the book itself, viz., Marketing Finance Interface. In sum, these Chapters bring Marketing and Finance closer to each other and attempt to bring out the independence as well as interdependence between these two disciplines, which in turn form the basis of two very important functional areas in the management of an enterprise.

CHAPTER 1

MARKETING MANAGEMENT—AN OVERVIEW

1. Definition of Marketing; 2. Role of Marketing in Society; 3. Market Orientation; 4. Market; 5. Marketing Mix; 6. Sales Management; 7. Sales Forecasting

1. DEFINITION OF MARKETING

Marketing has been defined in various ways. A few of such definitions commonly used are :

"......the system of value exchange". (Kotler)

"....... the process of discovering and translating consumer needs and wants into product and service specifications creating demand for these products and services, and then in turn expanding this demand." (Hansen)

"The management function which organizes and directs all those business activities involved in assessing and converting customer purchasing power into effective demand for a specific product or service, and in moving the product or service to the final consumer or user so as to achieve the profit target or other objectives set by a company." (The Institute of Marketing, USA)

If one reads between the lines, the definitions quoted above seek to highlight some basic features of marketing as an important function at the organisational level (micro) as well as the role of marketing at the societal level (macro). Peter Drucker presented an excellent synthesis of these two apparently divergent aspects viz.organisation and societal, when he observed, 'There is only one valid definition of business purpose: to create a customer', and also that, the very justification for the existence of a business unit in society is two-fold, viz innovation and marketing.

2. ROLE OF MARKETING IN SOCIETY

The purpose and role of marketing has undergone a sea-change during the current century. Till the early years of the 20th century, the concept of marketing was unknown. What was known was selling, to be more precise, trading. Traders were criticised severely for hoarding, charging high prices and exploiting the customers. Karl Marx saw in the 19th century little room for the middlemen who as parasites took away profits from the producers and caused increase in prices for the consumers. Even Galbraith in his The Affluent Society, wrote : "..... the fact that wants can be synthesized by advertising, catalyzed by salesmanship and shaped by the discreet manipulations of the persuaders shows that they are not very urgent. A man who is hungry need never be told of his need for food..."

We may identify here a few areas where marketing affects or influences society and consumer welfare in a rather undesirable manner.

Undesirable Impact of Marketing on Society :

(a) high prices; (b) manipulation of demand; (c) high pressure selling; (d) cultural pollution; (e) excessive political power; and (f) social rivalry.

Undesirable Impact of Marketing on Consumer Welfare :

(a) high prices; (b) manipulation of demand; (c) high pressure selling; (d) shoddy or unsafe products; and (e) minority discrimination.

However, the marketing concept is essentially a philosophy of service with mutual gain. In practice, it controls the economy by an invisible hand to carry out the mandates of consumer sovereignty.

Let us now examine the contribution of marketing to society and the social value of marketing which is closely related to this. It is accepted that the wealth of a society increases through increase in value added. Let us imagine how marketing could contribute towards value addition and increase society's wealth. Take, for example, handlooms and other handicrafts in India. Prices charged are usually many times more than the basic material cost. Therefore, a significant amount of value gets added. Sometimes, such value addition may be psychological than real; but when these products are marketed in India as well as abroad, society's wealth definitely increases. The economy benefits by the greater quantum of capital formation, greater revenue to the exchequer, higher employment and increase in the equity owners' wealth, which in turn helps accelerate capital formation. In the process, there is also some redistribution of wealth from the richer to the poorer sections of society. These phenomena are true, more or less, in respect of all products, in all countries. Marketing efforts could thus get credit for increased buoyancy in economic activities.

MARKET ORIENTATION

The essence of marketing lies in market-orientation as distinct from product orientation or, for that matter, any other orientation. A company that prefers to opt for the marketing approach looks to the market for the direction of its planning and decision-making and it redirects all aspects of the company activity towards satisfying the wants and needs of its customers at an optimum level of profit, though it may not be the maximum in the short run. It is said to be a 'market-oriented' approach. The traditional distinction is between the 'product-oriented company', with its emphasis on selling what the company can make, and the 'market-oriented company', which gears its efforts to producing what the market demands.

Essentially, market orientation has two important components viz., customer orientation and competitor orientation. Thus, a market-orientated company will have to be customer-centered in the first place. At the same time it should also necessarily be competitor-centered, that is, equipped with up-to-date information on competitors' strengths, weaknesses, objectives and strategies.

The question, "what business are we in ?" has influenced the marketing concept significantly. In his famous article 'Marketing Myopia', Theodore Levitt drew attention to the dangers of defining a company's business by its production capabilities rather than by the market in which it was competing. However, marketing myopia should not be a plea for indiscriminate diversification. It only points to the logic of taking the market as the focal point for the corporate enterprise to determine the most profitable area it can enter into, to make use of the expertise developed earlier in the fundamental activities. The continuous search for new products and opportunities could be systematic and useful through this approach.

Our effort to understand the marketing concept brings us immediately to some basic points of distinction between marketing and selling, as follows :

CRITERIA	SELLING	MARKETING
a. Orientation	Production capability	Market acceptability or Product-Market compatibility
b. Approach	Selling a product / Service	Need identification & fulfillment
c. Direction	*Push* (e.g.'push' sale of tickets for a theatrical performance of an amateur group)	*Pull* (e.g. sale of tickets for a multistarrer film or theater show — the spectators are pulled towards the venue)
d. Emphasis	*Aggressive Salesmanship* (An aggressive salesman is one who can sell refrigerators to the Eskimos and room heaters in the Gulf countries.	Creating a niche of monopoly or market niche.

e. Business Definition	In terms of the product services, the company sells / renders e.g.	In terms of the market, the company operates in e.g.
	Automobile	Transportation
	Bread	Nutrition
	Cash Registers	Protection
	Mattresses	Comfort
	Tea	Drinking satisfaction or Beverage
	Calculating machines	Business machines
	Computers	Problem solving Information Technology
f. Time-Frame	Short to medium run	Medium to long - run.

As a matter of fact, good marketing may eventually make selling superfluous. But we should not drag this distinction between marketing and selling too far and put these into two different water-tight compartments. In the final analysis, selling is an integral part of marketing. Philip Kotler has rightly observed, marketing is finding a product for the market and at its worst a market for the product. The latter is tantamount to selling. There are several other facets of marketing besides selling. These are promotion and advertisement, distribution and market researches, including market surveys with an eye on designing marketing strategies and tactics. But all these activities will ultimately have to boil down to or reflect in the sales graph of the company.

4. MARKET

In ordinary parlance, market means a particular location where buyers and sellers meet and transact purchases and sales. Taking a broader view than this, people understand market in terms of a geographical territory having identified customers. From the viewpoint of marketing management, the market has a very wide connotation. Market includes a location or a territory, a customer or a group of customers, a particular type or category of customers, specific application(s) or end-use(s) of a product, etc. Basically and essentially, market is people and marketing is influencing the buying decisions of people.

Different Types of Market

The distinction between sellers' market and buyers' market is commonly used to indicate the degree of control an enterprise could exercise at the marketplace in general and the customers in particular. In a sellers' market situation, an enterprise can have substantial control over the market whereas in a buyers' market, the enterprise can hardly exercise any control over the market and such a situation thereof demands great deal of marketing and selling skill..

Another broad distinction can be drawn between consumer goods market, industrial goods market, service market and social market. The main characteristics of these markets are given below :

Consumer goods market - refers to ultimate consumers who buy products for direct consumption.

Industrial goods market - where products are bought not for direct consumption but for intermediate uses. Industrial markets are again of two broad types viz, standard products and non-standard (custom - built) products. Another important factor relevant to industrial market is service after sales.

Service market - where some specific service is rendered like Banking, Insurance, Travel & Tourism, Consultancy etc.

Social market - where social service e.g.education, family planning, health care, literacy drive and rural development are rendered or marketed.

The influences operating on the buying decisions vary between different types of markets. Unlike the consumer market, where buying is guided more or less by need and impulse, the buying motivation for industrial products could be technical, financial and partly psychological. In service and social markets, buying is mainly based on the needs of the people and urge to serve the people respectively.

Market Segmentation

Market segmentation is basically concerned with dividing the market into several sub-markets or segments, each of which is of significant characteristics and together form a meaningful homogeneous group. The purpose of segmentation is to determine differences among buyers which may be consequential in choosing among them or marketing to them.

The various bases of market grouping or segmentation are as follows:

(a) Territorial, Regional or Geographical segmentation, viz., North, South, East and West Zones.
(b) Demographic segmentation - based on income, education, age, sex, etc.
(c) Social segmentation - in respect of social class and status.
(d) Psychological segmentation - based on attitudes, values, behavioural patterns, etc.
(e) Volume-wise segmentation - based on buying quantity.
(f) Quality-wise segmentation-based on quality consciousness.
(g) Use-wise segmentation - based on various uses of the same product.

The benefits of market segmentation are :

(a) The seller is in a better position to locate his target group and compare market effectiveness.
(b) The seller can make finer adjustments of his products and their marketing appeals.
(c) Segmentation is the key to economic or cost-effective market coverage.
(d) By identifying the target customer, it is possible to

reduce expensive sales and service time, cut down wasted calls and make advertising and promotion more purposeful and effective in communicating with the market.

(e) Specific products and policies can be designed for each target group and attempts made to penetrate those that appear most favourable, that is, ensuring in-depth market penetration.

Product Differentiation :

Product differentiation is securing a measure of control over the demand for a product by advertising or promoting the differences between the product and the other products of competing sellers. The aim is to differentiate a product from the competitors, products, by making it appear special in respect of quality, style or image. In markets characterised by product differentiation, the individual firm is more flexible in its pricing decision. Product differences whether in style or in functional features etc., serve to desensitize the buyer to existing prices.

Incidentally, in the Japanese system, there is an expression viz. DANTOTSU, meaning by far superior, something unique. When one likes to add some DANTOTSU features to a product, the purpose is actually product differentiation.

Market Segmentation (MS) and Product Differentiation (PD) are complementary with the aim of ensuring an enduring marketing effectiveness — MS is to identify the target group and PD to have a hold over the group.

MARKET SIZE VIS-A-VIS MARKET SHARE :

Let us study the following bar diagram, referring to the hypothetical market of a certain consumer product, say toothpaste.

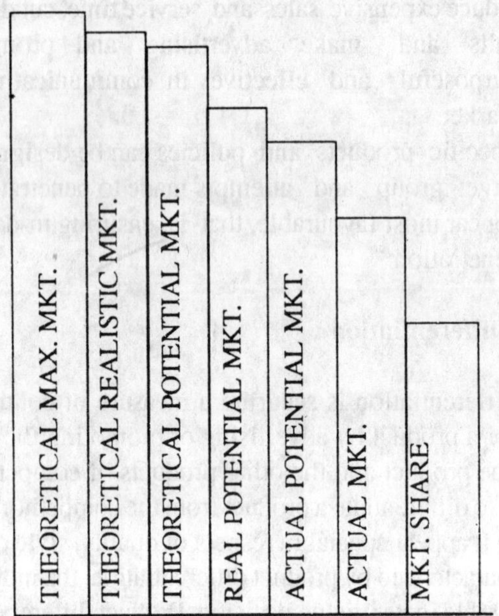

The theoretical maximum market could be the entire population of India, say 900 million. Leaving out children below the age group of 2/3 years we shall get theoretical Realistic Market. In this manner, through successive reductions, due to various reasons, we shall arrive at the actual market size and a particular firm's share of the market or its market share. The position depicted above is, however, likely to change over time at all the stages, due partly to population increase and partly to enhanced marketing efforts.

A company's share of the market is determined not just by the quantity the company sells but by the actual size of the market. If, suppose, the market size (actual market) increases by 30 per cent, and the particular company's sales increase by 20 per cent, its share of the market will come down. If this phenomenon is allowed to continue, after a certain period of time, say 5/7 years, the company's market share will have come down to a negligible level, though volume-wise and value-wise, the company might have increased its sales substantially.

5. MARKETING MIX

Marketing mix, to be more precise, management of the marketing mix, is explained here with the help of a conceptual model.

Marketing Mix

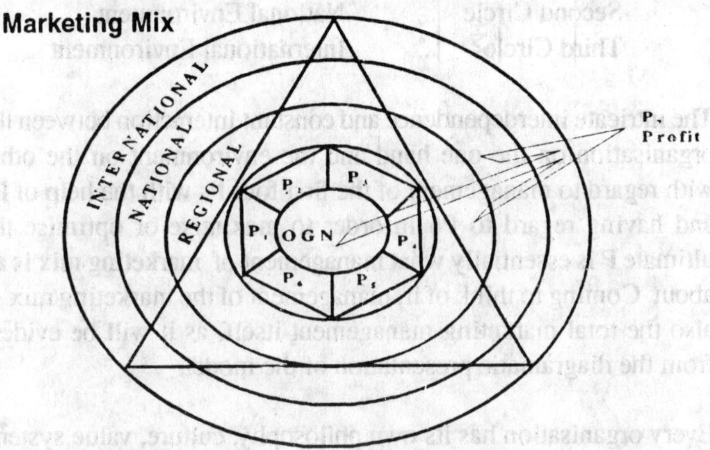

The model is developed around the nucleus, namely, marketing organisation at the centre. Over this, there are four Ps to be managed by the marketing organisation. These are :

P1 .... Product
P2 .... Price
P3 .... Promotion & Advertisement
P4 .... Placement or Distribution

In addition to these four Ps, a few more Ps also shown in the model need to be in our reckoning. These are :

P5 .... Packaging (for our purpose subsumed by P1— Product)
P5 .... People
P6 .... Public
P7 .... Profit (final and the ultimate P).

Management of the Marketing Mix thus implies management by the marketing organisation of Product (including packaging), Price, Promotion and Placement with the help of People, due regard being had to the Public, in order to maximise the last P that is Profit.

Outside the organisation, there is the environment. Three layers of environment are shown here through three circles viz.,

First Circle	...	Regional Environment
Second Circle	...	National Environment
Third Circle	...	International Environment

The intricate interdependence and constant interaction between the organisation on the one hand and the environment on the other with regard to management of the first four Ps with the help of P5 and having regard to P6 in order to maximise or optimise the ultimate P is essentially what management of marketing mix is all about. Coming to think of it, management of the marketing mix is also the total marketing management itself, as it will be evident from the diagramatic presentation of the model.

Every organisation has its own philosophy, culture, value system, beliefs and ethos. At a relatively mundane level, it has certain strengths and has also some weaknesses. From another viewpoint, one may have to look at the structure (shell) and the process (functioning) of an organisation.

The environment is a state of nature and is, as such, always in a state of flux. Environment promises opportunities and poses some threats as well to the organisation. From the marketing operations angle, environment may be classified into two types viz., task environment (where the task is accomplished) and macro environment (the larger environment, external to the task environment). The important point to note is that the happenings in the macro environment would very often have their impact on the task environment and thus, help or hinder the performance and achievements of the marketing people in their task environment itself.

As mentioned earlier, environment is always in a state of flux. In fact, there are innumerable factors and forces that are always at play in the environment. And such happenings transmit continuously to the organisation different types of stimuli and the organisation needs to respond to them. It is generally a stimulus-response paradigm.

When a stimulus is not responded to, the state of equilibrium at a given point in time with respect to first four Ps tends to be threatened with disturbances and marketing effectiveness of the organisation is likely to be impaired. Such impairment may still be there when a response of the organisation to a stimulus sent by the environment is not quick, adequate and effective.

The marketing organisation will therefore have to quickly, adequately and effectively make some adjustments in any or all of the four Ps in order to counter the threat of disturbance arising out of some turbulence in the environment, which is ipso facto outside the organisation. A response to a stimulus generally takes the form of an appropriate strategy with some long-term view or tactic (generally short-term in nature) or some tactical policy shift (of short or medium-term nature).

A very pertinent question that may be asked at this stage is : How does the marketing organisation come to know about the emergence and nature of a stimulus? The answer is : It does through a very effective instrument called "Marketing Research". Basically, market research serves to the marketing organisation exactly the same purpose as an antenna does to the television set. The performance of the set in terms of quality and coverage of programs it can capture is uniquely determined by the nature of the antenna — whether dish antenna or booster antenna or ordinary ones. In fact, effectiveness of a marketing organisation can also be gauged by the quality and intensity of its market research activities.

Coming back to the stimulus-response syndrome mentioned earlier, it may be noted that stimuli could be of varying degree of intensity, say, a ripple, wave, cyclone or tidal bore. The nature of response from the marketing organisation will also depend on the degree of intensity of the stimulus. In other words, the organisation may not like to respond to a ripple type stimulus, should respond reasonably well to a wave and will have to respond adequately and also fast enough to a violent cyclone or a tidal bore.

We have mentioned earlier about the factors and forces that are at play in the different layers of the environment. At this stage we may once again look at the triangle in the model, the three hands of which represent three different dimensions:

1st Dimension	......	Competitor's activities
2nd Dimension	......	Customer behaviour
3rd Dimension	......	Socio-cultural and eco-political milieu.

The disturbances in the environment resulting in the stimuli may arise in any or more of the three areas. But which area or areas a particular stimulus has emanated from is important for a marketing organisation to examine before it can plan to respond to the same and, as it has been said earlier, the response has to be timely, adequate and effective.

Before winding up the discussion on the subject of Marketing Mix, it would be useful to indicate the relative importance of the 5 Ps in the different types of marketing, as follows :

Type	P1 Product	P2 Price	P3 Promotion	P4 Placement	P5 Packaging
Consumer Goods	5	3	1	4	2
Industrial Goods	1	2	3	4	5
Services	2	3	4	1	-
Social Marketing	3	4	2	1	-

Notes :

i 1,2,3,4 etc.indicates ranking in terms of relative importance

ii This is a very broad approach only - wide differences may be there in specific cases.

6. SALES MANAGEMENT

Two important aspects we shall deal with here are viz., Sales Policy and Sales Force Management.

Policy is a statement of intention or approach that acts as the guiding star in coordinating and directing the activities of an organisation as a whole or any specific functional area. Just as we have personnel policy, financial policy, etc., a company should also have its own sales policy. Policies are, and should always be, linked with strategies from time to time. Policies should also be subjected to regular periodic reviews in the light of environmental changes.

Some of the areas in sales management in which clear-cut policies need to be formulated and communicated within the organisation are as follows:

a) Trade sales and Govt. or Institutional sales,
b) Direct sales and sales through middlemen/agents,
c) Domestic sales and export sales,
d) Sales to ultimate users and sales to OEMs (Original Equipment Manufacturers)
e) Sale to competitors,
f) Cash sales and credit sales,
g) Product sales and spare parts sales,
h) Sales of low value items/spares (e.g.minimum order value, free distribution),
i) Sale of one product by tagging it with another,
J) Sale against advance,
k) After-sales services, warranty etc.

It would be obvious that prior policy decisions in the above-mentioned areas will have a significant bearing on the company's sales efforts and of course, profitability. Some of these may also provide useful benchmarks for an objective evaluation of sales performances.

Sales force management is almost synonymous with sales management. This comprises, in broad outline, the following :

i) Determining and reviewing the size of sales-force
ii) Selection and recruitment of sales personnel
iii) Training, development and motivation of sales personnel
iv) Organisation of sales conferences and meetings
v) Sales personnel's reports
vi) Evaluation of sales personnel
vii) Compensation and incentive schemes for sales personnel.

7. SALES FORECASTING

Forecasting is an integral part of sales planning and is also used for monitoring sales. Basically forecasting the sales of a particular company depends on total demand forecasting on the one hand and the present as well as projected market share on the other - to be assessed separately for all major product-offerings of the company.

A) Financial and Semi-Financial Tools :

1) Historical analogy method - e.g.demand for steel in India now may be related with that in USA in the 50s.

2) Corresponding period comparison - e.g.demand for textiles in Oct/Nov'91 may be equal to demand for the same in Oct/Nov'90 plus a suitable percentage or growth factor.

3) End-users/buyers expectation method - e.g.demand for water filtration chemicals in metro cities, particularly during the rainy seasons.

B) Quantitative and Statistical Tools :

Time series analysis, including adjustments for seasonal and cyclical variations.

Trend extension or regression analysis — i.e. trend line fitted into the data for a number of periods in the past.

Multi-variable analysis

Exponential Smoothing

Probabilistic models

Input-Output tables/technique

Functional models — i.e. establishing a relationship between one dependent variable with one or more independent variable(s)

Linking factor — e.g.demand for spare parts may be linked with the population of the equipment, using an estimated 'factor' or percentage.

Establishing lead-lag relationship — e.g. heavy order booking of capital goods is an advance indicator of economic prosperity.

Technology Forecasting (TF) — particularly for products highly susceptible to technological obsolescence.

C) Qualitative Methods :

i) Opinions from experts,

ii) Brain-storming,

iii) Delphi Technique,

iv) Scenarios building.

D) Field Survey (Primary Data) :

i) Questionnaire based survey of representative samples, established preferably by stratified Random Sampling Technique.

ii) Bridging factor used in (2) above for estimating universe/ population from samples.

iii) Test marketing.

E) Literature Survey (Secondary Source) :

Through a judicious blend of some of the above-mentioned techniques sales forecasting exercise is to be completed first. Thereafter by applying the projected market share ratio the company's forecasted sales figures should be determined separately for each product or product-group. Target vis-a-vis Budget is the next issue to be tackled and finally sales quota are to be established.

Sales Budget is a realistic estimate of expected volume of sales, both in quantitative and financial terms, the basic inputs being obtained from Sales forecasts. The first and foremost budget is usually the sales budget because sales is the limiting factor in most cases. Other departmental budgets are, of course, to be co-ordinated with sales budget.

Sales Targets are generally set at slightly higher levels than the budget figures. A sales target should be set for each specific sales group and should be such as are within the sales people's capability of achievement, albeit with a good deal of efforts.

The sales target for a group is broken down into sales quota right upto the salesmen's level i.e.sales quota is fixed for each salesman. It is expected that by setting the quota on the higher side the salesman will put extra effort. The sales quota is usually accompanied by incentive plans, fixed product-wise and salesman-wise.

CHAPTER 2

BASIC FINANCE CONCEPTS

1. The Firm as an Economic Unit; 2. Financial Needs and Resources; 3. Role of Accountant in Modern Organisations; 4. Basic Principles, Conventions and Concepts; 5. Capital and Revenue; 6. Financial Accounting; 7. Cost Accounting; 8. Management Accounting; 9. Financial Management; 10. Other Finance Functions.

1. THE FIRM AS AN ECONOMIC UNIT

In order to survive and grow, a firm or business unit has to be economically viable - it has to run as an economic unit. In the first instance, the firm has to acquire or make available to itself some resources. Only then, through planned, systematic, efficient and effective use of such resources can the firm produce some results. The resources and the results may also be described as input and output, respectively. The balancing of such input and output should eventually leave some surplus. The surplus is called profit in commercial organisations. When profit does not accrue, the firm cannot be called an economically viable unit. Another interesting point to note is that both resources and results are external to the business and only through management skills can resources be exploited to produce results favourable to the business unit. Hence arises the need for efficient and effective management of resources.

Resources are of various types. They are, chiefly, men, materials, machines, market and money. Each of these resources needs efficient management. Slightly different management skills are required in respect of the various resources. This is how the different functional areas of management have been developed, namely, Personnel Management (men), Production Management or Operations Management (machines), Materials Management (materials), Marketing Management (market, which is also a resource in the form of opportunity to be explored and exploited) and Financial Management (money).

2. FINANCIAL NEEDS AND RESOURCES

Money is one of the most important resources, the others being men, machines, materials, etc. But the pivotal role of money is evident from the fact that, itself being a resource, money is also used for acquiring as well as having command over other resources and also for measuring the changes in them. This complex and multi-faceted role of money in an enterprise might sometimes appear confused to us. But this nevertheless, highlights how important resource money is. It necessarily follows, therefore, that the firm has to first acquire finance and then its other resources.

Accordingly, the financial needs of a unit primarily emanate from the need for acquisition of other resources like men, machines, materials etc. We all know the adage, "Money is what money does". It is true for a business unit also - it does not want money for its own sake. It wants money to be able to exercise command over various resources.

The requirement of finance for an enterprise arises mainly from two factors, namely, provision for acquisition of fixed assets and that for working funds or working (or circulating) capital. Fixed assets include land, building, plant, machinery, equipment, etc.,which are used (for a period of time longer than one year), to enable the business to earn profits through recurring purchases, production and sales. Working capital is necessary to meet the day-to-day revenue expenditures like material purchase, payment of wages, payment for overhead expenses etc. Working capital keeps the business going since physical assets (like plant and machinery) cannot by themselves effect any production or sales unless they are regularly fed with materials and services. The finance needed to provide continuously for such materials and services is actually the working capital. The two areas (namely, fixed capital and working capital) representing financial requirement differ widely in respect of both the source and servicing of finance and the modes of utilisation of the same.

The sources of finance are broadly two, namely, internal and external (also expressed as Own Capital and Loan Capital or Internal Equities and External Equities). Usually, internal finance is utilised in providing fixed assets and the hard-core or fixed element in arranging in working capital. External finance (short-term) is mostly utilised in arranging for working capital. Long-term external funds are needed to partly finance fixed assets in connection with expansion, replacement, modernisation and diversification programs. These principles, however, should not be taken to be rigid. Depending on the nature of the business and the financial policy and planning of a particular enterprise, there may be a variance in the approaches to sourcing decisions.

3. ROLE OF ACCOUNTANT IN MODERN ORGANISATIONS

A modern organisation, especially one engaged in industrial or business activities, should have three basic functions : marketing, production and finance. There are other functions as well such as purchase, commercial, materials management, personnel management, administration, R&D, etc., but these are, by and large, subservient to the three main functions. Of these various functions, the accounting and finance functions is all-pervasive in nature. All departments or functions are by and large, dependent on and influenced by the accounting and finance department.

In the earlier days, an accountant's role in the organisation was of a very limited nature. Consequently, his position in the organisation was also not of great significance. His main function was that of a treasurer. He was the custodian of the cash resources of the enterprise. In addition to this, he used to maintain the 'score card' of the business. He used to religiously record all purchases and sales transactions of the enterprise. And in maintaining such records, he used to abide by the instructions of his employers. But over the last few centuries, an accountant's functions and consequently, his position in the organisation have undergone a sea-change. The factors that have contributed to this are, to mention but a few, growing industrialisation since the nineteenth century, the enactment of the Companies Acts and formation of joint stock companies in different countries, the two World Wars, world-wide depression in the '30s post - War booms and inflationary pressures and spectacular technological advancements. Some other factors, specially from the marketing angle, which have added further dimension and complexity to the finance function are growing competition, transition from sellers' market to buyers' market and increasing state participation in and control of industrial as well as commercial activities.

Today's accountant is not, therefore, just a treasurer and a score-keeper. He has to discharge, in addition to these, a host of diverse functions, complex and interdependent in nature. Consequently, he has come to occupy a key position as an executive in the modern organisation. Professional accounting bodies have been formed, with state patronage and regulations, almost all over the world. As a result, accountants are today guided not so much by the dictates of their employers as by the various statutes of the country and professional obligations and ethics. Besides these, accountants have developed, over a period of time, some basic principles which are built on the foundation of certain sound concepts and conventions to which they are committed.

4. BASIC PRINCIPLES, CONVENTIONS AND CONCEPTS

One time-honoured principle in accounting is that of dual aspects. This signifies that accounting has to take cognisance of both the aspects involved in each transaction. Accounting, therefore, is not complete and scientific until and unless both the aspects of a transaction are duly recorded in the books of accounts. This principle is somewhat similar to Newton's Third Law of Motion.

Over a fairly long period of time, quite a few healthy conventions have been developed in accounting that are, by and large followed by accountants all over the world. Some of these are :

i) Conversatism in estimating profits earned;

ii) Consistency in treatment of the same type of transactions;

iii) Disclosure or full disclosure of all information of material nature;

iv) Objectivity in analysing; recording and summarising business transactions;

v) Materiality, that is, disregarding what is immaterial, judged by 'accounting cost' involved.

Then there are certain concepts or necessary assumptions and conditions upon which accounting principles and practices are based. Some of these concepts are:

i) Business entity - treating each business unit as an independent entity, quite distinct from its owners.

ii) Money measurement - taking cognisance of only such transactions as are amenable to strict monetary measurement.

iii) Continuity or going concern - ignoring fluctuations in market value of fixed assets (particularly)

iv) Historical cost - recording transactions at past or historical money values only.

v) Costs attach - merger or pooling of product costs in a manufacturing activity.

vi) Periodic matching of costs and revenues - this includes :

(a) accounting period concept and
(b) accrual theory of accounting.

5. CAPITAL AND REVENUE

The distinction between capital and revenue is a logical requirement of the accounting period concept. By capital and revenue, we mean capital and revenue transactions respectively. Capital transactions mean transactions involved in the purchase, acquisition, sale or disposition of assets which have a life of at least more than one year.

Revenue transactions, on the other hand, relate to the incomes and expenses connected with the normal day-to-day operations of the business.

If the life of a business is not divided into a number of distinct accounting periods or years, the distinction between capital and revenue losses its significance. All the expenses (both capital and revenue) will be deducted from all the incomes (both capital and revenue) to arrive at the total profit or loss during the lifetime of the business, under such a situation. But in reality we do go by the accounting period concept. Hence the necessity of differentiation between capital and revenue.

We come across four types of transactions ; (1) Capital Expenditures, (2) Capital Incomes or Gains, (3) Revenue Expenditures and (4) Revenue Incomes or Gains.

Capital Expenditures are those incurred for acquisition of some assets intended to be used in the business at least for more than a year to maintain and /or enhance its profit earning capability. Expenditure for the purchase of land, building, plant, machinery, etc. are accordingly capital expenditures.

Capital Incomes or Gains mean gains accruing from the sale or disposition of capital assets. Examples of some capital incomes are sale of old machinery, sale of land or building, etc., at a price higher than the respective original cost of their acquisition.

Revenue Expenditures relate to those connected with the normal operations of the business and which do not result in some 'enduring benefits' to the business through the acquisition of something tangible. Purchase of goods (for being used in manufacturing and sale or resale in as it is condition), payment of salaries and wages, all operating expenses and losses like commission, discount, carriage, travelling, depreciation of assets, bad debts,etc., are examples of revenue expenditures.

Revenue Incomes or Gains are similarly those that accrue from the normal operations of the business, for example sales, interest received, commission earned, discount received, etc.

Though the distinction between capital and revenue, as explained above, is apparently very easy to understand, there are some items or types of transactions which can be treated either way. There are some borderline cases, the treatment of which depends on particular facts and situations obtaining commercial expediency and finally, the approach of the accountant concerned. He has, however, to take into consideration the acceptability of his decision by auditors and tax authorities besides adhering to the accounting principles involved.

Deferred Revenue Expenditure is expenditure strictly of a revenue nature, but the full amount involved is not treated as such expenditure in the particular year in which it is incurred since the benefits therefrom do not cease to exist in that particular year itself. Expenditure on a massive advertisement campaign, involving a huge sum of money, may be treated as deferred revenue if it is found that the benefits from such advertisement will be available during subsequent years. The expenditure is, in such case, divided into say, three, five or ten parts (depending on the estimate of the number of years during which such benefits would be available) and each part is charged as revenue expenditure in each of these years. Such spreading of the revenue expenditure over a number of years closely resembles pure capital expenditure, which too, is spread over a number of years through what is called depreciation. Some other examples of deferred revenue expenditures are preliminary expenses, discount or loss on issue of debentures, research and development expenses (including expenses on the development of a new product or process), etc.

6. FINANCIAL ACCOUNTING

Till probably World war I, accounting meant only financial accounting. Even today this is the most important and basic branch of accounting. The oft-quoted definition of accounting is : "... the art of recording, classifying and summarising in a significant manner and in terms of money, transactions and events which are, in part at least, of a financial character and in interpreting the results thereof." (Accounting Terminology Bulletin No.1, American Institute of Certified Public Accountants). The definition is applicable more to financial accounting than to any other branch of accounting. Similarly, all the basic principles and conventions and concepts of accounting as well as the capital revenue allocation, discussed above are essentially applicable to financial accounting.

Financial accounting practices can be traced back to the dawn of human civilization. But it was given a more or less scientific framework in 1494 when Luca Pacioli of Italy first published in printed form the Double Entry Book Keeping. The Double Entry System is, in fact, the bedrock of financial accounting system. This is the only scientific system which takes into accounting both the aspects of every transaction and thus ensures a complete record.

Book keeping is an integral part of the financial accounting process. Book keeping is simply the keeping of books-the books of accounts of an enterprise. 'Keeping' means the recording of transactions in the 'books' in keeping with sound accounting principles.

Financial accounting, including book keeping, is both a science and an art. The science part of the entire gamut of recording transactions and providing information to various interests is called Accountancy. Book keeping on the other hand, is the art part in the process, that is, the application of the principles of accountancy to actual situations.

Financial accounting primarily meets the external needs of the enterprise. A complete record of all business transactions maintained under the financial accounting process should satisfy the requirements of various legislations (for example, the Companies Act) as well as auditors, shareholders and other Government authorities. For this reason, financial accounting is often looked upon as Statutory Accounting or Custodian Accounting.

7. COST ACCOUNTING

It is the internal needs of management rather than external (which was primarily responsible for the development of Statutory Accounting) that led to the emergence of Cost Accounting around the World War I period. The main emphasis at that time was on finding the accurate and factual cost of products, jobs or processes. Due to the popularity of 'Cost plus contracts' in different countries during World War I, actual cost-finding became imperative. There was an urgent need felt for principles governing decisions as to which items were to be charged to and which ones excluded from costs and reasons for such treatment in a 'cost plus contract'.

The method of actual cost-finding came to be well-developed right in the earlier stage. Costs were to be ascertained element-wise. And in the entire gamut of cost-finding, costs would be channeled, divided and re-chanelled, involving what are called allocation and apportionment of costs. The results of all such efforts would be 'actual cost.'

However, it did not take long to realise the actual cost or factual cost is nothing more than an accidental cost when judged for one product or job. The concept of cost-finding thus came in for a thorough review. The emphasis in cost-finding effort was then shifted from the so-called true cost or actual cost to equitable cost-from factual cost to decision-oriented or purposeful cost. It was found that purposeful cost was more helpful in comparing costs, offering quotations, measuring performance and profitability and so on. But actual costs have still got to be ascertained for measuring actual profits or losses on an historical basis.

The actual cost-finding exercise was found also to suffer from serious limitations in the face of free competition. As a result, cost accounting was further developed as a tool for improving profitability through cost control and also cost reduction through improved productivity.

Thus, what began as a set of methods for actual cost finding in 'cost plus contract' have now come to stay as a well-developed discipline covering cost-finding-both actual and purposeful cost control and cost reduction aimed at improved performance and profitability.

8. MANAGEMENT ACCOUNTING

The term management accounting or managerial accounting is comparatively of recent origin. It has been generally in use since World War II. Management accounting is defined as the presentation of accounting information in such a way as to assist management in the creation of policy in day-to-day operation of an undertaking. Another good definition of management accounting is given by the Institute of Chartered Accountants of England and Wales : 'The active contribution which accountants, whether in public practice or in industry can make to the daily conduct of business, whether they be large or small.' To sum up, we may define management accounting as a discipline which comprises all those accounting activities that assist management functions at all levels and include all available techniques for improvement of efficiency. The scope of management accounting is, therefore very broad-broader than that of either cost accounting or financial accounting or even both put together. The emphasis here is more on the internal needs of the management than the external, more on the non-routine aspects of accounting than the routine. The very concept and philosophy of management accounting is to render assistance to all levels of management so that efficiency and productivity can be improved through better planning, improved decision making and more effective control.

The distinction between the three branches of accounting has been brought out in the following table :

	Financial Accounting	**Cost Accounting**	**Management Accounting**
Need	External-law audit,society	Internal-cost finding,cost control productivity	Internal profitability, improvement in efficiency and overall performance
Responsibility	Watchdog of shareholder	Watchdog of management	Watchdog of management,in particular (lower and middle levels)
Effectiveness	Control through budgets	Control by setting standards and operating cost control.	Challenging the various standards productivity.

Thus while financial accounting and cost accounting operate in somewhat restricted areas, management accounting has almost an unrestricted field of operation, since it is concerned with the system as a whole and the overall vitality of the organisation. Financial accountants and cost accountants prepare the year's profit and loss accounts and balance sheet. The management accountant looks ahead to prepare future profit and loss accounts and balance sheets of the Company, that too under different sets of parameters and assumptions.

However, we should not stretch the distinction too far. Management accounting and cost accounting are not mutually exclusive. Management accounting is rather a logical extension of cost accounting. Again, management accounting cannot be divorced from financial accounting and financial management. The efficient cost accountant, financial accountant or even finance manager very often has to undertake, in the ordinary course of his work, those tasks that fall broadly in the area of the management accountant. Similarly, management accounting cannot work successfully in an organisation where one of the other two functions, namely, cost accounting and financial accounting, is weak. Thus,these three branches of accounting are closely interdependent and complementary to each other.

9. FINANCIAL MANAGEMENT

Money can be viewed from two different angles, money as a measure and money as a resource. The first role of money (money as a measure) is important in accounting, specially since financial accounting is based on the underlying assumption of treating money as a measure. However, for financial management, money is looked upon as a resource.

Further, the source discipline of financial management is economics, while that of financial accounting is mathematics or arithmetic, to be more precise. Financial management comprises essentially the planning and control of financial resources, that is money. But to be good finance manager one has to cultivate the art of analysing and interpreting financial statements which are prepared using money as a measure. It is felt that an ability to read the financial statements between the lines and tabulate, analyse and interpret them, to arrive at valid and meaningful conclusions, is a precondition to successful planning, organisation and control of financial resources.

The paramount importance of finance in an enterprise has led to the development of the discipline of financial management. Initially it was considered to be an integral part of financial accounting. But during the last couple of decades, the tools and techniques of financial management have been so well developed that it has come to be regarded as a separate branch of accounting - sometimes even treated as a separate branch of study. Financial management is today considered to be different from financial accounting, cost accounting and even management accounting, though financial management is closely related to and to a great extent dependent upon, all these facets of accounting.

Financial Management has three broad elements, namely Planning, Organisation and Control. The details of these elements are as follows :

i)	Ascertainment of financial needs	Planning
ii)	Determination of sources of finance	
iii)	Procurement of funds	Organisation
iv)	Allocation of funds	
v)	Monitoring of funds (through 'financial discipline' with regard to funds utilisation)	Control

Accounting is by and large a service function - a staff function in management terminology. But financial management is at least one area which represents more a line function than a staff function. The modern finance manager is no less an 'operating' person than the marketing manager or the production manager.

10. OTHER FINANCE FUNCTIONS

Besides the major finance functions discussed above (namely, financial accounting cost accounting, management accounting and financial management), there are various other finance functions also. Special mention may be made of two of them - audit and taxation.

Auditing means a critical examination of the books of accounts to check their accuracy and also detect and prevent errors and frauds. Audits are of two types, external audit and internal audit. External audit is undertaken by outsiders. In the case of joint stock companies, the financial accounts have to be audited every year by independent external auditors who must be qualified chartered accountants. Similarly, in the case of certain manufacturing units, cost accounting records have to be audited by external auditors who must be qualified cost accountants. External audit is also called statutory audit since it is always conducted in conformity with the provisions of various statutes, specially the Companies Act. The statutory auditors are appointed by the companies concerned. But the Companies Act lays down various provisions covering the appointment, removal, renumeration, qualification, disqualification, status,powers and duties, as well as obligations and liabilities of the statutory auditors. Consequently, such auditors are bound by the Companies Act provisions and not by the requirements or dictates of the companies that hire them. This ensures professional independence of external auditors which in turn is a must for the healthy functioning of the corporate sector.

Internal audit is an independent appraisal and review within the business house by its own staff of accounting, financial and even other operations. Internal audit system normally envisages a continuous audit carried on throughout the year, as opposed to the periodic audit carried on by the external auditors. The scope on internal audit is also very wide. Besides setting right the books of accounts in the manner acceptable to the external auditors, internal audit can prevent errors and frauds to a significant extent and can also render various protective and constructive services to the management. The scope of internal audit has been broadened by progressive business houses to cover not only the audit of accounting records but also the areas of operational audit, systems audit, information audit, procedural audit, etc.

The last major function is taxation. There are two types of taxes, direct taxes and indirect taxes. The only direct tax payable by company is income tax. There are various indirect taxes which have a significant bearing on the operations of a company. There are sales tax, excise duty, octroi, etc. The function of taxation can also be considered from the same two angles as for audit function, namely, external and internal. The external taxation function relates to dealing with taxation authorities, namely income tax authorities, sales tax authorities, excise duty authorities etc. and complying with the various procedural requirements with regard to submission of returns, payment of taxes, etc.

Internal taxation function includes providing the necessary guidance to the operating management, specially marketing and production departments, in respect of sales tax, excise duty, octroi, etc. There is also a scope for tax planning, specially in the area of sales tax, to legally reduce the impact and incidence of sales tax and thereby make the product of the company more competitive in respect of prices. Another important internal taxation function is corporate tax planning.

There are yet other functions coming under the accounting and finance department. First, mention may be made of insurance - insurance of different types ranging from assets and property,including vehicles and stocks insurance to loss of profit insurance. Then there are various personnel schemes, namely, provident fund, superannuation, gratuity, group and accident insurance, executive commission, etc. The framing-up, review and implementation of all such schemes and rendering diverse services to the staff also fall within the purview of accounting and finance functions, although these have to be handled in close co-ordination with the Personnel Department. There is also marketing and sales accounting concerned with the accounting of the related aspects, Some companies have even formed a marketing-finance cell, within the marketing function itself, for this purpose.

CHAPTER 3

MARKETING FINANCE INTERFACE

1. Introduction ; 2. Marketing Finance Independence; 3. Marketing Finance Interdependence; 4. Cost-Revenue-Investment Framework in marketing.

1. INTRODUCTION

The preceding two chapters conveyed a general idea about the nature and purpose of marketing on the one hand and the role and functions of finance on the other, besides a bird's-eye view of the various sub-functions broadly covered under both marketing and finance functions in an organisation. This Chapter will endeavour to synthesise these ideas and examine to what extent these two important functions are independent and also interdependent. An attempt will also be made to highlight how the success of an enterprise would, to a great extent, depend upon the closest possible coordination between marketing and finance.

There has been a tendency, for a long time now, to treat marketing and finance as two completely different functions and separate them into water-tight compartments. Unfortunately, this tendency has been more evident among typical Indian enterprises. Marketing people have tended to create an impression that they are the money - spinners and accounting and finance, just as many other functions, are unproductive staff - parasites living on their (i.e.marketing peoples') earnings and with no contribution of their own. Finance people, on the other hand, with rigorous professional qualifications in most cases, have tried to find faults with marketing people and despised their lack of knowledge of finance and even sometimes condemned openly their high-handed attitude of frittering away the company's precious financial resources.

There is, however, a welcome sign of such tendencies steadily yielding place to an attitude of co-operation and co-ordination with a view to fulfilling the overall corporate objectives. By now they might have learnt the moral of the time-honoured fable that if the limbs of the body fight with one another the overall health suffers and consequently all the limbs, too!

Yet, some conflict does exist between marketing functions and finance functions in most of today's organisations. The marketing manager is unhappy with the accountant when the latter tightly controls the marketing staff's travelling expenses or the sales promotion budgets. An accountant's financial wizardry of keeping the company's interest cost low is frustrated by the marketing managers expertise at extending credit to the valued customers or holding more stocks at distribution points. The attempt of the management accountant to prepare a realistic budget for the company is seriously hampered by the marketing manager's highly optimistic or highly pessimistic predictions. At the end of the year the actual sales are very much different. When they are below the prediction level, the marketing manager is sure to produce his 'Magna Carta' of reasons to justify the dismal results which, had it not been for him, would have been even more dismal ! And next year once again come the unrealistic predictions which the marketing manager insists are realistic and there begins the management accountant's predicament.

2. MARKETING FINANCE INDEPENDENCE

Let us first examine to what extent marketing and finance functions are independent of each other. If you analyse the nature of these functions, you will find that there exists a great deal of independence.

Marketing functions by and large lie outside the organisation. On the one side, there is the marketplace and on the other, there is the organisation. In the marketplace there are customers, negative customers and neutral or potential customers. The marketplace is always in a state of flux. It is also continuously affected by economic, political and social changes. Such changes are again of a very complex and interdependent nature. All such changes and forces and interactions at the marketplace are transmitted to the organisation through one important function of marketing, viz., market research. Based on such factors and forces the organisation takes certain decisions which are again reflected in the marketplace.

Finance function by its very nature is internal to the organisation. An important part of the finance function, i.e., statutory accounting or custodian accounting, is responsible to outsiders, viz., shareholders, Government authorities, auditors,etc. But all other functions under finance do not owe any allegiance to outsiders and the degree of dependence, too, is little. Financial management, particularly to the extent it relates to making available financial resources from outside, is influenced rather widely by external factors, especially capital market situations. But this influence is significantly different both in character and quality from the influences that market forces constantly exert on the marketing functions.

These points would lead us to believe that the nature of marketing is completely different from that of finance. And these two functions have to be discharged more or less in an isolated manner. Also these two functions require completely different types of technical and human skills. This would be evident from the fact that a very successful salesman often turns out to be an utter failure as an accounts assistant just as a very efficient accounts man may make a mess of sales if he is asked to handle this.

3. MARKETING FINANCE INTERDEPENDENCE

A general tendency to treat marketing and finance as two different functions and separating them into water-tight compartments is happily yielding place to the coming together (of these two functions) with an attitude of mutual cooperation and coordination. This welcome change may be traced to two reasons. First, these two sets of people have generally realised that they are working for a common cause in order to fulfill common corporate objectives of survival, profitability and growth. Second, there are quite a few important areas where marketing and finance specialisations tend to overlap. Some of these are :

i) Product planning including product selection, retention and abandonment as well as dilution in product portfolio;

ii) Product pricing including both short-range and long-range pricing policies and strategies.

iii) Evaluation of marketing performance - both general and specific marketing functions like product profitability analysis.

iv) Functional Cost Analysis to achieve cost effectiveness and also for exercising a systematic and meaningful control over marketing costs and expenses;

v) Introduction and operation of an effective budgetary control system in marketing;

vi) Control of marketing operations - both the employment of funds and the cost of inputs; and

vii) Marketing investment decisions including monitoring their implementation.

Then there are several commercial and fiscal issues (also under the domain of Finance) that should be addressed jointly by Finance and Marketing people. Some of these — illustrative and by no means exhaustive — are :

i) Sale on consignment basis, sale on approval or sales or return type of transactions.

ii) Leasing and hire purchase transactions.

iii) Interest element on credit granted and the related concept called average due date.

iv) Bills of exchange and hundies.

v) Recovery of excise duty through invoicing and keeping the said duty undisturbed even when the sale is made at a discount.

vi) Recovery of sales taxes-both Central and State — through invoicing and collection of sales tax declaration forms (Forms C & D, as the case may be)

Some progressive companies in India have therefore set up Marketing Finance Cell on the same lines as Market Research Cells. A Marketing Finance Cell is staffed by personnel possessing expertise in both finance and marketing, so that they can provide staff assistance to marketing management at all levels in all the important areas listed above, as and when necessary.

4. COST-REVENUE-INVESTMENT FRAMEWORK IN MARKETING

This is a perspective view of marketing finance, comprising three components. The term cost has a broad meaning here and covers in its ambit all costs of setting up as well as running a marketing organisation. Some of these costs are of one-time nature — "the capital costs" in accounting terminology. Other costs are "revenue" or of recurring nature. But even those one-time capital costs become a part and parcel of the recurring costs through the process of depreciation or amortization, so that in the end all costs get absorbed or recovered through operations.

Revenue is what the organisation earns by selling its products and /or services to customers outside the organisation. The sum-total of all revenues is matched against the sum-total of all costs, both direct and indirect and the difference is worked out. When the difference is on the positive side (i.e. total revenue exceeds total cost), it means a positive surplus or profit. The negative difference means a loss.

To keep the recurring operations going in marketing there has to be some investments. These are broadly of two types viz., investments on capital assets (e.g.motor cars, warehouses, office equipment, etc.) and those on working capital (e.g.inventory,accounts receivable, etc). The recurring costs of such investments have to be absorbed, as stated above, along with the direct costs, by revenues earned through marketing efforts. Recurring cost due to investments in marketing usually takes any or both the following forms :

(a) depreciation or diminution in respect of capital assets, inventory, value of amounts to be collected from customers, etc.

(b) financing or interest charges (actual or notional), covering all investments both in fixed assets and in working capital.

The cost-revenue-investment inter-relationship discussed above is succinctly represented by a financial ratio called the Return on Investment (ROI). This ratio has broadly two components, viz., Return on Sales (ROS) or Margin Ratio and the Turnover of Capital Employed (Times). Return on Investment improves or deteriorates not due to just the higher or lower earning in the form of gross margin percentage on sales. Even with the same margin percentage, ROI can improve or deteriorate drastically through efficiency or otherwise in the deployment of funds or capital employed in marketing operations. In fact it is quite possible to improve ROI percentage by dramatically improving the rate of capital turnover (times), margin percentage remaining the same. This is what is called' "Turn and Earn".

SECTION II

MARKETING FINANCE AND COST

If the preceding section was devoted to 'clearing the ground', the purpose of this section is to 'lay the foundation'. In the first of the five Chapters included in this section, an attempt is made to expose the reader to the Financial Accounting process, to be more precise, the rather mechanical but important framework of what is popularly known as 'Book Keeping'. The subsequent three Chapters seek to explain and illustrate the various tools and techniques of interpretation of financial statements including the very widely-used techniques like financial ratio analysis and funds flow analysis. In Chapter 8 (fifth Chapter in this section), the reader will be exposed to the basic principles and concepts of a very important branch of accounting, viz, cost accounting. All these five Chapters have been so designed as to enable the reader to acquire basic knowledge of finance and cost, absolutely necessary for him to understand the subsequent sections of the book. And throughout the discussion, relevance of various principles and techniques to marketing operations has been kept in view.

CHAPTER 4

FINANCIAL ACCOUNTING PROCESS

1. Double Entry System; 2. The Ten Point Programme in Book Keeping; 3. Journal; 4. Ledger; 5. Cash Book; 6. Trial Balance; 7. Final Accounts.

1. DOUBLE ENTRY SYSTEM

Double Entry System does not imply that every transaction is entered twice. It really means entry of both aspects of every transaction must have two different axiom in accounting, that every transaction must have two different (and mostly opposite) aspects.The system is geared towards ensuring a complete record of every transaction since both of its aspects are recorded in the books of account.

Because this system is scientific, it enjoys the faith and confidence of everybody connected directly or indirectly with the operations of an enterprise. Bankers, Auditors, taxation authorities and other government agencies accept only such book of accounts as are maintained under the double entry system. Under this system alone, records are comprehensive and complete, errors and frauds are minimum and these can be easily detected and prevented.

Under the double entry system, there are two sets of books of accounts namely, Journal and Ledger. The Journal is also called the 'books of prime entry' or 'book of original entry'. In this book are recorded all the transactions as and when they occur in the form of what is called 'journal entry'. Since there is no entry immediately after a transaction, the journal has to be a chronological record. The ledger is also called the 'book of final entry'. In this book transactions (originally recorded in the journal) are entered from the journal by 'ledger posting'. The question arises as to why should the same transaction be recorded in two different sets of books, thus involving duplication of efforts. The reasons are as follows. Firstly the journal is more or less a rough book for recording running transactions as and when they take place, while the ledger is a fair and final book wherein transactions are subsequently recorded with reduced chances of error. Secondly, the journal provides more details of each transaction by way of a narration which serves the purpose of future reference, while the ledger records a transaction in a precise manner. Thus, there is not much of duplication in recording the same transaction in two books.

The language or medium of accounting is account. All transactions or events are recorded in the books only through its medium. An account may be defined as a word or a group of words by which an aspect of a transaction is represented for the purpose of recording the transactions in the books of accounts. Every transaction thus involves at least two accounts because of its two-fold aspects.

Accounts are broadly classified as personal and impersonal. Personal accounts are those accounts which relate to persons such as individuals, firms, bodies corporate, etc. In most cases personal accounts are the accounts of the customers and suppliers (of both goods and services) maintained in the books of business. Some examples of personal accounts in the books of say, X Ltd., are:.Y Ltd. a/c, Z Ltd. a/c and X Ltd. Calcutta branch a/c (but not 'X Ltd. a/c' as such).

All accounts which do not relate to any 'person' as explained above, should be regarded as impersonal, accounts. Impersonal accounts are further classified into two types : real accounts and nominal accounts. Real accounts are accounts relating to the assets and liabilities of a business. Some examples are : plant and machinery a/c, 10 per cent debentures a/c, etc. All accounts representing revenue incomes, receipts or gains and revenue expenses, payments or losses of a business, are called nominal accounts. Some examples are : sales a/c, purchase a/c, salary a/c and bad debt a/c.

Whenever a transaction occurs, a basic document has to be prepared which initiates the necessary accounting operations. This document is called a voucher. In case of sales, an invoice (for credit sales) or a cash memo (for cash sales) serves the purpose of a voucher. In case of a purchase, it is the purchase order. If it is a cash transaction, a cash voucher (receipt voucher or payment voucher) or petty cash voucher, as the cash may be is required. And if the transaction has to be entered in the journal proper, a journal voucher should be prepared. Similarly, debit notes and credit notes also serve the purpose of a voucher.

A voucher serves the important purpose of intimation of a transaction soon after it takes place. This is how accountant sitting at the head office is able to keep a track of all the business transactions that are taking place throughout the area of operation of the company. However, just intimation is not enough. The accountant will also have to classify and record every transaction and to enable him to do so, the voucher (which is the medium of communication of a transaction) has to provide all the relevant details. In the absence of such details, the accountant will have to return the voucher to the originator with a request to provide the missing information. To sum up, a voucher serves the following three important purposes

(i) Intimation or communication of a transaction;

(ii) Classification of the same from accounting point of view; and

(iii) Authorisation for its treatment in the book of accounts.

2. THE TEN-POINT PROGRAMME IN BOOK KEEPING

Right from the time a transaction takes place, upto the preparation of the balance sheet, the entire process in book keeping under the double entry system may be envisaged in ten logical step. This ten-point program in the right sequence is explained below . One point which is to be made clear is that finally, each and every transaction will eventually be reflected in the balance sheet of the enterprise in some way or other.

(i) *Analysis of facts and events into independent transactions :* In every enterprise there is a stream of events. Not all such events are business transactions. Business transactions may be defined as a single fact or event which introduces or is, by itself, capable of introducing some sort of financial change in the business. For example while booking of an order is not a transaction, effecting a sale is. Or, while appointing a clerk by a letter (even though duly accepted by the incumbent) is not a transaction, utilising the clerk's services for a certain period, say, a month (even though the salary is not paid yet) is.

Once a business transaction occurs, it has to be identified and segregated from the stream of other business events. The counting process starts with such identification and segregation. Communication of the transaction through a voucher, as mentioned earlier, closely follows this.

(ii) *Determination of the two aspects involved in each transaction :* After the communication of a transaction is complete, the accounts staff will analyse it to determine the two aspects involved in the transaction. This is explained with the help of some illustrations :

	Transaction	**The Two Aspects Involved**
1.	Starting of a business by Mr. X on paying some money in a bank account opened in the business name.	i) Introduction of capital by the proprietor, Mr .X ii) Money in bank (business bank account)
2.	Purchase of machinery to be used in the business on payment by cheque bank account)	i) Acquisition of machinery ii) Money in bank (since a part of it is going out)
3.	Purchase of materials to be used in the business from Mr.Y on credit - amount payable in a month	i) Purchase of goods/materials ii) Credit enjoyed from Mr.Y
4.	Purchase of some furniture to be used in the business from Mr. Z on credit	i) Acquisition of furniture ii) Credit enjoyed from Mr.Z

5.	Sales made to M/s.P, Q & R for cash.	i) Cash or money in bank ii) Effecting a sale
6.	Sales made to both Mr. S & Mr. T on credit for equal amount. *(N.B.-This contains two transactions)*	i) Credit allowed to Mr. S ii) Effecting a sale i) Credit allowed to Mr. T ii) Effecting a sale
7.	A part of the goods sold to Mr.T was returned	i) Goods received back as returns ii) Party returning the goods (Mr.T)
8.	A part of the goods purchased from Mr.Y was returned.	i) Goods sent back as returns ii) Party to whom returned (Mr.Y)
9.	Withdrawal of cash from business bank account	i) Money in bank (going out) ii) Money in cash (coming in)
10.	Payment of wages to workmen	i) Payment of wages ii) Money in cash (going out)

While dealing with third parties, in the case of cash transactions, cash account or bank account is one aspects (for example no. 5) while in case of credit transactions, the party concerned is one of the aspects (examples no.3, 4, 6)

iii) *Deciding upon suitable account heads to represent the two aspects of a transaction :* As mentioned earlier, every transaction has to be recorded in the books of accounts through the accounting language, the chief medium of which is accounts or account heads. Once the two aspects of a transaction are determined (as above) each of these two aspects has to be designated by a suitable account-head before any attempt is made to record the transaction in the books. To illustrate how account-heads are determined, we take the same ten transactions mentioned. Considering the two aspects involved in each of these transactions, the appropriate account-heads should be as follows :

No. 1	(i) Capital a/c (ii) Bank a/c	No. 6	(i) Mr. S a/c (ii) Sales a/c (i) Mr. T a/c (ii)Sales a/c.
No. 2	(i) Machinery a/c (ii) Bank a/c.	No. 7	(i) Returns inward a/c (ii) Mr. T a/c
No. 3	(i) Purchase a/c (ii) Mr. Y a/c	No. 8	(i) Returns outward a/c (ii) Mr. Y a/c
No. 4	(i) Furniture a/c (ii) Mr. Z a/c	No. 9	(i) Bank a/c (ii) Cash a/c
No. 5	(i) Cash a/c, or Bank a/c (ii) Sales a/c	No. 10.	(i) Wages a/c (ii) Cash a/c

iv) *Decision as to the account to be debited and the account to be credited :* Such decision have to be taken following certain rules. The golden rules of debit and credit, as they are called are based on the type or classification of the account. Each classification of accounts has got a separate set of rules. They are :

(a)	Personal : Accounts	Debit (Dr) the receiver (of money, goods or services) and credit (Cr) the giver (of money, goods or services)
(b)	Real : Accounts	Debit what comes in and credit what goes out or to put it a bit differently, Debit all assets, that are acquired or liabilities that are discharged and credit all liabilities that are created or assets that are disposed of.

(c) Nominal : Accounts — Debit all expenses, losses, etc.and credit all incomes gains, etc.

To illustrate the application of these rules of debit and credit we may again consider the same ten transactions :

No.	Debit (Dr)	Credit (Cr)
1	Bank a/c	Capital a/c
2	Machinery a/c	Bank a/c
3	Purchase a/c	Mr. Y a/c
4	Furniture a/c	Mr. Z a/c
5	Cash or Bank a/c	Sales a/c
6	Mr .S a/c	Sales a/c
	Mr. T a/c	Sales a/c
7	Returns Inward a/c	Mr. T a/c
8	Mr. Y a/c	Returns Outward a/c
9	Cash a/c	Bank a/c
10	Wages a/c	Cash a/c

v) *Entry of the transaction in the journal* - explained in the next topic.

vi) *Posting from the journal into the accounts in the ledger* - illustrated in topic No.4

vii) *Balancing of ledger accounts* - illustrated in topic No.4

viii) *Preparation of trial balance* - explained in topic No.6

ix) *Preparation of profit and loss account* - explained in topic No.7

x) *Preparation of balance sheet* - explained in topic No.7

3. JOURNAL

To explain clearly how entries are made in the journal or how the journal is written up, we shall use the same ten transactions as given above, assuming hypothetical amounts in figures against each.

In the Books of Mr.X (that is Mr.X's Business)

Date 19x3	Particulars	L.F.	Amount Dr Rs.	 Cr Rs.
Jan 1	Bank a/c Dr To capital a/c (being the capital brought in by Mr .X to start the business with)		1,00,000	 1,00,000
2	Machinery a/c Dr To bank a/c (being the acquisition of machinery from.....against payment to cheque no....)		40,000	 40,000
3	Purchase a/c Dr To Mr. Y a/c (being the purchase of raw materials from Y on credit-terms of payment being one month)		20,000	 20,000
4	Furniture a/c Dr To Mr .Z a/c (being the purchase of furniture on credit)		8,000	 8,000
5	Cash (for Bank) a/c Dr To Sales a/c (being sales made in cash to M/s P, Q & R)		12,000	 12,000
6	Mr. S a/c Dr To Sales a/c		5,000	 5,000

	(being sales made on credit)		
	Mr. T a/c Dr	5,000	
	To Sales a/c		5,000
	(being sales made on credit)		
7	Returns Inward a/c Dr	1,000	
	To Mr.T a/c		1,000
	(being a part of goods sold on 6.1 x 3 returned)		
8	Mr.Y a/c Dr	3,000	
	To Returns Outward a/c		3,000
	(being a part of goods purchased on 3.1 x 3 returned)		
9	Cash a/c Dr	4,500	
	To bank a/c		4,500
	(being cash withdrawn from bank)		
10	Wages a/c Dr	4,300	
	To Cash a/c		4,300
	(being the payment of wages)		

The journal entries as shown above have been made under the basic assumption that the business is maintaining only one book to serve the purpose of a Journal. This assumption is,however,not realistic. Because of the multiplicity of transactions, the journal has to be subdivided usually into three sets, namely, (a) Subsidiary Books, (b) Cash Book and (c) Journal Proper. The names of the more important subsidiary books of a business and the type of transactions that are recorded in each such book are as follows :

	Subsidiary Book	To Record Only
1.	Purchase Book	Credit purchases from all suppliers
2.	Sales Book	Credit sales to all customers
3.	Returns Outward Book	Returns sent out of previous credit purchases

4.	Returns Inward Book	Returns received back out of previous credit sales.
5.	Bills Receivable Books	Bills of exchange accepted by various parties in our favour.
6.	Bills Payable Book	Bills of exchange accepted by us in favour of various parties.

There may be other subsidiary books depending upon the special needs of each business unit. Those mentioned above are the more common ones. The format and design of different subsidiary books differ from business to business.

Cash Book is an important subdivision of the journal. All cash transactions, irrespective of their nature and type (for example, big or small, capital and revenue), are recorded in the cash book. It is to be mentioned in this connection that the cash book has a distinct and dignified place under the double entry system, since it is as much a part of the ledger, as of the journal. The format and design of a cash book is such that it can serve the purpose of both journal and ledger. The cash book may, therefore, be called both a journal and a ledger.

4. LEDGER

Ledger is the Book of Final Entry. All transactions are ordinarily posted from the journal to the ledger. And once such posting is complete, accounting takes it own course through the ledger alone-the utility of journal ceases thereafter (excepting for providing details in case of future reference only). One of the main objectives of accounting operations, namely, preparation of the final accounts relative to an accounting period is also based primarily on ledger accounts. Thus the importance of correct maintenance of all ledger accounts need not be overemphasised. Maintaining all accounts in a correct and proper manner in the ledger requires that accuracy should be ensured in respect of (i) all posting to accounts (ii) all casting of accounts (iii) all balancing of accounts and (iv) bringing down all balances.

All these operations of ledger accounts are explained below with hypothetical illustrations :

1.

Dr.	Cash A/C		Cr
	Rs		Rs.
To Sales a/c	3,000	By Wages a/c	2,000
To Debtors a/c	12,000	By Purchases a/c	3,000
		By Rent a/c	4,000
		By Balanced c/d	6,000
	15,000		15,000
To Balance b/d	6,000		

Notes :

(a) Taking all the postings (hypothetical) on the two sides of the above account, the total amount comes to Rs.15,000 in the debit side and Rs.9,000 in the credit side-operation casting.

(b) Difference between the two totals is Rs.6,000. This is a Debit Balance (since total of the debit side is higher than that of the credit side). The amount is shown on the credit side against balance c/d-operation balancing.

(c) In the next operation this debit balance is brought down to its proper place (that is, debit side) with the opening of the account for the next period. The expression used in 'Balance b/d or b/f' - operation bringing down the balance.

(d) Here is a case of debit balance - shown in the credit side first and then brought forward to the debit side. The mode in case of a credit balance will be the same - shown first in the debit side and then to be brought forward to the credit side.

2.

Dr.	M A/C		Cr.
	Rs.		Rs.
To Bank a/c	14,000	By Balance b/d	10,000
To Discount a/c	1,000	By Purchase a/c	20,000
To Balance c/d	15,000		
	30,000		30,000
		By Balance b/d	15,000

3.

Dr.	Sales A/c		Cr
	Rs.		Rs.
To Balance c/d	27,000	By Balance b/d	17,000
		By AB a/c	3,000
		By BC a/c	2,000
		By CD a/c	5,000
	27,000		27,000
		By Balance b/d	27,000

Notes :

The opening balance was Rs.17,000, closing balance is Rs.27,000. Total of the credit side itself (including the opening balance) is the credit balance Rs.27,000 - shown first in the debit side and then brought to the appropriate place (that is credit side).

A careful scrutiny of classifications of the Journal would reveal it is classified by the nature of transactions. Classification of ledger is made on a different basis - it is in accordance with the class of accounts. Accordingly, a ledger is broadly classified as personal ledger and impersonal ledger.

In the personal ledger, only personal accounts will be maintained. This ledger may be subdivided into debtors ledger (or sales ledger) and creditors ledger (or purchase ledger).

Depending on the volume of business (with consequently increased number of customers and suppliers) a debtors' ledger as also a creditors' ledger may have to be further subdivided, each into several ledgers. Such subdivision may be based on :

(a) geographical territories of the respective parties;
(b) alphabetical order of the names of the parties; and
(c) nature of specific product sold/purchased.

Impersonal Ledger will keep only the impersonal accounts. This ledger may also be subdivided into real ledger and nominal ledger, just as impersonal accounts are subdivided into real accounts and nominal accounts. These two ledgers will maintain all real accounts and nominal accounts respectively. Excepting for a very big business, further subdivision of real ledger and nominal ledger may not be deemed necessary, since even with the increasing volume of business, the number of real and nominal accounts does not tend to increase appreciably - the amounts involved will only increase.

5. CASH BOOK

Cash Book is a Book of Original Entry used to record all cash transactions only. By a cash transaction we mean the one in which, out of the two aspects (or two accounts) involved at least one is cash. A cash transaction involves, either a cash receipt or a cash payment. As already indicated earlier, a cash book is both a journal and a ledger. It is,however, to be kept in mind that a cash book in itself serves the purpose of a ledger only in respect of the cash aspect of the transaction. But even in a cash transaction there must be another aspect (usually a non-cash). Ledger posting should be made in respect of this other aspect or account. No ledger posting would be necessary for the cash aspect only.

Cash transactions include transactions through the bank also. Bank transactions are very common in business. Such transactions may be broadly of four types :

(i) Paying in (depositing) cash, cheques, bills of exchange (for collection and credit), etc.

(ii) Issue of cheques to make payments or to meet obligations.

(iii) Interest paid to bank on overdrawn money or interest received from bank on deposits.

(iv) Bank charges, commissions, etc. paid to bank.

While transactions (i) and (ii) are through cheques or other instruments, those under (iii) and (iv) are effected through accounting adjustments and advice by bankers, without the use of cheques.

If it is assumed that the business has only one current account (with or without other types of accounts in the same and /or in other banks) in one particular bank, then it would be convenient to record transactions relating to this bank accounting in the cash book itself. It may be possible thereby to avoid duplication of work and also confusion and errors. But to do so the cash book has to be designed a bit differently to provide for both cash and bank amount columns on both the debit and the credit sides. Such a cash book is called a double column cash book. It is to be noted that in a double column cash book there are double amount columns only on both the sides - one column for the cash amount and other for bank amount figures. Even when a business maintains a double column cash book, it may have to maintain a separate cash book with bank columns only, for each of the other bank accounts it operates if any. The main cash book is used to record cash and main bank account operations.

An addition of a third amount column on either side of a cash book (so as to make it triple column) is sometimes necessary to record the discount element along with all receipts and payments, for the sake of convenience. The discount we are speaking of here is cash discount. This may be allowable when we receive money and receivable when we pay money (in both the cases within the stipulated period and at a rate agreed upon by the parties).

Mention may be made here of yet another discount, namely, trade discount, receivable or payable at the time of purchases or sales respectively. Ordinarily no separate accounts are maintained for such discounts since only the net purchases or sales figures, as the case may be, are taken into account. In any case, there is no possibility of trade discount being treated in cash book.

When cash discount are intended to be treated in the cash book itself, the discount column on the debit side of the cash book records all discounts allowed on cash receipts (such discount is a nominal a/c - a loss, hence debited). And in the credit side discount received on cash payments are recorded (discount in such a case is a gain, hence credited). Cash receipts and payments here include receipts or payments through cheques also.

It is to be noted, however that, in a triple column cash book, while cash and bank columns serve the purpose of cash and bank accounts (ledger) respectively, the discount column is only a journal so to say - it does not serve the purpose of discount account(s) which is required to be separately provided in the ledger.

Illustration

From the following details is to be prepared a triple column cash book of Mr XY's business. Necessary ledger postings have also to be shown thereafter.

19 x 3			**(Rs. in 000's)**
Jan	1	Balance : Cash	1
		Bank	29

2	Cash sales	10
3	Cash deposited in bank	7
4	Paid by cheque Mr PQ (in full settlement of our dues of Rs.15,000 to them)	14
5	Paid wages to workmen	1
6	Received from Mr RS (who purchased from us last month -Rs 10.000 cheque which was immediately sent to bank)	6
7	Withdrawn cash from bank	2
8	Met sundry office expenses	2
9	Received from Mr TU in cash and he was allowed discount - Rs 2,000 (the account was closed thereby)	17
10	Cash purchase (paid by cash)	12
11	Deposit to bank	5
12	Paid Mr VW by cheque and he allowed a discount Rs 5,000 - The balance (Cr) in this account before this payment was Rs 5000 on account of several purchases in the past	20
13	Mr XY withdrew cash from business for personal purpose	2

MR XY
TRIPLE COLUMN CASH BOOK

(FIgures: Rs.000's)

Dr.						Cr.					
Date	Particulars	LF	Disc	Cash Rs.	Bank Rs.	Date	Particulars	LF Rs.	Disc Rs.	Cash Rs.	Bank Rs.
19x3						19x3					
Jan.1	To Balalnceb/d			1	29	Jan.3	By Bank a/c	C		7	
Jan.2	To Sale a/c			10		Jan.4	By MrPQ a/c		1		14
Jan.3	To Cash a/c	C			7	Jan.5	By Wages a/c			1	
Jan.6	To MrRS a/c				6	Jan.7	By Cash a/c	C			2
Jan.7	To Bank a/c	C	2			Jan.8	By Office Expenses a/c			2	
Jan9	To TU a/c		2	17		Jan.10	By Purchase a/c			12	
Jan.11	To Cash a/c	C			5	Jan.11	By Bank a/c	C		5	
						Jan.12	By Mr VW a/c		5		20
						Jan.15	By Drawings a/c			2	
						Jan.15	By Balance c/d			1	
			2	30	47				6	30	47
19x3											
Jan.16	To Balance b/d			1	11						

Notes :

(i) Transactions dated 3rd, 7th and 11th are contra entries; hence shown on both sides with 'C' in LF columns against respective entries.

(ii) LF columns against all entries have been left blank excepting for the 'C' as per (i) above.

(iii) Discount columns have not been balanced; but totals have been shown on both sides. Posting to the Ledger Accounts (as shown later) will be on the basis of these total figures.

(iv) The cash book has been closed on 15th January and hence it is reopened on 16th with the balance brought down on this date. The peridicity of closing (daily, weekly, forth nightly, monthly, etc.) depends upon the volume of transactions and convenience of a particular business unit.

(v) There are differences of opinion as to the treatment of cheques received.
Two treatments are available viz.,
(a) Treat it as cash first (Dr Cash a/c) and if and when it is sent to bank for collection, Dr Bank a/c & Cr Cash a/c (by a contra entry).
(b) Treat it in bank column (Dr Bank a/c) straight away.

The logic behind the first treatment is that the receipt of a cheque does not automatically imply that the bank balance has increased (since the cheque, instead of being deposited into bank, may be endorsed to a third party). But any cheque issued always results in a decrease in bank balance.

The argument behind the second treatment is that practically all cheques received are subsequently (in a day or two) paid into the business bank a/c for collection and credit.

Which of the two treatments a company should follow would depend upon its own system of bank lodgements. To avoid any confusion in this respect, we have clearly stated, in the transaction dated 6th, the treatment

to be made of the cheque received and have also shown the workings accordingly.

LEDGER ACCOUNTS
(Postings shown only)

'T' Form is used in all cases (Figures in Rs.000's)

Dr			SALES a/c		Cr
			2/1	By Cash a/c	10

Dr.			Wages a/c		Cr
5/1	To Cash a/c	1			

Dr.			Purchases a/c		Cr
10/1	To Casha/c	12			

Dr.			Office Expenses a/c		Cr
8/1	To Cash a/c	2			

Dr.			Drawings a/c		Cr
15/1	To Cash a/c	2			

Dr.			MR PQ a/c		Cr
4/1	To Bank a/c	14	1/1	By Balance b/d	15
4/1	To Discount a/c	1			

Dr.			MR RS a/c		Cr
1/1	To Balance a/c	10	6/1	By Bank a/c	15

Dr.		MR TU a/c			Cr
1/1	To Balance a/c	19	9/1	By Cash a/c	17
			9/1	To Discount a/c	2

Dr.		MR VW a/c			Cr
12/1	To Bank a/c	20	1/1	By Balance b/d	50
12/1	To Discount a/c	3			

Dr.		Discount Allowed a/c			Cr
15/1	To sundries (as per cash book 1/1 to 5/1)	2			

Dr.		Discount Received a/c			Cr
			15/1	To sundries (as per cash book 1/1 to 5/1)	6

Notes :

(i) There is no cash a/c or bank a/c in the ledger since the cash book itself serves the purpose of these ledger accounts (besides serving the purpose of a journal)

(ii) But there are discount accounts in the ledger. The two accounts shown above may be (if desired) consolidated into one discount a/c . In that case the debit and the credit posting shown above will appear in the same manner in the respective sides of the accounts.

(iii) The opening balance (balance b/d - Dr or Cr) in Mr PQ a/c, Mr RS a/c, Mr TU a/c and to Mr. VW a/c, have been found cut from the information given in the problem at appropriate places.

(iv) Though no balancing has been done above it is obvious that Mr PO a/c and Mr TU a/c will be closed with no balance left in either case. (This conforms to the information given in the problem).

ABC CO (A PARTNERSHIP FIRM)

TRIAL BALANCE AS AT 31.12.19 X 3

	Name of Account	L.F.	Debit Balance Rs.	Credit Balance Rs
1.	Land and Building		2,00,000	
2.	Plant and Machinery		1,00,000	
3.	Furniture and Fixture		40,000	
4.	Commission		15,000	
5.	Discount		5,000	8,000
6.	Wages and Salary		21,000	
7.	Opening Stock		17,000	
8.	Purchase		1,02,000	
9.	Sales			2,00,000
10.	Returns			2,000
11.	Office Expenses		11,000	
12.	Sundry Debtors			34,000
13.	Sundry Creditors			22,000
14.	Bank			18,000
15.	Cash			5,000
16.	Capital : A			80,000
	B			1,30,000
	C			90,000
	Total		5,50,000	5,50,000

Note :
Sundry debtors is actually the sum total of the debit balances of all our debtors (usually customers). Similarly sundry creditors is the sum total of all the credit balances of our creditors (usually suppliers of goods and services).

6. TRIAL BALANCE

Trial Balance may be defined as a statement prepared after the balancing of all ledger accounts, showing the balances of all the accounts arranged as debit balances and credit balances respectively. Since the books of accounts are maintainedunder the double entry system, trial balance must agree - that is the total of debit balances must be the same as the total of the credit balances. Thus, if the trial balance does not agree it can be concluded without hesitation that there are errors, whatever be their nature in the books of accounts.

Besides checking the accuracy of the book of accounts as above, the trial balance serves another important purpose.The statment greatly facilitates the preparation of final accounts, Profit and Loss Account and Balance Sheet. The final accounts can be (and are actually) prepared straight from the trial balance without any further reference to the ledger accounts.

An illustrated trial balance is shown on page 60.

FINAL ACCOUNTS

Before going into the mechanism of finalisation of accounts, let's recapitulate what has been discussed earlier. Let us first study the following simple tabular layout :

FRAMEWORK OF BOOK KEEPING

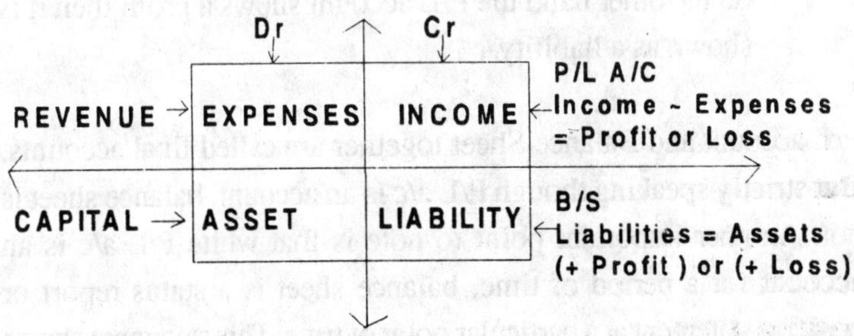

A transaction once intimated to the accountant will be classified under any one of the four categories; expense, asset, income or liability. In case it is expense or an asset, the relevant account will be debited and with all probability the account, when closed, will show debit balance. On the contrary, if the transaction is an income or a liability, it will be credited and the resultant balance will usually be a credit balance. The accounts finalisation stage begins with the preparation of trial balance. From trial balance, the following two statements are prepared.

(1) A revenue statement called Profit and Loss Account (P & L a/c) which takes up only the expenses and the income accounts of trial balance and shows up the difference of the total of the two sets. This difference is either a profit (if total income is higher than total expenses) or loss (if total expenses is higher that total income). In a rare case if total income equals total expense, then there is no profit and no loss.

(2) A statement called the Balance Sheet which shows the asset on one side and the liabilities on the other side. Also by including the net result of the previous statement (profit or loss shown by the P/L account) the two sides of the balance sheet are made to agree in total. In case the P/L account shows a loss then it is treated as an asset. If on the other hand the P/L account shows a profit then it is shown as a liability.

P/L account and Balance Sheet together are called final accounts. But strictly speaking though P/L a/c is an account, balance sheet is not. Another important point to note is that while P/L a/c is an account for a period of time, balance sheet is a status report or position statement at a particular point of time. This statement shows the assets of the business on one side and the liabilities of the business on the other side, both as on a particular date, the date of its preparation.

Based on the trial balance given in the previous topic we show here the Profit and Loss account and the Balance Sheet.

ABC CO

Profit and Loss A/C for the year ended on 31.12.19 x 3

Dr **Cr**

Particulars		**Amount Rs.**	**Particulars**	**Amount Rs.**
To Opening stock		17,000	By Sales	2,00,000
" Purchases	1,02,000		" Closing Stock	12,000
Less : Returns outwards	2,000	1,00,000	(vide note i)	
" Wages & Salaries		21,000	" Discount (Received)	8,000
" Commission		15,000		
" Discount (allowed)		5,000		
" Office Expenses		11,000		
" Net Profit c/d		51,000		
		2,20,000		2,20,000

ABC CO

BALANCE SHEET AS AT 31.12.19X3

Liabilities		Rs.	Assets	Rs
Sundry Creditors		22,000	Land & Building	2,00,000
Bank overdraft		18,000	Plant & Machinery	1,00,000
Capital :			Furniture & fixtures	40,000
A	80,000		Sundry Debtors	34,000
B	1,30,000		Cash	5,000
C	90,000		Closing Stock	12,000
	3,00,000			
Add Net Profit (undistributed)	51,000	3,51,000		
		3,91,000		3,91,000

Notes :

(i) The closing stock of Rs. 12,000 shown in the P/L a/c does not appear in the trial balance. This is a figure assumed for the purpose of the preparation of the P/L a/c. Similarly, closing stock with the same amount figure has been shown as an additional item in the assets side of the balance sheet.

(ii) Net profits in the liability side of the balance sheet, since it increases the liability of the business unit to the owners or partners. We have not shown Qthe distribution of the net profit. In reality, however, the ne. profit will be distributed among the partners in the profit sharing ratio agreed upon by them (equally, in case there is no such agreed ratio).

(iii) The P/L a/c shown above is highly oversimplified. P/L a/c may be divided into a number of sections or parts. The end result of one part is the starting point of the next part. The different parts or sections are as follows :

(a) Trading section : It shows the gross profit or loss during the accounting period. Gross profit or loss (a controversial term in accounting) ordinarily means the direct profit or loss from manufacturing and/or selling activities of the business.

(b) P/L Proper Section : This section shows the net result of business operations during an accounting period in the form of net profit or loss. This is the most important section in the P/L a/c.

(c) P/L Appropriation Section : This is the last section of a P/L a/c applicable to every enterprise other than a proprietorship and distribution of Net Profit found out in the preceding section.

During the preparation of annual P/L a/c and Balance Sheet some adjustments become necessary mainly due to two reasons :

(a) to ensure that the accounting period concept has been strictly adhered to, and

(b) to treat some such items as are accounted for correctly only during the closing; for example, description, bad debt, reserves and provisions, and most important, closing stock.

A detailed discussion of such adjustments is outside the purview of the book, since this is not so important for non-finance people.

CHAPTER 5

INTERPRETATION OF FINANCIAL STATEMENTS

1. How to Read a Balance Sheet; 2. Reliability and Authenticity of Balance Sheet; 3. Analysis of Financial statements; 4. Limitations of published Accounts; 5. Illustrative Case.

1. HOW TO READ A BALANCE SHEET

The balance sheet is the most important of all financial statements since it forms the basis and the bedrock of all subsequent financial analysis. An ability to understand and interpret a balance sheet - to read a balance sheet between the lines - is therefore considered to be a must for all, especially executives charged with decision-making and control.

Essentially, a balance sheet is a statement embodying a pictorial representation of the position of assets and liabilities of a business as on a particular date. Assets mean what the company owns and liabilities are what the company owes. Thus, a balance sheet is a statement showing what the company owns and what it owes. And this statement should be presented in a manner that the layman should be able to understand and interpret it. However, some conceptual background and also some idea of the implication of different items included in a balance sheet is required to understand it, just as some power of appreciation of art is required to interpret and appreciate a picture. An attempt is made in this section to help develop this power of interpretation and appreciation of our readers. For convenience of understanding, we shall discuss this under the following heads: form of balance sheet, assets side, liabilities side, the complete balance sheet, balance sheet as a valuation of statement and reliability of balance sheet.

(i) Form of Balance Sheet : Here is an imaginary balance sheet :

NOWHERE LIMITED - BALANCE SHEET

AS ON 31ST DECEMBER 19x0

(FIgure in Rs./Lakhs)

Previous Year	**Liabilities**		**Previous Year**	**Assets**	
40	Share Capital			Fixed Assets	
	Equity Share Capital (Rs. 100 shares)	40	10	Goodwill	5
			5.5	Land & Building	10
15	5 % Preference Share capital (Rs. 100 shares)	15	28	Plant and Machinery	30
			11	Furniture and	10
			5.5	Patents	
	Reserves and Surplus			Investment	
2	Capital Reserve	2	0.9	6 % Deposit Certificates	1
2	General Reserve 2 Add : P& L A/C Balance 5	7	8	Share in subsidiaries	8
0.9	Debentures Redemption Reserve Fund	1			
	Secured Loans			Current Assets, Loans And Advances	
5	10 % Debenture Bonds	5	14	Sundry Debtors	24

(Figure in Rs./Lakhs)

Previous Year	Liabjlities		Previous Year	Assets	
16.1	Bank Overdraft	20	20	Inventory	30
		4		Bills received	5
		2		Cash	1
	Unsecured Loans				
19	4 % Public Deposit	20			
	Current Lilabiliies and Provisions			Miscellaneous Expenses	
7	Sundry Creditors	15	1.1	Advertisement Suspense	1
2	Bills payable	3			
1	Provision for Tax	2			
110		130	110		130

The following points are worth mentioning regarding the form and general features of a balance sheet :

(a) Name of the company or enterprise must appear at the top of the balance sheet.

(b) The date of the balance sheet must also appear at the top. It is to be noted in this connection that a balance sheet is a position statement as on a particular date - it is a statement of a point of time, not for a period of time.

(c) As per the requirements of the Companies Act a balance sheet should show two sets of amount figures - one set for the last date of the relevant accounting year and another for the last date of the previous accounting year.

(d) Again, as per the requirements of the Companies Act in India, a balance sheet may show figures to the nearest rupee (Paise figures may be ignored in conformity with the principle of Materiality). However, for convenience of handling we have shown the above figures in Rs.lakhs only. Though the annual balance sheet meant for publication and submission as per legal requirements has to show figures to the nearest rupee, to meet various internal needs from time to time, a balance sheet may have to be prepared sometimes in a summary manner and with figures to the nearest thousand or even lakhs, depending upon the purpose.

(e) To avoid confusion due to the numerous data in the balance sheet, it is customary to show only the group totals in the main balance sheet with a reference to accompanying schedules. These schedules provide the break-down and all details of the respective group totals.

(f) Besides the schedules, some notes are also added at the end. These notes are meant for providing further explanation about the implications or interpretation of a particular item or items and the amount involved.

(g) The classification of the various items in the assets and liabilities sides of the balance sheet shown above has been made in conformity with the form of balance sheet as per Schedule VI part I of the Companies, Act.

A question may arise whether this form of balance sheet has to be rigidly adhered to. Dogmatic adherence to this form under all cases may be neither desirable nor practicable. A company, if it so desires, may deviate from such requirements provided they get prior approval from the Central Government. Thus, these days, we come across quite a few balance sheets of different companies laid out not strictly in accordance with Schedule VI Part I, but in the form of Proprietary Statement or Statement of Sources and Uses of Funds.

(ii) Asset Side : A business enterprise earns profit only by efficient 'assets management'. Whenever profit is generated, it is reflected through an accretion of assets, to be precise, the current assets in the first instance. To balance the two sides of a balance sheet, such an accretion in assets is counter balanced by similar accretion in liabilities, usually reserves and surplus. If and when such profit is distributed to the owners, reserves and surplus will deplete to that extent with the consequent reduction also in the assets value, usually cash and bank balances.

Out of the four groups of assets, true assets employed in the business or trading assets as they are called, are in the first and third groups, namely, fixed assets and current assets, loans and advances. Investment represents money invested outside the business. it is, nevertheless, an asset and can be converted into cash more or less easily. But since it is not invested in the business itself, it is not considered to be a trading asset.

Confusion may arise regarding miscellaneous expenses being called assets. These expenses in reality are prepaid expenses. To the extent such expenses have not been written off against revenue, they are assets assets of an intangible nature, for the purpose of the balance sheet. The simple reason for this is that the benefits out of these expenses would be available during the subsequent accounting year or years. When any such items is fully written off it would no longer appear as an asset in the balance sheet.

The most controversial item in the list of fixed asset is goodwill. Goodwill is a term easy to describe but difficult to define. From an accounting point of view, goodwill indicates the super profit earning capacity of the business. it is an intangible asset. It may be a fictitious asset also (for example, when the goodwill has been lost and yet we find a substantial amount under the head goodwill '.. 'he balance sheet).

The inclusion of goodwill in a balance sheet does not necessarily mean that the company possesses goodwill of equivalent value. On the other hand, the non-inclusion of goodwill in a balance sheet may signify that the company has goodwill of considerable value. Goodwill appears in the balance sheet usually in the case of acquisition of a going concern after payment of an amount towards the value of its goodwill over and above the amount paid for its net assets. In the balance sheet of Nowhere Ltd., an amount of Rs. 5 lakhs has been shown against goodwill. The appearance of such goodwill in a balance sheet, whatever may be its source of origin, results in an equivalent reduction in the amount of reserves and surplus or even equity shares (and for that matter, in the shareholders' fund). The net reserves and surplus in the illustration would, therefore, be Rs.5 lakhs only (Rs. 10 lakhs minus Rs. 5 lakhs).

(iii) Liabilities Side : The total liabilities of Nowhere Ltd., as the end of the currently year is Rs 130 lakhs, as against Rs.110 at the end of the year. All the five groups of liabilities can broadly be divided into two categories :

(i) Liabilities to owners/members - share capital and reserves and surplus.

(ii) Liabilities to outsiders - secured loans, unsecured loans and current liabilities and provisions.

Liabilities to outsiders are the true liabilities. But those in the first category, to owners or members are shown as liabilities only to fall in the line with the business entity concept of accounting. Let us consider the same five groups of liabilities from a different angle. We may exclude for this purpose the last group, namely current liabilities and provisions (since it represents in effect the negative side or neutralising element of working capital or to be more precise, a part finance towards working capital of the business). The other four groups together broadly represent the total capital employed by the business which can again be viewed from two angles:

(i) Own Capital — Share capital and reserves and surplus

(ii) Loan Capital — Secured and unsecured loans

Loan capital is sometimes expressed as debt, funded debt, etc. though all such expressions are not strictly synonymous. Own capital, if it does not contain preference shares, is also called the owners' equity or the equity fund. If share capital consists of both equity and preference shares, then usually the face value of preference shares is deducted from the own capital to arrive at equity fund or equity.

One important point to be noted in connection with capital (both own capital and loan capital) is that it represents only one side — the abstract side of the business, the concrete side being the assets. In other words, capital remains invested in the different assets of the business. Thus, at any point of time the own capital may be arrived at by subtracting the total outside liabilities of the business from its total assets, excluding, of course, intangibles like goodwill, etc.

There is a lot of confusion (especially among non-accountants) about reserves and surplus (one of the elements of total capital employed). Reserves ordinarily mean undistributed profits or unappropriated income. But it does not necessarily lead us to the conclusion that such undistributed profits or income are separately kept as liquid cash or in the form of bank balance which can be withdrawn at any time. In fact, like share capital or loans, reserves and surplus also remain invested in different types of assets of the business, mostly beyond recognition and defy precise segregation. There is one exception to this. If the word 'fund' is used after any reserve, then such reserve has to be represented in specifically earmarked assets of similar amount in the assets side of the balance sheet. In the illustrative balance sheet of Nowhere Ltd., there is a liability (under reserves and surplus) of debenture redemption reserve fund and also an asset (under investments) of 6 per cent deposit certificates —both amounting to Rs. 1 lakh. Here the reserve fund in the first case is represented by a specific investment (Outside the business) for a similar amount, in the second case.

(iv) The Complete Balance Sheet: We now focus our attention on the balance sheet as a whole considering liabilities and assets together. We shall discuss and illustrate consecutively other four concepts namely, working capital, capital employed, net worth or shareholders' fund and owners' equity.

Working capital is defined as current assets less current liabilities. The working capital of Nowhere Ltd., is Rs. 40 lakhs (Rs. 60 lakhs minus Rs. 20 lakhs). Strictly speaking, working capital is the total of the current assets (Rs. 60 lakhs in this case). This may be called gross working capital. However, out of this Rs. 60 lakhs, Rs. 20 lakhs representing current liabilities has been financed, so to say freely, by ordinary creditors. As a result, the net working capital has come down to Rs. 40 lakhs. By working capital, we usually mean the net working capital only.

Let us analyse the composition of the working capital of Nowhere Ltd. Money locked up with customers is actually Rs. 29 lakhs (sundry debtors Rs. 24 lakhs and bills receivable Rs 5 lakhs). Then we have inventories (representing raw materials, work-in-process, finished goods etc.) valued at Rs. 30 lakhs. Additionally we have cash of Rs. 1 lakh. Thus the total current assets is Rs. 60 lakhs. Against this, however, we owe our suppliers for goods and services, an amount of Rs. 18 lakhs (Sundry creditors Rs. 15 lakhs and bills payable Rs. 3 lakhs). We also have a provision for tax Rs. 2 lakhs, which represents our liabilities, and provisions thus come to Rs. 20 lakhs.

It may be noted that working capital at the end of the previous year was Rs. 40 lakhs (current assets Rs. 50 lakhs less current liabilities

Rs. 10 lakhs). Thus over the previous year there has been an increase of Rs. 10 lakhs in the net working capital. This is a common feature — working capital tends to increase in keeping with (though not in exact proportion to) an increase in activity, usually represented by turnover or sales.

Capital Employed may be looked at from two angles — the total capital employed by the business and capital employed in the business itself. In the Nowhere Ltd. balance sheet, there is an outside investment of Rs. 9 lakhs, which is not being used in the business itself. For the purpose of arriving at capital employed in the business, this Rs. 9 lakhs should be deducted (since this represents funds invested outside the business). The capital employed in the business would therefore be Rs. 95 lakhs (Total investments of Rs. 104 lakhs minus outside investment of Rs. 9 lakhs).

This Rs. 95 lakhs capital employed in the business can be arrived at in two ways:

(i)	Net block working capital	=	Rs. 99 lakhs + Rs 40 lakhs
		=	Rs. 95 lakhs
(ii)	Share capital plus reserves and surplus (less goodwill and miscellaneous expenses) plus loans minus investments.	=	Rs. 55 lakhs + Rs. 10 lakhs-(Rs. 5 Lakhs + Rs. 1 lakhs) Rs. 45 lakhs - Rs. 9 lakhs +
		=	Rs. 95 lakhs

Net worth of the business (also called shareholders fund) is nothing but the total of share capital and reserves and surplus. In Nowhere Ltd. this is Rs. 59 lakhs (share capital Rs. 55 lakhs and adjusted reserves and surplus Rs. 4 lakhs). As the very name suggests this Rs. 59 lakhs is the net worth of the business. The net worth would be accordingly, the total capital employed minus loans or Rs. 104 minus Rs. 45 lakhs. Strictly speaking, this represents the shareholders share of the total business. That is why, it is also called shareholders fund.

Owners Equity (also called Equity Net Worth or Equity Fund or only Equity) represents that part of the net worth or shareholders only. By deducting preference share capital from the net worth, one can arrive at the owners equity.

In the case of Nowhere Ltd., owners equity is Rs. 44 lakhs (shareholders fund Rs. 59 lakhs less preference share capital Rs. 15 lakhs). Equity fund can also be worked out as follows:

	Rs. in lakhs		
Equity Share Capital			40
Add: Reserves and Surplus		10	
Less: Goodwill	5		
Miscellaneous Expenses	1	6	4
			44

NOTE: Miscellaneous Expenses is also to be deducted from reserves and surplus in arriving at equity fund (since these are intangible assets).

2. RELIABILITY AND AUTHENTICITY OF BALANCE SHEET

The questions relevant here are how reliable is the balance sheet and how authentic is the statement. In the case of the balance sheet of a proprietary concern or a partnership firm, there is no provision for statutory audit by qualified accountants. For this reason, the reliability and authenticity of such balance sheets are of a very limited nature.

In the case of limited companies, however, balance sheets are more reliable and authentic documents, simply because the accounts are audited by independent and qualified auditors, whose rights, duties and liabilities are statutorily determined (that is, provided in the Companies Act.) The auditor in his report has to certify inter alia that the balance sheet presents a true and fair view of the state of affairs of the business as on the relevant data (that is, the date of the balance sheet).

A company balance sheet is also reliable because it is signed by the company secretary and some of the directors of the company, besides the auditors. Auditors may also add some notes before signing the balance sheet to cover some special points requiring explanation or opinion from them. Sometimes the auditors even qualify their audit report accompanying a balance sheet and profit or loss account, mentioning in particular some irregular or improper transactions or accounting treatments as 'qualifications'. (An unqualified audit report means a clean report and that there are no irregularities).

However, even such provisions for independent audit and audit report do not per se render a balance sheet fully reliable and authentic. This is due to the fact that the conventional accounting structure itself suffers from some serious limitations (discussed later in this chapter).

3. ANALYSIS OF FINANCIAL STATEMENTS

Published accounts and for that matter, any financial statement, presents only some figures, but facts lie hidden behind the figures. Unless these facts are brought out in proper perspective, any conclusion derived from the figures as such may be erroneous and sometimes misleading. Hence, the importance of proper analysis and interpretation of financial statements. Analysis of financial statements means rearrangement of figures following some specific techniques facilitating subsequent interpretation. Analysis also includes some further accounting operations relevant to the particular technique or techniques adopted and the specific purpose to be served.

Interpretation of data to arrive at valid conclusions usually follows analysis of figures. Many tools and techniques of analysis of financial statements have been evolved to arrive at correct conclusions through a proper interpretation of the financial data. The more important techniques are as follows:

(i) Comparative Statements (in respect of both profit and loss account and balance sheet)

(ii) Trend analysis (say, of sales, expenses, etc) (The two techniques mentioned above can be effective when the indexing method is used — vide an illustrative case at the end of this Chapter).

(iii) Statement of proprietary fund

(iv) Financial ratio analysis

(v) Cash flow analysis

(vi) Funds flow analysis (including the statement of increase and decrease in working capital).

(The last three techniques mentioned above will be explained in the subsequent chapters).

4. LIMITATIONS OF PUBLISHED ACCOUNTS

In examining the limitations of published accounts we should be clear about two things, namely, the objective of published accounts and the expectations therefrom of the different classes of people and interests. The prime objective of a published account is to present a true and fair view; (a) in the case of the balance sheet, of the state of affairs and (b) in case of the profit or loss account, of the profit or loss of the company for the accounting year.

Let us take the expectations from the published accounts. Published accounts ought to present a true and fair view to all concerned directly or indirectly. Classes may run at cross purposes or may clash with one another. But every class has some expectations from the published accounts. These classes of interest are as follows:

Owners or shareholders, employees (and trade unions), prospective investors, prospective merger candidates, financiers, creditors, management, government and public.

If one goes deep into the subject, one will be dismayed to discover that published accounts suffers from serious limitations in as much as the above-mentioned objectives are hardly fulfilled and the expectations of the different classes of interest are mostly belied.

It has been said that "the Balance Sheet is like a bikini suit... what it reveals is interesting, but what it conceals is vital." In fact, anybody who can read a balance sheet between the lines will be able to come out with quite a few interesting facts and figures to the affairs of the company concerned. To an intelligent financial analyst, a balance sheet can present a neat and comprehensive picture depicting the financial position of the company and consequently, help him draw conclusions which could be purposeful, meaningful and by and large valid. But that we should not expect too much from published accounts, since our disappointment is bound to be greater if we do so.

5. ILLUSTRATIVE CASE(S)

(a) (Summarised) Balance Sheet as on 3.12.19x6

(Rs. in Lakhs / Crores)

Liabilities			Assets		
Share Capital:			**Fixed Assets :**		
Equity	40		Goodwill	7	
Preference	10	50	All others	58	65
Reserve & Surplus		20	**Investment**		12
Secured Loans			**Current Assets, Loans & Advances**		
Term Loans	16		Inventory	34	
Working Capital Borrowings	19	35	Debtors	35	
			Cash/Bank	3	72
Unsecured Loans		18	**Misc. Expenses**		
Current Liabilities & Provisions					
Current Liabilities	24		Preliminary Expenses	6	
Provisions	8	32			
Total		155			155

(b) Matching of Sources and Deployment of Funds.

Sources	Deployment				
	Fixed Assets	Investment	CA Loans & Advances	Misc Expenses	Total
Share Capital	44			6	50
Reserves & Surplus	5	12	3		20
Secured Loans	16		19		35
Unsecured Loans			18		18
Current Liabilities & Provisions			32		32
Total	65	12	72	6	155

Notes :

i) Some of the principles followed in the above matching exercise are :

(a) long-term finance should be used for long-term assets primarily and partly for working capital also;

(b) short-term finance should be used only for short-term assets, mainly working capital;

(c) investments should be financed from own funds only; so also miscellaneous expenses (e.g. preliminary expenses on company formation);

(d) The above table presents one possible matching. There could be some variations consistent with the principles underlying such matching exercise.

(c) Primary Analysis of Balance Sheet

	To find out	Workings		Results
(1)	New Worth (Shareholders Fund)	50+(20-7-6)		57
(2)	Equity Net Worth (Equity Fund or Equity)	57-19 Or 40+20-7-6		47
(3)	Working Capital	72-32		40
(4)	Capital Employed :			
	(a) by the business	58+12+40 Or 50+20+35+18-7-6		110
	(b) in the business	110-12		98
(5)	Break-up of Capital Employed into:			
	(a) Own capital (own fund or shareholders fund	Same as 1	57	
	(b) loan capital (loan fund or borrowed fund)	35+18	53	110

CHAPTER 6

FINANCIAL RATIO ANALYSIS

1. Classification of Ratios; 2. Critical Analysis of a Few Ratios; 3. Return on Investment (ROI); 4. Marketing ROI; 5. Check-List of Purpose-Based Ratios.

1. CLASSIFICATION OF RATIOS

Financial or Accounting Ratio may be defined as relating one accounting figure to another to provide better comparison - a comparison on an 'apples to apples' basis. The rationale behind ratio analysis is that absolute figures do not and cannot disclose true facts or real position.

Ratios can be classified from different viewpoints. From the viewpoint of the source of components, a ratio may be :

(a) Revenue Statement Ratio — if both the components are available from the P/L account or revenue statement (e.g. gross profit ratio, net profit ratio, expenses ratio, etc.)

(b) Balance Sheet Ratio — if both the components are available from the balance sheet (e.g. current ratio, liquid ratio, debt equity ratio, etc.)

(c) Composite Ratio or Revenue Statement and Balance Sheet Ratio — if one of the components is available from the balance sheet and the other from the revenue statement (e.g. inventory turnover, accounts receivable turnover, return on investment, etc.)

From the viewpoint of accessibility, ratios could be external and internal. External ratios are those which can be worked out from the published statements alone. Internal ratios can be prepared not from published statements alone, but from other data with or without the help of such statements. All cost ratios (materials cost to total cost, labour cost to total cost, overhead cost, etc.) fall in this category. Also included in this category are some physical financial relationship (working capital per unit of product, fixed capital per unit of productt, etc.) and some productivity ratios (contribution per salesman, value added per worker, etc.).

The most useful classification is from the viewpoint of the nature and purpose of financial ratios. A more or less comprehensive list of ratios classified accordingly is given on following pages, showing also, side by side, the mode of calculation in each case.

A. ACTIVITY RATIO

1. Inventory Turnover (Times) = $\dfrac{\text{Cost of goods sold (or sales)}}{\text{Average Inventory}}$

2. Average Inventory Period = $\dfrac{\text{Average Inventory}}{\text{Cost of sales per day (Month)}}$

3. Accounts Receivable Turnover (Times) = $\dfrac{\text{Sales}}{\text{Average Accounts Receivables}}$

4. Average Collection Period (Days/Months) = $\dfrac{\text{Average Accounts Receivables}}{\text{Credit Sales per day (month)}}$

5. Sundry Creditors Turnover (Times) = $\dfrac{\text{Cost of goods purchased}}{\text{Average Sundry Creditors}}$

6. Average Payment Period (Days/Months) = $\dfrac{\text{Average Sundry Creditors}}{\text{Credit purchases or cost of goods purchased per day (month)}}$

B. COST RATIOS (Percentages)

1. Materials consumed as percentage of Sales or Total Cost
2. Employee expenses as percentage of Sales or Total Cost
3. Marketing expenses as percentage of Sales or Total Cost
4. Fixed costs as percentage of Sales or Total Cost
5. Variable costs as percentage of Sales or Total Cost.

C. PROFITABILITY RATIOS (Percentages)

1. Gross Operating Margin = $\dfrac{\text{Gross Operating profit before depreciation, interest and tax} \times 100}{\text{Sales}}$

2. Net Operating Margin = $\dfrac{\text{Net Operating profit before depreciation, interest and tax} \times 100}{\text{Sales}}$

3. Return on Equity = $\dfrac{\text{Net profit after tax and Preference dividend} \times 100}{\text{Equity paid up and free reserves}}$

D. LIQUIDITY RATIOS (Times)

1. Current Assets/Current Liabilities (= Current Ratio)
2. Current Assets Less Inventories/Current Liabilities (= Liquid Ratio or Acid Test Ratio)

E. LEVERAGE RATIOS

1. Debt-Equity Ratio $= \dfrac{\text{Total Debt (Short-term + Long-term + Redeemable Preference share Capital)}}{\text{Equity + Reserves}}$

2. Total Debt/Annual Fund (i.e. Profits + Depreciation + Interest)

3. Debt Servicing Coverage Ratio (DSCR)* $= \dfrac{\text{Interest + Preference Dividend}}{\text{Annual Fund}}$

*This is a very important ratio from the viewpoints of outside financiers, especially Banks and Financial Institutions.

F. VALUATION RATIOS

1. Earning-price Ratio $= \dfrac{\text{Market price of equity share}}{\text{Earnings per share (E.P.S)*}}$

2. Price/Earning (%) $= \dfrac{\text{Earnings per share x 100}}{\text{Market price of equity share}}$

3. Dividend rate per cent $= \dfrac{\text{Dividend per share x 100}}{\text{Paid up value of share}}$

4. Yield per cent $= \dfrac{\text{Dividend amount per share x 100}}{\text{Market price per share}}$

---

*E.P.S. is found out as : $\dfrac{\text{Profit after tax less preference Dividend}}{\text{Number of equity shares}}$

2. CRITICAL ANALYSIS OF A FEW RATIOS

An attempt is made here to critically analyse a few commonly used ratios and indicate some controversial aspects in their mode of computation. We have chosen only four ratios for this purpose — gross profit ratio, debt equity ratio, inventory turnover ratio and debtors turnover ratio.

Inventory Turnover Ratio: The usual definition is cost of sales divided by average inventory. Usually this ratio is used not so much for interpretation as for internal control, or to be more precise, for inventory control. Thus the need for computation of the ratio at different points of time at shorter intervals, say at the end of each month, is urgently felt.

If we calculate the ratio taking a particular period figure of cost of sales and the same period-end figure of inventory, the ratio may not be comparable from time to time. The best method would, therefore, be to go by the moving annual total of cost of sales and to take the average of the beginning and the end values of inventory in respect of the same twelve-month period. However, this approach is seldom adopted in practice.

A further refinement of the above approach could be to take only a month-end inventory figure and relate it to subsequent twelve months cost of sales-actual costs (for ex-post analysis) projected cost (for ex-ante analysis). The logic behind this statement is that inventory as at the end of a particular period is meant for consumption during the subsequent period and not the preceding one. The same moving annual total approach may be adopted in calculating the cost of sales. The procedure has been explained with the help of an illustration later. This shows the conventional treatment and the one suggested for inventory turnover ratio as well as debtors turnover ratio.

Debtors' Turnover Ratio : This ratio, commonly expressed in terms of month (or days), is calculated as closing receivables divided by average monthly (or daily) sales, which is usually the annual sales divided by twelve (or 365). However, like the inventory turnover ratio, this method also cannot give a full picture of the real turnover of debtors. First, the position may be veiled because of window-dressing at the end of the accounting year. The ratio may also be vitiated to a significant extent when sales are highly seasonal in nature.

A more refined approach is to relate month-end receivables to sales of the immediately preceding month or months, considering the fact that the receivables arise because of past sales, unlike inventory which is held to meet future sales.

Let us now illustrate our suggested methods of computation of both inventory turnover ratio and debtors turnover ratio, using hypothetical data :

(Figures in Rs. Lakhs)

	Actual 19 x 5				Projected 19 x 6	
	Sales	Cost of Sales	Monthend Inventory	Monthend Receivable	Sales	Cost of Sales
January	8	6	30	20	8	6
February	12	9	35	25	16	12
March	16	12	40	30	20	15
April	20	15	40	49	24	18
May	20	15	45	45	24	18
June	12	9	40	42	16	12
July	12	9	35	40	16	12
August	8	6	35	40	12	9
September	8	6	30	38	16	12
October	12	9	30	36	16	12
November	12	9	35	40	16	12
December	8	6	35	40	16	12
Total	148	111	-	-	200	150

Workings :

Conventional Method

Inventory Turnover Ratioo (19 x 5- end) $\frac{(111)}{35}$ = 3.17

Debtors' Turnover Ratio (19 x 5 - end) $\frac{(40)}{148/12}$ = 3.24 months

Months' Sales Outstanding

Suggested Methods

Inventory Turnover Ratio

March 19 x 5

Cost of Sales for April X5 to March X6 / March X5 Inventory = 117 / 40 = 2.93

December 19 X 5

Cost of sales (Budgeted for Jan to Dec. 19 x 6 / December 19 x Inventory = 150 / 35 = 4.29

Months Sales Outstanding

	Outstanding	Sales		Month
March 19x5	30	March	16	1.00
		Feb	12	1.00
		Jan	2	0.25
		(of 8)		
			30	2.25
December 19x5	40	Dec	8	1.00
		Nov	12	1.00
		Oct	12	1.00
		Sept.	8	1.00
			40	4.00

(Only two examples of working in each case are shown here)

Interpretation (19x5 Results)

Inventory Turnover Ratio

Actually much better than what is shown under conventional method (4.29 as against 3.17)

Months' Sales Outstanding

Actual position is not disclosed under the conventional method, since the position is four months actually and not 3.24 months, as arrived at under the conventional method.

3. RETURN ON INVESTMENT (ROI)

This is perhaps the most commonly used ratio—both for interpretation of the published accounts and also for control of internal operations. By definition, the ratio is between return and investment or capital employed. The ratio is usually broken down into two components, as follows :

$$\text{ROI} = \frac{\text{Net Profit}}{\text{Capital Employed}}$$

$$= \frac{\text{Net Profit}}{\text{Sales}} \times \frac{\text{Sales}}{\text{Capital Employed}}$$

= Net Profit Ratio x Capital Turnover Ratio

As has been rightly observed, ROI is like a rubber with infinite elasticity. There are various methods of calculating both returns and investment or capital employed. For example

Return : Net profit after tax, net profit after tax but before depreciation and interest, net profit tax, operating profit before tax, earning before interest and tax (Ebit), contribution (that is sales revenue less variable cost of sales), cash flow (for project evaluation purpose), etc.

Investments : Total of fixed assets and total of current assets, fixed assets plus working capital, net worth, equity net worth, own capital plus working capital, only own capital, only working capital and so on.

We thus get several combinations of return and investment resulting in quite a few ROIs is based on the same set of data. However, it needs to be purposeful and all such workings may be correct considering the particular purpose or purposes in view.

For example, ROI may be worked out as ROSE, that is, Return On Shareholders Equity, when one is interested in evaluating profitability of the enterprise strictly from the equity shareholders point of view. ROSE should be calculated by taking after-tax profit, less preference divided, if any, as percentage to equity net worth or equity shareholders fund.

Let us now illustrate and examine some interesting implications of the RΘI. As we have already indicated, ROI has two major components. Net Profit Ratio (percentage) and Capital Turnover Ratio (Times). The result arrived at after multiplying these two components will be ROI. For example, 5 percent net profit ratio and a capital turnover of our four times will result in an ROI of 20 percent. This 20 percent ROI could be achieved by any combination of the two components say, only 2 percent net profit ratio and a capital turnover of ten times or 10 percent net profit ratio with a capital turnover of 2 times only.

As is well known, a manufacturing-cum-marketing organisation will have relatively larger amount of capital investments than that of a similar company in the same industry which is a purely trading concern. Both the companies may have around the same ROI but the composition of the ROI will be significantly different. In case of the manufacturing-cum-marketing organisation, the net profit ratio will be relatively high but the capital turnover rather low (because of high capital investments relative to turnover). The purely marketing organisation will, on the other hand, achieve a higher rate of capital turnover but relatively low net profit ratio (since their net profit is restricted to only the earnings from trading operations).

Net profit ratio, one of the two components of ROI, can again be broken into two ratios as follows :

$$\frac{\text{Net Profit}}{\text{Sales}} = \frac{\text{Contribution}}{\text{Sales}} \times \frac{\text{Net Profit}}{\text{Contribution}}$$

$$= \text{C/S Ratios x Margin of Safety}$$

The concepts of C/S Ratio and Margin of Safety have been explained in detail in chapter 13. The mode of calculation of these ratios, as shown above, will be adequate for our present purpose.

We may now consider the total ROI model and its major components with the help of an illustration, using imaginary figures :

	Rs.Lakhs	Rs.Lakhs
1. Capital Employed		
Net Block	100	
Working Capital	100	
Total		200
2. Sales		400
3. Marginal Cost of Sales		300
4. Contribution (2-3)		100
5. Fixed Cost		
Operational	40	
Finance Charges	20	
Total		60
6. Net Profit (4-5)		40

$$\text{ROI} = \frac{\text{Net Profit}}{\text{Capital Employed}} = \frac{40}{200} = 0.2$$

$$\text{Marginal Ratio} = \frac{\text{Net Profit}}{\text{Sales}} = \frac{40}{400} = 0.1$$

$$\text{Capital Turnover} = \frac{\text{Sales}}{\text{Capital Employed}} = \frac{400}{200} = 2$$

$$\text{C/S Ratio} = \frac{\text{Contribution}}{\text{Sales}} = \frac{100}{400} = 0.25$$

$$\text{Margin of Safety} = \frac{\text{Net Profit}}{\text{Contribution}} = \frac{40}{100} = 0.4$$

Check (i) 0.1x2 = 0.2 or 20 per cent (ROI)

(ii) 0.25x0.4 = 0.1 or 10 per cent (Margin Ratio)

4. MARKETING ROI

From the point of view of marketing management it will be both interesting and useful if an attempt is made to arrive at the marketing ROI, as distinct from the corporate ROI. For this purpose, marketing ROI may be defined as the relationship between marketing net profit or net marketing margin and the capital employed only in marketing operations. This ROI also can be expressed either as a ratio or as a percentage.

Continuing with the same illustrations given in the previous topic and with some further imaginary data, an attempt is made here to work out the marketing ROI in the above case, using the formula :

$$\text{Marketing ROI} = \frac{\text{Net Marketing Margin (NMM)}}{\text{Investments in Marketing Operations}}$$

(Figures are in Rs. Lakhs)

	Total	Non-Marketing	Marketing	Remarks
1 Capital Employed				
Fixed Assets	100	90	10	10% represents automobiles, warehouse, office equipment, etc. used by Marketing Department.
Working Capital	100	40	60	60% represents finished Inventory and Net Receivables
Total	200	130	70	
2. Financial Charges	20	13	7	10% is the assumed effective rate taking into account both own funds and loan funds employed.
3. Sales	400	320	400	320 is the transfer price of goods from Manufacturing to Marketing.
4. Marginal Cost	300	270	350	350 includes 320 and another 30 are variable marketing expenses.
5. Contribution(3-4)	100	50	50	
6. Fixed Cost:				
Operational	40	18	22	break-up assumed
Financial charges	20	13	7	break-up as per 2 above
Total	60	31	29	
7. Net Profit (5-6)	40	19	21	NMM is 21
8. ROI (7 on 1)	20%	15% (appr.)	30%	

In the above illustration we have assumed a manufacturing-cum-marketing company and a system of performance evaluation treating manufacturing and marketing departments as two independent profit centres. Incidentally, the marketing ROI is higher than that for non-marketing (i.e.primarily manufacturing) operations. A point to note in this connection is that the two ROI percentages cannot be added up due to mathematical reasons and also due to the fact that the marginal cost figures involve some duplication. Ordinarily marketing ROI., as it is in the above case. But what is more important is not the marketing ROI percentage figure per se but a trend of the percentages worked out from time to time following uniformly the same approach. This trend can indicate broadly whether there is an upward or downward swing in overall efficiency in the marketing operations of the company.

In a purely trading concern application of the above model will be relatively easy, since there will be practically nothing under non-marketing. And in such a situation the marketing ROI will be equal to, or at least very close to, the corporate ROI. Further, this approach of arriving at marketing ROI percentages and comparing the same from time to time can be extended to various marketing divisions within a company and this can form a good criterion for overall evaluation and comparison of inter-divisional and even inter-product performance.

5. CHECK-LIST OF PURPOSE-BASED RATIOS

Accounting ratios should not be computed simply for the sake of computation. In fact, a large number of ratios might cloud and confuse people and thus defeat the main purpose. Significant ratios relevant to a particular purpose have only to be selected and computed and only then can some meaningful conclusions be drawn.

A check-list is provided here to enable one to select the ratio or ratios suited to some specific purpose/s :

Test/Purpose		Significant Ratio/Ratios
1.	Financial stability (Short & Medium term)	Liquid Ratio Current Ratio
2.	Financial stability (Long-term)	Debt-Equity Ratio Proprietary Ratio (i.e.fixed assets to share-holders fund)
3.	Adequacy of working capital, Overtrading/ undertrading total	Current Ratio Working capital to sales Working capital to total assets.
4.	Working Capital Management	All against 3 above and Inventory to working capital, Receivables to working capital. Cash to working capital
5.	Debts management and Collection efficiency	Current debt to total debt Debtors Turnover Ratio
6.	Creditors management	Creditors to cost of goods or credit purchase
7.	Inventory management	Inventory Turnover Ratio
8.	Investment in fixed assets	Proprietary Ratio Sales to fixed assets
9.	Capital Structure	Debt Equity Ratio
10.	Assets Structure	Fixed Assets to Working Capital Ratio
11.	Profitability	Gross Profit Ratio Net Profit Ratio Operating Ratio ROI Return on Net Worth/ Shareholders Equity (ROSE)

12.	**Productivity**	**Output to input (Physical units or value)** **Output to capital (unit or money)** **Sales per salesman** **Contribution per salesman** **Fixed assets per unit of product/ Re. of sale.** **Working capital per unit of product/ Re. of sale.**

Finally, it is important to note that there is nothing called an 'ideal ratio'. There could be of course be norms of different ratios that should be set and reviewed from time to time by a company. Ratios should be compared against several bases or reference points namely:

i) actual ratio vis-a-vis the relative norm;
ii) trend of the particular ratio in the same company over the recent past period;
iii) industry norm with respect to the particular ratio; and
iv) same ratio of several other companies in the same industry, particularly that of the close competitors.

CHAPTER 7

FUNDS FLOW, CASH FLOW AND CASH BUDGET

1. Meaning and Significance of Funds Flow Statement; 2. Cash Flow Analysis; 3. Is Depreciation a Source of Funds ? 4. Cash Budget; 5. Illustrations.

1. MEANING AND SIGNIFICANCE OF FUNDS FLOW STATEMENT

For purpose of financial analysis, three types of 'flows' are used, namely, Income Flow (i.e.Profit & Loss or revenue statement), Cash Flow and Funds Flow. Each such statement reflects changes over a period of time, unlike a Balance sheet which is a status report as at a particular point of time.

A number of expressions are used to designate a funds flow statement. Some of these are :

> Sources and Application (or Uses, Employment, Disposition or Utilisation) of Funds, Funds Statement, Where Got and Where Gone Statement, Movement of Funds, Movement in Working Capital, Sources of Increases and Application of Decreases, Statement or Changes in Financial Position etc.

Each of the above expressions explains in some way or the other the meaning of funds flow statement. The statement shows on the one hand all inflows and on the other all outflows (or dispositions or applications) of funds. The net result of all such inflows and outflows is reflected through an increase or decrease in working capital. Consequently, for a given period, the total of all inflows must equal the total of all outflows.

The significance of funds flow statement lies in the fact that while the balance sheet is a static statement (prepared as it is on a particular date), the former is a dynamic one. Following a commonly used analogy, it may be stated that while a balance sheet is a snapshot or still picture, a funds flow statement, with an element of dynamism, can tell us many financial facts and figures which a balance sheet cannot.

Again, while a balance sheet is the end product of all normal and routine accounting operations for a period of time, a funds flow statement is essentially a post-balance sheet exercise. This exercise is usually undertaken to bind the static balance sheet with the dynamic stream of the flow of funds.

A typical funds flow statement would be as follows :

TYPICAL LIMITED
FUNDS FLOW STATEMENT FOR THE YEAR 19X3

Sources of Funds	Rs.	Uses of Funds	Rs.
Proceeds of issue of shares		Acquisition of Fixed	
Proceeds of issue of Debentures		Investment outside	
Long Term Borrowings		Redemption of Debentures or Preference shares	
Disposal of Fixed Assets			
Sale of Investments		Repayment of long term loans	
Non-Operational Income			
Casual Income		Payment of Dividends	
Operating Income *1 (Adjusted for funds flow)		Payment of Tax	
Decrease in working Capital *2		Operational Losses *1	
		Increase in Working Capital *2	
Total..		Total..	

Note :

*1 figures are mutually exclusive, that is, either profit or loss will appear on one side, as the case may be. So are *2 figures which will appear on either side (not both) as a balancing item so that the total of the two sides agree.

2. CASH FLOW ANALYSIS

The word 'fund' has a wider purview than cash. Fund includes cash and also non-cash elements. If non-cash elements are removed, and a similar statement is prepared, it will be called cash flow statement. Sometimes, it is necessary to analyse the inflow and outflow of cash for a particular period rather than the inflow and outflow of funds. Such analysis is facilitated by the preparation of a cash flow statement. Moreover, the preparation of a cash flow statement will automatically highlight the cash position as at the end of the concerned period vis-a-vis at the beginning and thereby clearly indicate the change in cash position between the two points of time. It may also be noted that a cash flow statement is generally prepared for the company as a whole and that this can be based on actual data for a past period or projected data for a future period.

The mode of preparation of cash flow statements will be evident from the standard format given here :

CASH FLOW STATEMENT (FORMAT)
Period......................

Rs.

Opening Cash Balance
Add ('Generation' of cash):
(i) Adjusted Net Profit:
Net Profit for the period
Add (less) * Depreciation written off
* Provisions
* Accrued expenses
(accrued income)
* Write-offs
(ii) Decrease in current sales
(iii) Increase in current liabilities
(Including bank borrowings)
(iv) Receipts from other Sources
* Issue of share capital
* Issue of debentures
* Term Loans
* Sale of Plant & Machinery

* Invesunent
Total Cash (A)
Deduct ('Consumption' of cash) :
(i) Increase in current assets
(ii) Decrease in current liabilities
(iii) Other Payments
* Capital Expenditures
* Repayment of loans
* Payment of taxes
* Payment of dividends ——— ———
Total Deduction (B)
CLOSING CASH BALANCE (A-B)

---

3. IS DEPRECIATION A SOURCE OF FUNDS ?

It is to be noted at the outset that depreciation does not directly lead to generation of funds except to the extent by which it helps the business concern to effect savings in tax and dividend payment. Charging depreciation merely amounts to withholding a part of the funds generation through normal business operations. Thus, depreciation can at best be regarded as an indirect or remote source of funds, that too, not always.

If an enterprise is either incurring loss or earning not enough operating income to cover tax depreciation, then any debit to P/L a/c on account depreciation does not effect any generation of funds for the current accounting period. Depreciation is, therefore, not a source of funds in such a situation.

Depreciation is nothing more and nothing less than an amortization of prepaid expense which is incurred for the asset concerned. To acquire an asset, a lumpsum amount is spent in advance and the amount is recoverable over subsequent years through what is called depreciation.

Depreciation really represents a non-cash expense in the current period (since cash expense was incurred in earlier years). This is precisely the reason why for the purpose of a funds flow statement, depreciation is added back to show the amount of real funds inflow on account of operating profit. All non-cash debits in P/L a/c (for example, preliminary expenses, advertisement suspense, provision for doubtful debts, gratuity provisions and obviously, depreciation) are added back to arrive at the adjusted operating income which is an important source of funds. The logic behind such add-back is that there is no funds outflow against such debts, at least in the period for which the funds flow statement is being prepared.

4. CASH BUDGET

A Cash Budget is a forecast of cash position over a period of time, to reflect changes in the position within the same period. Conventionally, cash budget is considered to be an integral part of the total budgeting process and it is prepared only after all sectional or functional budgets are in. However, to install better control on cash flow, the scope of operation of cash budgets can control on cash flow, the scope of operation of cash budgets can be expanded to cover each function or sub-unit separately and to develop a rolling cash flow plan for each sub-unit as well as the company as a unit. A format for such rolling plan is included here. If a company adopts, say, a 12 month rolling plan, every month the figures in the format will be updated to cover the subsequent twelve months. For the purpose of effective control, budget-actual comparison pertaining to the immediate previous month has also been shown in the format.

Since cash budget occupies an important position in the overall budgeting process of a company, the technique of its preparation is illustrated below using a relatively simplified format

CASH BUDGET (FORMAT)
(Under Rolling Period Basis)

Period.............

Budget	Actual	Comparison			
	Month 1				
Budget	Actual	Item	Month 1	Month 2	Month 3 etc.
		A. Sales Receipts :			
		(1) Cash Sales and advances			
		(2) Sundry debtors collected			
		(3) Cash subsidies, rebates etc.			
		Total of A			
		B.Operating Disbursement :			
		(1) Cash purchases and advances			
		(2) Sundry creditors paid			
		(3) Wages, Salaries, PF, Bonus, etc.			
		(4) Rents, Electricity, rates insurance etc.			
		(5) Selling expenses			
		(6) Administration Exp.			
		(7) Income Tax			
		Total of B			
		C. Cash Flow through Operations (difference between A&B)			
		D. Miscellaneous receipts (rents, dividends, royalties, etc.)			
		Total of C&D			
		E. Capital Receipts :			

(1) Debentures issue
(2) Term Loans
(3) Issue of share capital
(4) Sale of assets

Total of E

F. Non-Operating Disbursements
(1) Interest & Financial costs
(2) Donations
(3) Dividends
(4) Capital expenditure
(5) Debt redemption

Total of F

G. Net Cash Flow (C+D+E-F)
H. Add: Cash Balance : beginning of month

I. Cash position
J. Less : Minimum cash balance required

K. Bank Loan position (increase/decrease)
L. Cumulative bank loan position Drawing power

5. ILLUSTRATIONS

1. A simple illustration showing all the three flows

Mr.A has Rs.1000 in cash on 1st January 19x0. He enters into a trading business and purchases on the same day goods worth Rs.1600 paying half the amount in cash. During the month, he sells three-fourths of the goods at Rs.2500, 20 per cent of which is in cash and the balance on credit. His business expense for the month is Rs.500.

		Rs.	Rs.
(A)	INCOME FLOW STATEMENT :		
	Sales	2,500	
	Add: Closing stock at cost	400	
			2,900
	Less: Purchase	1,600	
	Expenses	500	
			2,100
	Income (Profit) earned during the month		800
(B)	CASH FLOW STATEMENT:		
	Opening balance of cash		1,000
	Add: Cash in (receipts)		500
			1,500
	Less: Cash out (Payments):		
	Creditors for goods	800	
	Expenses	500	
			1,300
	Closing balance of cash		200

(C) FUNDS FLOW STATEMENT:

(i) Working Capital change as on	1.1.10x0	31.3.19x0
	Rs.	Rs.
Stock	--	400
Debtors	--	2,000
Cash	1,000	200
Current Assets	1,000	2,600
Less: Current Liabilities		800
Working Capital	1,000	1,800
Working capital Increase	800	

FUNDS FLOW STATEMENT

SOURCE	Rs.	USE	Rs.
Profit	800	Increase in Working Capital	800
	800		800

We may also show here, as on 31.1.19x0 Mr.A's Balance Sheet

Liabilities			Assets	
		Rs.		Rs.
Capital (Opening)	1,000		Stock	400
Add: Profit	800		Debtors	2,000
		1,800	Cash	200
Creditors		800		
		2,600		2,600

2. Preparation of funds flow statement and cash flow statement from the same data.

FINANCIAL MANAGEMENT LIMITED
(Summarised) Balance Sheet as at 31-12-XX

Figures in Rs.Lakhs

	19x7	19x8		19x7	19x8
Share Capital			Fixed Assets		
Equity Shares (Rs.10 each fully paid)	6	10	Goodwill	1	1
10 per cent preference Shares	2	2	Other fixed assets	5	9
Share Premium		1	Investments (Interest @ 5%)	3	3
Reserves & Surplus			Current Assets		
General Reserves	4	6	Loans & Advances		

Secured Loans			Sundry Debtors	7	10
12% Debentures	6	6	Stock	9	14
Bank Borrowings			Cash	2	1
(Short-term,					
interest @ 15%)	2	4	Miscellaneous		
			Expenditures		
Unsecured Loans			Preliminary	3	2
14% Public deposits	6	4	Expenses		
Current Liabilities					
and Provisions					
Sundry Creditors	3	4			
Income tax payable	1	3			
	30	40		30	40

Additional information provided:
(i) Depreciation charged to P/L a/c for 19x8:Rs.2 lakhs.
(ii) There has been no disposal of fixed assets or Investments in 19x8.

CASH FLOW (OR FUNDS FLOW) FROM OPERATIONS

	Rs. Lakhs
Increase in General Reserve 19x8 over 19x7 (6-4)	2
Add: Provision for depreciation 19x8	2
Preliminary expenses written off in 19x8 (3-2)	1
Provision for income tax in 19x8	3
Total.....	8

FUNDS FLOW STATEMENT

(For the Year 19x8)

Rs. Lakhs

Sources of Funds		Uses of Funds	
Proceeds from equity shares		Acquisition of fixed	
(Face Value + Premium 10	5	assets * 1	6
Increase in bank borrowings	2	Public deposits	

		refunded	2
Funds flow from Operations (as shown above)	8	Income tax (for 19x7) paid	1
		Increase in working capital * 2	6
Total....	15		15

Workings

		*** 2**	19x7	19x8
* Balance end 19x7	5	Current Assets	18	25
Less: Depreciation	2	Current Liabilities	3	4
	3	Working Capital	15	21
Balance end 19x8	9			
Acquisition	6	Do-Increase	6	-

CASH FLOW STATEMENT
(For the Year 19x8)

		Rs.Lakhs	
Opening Cash and Bank balance		(2-2)	0
Add:	Cash inflow:		
	Through Operations	8	
	Proceeds of Share issue	5	
	Increase in Sundry Creditors	1	
			14
			14
Less:Cash Outflow:			
	Acquisition of fixed assets	6	
	Payment of Income Tax	1	
	Refund of public deposits	2	
	Increase in current assets (excl. cash)	8	
			17
	Closing Cash & Bank balance	(1-4)	(3)

3. Illustration on Cash Budget

Required from the following information a monthly cash budget for the fourth quarter ending 31st December:

1. Extracts from Sectional Budgets

(Figures in Rs.Lakhs)

Month	Sales	Materials	Wages	Production overheads	Administration & Selling overheads
	Rs.	Rs.	Rs.	Rs.	Rs.
June	60	36	13	4.5	3.2
July	65	40	15	4.5	3.2
August	70	48	15	5.0	3.6
September	75	45	15	6.0	3.5
October	80	46	16	6.0	4.0
November	85	50	18	7.0	4.0
December	90	52	20	7.0	4.5

2. Credit terms :

Sales-three months to debtors: 10 percent of sales are on cash. On an average 50 per cent of credit sales are paid on due dates and the balance in the following month.

Creditors (Materials) - two months

3. Lag in Payment :

Wages-quarter month, Overheads-half month

4. Cash and bank balance on 1st October is estimated to be Rs.30 lakhs.

5. Other Information :

(i) Plant and machinery to be installed in August at a cost of Rs.480 lakhs will be paid for by monthly installments of Rs.10 lakhs from 1st October.

(ii) Preference divided @ 5 per cent on capital Rs.100 lakhs payable in December

(iii) Call on 50,000 equity shares @ Rs.20 each receivable in November

(iv) Dividends (from investments) of Rs.5 lakhs receivable in December.

(v) Income-tax (advance) payable in December, Rs.10 lakhs.

CASH BUDGET
Period ending 31st December

Details	October	November	December
Balance b/d	30.00	10.75	7.00
Receipts:			
Sales	64.25	69.25	74.25
Call on Shares	-	10.00	-
Dividends	-	-	5.00
Total (x)...	94.25	90.00	86.25
Payments:			
Creditors (materials)	48.00	45.00	46.00
Wages	15.75	17.50	19.50
Overhead-Production	6.00	6.50	7.00
Overhead-admn. and selling	3.75	4.00	4.25
Preference dividend	-	-	5.00
Income tax	-	-	10.00
Plant and machinery	10.00	10.00	10.00
Total (Y)	83.50	83.00	101.75
Balance c/d (X-Y)	10.75	7.00	(15.50)

Notes:

(i) The balance of Rs.15.50 lakhs at end-December indicates overdraft.

(ii) Closing balance of October becomes the opening balance of November, and so on

(iii) Wages for October would be one-fourth of September wages plus three-fourths of October wages. Similar would be the treatment for November and December.

(iv) Overheads for October would be half of September overheads plus half of October overheads. Similar would be the treatment for November and December.

(v) Receipts from Sales are found out as under:

COLLECTIONS

Month	Sales	October	November	December
June	60	27.00		
July	65		29.25	
August	70			29.25
September	75		31.50	31.50
October	80	8.00		
November	85		8.50	
December	90			9.00
Total		64.25	69.25	74.25

(iv) August purchases (materials) for Rs.48 lakhs has been shown as payment in October, and so on (because of two months credit term enjoyed from suppliers).

CHAPTER 8

BASIC COST CONCEPTS

1. Introduction; 2. Basic Concepts; 3. Selling & Distribution Overheads; 4. Diverse Viewpoints of Costs; 5. Methods of Costing; 6. Techniques of Costing.

1. INTRODUCTION

Costing, Cost Accounting, Cost Management etc. comprise a package of methodology that was developed during the first World War, thanks to the pioneering efforts of some British Cost and Management Accountants.

Financial accounting was developed primarily to serve the external needs of an enterprise and it still is oriented towards meeting the needs of such people like shareholders, government authorities and the different cross-sections of the society. Cost accounting was developed on the other hand to fulfill the internal needs of management, particularly those in operations.

Over the years, the discipline has made substantial headway. The important milestones of its development are as follows :

1. Cost Finding : Actual/Historical
   Scientifically Projected/Estimated
   (e.g. Standard Cost)
2. Cost Control, Cost Reduction & Cost Effectiveness
3. Cost Analysis — Decision-Oriented

We shall briefly discuss here the salient features and basic tools of Cost Management :

2. BASIC CONCEPTS

The first and foremost area is cost determination or cost finding. The underlying principles may be expressed as 2+3+4. This means there are two types of costs, three elements of costs and four stages of cost determination.

Costs are basically of two types namely, Direct and Indirect. Direct Cost is also called Prime Cost and Indirect Cost is called Overhead. Three elements of costs are Materials, Labour and Expenses (generally Overheads).

When any of these three elements are direct in nature and are traceable to a product, job or process it will be a direct cost. When these cannot be so traced and therefore are of an indirect nature, these will be called indirect costs or overheads.

In the traditional costing methodology there are four stages in cost finding. These are Prime Cost, Factory Cost (or Works Costs or Manufacturing Cost), Total Cost and Cost of Sales. The progressive cost build-up on these lines is illustrated below, using hypothetical figures.

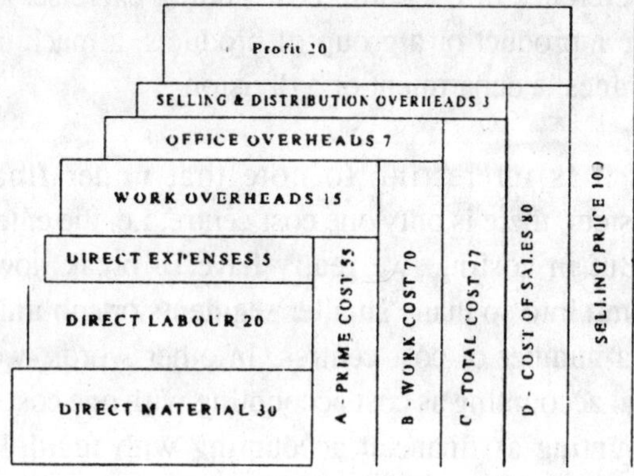

Sometimes, there is a misconception about indirect costs or overheads — these are considered to be extraneous to the mainstream of operations. But this is not correct. Indirect costs or overheads are incurred not directly for the job or product but for running the set-up or establishment and provide diverse services without which the job cannot be done or the product cannot be produced. Indirect costs are, therefore as complete, genuine and full costs as the direct ones, but these are to be distributed or apportioned in as equitable a manner as possible among the various jobs or products.

There can be no accurate basis for apportionment of indirect or common costs among different products or jobs, because in that case such costs will no longer remain indirect in nature. What we should endeavour, therefore, is to choose a good basis for apportionment of each item of indirect cost. The guiding principles in such choice of basis should be simplicity, measurability, equity and, fair costing of course, cost of costing.

Another very important concept is that of Cost Centre. The financial accounting process starts with Vouchers. Likewise, determination of Cost Centres is the starting point of Costing and Cost accounting. Cost Centre means any section or activity-unit around which costs are ascertained and collected. It is, so to say, the frame of reference of the entire cost finding exercise. A Cost Centre may be a product or a group of products, a machine or a group of machines, a department or a division.

Incidentally, it is interesting to note that under financial accounting system, there is only one cost centre, i.e. the enterprise as a whole. But in costing, we really have to break down the enterprise or unit into so many smaller segments or sub-units and thus identify a number of cost centres. In other words, we may define financial accounting as cost accounting with one cost centre and cost accounting as financial accounting with multiple cost centres.

Closely related to this is another important point of distinction between financial accounting and cost accounting. The former adopts a macro approach and thus relates to the enterprise as a whole, while cost accounting is of a micro nature and enables us to obtain the financial data separately with respect to different divisions or segments of activity or even products of the enterprise.

Out of the three elements of costs, it is the overheads (or indirect costs or common costs) that poses major problems in cost finding. Overheads or common costs need to be identified, classified, divided and sub-divided, channeled and rechanneled, involving what is called allocation and apportionment of overheads. The degree of accuracy in costing as well as cost data depends primarily on :

a) Definition of Cost Centres

b) Adoption of appropriate and rational bases for allocation of common cost or overheads.

Overheads comprise three elements, namely, indirect material, indirect labour and indirect expenses, as mentioned earlier also. Overheads are classified on functional basis as manufacturing (or factory or works or production) overhead, administrative (or general & office) overhead and selling & distribution overhead. This is necessary for both cost ascertainment and cost control.

Another important concept related to overhead is that of service department. A factory is not just production departments only— there may be a number of service departments which do not produce anything but without which production would come to a standstill. Examples of such service departments are boiler, canteen, water, maintenance etc. Common sense tells us that all costs - not only of production departments but of all service departments - have to be collected or recovered through the jobs of products.

Since cost finding is an on-going exercise (which is not generally the case in financial accounting), for purpose of overhead recovery through products or jobs, we have to necessarily adopt some predetermined overhead recovery rates. The predetermined rates may be based on units (i.e., overheads per unit of product), as percentages (say, manufacturing overheads as percentage of direct labour, office and administrative overheads as percentage of works cost, etc.),on machine hour rate (i.e. the average of all costs and indirect expenses in connection with the running of a machine or machine centre for one hour) or on labour hour rate (i.e., the average of all indirect expenses per direct labour hour).

The traditional four-stage cost build-up mentioned and illustrated above is based on what is called Full-Cost technique, also called Absorption Costing technique. The stages have since been restructured by CIMA, London and according to their official terminology the stages of revenue and cost build-up are as follows:

1. Net Turnover
2. Production Cost of Sales :
    - Direct Material
    - Direct Labour
    - Production Overhead
3. Gross (or Factory) Profit (1—2)
4. Non-Production Overheads :
    - Selling Overhead
    - Distribution Overhead
    - Administrative Expenses
    - Research & Development Cost
5. Net Profit before Tax (3—4)

A more logical technique of cost determination as well as cost management is Marginal Costing, under which the mode of profit build-up is as follows :

1. Net Turnover
2. Variable Cost of Sales :
    - Direct Material
    - Direct Labour (only variable content, if any)
    - Variable Production Overhead
    - Other Variable Overheads (if any)
3. Contribution (1—2)
4. Total Fixed Cost :
    - Production Overhead
    - Selling & Distribution Overhead
    - Office & Administrative Overhead
    - Research & Development Cost
    - Interest (Fixed element generally)
5. Net Profit before Tax (3—4)

3. SELLING AND DISTRIBUTION OVERHEADS

Selling overheads are defined as all expenses for stimulation to retain custom as also to increase custom. Selling overheads thus include selling expenses, advertising expenses and marketing expenses. Distribution overheads relate to all expenses incurred in the entire operation beginning with making the packed goods available for dispatch and ending either with the goods finally reaching the ultimate consumers, or — in case of returnable containers system — with the reconditioned returned empty packages being made available for reuse. Cost of maintaining distribution centres and running delivery vans, outward freight, transport and insurance of goods and distribution commission are some of the examples of distribution overhead expenses.

In today's business parlance, the expression 'Marketing Overhead' is commonly used. Marketing Overhead essentially comprises both Selling Overhead and Distribution Overhead put together.

Selling and distribution overheads are usually recovered through sales either on unit basis or as percentage of sales value. More important is, however, the control of such overheads. Comparison is a weapon of control. Comparison of present actuals may be made with past actuals, budgets, standards or norms. But to provide better comparison and also to locate control areas, proper analysis of selling and distribution expenses is a must. There are different methods or bases of such analysis. Mention may be made of:

- (i) Expense items (salary, commission, freight etc.).
- (ii) Expense behaviour (fixed, variable, semi-variable).
- (iii) Functions (direct selling, advertising, marketing and transportation).
- (iv) Geographical location (area, region, territory or zone).
- (v) Productwise or product-groupwise.
- (vi) Salesmen.
- (vii) Channels of distribution (consumers, retailers, wholesalers).

(viii) Nature of sales (e.g. inland and export, cash and credit, etc.).

(ix) Types of customers (e.g. government, trade, institutions).

Each such method has its own advantage. But for the purpose of cost control through comparison, one or a few of such methods only have to be chosen, regard being had to the situation and the nature of control in view. Under mechanised accounting systems, analysis of sales and selling and distribution expenses are immensely facilitated.

4. DIVERSE VIEWPOINTS OF COSTS

Financial accounting is generally a straight-jacketed system — the books of records are about the same for all types and sizes of enterprises. But costing is a dynamic system in that there are varied viewpoints to look at even the same set of cost data. This is the most important reason why cost accounting provides the necessary foundation of management accounting or managerial accounting.

We may broadly summarise here the more important viewpoints of costs :

A) Classical Approaches —

The 2, 3+4, mentioned earlier.

B) Neoclassical Approaches —

Generally based on Marginal Costing and Break Even Analysis and Standard Costing.

C) Modern Approaches —

* Controllable and Non-controllable costs.
* Cost of a product/job and cost of a department/ section (the former for decision-making and latter for cost control).
* Engineered, Committed and Managed costs (useful in Management Control System).

* Relevant Cost (essentially decision-oriented).
* Several other cost analysis techniques, mentioned later.

D) Latest Approaches —

Activity Based Costing (ABC) and the allied tenets like Value Chain Analysis, Strategic Cost Analysis etc. which are very useful in the field of business strategy formulation.

5. METHODS OF COSTING

The type of output and nature of production vary from industry to industry. Accordingly, different procedures are necessary for arriving at the cost (specially, manufacturing cost) of a product or job, though the basic principles of fair costing underlying all such procedures remain unchanged. Different procedures have thus resulted in different methods of costing applicable to different industries. The method of costing applicable to a job order type of business would be significantly different from that followed in, say a pharmaceutical company.

Job Costing and Process Costing are the two basic methods of costing. The emphasis of the former is on the 'product' but that of the latter is on the 'period' first and then the product.

Job costing method is applicable to job order type of business, both in respect of tailor-made jobs against specifications and standard jobs made for stock and sale. Materials. labour and directly allocable expenses are separately ascertained for each job (against order or of standard type). And overheads are apportioned to the job based on some predetermined recovery rates. The basis of such rates may be percentage (past actuals), labour hour rates or machine hour rates.

Process costing is a method of arriving at the cost of conversion of raw-materials into finished products in a production system where more than one operation or process is involved and where usually the finished product of one process becomes the raw-material for the subsequent one, till the final product is ready. Under the process costing method, cost of operation of each process or operation is worked out separately for each period with the ultimate object of arriving at the average total cost per unit of product.

Following is a list of the important Methods of Costing :

Methods		Examples of Application
(1) Job Costing	(i) Batch Costing	Toy, garments, biscuit manufacturing
	(ii) Contract Costing	Erection of bridges, buildings etc.
(2) Process Costing	(i) Output or Unit Costing	Collieries, paper mills breweries, etc.
	(ii) Departmental Costing	Costing of operating a department or cost centre
	(iii) Operation Costing	Cost of each operation at each stage of production or process
	(iv) Operating Costing	Transport, canteen, hospital (i.e.all service functions)
(3) Multiple or Composite Costing (combination of 1&2)		Pharmaceuticals, engines, motor cars, etc.

(4) Farm Costing	Agriculture, poultry etc.

6. TECHNIQUES OF COSTING

There are several techniques of costing, the scope as well as application of which, unlike that of the methods of costing, is very wide — not bound by the limitations of technicalities of different industries. These techniques aim not so much at cost-finding as at cost control and for that matter, generation of decision-oriented cost data.

A list of important techniques of costing follows:

Techniques	Purpose and Application
1 Absorption (or Total or Traditional) Costing	Ascertainment of costs after they have been incurred — product cost includes fixed costs — fixed cost spread over more than one accounting period through inclusion in closing stock.
2 Standard Costing	Ascertainment and use of standard cost and measurement (predetermined) — purpose:analysis of variance for cost control
3 Marginal Costing and 4 Break Even Analysis	Ascertainment of costs after segregating and keeping aside the fixed elements in costs — Use : assist management in various decisions.
5 Standard-Marginal Costing	Combination of 2 and 3 — Use : both cost control and assisting management in decision- making.
6 Uniform Costing	Adoption of the same costing methods and principles by a number

	of firms in the same industry. Use : improvement in operating efficiency through inter-firm comparison.
7 Other techniques	Used in various decisional problem as also for cost control and cost reduction.

(a) Differential Cost and Incremental revenue analysis
(b) Cost relevance study
(c) Cost effectiveness analysis
(d) Opportunity costing techniques
(e) Cost benefit analysis.

Standard Costing is closely linked with another technique called Budgetary Control, even though the latter is not a costing technique, to be precise. Standard Costing cannot be put into operation without Budgetary Control; but Budgetary Control can be used independent of Standard Costing, Definitions of these two follow:

Standard costing is a set of techniques which involves the establishment of standard costs, measurement of variations of actual costs from such predetermined standard costs, analysis of the reasons for variations and indicating ways to maintain and improve efficiency.

Budgetary Control is a set of techniques which involves the establishment of departmental or functional budgets, comparison between actual and budgeted results and analysis of the reasons for variations, either to fulfill the planned activities through control actions or to provide a basis for their revision.

Certain basic principles and steps are common to both, Budgetary Control and Standard Costing. They are :

(a) Establishment of a predetermined standard, target or yardstick of performance;

(b) Measurement of actual performance vis-a-vis the yardstick;

(c) Location of variances between actual and standard performances;

(d) Disclosure of reasons of such variations

These two and the several other techniques mentioned above are generally applied to achieve diverse objectives, irrespective of the nature of the industry and the particular method of costing in vogue. The objective could be cost determination, cost management or improving the decision-making process in operations.

SECTION III

MARKETING PLANNING

Discussions on planning included in this section cover both long-range strategic planning and short-term operational planning, but the focus all the way is on marketing. The section starts with Corporate Planning in Marketing (Chapter 9) emphasising the fact that marketing planning is the forerunner of corporate long-range planning.

The next Chapter encompasses relatively short-term marketing planning, viz., Budgetary Control in Marketing.

The third Chapter in the series (Chapter 11) takes a hard look at product planning and development which is an integral part of long-range planning and is also closely connected with short-range and medium-range planning.

Chapter 12, last in the section, explores the various considerations involved in planning the marketing organisation.

In all the Chapters of this section, an attempt has been made to keep in view the 'systems approach', a very important ingredient in any modern planning process.

CHAPTER 9

CORPORATE PLANNING AND MARKETING

1. Backdrop; 2. Corporate Planning — the Basic Concepts; 3. The Process of Corporate Long Range Planning (CLRP); 4. The Role of Marketing in CLRP Process; 5. Corporate vis-a-vis Marketing Objectives; 6. A few More Pertinent Observations.

1. BACKDROP

"Planning deals with what has to be done to be ready for the uncertain tomorrow" (Drucker). Planning could be for different time frames - short-range, medium-range and long-range. Generally Corporate Planning implies long-range planning with the corporate entity as a whole as the frame of reference.

Conceptually, the expression corporate planning, long range planning, corporate policy planning, strategic planning, etc., are different from each other in terms of their respective ambit, methodology and thrust areas. For practical purposes, however, the expression Corporate Long Range Planning (CLRP) may be assumed to subsume all these tenets. And this is an underlying assumption in our entire discussion under this chapter.

For obvious reasons, a great deal of emphasis of any CLRP exercise needs to be placed on Marketing. The purpose of this chapter is, therefore to take both a perspective view of CLRP as a whole and a ring-side view of long-range marketing planning as an integral part and within the overall framework of corporate planning. However, an important tenet viz., Strategic Planning, in marketing requires a more elaborate treatment and is, therefore, dealt with in the immediate next chapter (Marketing Strategies).

2. CORPORATE PLANNING — THE BASIC CONCEPTS

Before we suggest what corporate long-range planning (CLRP) is, let us first understand what it is not. First, CLRP is not just forecasting. Second, CLRP is not even budgeting. Third, CLRP is not painting a rosy picture of the future of a corporation based on mere wishes and hopes and gilded expectations. Fourth, CLRP is not an attempt to eliminate risk. More often than not, CLRP is mistaken to be any one or combination of these. Consequently, there emerges an annual budget extended over the next five or ten years, missing as it does the essence and the raison d'etre of the CLRP system.

Various experts have tried to define CLRP in different ways. We could have quoted a few of these here. But it is preferable, to draw up our definition:

CLRP as a *top management tool* is a *continuous process* of presenting the *strategic decisions* of an *enterprise as a whole*, with the best available *knowledge of the future* and *coordinating the efforts* needed to implement such decisions through an effective *monitoring mechanism*.

Notes:

1) The seven expressions highlighted above are the seven component elements in the definition.
2) CLRP is essentially a strategic planning — a planning exercise to frame strategic decisions.
3) CLRP requires inter alia building up a reservoir of knowledge about the future and to this end an intellectual analysis called SWOT Analysis (discussed below) is required.
4) Monitoring mechanism implies Management Information Control and Reporting System (MICRS).

There is one school of thought which believes that in these days of grave uncertainties about the future the complexities in operations that beset particularly developing countries like India, long-range planning is nothing but an exercise in futility. But this is not true. There are uncertainties about the future. Yet strategic decisions need to be taken and taken to-day – in order to manage rather than being managed by the uncertain tomorrow. According to Drucker again it is not the present decisions per se but the futurity of all such decisions that should be primary consideration in LRP.

Many a manager complains that he has no time to plan since he is always busy putting out fires. He also might believe in the Keynesian saying that in the long run we are all dead! But, as observed by T.S. Elliot, we are so much concerned about our present difficulties, that we continuously ignore the permanent ones but it is these permanent difficulties that are with us every moment of our existence. CLRP actually seeks to tackle the permanent or long term issues of an enterprise. But this requires more than anything else deliberate thinking on the part of its managers. Particularly, when there are frequent and heavy bombardments from the environment, managers ought to think hard, think through and think ahead.

Experts debate also on the time-horizon of CLRP-how long is long-range? The answer is: it depends — say, 40 years for paper and pulp, 20 years for ship-building and 2 years for garments, electronics, etc. But most companies seem to have settled with a 5 year time-horizon mainly because four years is perhaps too short and six too long! There is, of course another concept called Perspective Planning that can range up to say 50 years. Perspective Planning in fact provides a broad set of basic and secular planning premises. But for CLRP as such the outer limit should be 10 years since beyond that period the validity of forecasts is keyed with doubts.

3. THE PROCESS OF CORPORATE LONG-RANGE PLANNING (CLRP)

The process involved in any systematic, organised, strategic planning, which the CLRP is, starts with an understanding and articulating the corporate philosophy, values and ethos on the one hand and the business we are in and we would like to be in, on the other.

From these emanates the *Corporate Mission Statement* which is qualitative in nature but based on well-developed logic. The next step is to arrive at a set of *Objectives.* Objectives are detailed into targets and further broken down into a set of forecasts. The first set of targets and forecast may be called *Forecast I.* This should be essentially quantitative in nature. Unfortunately, corporate planning of many companies stop here. But there are a few more important steps to be taken in the process of development of the CLRP. The targets once fixed provide only some intentions or aspirations. Some intellectual analysis is required to critically review how far the targets are realistic and attainable. Two important aspects are to be considered at this stage viz., organisational (internal) and environmental (external). The organisation may have some strengths and weaknesses. Similarly, the environment might promise some opportunities and pose some threats. A critical analysis of such Strengths(S), Weaknesses(W), Opportunities(O) and Threats(T) is called SWOT Analysis. It is to be noted, however, the *SWOT analysis* is not and should not be undertaken in isolation-this has to be anchored to the targets initially set, detailed in the form of Forecast I.

The organisational analysis under the SWOT analysis should cover the following important areas, viz., leadership, organisational structure, production, marketing, finance, personnel, company image and standing etc. Environmental scanning on the other hand should deal with external factors like political and social as well as state of competition, state of technology, emerging trends in consumer needs, import, export and foreign exchange position, etc. SWOT Analysis may be undertaken very effectively through a brain-storming session which should be attended by all key executives and functional heads.

SWOT analysis will necessarily lead to another set of forecasts, viz., *Forecast-II.* It will be evident at this stage that there is a gap between Forecast-I and Forecast-II. This is called the planning gap, representing the divergence between what we would like to be and what we are likely to be. Some *Strategies* have to be developed now for closing the gap as much as possible. It may be necessary after that to develop yet another set of forecasts say, *Forecast-III* which would be the basis for a realistic plan, backed by detailed strategies and action plans. This logically leads to the development of the *Master Plan.* Thereafter *Functional Plans* are developed through detailed exercises in respect of each functional area, viz., marketing, production, personnel, finance, R&D, etc. Finally monitoring mechanism for implementing the plan needs to be developed through an appropriate *MICRS.*

The process of CLRP discussed above, as also the various steps and the sequence involved, is one commonly adopted. But there are many other ways of or models for developing a corporate plan. But this process or any other process should not be taken to be too rigid-this should provide for an ample scope of alteration and back and forth movement as one goes along. For example, during or after the SWOT analysis it may be necessary to redefine the Corporate Mission statement which in turn will mean restating the corporate objectives themselves. Similar needs might arise even at the time of formulating strategies for bridging the planning gap. What is more important, therefore, is to keep the questioning mind always alert and active so that the process of developing corporate plan does not degenerate into a purely mechanical exercise in a rigid sequence.

Another very useful approach in developing CLRP is contingency planning. Particularly in a situation when forecasts tend to be nothing more than crystal ball gazing-future appearing to be so volatile-contingency planning is a must. The idea here is to develop two or three alternative sets of CLRP rather than taking one deterministic set and watch which of these alternatives is veering close to the emerging reality so as to firm up the plan at an appropriate later stage accordingly. The process thus would require building alternative scenarios for planning purpose.

4. THE ROLE OF MARKETING IN CLRP PROCESS

From the process of corporate planning outlined above, it would be evident that any corporate plan has eventually to be built up through a process of integration and amalgamation of all the individual functional plans of the organisation, and the corporate plan must cover every facet of the business. Marketing being one of these, marketing planning must clearly be an integral part of the whole corporate planning process. If marketing, production, personnel, finance and research plans were drawn up independently, the result would compare with a team of horses pulling in different directions.

The second important aspect to be considered is that, while various other functional plans are by and large under the firm's control, a marketing plan is not. The reason for this is marketing plans depend on market conditions which are outside the control of the management and are externally determined. At the same time they represent a restraint on what the company can hope to achieve and the challenge to optimise the yield of resources thrown into a given market situation.

Marketing's role in corporate planning is thus crucial. Whatever be its business, a company must decide what opportunities it wants to pursue and what risks it is willing and able to take. Having expressed these general aspirations in terms of specific objectives, its management must define the strategies and tactics to achieve them. It is therefore rightly stated that, "marketing planning is the forerunner of any corporate planning."

If we refer back to the stages in the development of CLRP discussed earlier it would be apparent that marketing function is predominant all the way, from the beginning to the end. Right from the stage of defining the Corporate Mission, marketing gets integrated in the process. In fact, marketing objectives should form the bed-rock of the corporate objectives. The various other stages thereafter, viz., Forecast-I, Forecast-II, Forecast-III, etc., have to necessarily depend on marketing. Even in the SWOT analysis, the most important part is perhaps market analysis, specially the process of identifying opportunities that lie ahead. As many modern corporate planners suggest rightly, long-range planning has to be essentially oriented towards opportunities and needless to say, corporate opportunities can by and large be equated with marketing opportunities. The strategies that are to be developed for closing the planning gap as far as practicable, are mostly of the nature of marketing strategies. This is how corporate planning and marketing strategies are considered to be very closely inter-related.

For marketing to play its dominant role in corporate planning process, the marketing department in general and the marketing services function in particular, needs to be sufficiently and systematically organised. The most important requirement to this end is development of marketing intelligence and data base. Though it is believed that planning based on past data and performance is nothing but driving a vehicle with eyes fixed on the rear view-mirror, the past could still be a never-failing guide. And therefore, creation of a systematic and properly analysed data base or data bank is one of the important functions of marketing services.

Another important function is the development of systematic and well-designed formats for streamlining the collection of various data and forecasts at various stages and the presentation of the results of SWOT analysis, specially the market analysis.

However, all these require earmarking a certain part of the resources, manpower and others, for use in the long-range marketing planning, as distinct from the day-to-day operational planning and control of marketing efforts.

5. CORPORATE VIS-A-VIS MARKETING OBJECTIVES

The development of corporate objectives, as stated earlier, is one of the first basic steps in the process of CLRP. "Objective" is admittedly an elusive term, perhaps even a metaphysical one. It may be as difficult for Management science to define "objectives" as it is for Biology to define "life". Yet, it cannot do without objectives as muc' 's biology cannot do without life. Today even entrepreneurial decisions, let alone the integrated decision system we call long-range planning, must have objectives. Objectives should always be there to ensure effectiveness and efficiency. Sometimes, there is a confusion between objectives and activities. The activities, as set out in the Memorandum of Association of a company, are only the means of achieving some ends. Objectives are actually the ends. For every company there are some primary objective or objectives and there are also a series of secondary objectives.

Corporate objectives can broadly be classified into two groups, namely, economic and social. Economic objectives are a must for commercial enterprises and these are nothing but owners' or shareholders' expectations in terms of dividends, bonus shares,right shares and capital appreciation. Social objectives are also important and of ten they influence the economic objectives also. Obligations of a company of the society include those to its employees, customers, suppliers, public at large and the government.

Marketing objectives should be logically derived from and be an integral part of the corporate objectives - there has to be consistency and matching between these two. In specific terms marketing objectives can be set along the following criteria:

i) Rupee growth in sales (e.g. Rs. 5 crore extra sales per year)

ii) Percentage growth in sales (say, 20%]compounded annual growth in sales at current/ constant price or on inflation-adjusted basis.)

iii) Volume growth in sales (e.g. additional 10 MT production and sales every year.)

iv) Percentage growth in volume sales (e.g. 15% increase in volume sales per year)

v) Product leadership - for important products, based on quality as perceived and recognised by the market.

vi) Brand leadership - for certain specific products, judged by market recognition again, but need not necessari'y be quality-based.

vii) Market leadership - measured by market share, (e.g. increasing the market share from the present level of 20% by 5% each year).

viii) Price leadership - for certain products, based on customers' perception about quality, performance and of course image.

ix) Profitability or Marketing ROI - defined as Net Marketing Margin related to total Investments in Marketing operations (explained and illustrated in chapter - 14).

Two observations are pertinent at this stage :

a. Several objectives, on this lines suggested above, should be set, instead of having a single objective. But these have to be given priority-ranking-it is not possible to achieve several objectives with the same prioritisation in a given time-frame.

b. In course of prioritising the objectives, one will have to accept some trade - offs. For examples, there is invariably a trade-off between market share objective and marketing profitability objective - if market share were to be increased substantially, one has to accept a dip in marketing profitability, at least for some time, the extent of which vis-a-vis the increase in market share envisaged can and should be estimated at the planning stage itself.

6. A FEW MORE PERTINENT OBSERVATIONS

Nobody expects that a CLRP system, and for that matter any system, would yield results right from its inception. Mistakes may be made at various stages and in many ways - more so when one is dealing with the future imponderable. What is more important is to learn from past mistakes and progressively improve the CLRP system in the enterprise. "To err is human but when the eraser wears out ahead of the pencil you're overdoing it" (J. Jenkins).

CLRP is an on-going process, not just a one-off situation or sporadic exercise. It also needs a system by which it is revised and updated regularly by incorporating changes that have occurred (but which could not be foreseen) during the period between the last CLRP exercise and the current one. *The rolling plan concept* has been found to be well-suited to corporate LRP's. If this concept is adopted, at the time of annual review and updating, the first year of the last CLRP would be removed and a new year (the year immediately following the last CLRP period) would be included. Thus at any point of time a complete and updated CLRP for say, a 5 year or 10 year period, would be available. We may sound a note of caution here : the emphasis in the rolling plan should be on "planning" and not on "rolling".

Similarly, by a suitable system, the CLRP exercise, usually preceding the annual budget exercise, may be linked up with the annual budget. Usually forecasts under CLRP in the Plan Year I would broadly serve the purpose of the next annual budget. Only some new schedules may have to be prepared and greater details worked out for the purpose of the annual budget. There may be even changes between the Plan Year I forecasts and the budget estimates. But the reasons for all such changes should be adequately explained, quantified and included in the budget narratives. This will ensure that the most important element in CLRP viz., monitoring and control system, is not lost sight of. This will also create a situation whereby long-range corporate plan gets broken down into short-range operational plans for effective implementation, progressively.

CHAPTER 10

BUDGETARY CONTROL IN MARKETING

1. An Overview; 2. Process of Budget Setting; 3. Parameters for Developing Marketing Budgets; 4. Flexible Budgeting; 5. Administration of Budgetary Control System; 6. Probability Concept in Budgeting.

1. AN OVERVIEW

Budgeting and budgetary control are perhaps the oldest and most popular instruments used in planning as well as monitoring the operations of an enterprise over a short and medium-term time-frame. Particularly with respect to marketing operations of an enterprise, these seek to direct the activities of the enterprise in a certain logical sequence and answer some basic issues, as follows

Objectives	—	Where do we want to go?
Diagnosis	—	Where are we?
Prognosis	—	Where are we heading?
Strategies	—	How do we go?
Tactics	—	How do we implement the strategies?
Control	—	How do we monitor our course?

2. PROCESS OF BUDGET SETTING

There are important issues that need to be examined and sorted out before starting the detailed budget setting exercise :

i) Corporate Objectives— Companies having systematic and organised long range planning (LRP) process will always have before them such long-term objectives, spelt out clearly and quantified. The companies which do not have a LRP system should also develop broad outline about its objectives on a long-term basis, at least for two or three years. The objectives should be set specially in two respects, growth and profitability. Preferably these should be broken up into present products and lines of activities on the one hand, and proposed new products and new lines of activities on the other.

ii) Corporate Profit Planning — Profit planning and budgeting are two ifferent things. They are rather interdependent and more precisely, complementary to each other. Profit planning should precede the detailed budgeting exercise. Basically, profit planning provides a general blue - print of the expected profit and the broad elements through which this can be achieved during a particular budget period. By its very nature, it is a summary plan, not backed by a detailed action plan. From the practical point of view it is always convenient to develop a broad profit plan and get it approved by the top management before a detailed budgeting exercise is taken up. This will obviate confusion and back and forth referrals which are common in a budgeting exercise.

iii) Nature of Markets — By nature of markets, we mean the buyers' market and sellers' market. Rarely it is found that a company is operating exclusively in the buyers' market or exclusively in the sellers' market. If that be so, then the budgeting exercise would be relatively a simple one. More often than not, a company will be found to operate under a combination of these two types of markets - some of its products being in the buyers' market and some others enjoying the privilege of being in the sellers' market. This combination has to be broadly determined since it has a bearing on the marketing budgets.

iv) Principal Budget Factor — This is also called a key factor, limiting factor, critical factor or governing factor. It is defined as the factor, the extent of whose influence must first be assessed to ensure that the functional budgets are reasonably capable of fulfillment. Limiting factor may be in any of the operational areas, namely sales activity (demand, sales efficiency, warehouse space); plant capacity (machine hour, space, bottlenecks in key process); raw materials (shortage, import restrictions); labour (general shortage, shortage of skilled labour); management (technical knowhow, efficient and effective executive) and capital (fixed capital, working capital). Key factor may be of an enduring nature or of a purely temporary nature (that is those which may be overcome by suitable management actions). But an adequate consideration of the magnitude or impact of such factors in existence during the budget year is a must in realistic budget-setting.

v) Sales Forecasting — Since more often than not sales is the limiting factor, preparation of sales budget is generally the starting point in the budgeting exercise. Sales estimate or sales forecast, is the basis of sales budget. Here is a list of the various factors to be considered in arriving at sales estimate or sales forecast :

a) Analysis of the past sales to understand the trends of sales and also forecast the future trends.

b) Demand Analysis and market analysis to ascertain market potential, market growth, the company's share of the market, emergence of competition, competitors' strategy, product design, pricing trends, customers' habits and preferences, etc.

c) Analysis of reports by salesmen as to expected sales - first hand and fresh from the field reports.

d) Examination of general business conditions.

e) Examination of special business conditions.

f) Production capacity study (or availability study, in case of a pure trading concern.

g) Profitability analysis through sales mix planning to ensure that the profit objective is fulfilled by the proposed sales forecast.

vi) Spending for the future — There could be quite a few items of spending for the future like training and development of people, new product development and launch, developing an infrastructure for providing marketing intelligence and undertaking marketing research, etc. Such expenses may not contribute directly to profit during the budget year and may often bring down the profitability, sometimes significantly. It is therefore, necessary to segregate such expenses from pure operational expenses, at least for the purpose of understanding the budget-year performance and profitability in the right perspective. Management may still commit such expenses on long-term considerations knowing fully well the extent to which this would reduce the profit for the budget year.

After having thoroughly evaluated the above issues and prepared some basic inputs as a sequel, one might go about developing the detailed budgets. Efforts should be made of course to direct the entire budget setting activities along a systematic and logical approach, vide a schematic presentation given on page 138

3. PARAMETERS FOR DEVELOPING MARKETING BUDGETS

Budgeting essentially involves developing a chart, a map or integrated and well-knit plan of action-as much detailed as possible-for a definite period of time to achieve some definite objectives. Budgets are nothing but specific estimates of future events and

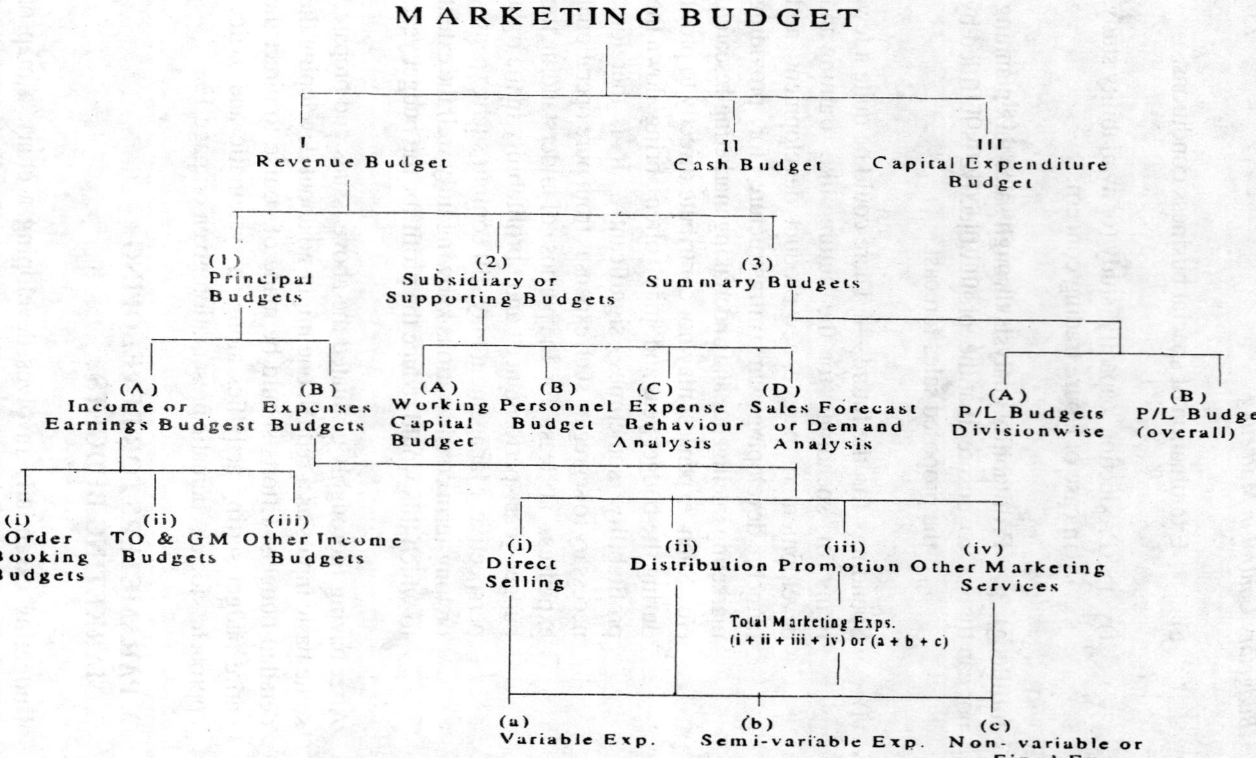
MARKETING BUDGET
I Revenue Budget
II Cash Budget
III Capital Expenditure Budget
(1) Principal Budgets
(2) Subsidiary or Supporting Budgets
(3) Summary Budgets
(A) Income or Earnings Budgest
(B) Expenses Budgets
(A) Working Capital Budget
(B) Personnel Budget
(C) Expense Behaviour Analysis
(D) Sales Forecast or Demand Analysis
(A) P/L Budgets Divisionwise
(B) P/L Budgets (overall)
(i) Order Booking Budgets
(ii) TO & GM Budgets
(iii) Other Income Budgets
(i) Direct Selling
(ii) Distribution
(iii) Promotion
(iv) Other Marketing Services
Total Marketing Exps. (i + ii + iii + iv) or (a + b + c)
(a) Variable Exp.
(b) Semi-variable Exp.
(c) Non-variable or Fixed Exp.

situations. All such estimates have to be based upon some logic, some chain of reasoning, a set of assumptions and a number of parameters. Good budgeting practice requires that all such assumptions and parameters should be laid down in precise terms with quantification wherever possible. If this condition is not fulfilled, the credibility of budget estimates cannot be established, nor can there be a scientific budgetary control system or objective evaluation of performance and effective control of operations. The subsidiary or support budget mentioned in the table do provide some basic data and worksheets, including some important norms and assumptions, in support of the principal budgets. Besides these, there could be a number of other assumptions and parameters of varied types. We give below only a few such important parameters which would lie behind the framing of the market budgets.

i) Distribution Plan : The existing distribution system and any proposed changes in it during the budget year (e.g. change-over from distributorship to distribution through the company's own sales depots, changeover, partial or full, from sole selling agency system to company's own marketing, etc.)

ii) Advertisement Plan : The usual advertisements through media etc., as well as any extraordinary promotional campaign envisaged during the budget year with detailed cost-benefit analysis in respect of each such plan, change over from advertisement through agencies to the company's own advertisement through agencies to the company's own advertising set-up again with a suitable cost-benefit analysis in this regard, etc.

iii) Salesmen's recruitment and training scheme with its financial implications.

iv) Salesmen's and executives' travel plans, with estimated expenses against each, showing separately inland travel and foreign travel.

v) Salesmen's incentive scheme.

vi) Inventory policy and any changes therein.

vii) Credit policy and any changes therein.

viii) After sales service set up and basis of charging for services.

ix) Import and export policy of the Government.

x) Breakdown of sales plan into quota in respect of the various profit centres as well as various sales executives under each. Budgets have to be approved by the top management or the budget committee. A detailed review of the budgets should precede the approval. For review and approval, budget figures should be presented along with some of the important parameters as stated above. Also, for comparison during review, budget statements should include various other sets of figures. Each budget statement should contain at least the following sets of figures :

a) Previous year - 1 actuals;
b) Current year latest best estimates; and
c) Budget year estimates.

Sometimes, to gain a better idea of the trend for the purpose of budget review, previous year-2 and even previous year-3 actual figures are required in each budget statement. Once the annual budgets are framed, finalised and approved, the budgets have to be broken up into shorter-period budgets to ensure more effective budgetary control. Usually annual budgets are broken into monthly budgets. Some companies restrict themselves to quarterly budgets because of the special nature of their business operations, while some other companies may like to develop fortnightly, weekly or even daily budgets.

4. FLEXIBLE BUDGETING

While fixed budgets portray a more or less rigid plan based on one set of conditions and one level of activity, flexible budgeting system attempts to develop a series of budgets for various levels of activity and under varying sets of assumptions. Conventionally. flexible budgeting system is associated with production budgets. But there is no reason why this concept should not apply to the marketing budgets also. Infact, marketing budgets could be framed on a more realistic basis and their control made more meaningful and effective with the help of this concept.

The expense behaviour analysis suggested earlier should form the bedrock of flexible budgeting in marketing, specially for marketing expense budgets. For example, we give here a summary of the marketing expenses broken up into the four functions and indicating the behaviour of expenses :

Illustration : Flexible Budgeting

The marketing expenses of P. Ltd., have been budgeted at Rs.100 lakhs for the current year and their functional allocation is shown below :

Functional Allocation of Budgeted Expenses :

(Rs.in lakhs)

	Fixed	Variable	Total
Direct Selling	10	30	40
Distribution	15	20	35
Promotion	5	10	15
Other Marketing	10		10
	40	60	100

The sales were budgeted at Rs.1000 lakhs and the quarterly break-up of the budgeted sales is,

Quarter	I	Rs.160 lakhs
	II	Rs.240 lakhs
	III	Rs.280 lakhs
	IV	Rs.320 lakhs

The actual sales during the I and II quarters were Rs.200 lakhs and Rs. 180 lakhs respectively and the actual marketing expenses were, quarter I - Rs.26 lakhs and quarter II - Rs.23.5 lakhs.

A. Fixed Budgeting

Under fixed budgeting, no distinction will be made between fixed and variable marketing costs and the total budgeted marketing costs of Rs.100 lakhs would be assumed to be incurred uniformly throughout the year. So, quarterly budgets for marketing costs would be Rs.25 lakhs for each quarter. The report on sales and marketing costs would be as given below :

(Rs.in lakhs)

	Quarter I			Quarter II		
	Budget	Actual	Variance	Budget	Actual	Variance
Sales	160	200	40(F)	240	180	60(A)
Marketing expenses	25	26	1(A)	25	23.5	1.5(F)

(F) Favourable
(A) Adverse

B. Flexible Budgeting

If a flexible budgeting is followed, the fixed marketing costs of Rs.40 lakhs would be assumed to be incurred uniformly throughout the year. The variable marketing costs would vary with the sales value in each quarter. Since Rs.60 lakhs of variable costs represent 6% of budgeted sales, the budgeted marketing costs would be as follows :

(Rs.in Lakhs)

	Total	Qtr.I	Qtr.II	Qtr.III	Qtr.IV
Fixed expenses	40.00	10.00	10.00	10.00	10.00
Variable expenses	60.00	9.60	14.40	16.80	19.20
	100.00	19.60	24.40	26.80	29.20

When actual expenses are to be compared with the budget, the budgeted variable expenses will have to be flexed for the actual sales volume achieved to work out the variances.

Marketing Expenses Allowed for Sales Achieved

(Rs.in lakhs)

	Quarter I	Quarter II
Fixed expenses	10	10
Variable expenses (6% of actual sales)	12	10.8
Total	22	20.8

The control report under flexible budgeting would be as follows :

	QUARTER I			QUARTER II		
	Budget	Actual	Variance	Budget	Actuals	Variance
Sales	160	200	40(F)	240	180	60(A)
Marketing Expenses	22	26	4(A)	20.8	23.5	2.7(A)

During the first quarter, the adverse expense variance is only Rs.1 lakh under the fixed budgeting method. It will be easy for the marketing department to justify this increase on the ground of sal^^

being higher than budgeted. Similarly, in the second quarter, the marketing department will be complimented for showing a favourable expense variance of Rs.1.5 lakhs. However, when we apply the flexible budgeting concept, the position changes significantly. The adverse variance in the first quarter is Rs.4 lakhs and not Rs.1 lakh. Similarly during the second quarter there is again an adverse variance of Rs.2.7 lakhs and not a favourable variance of Rs.1.5 lakhs.

In order to judge expense variance in the right perspective, the flexible budgeting approach would obviously be the correct one. For more effective control of expenses, the same approach of arriving at the revised budgeted expenses figures - the expenses should be allowed with reference to the actual activity - can be extended to each functional area. And for this purpose, the budget should also be broken up department-wise as shown at the beginning. Further, to introduce more intensive control, the technique can be adopted on a monthly basis instead of quarterly as shown here. The mode of working will however, remain the same.

5. ADMINISTRATION OF BUDGETARY CONTROL SYSTEM

Many organisations in India have a reasonably good budgeting system, but the budgetary control system is either non-existent or ill-structured or haphazardly implemented by them. In fact, no matter how systematically it is done, budgeting loses much of its significance and utility unless a budgetary control system is operated in proper perspective. This comprises several important steps that need to be taken up in a logical sequence, as follows:

i) Developing the budgets as well as breaking these up into departmental/section wise details and also for shorter periods;

ii) Continuous comparison at regular periodic intervals, say, monthly or quarterly, between the budgeted figures and the corresponding actuals, using suitably designed formats;

iii) As a sequel to (ii) above, location of divergences between the budgeted figures and actual figures and pinpointing those that are adverse in nature and higher in magnitude;

iv) Analysing the reasons for the divergences so pinpointed;

v) Initiating remedial measures, again through the active involvement of the operating people, in order to correct the adverse divergences in the immediate next time-period; and

vi) If any major divergence, whether favourable or adverse, is found to be beyond control during the budget period, then working out a rational basis for revising the budget itself.

It is important to use suitably designed formats for presentation of budget-actual comparison. It should provide preferably a multiple frame of comparison and the following column-heads may be suggested to this end :

Budget TM (This Month)	Actual TM	
Budget YTD (Year-to-date)	Actual YTD	Actual YTD LY (Year-to-date last year)
Variance TM	Variance YTD	Variance YTD LY

Review and comparison between budgets and actuals on a regular and continuing basis and generating budgetary control statements form only one part of the story. But the other part, perhaps the more important part, is the process through which these statements trigger off control actions. The most vital requirement for this is that somebody has to take up the responsibility of initiating the corrective actions. More often than not it is found that people do not like to shoulder the responsibility for taking corrective measures and budgetary control ends there. The reason for the above may be attributed to the human factor in budgetary control system, or in any other control system for that matter.

People have been found to be a bit too sensitive to adverse variance. confronted with the same, they start building up defence mechanisms in their own mind, rather than thinking constructively how to correct the situation. They start finding scapegoats, alibis and excuses to justify non-performance.

An atmosphere of mutual faith and confidence has, therefore, to be created in the orgainsation whereby people will look upon variance analyses not as fault-finding or witch-hunting exercises, but engage themselves, in a genuine and constructive manner, in coordinated efforts so as to correct the adverse variances. This is of paramount importance, otherwise budgets and standards will continue to go wrong and the entire control mechanism will degenerate into mechanistic rituals with nothing coming out of these.

6. PROBABILITY CONCEPT IN BUDGETING

Budgeting in marketing area can be rendered more meaningful if the elementary concepts of statistical probability theory are introduced in the budgeting system. This may be explained with reference to a simple budgeting situation as indicated below :

Profit Budget for the Year 19x5

(Rs.lakh)

	Pessimistic	Moderate	Optimistic
Sales at Rs.10 per unit	500	700	800
Variable costs :			
Manufacturing	Rs.5.10 per unit	Rs.5 per unit	Rs.4.80 per unit
	255	350	384

Marketing Rs.0.50 per unit		25		35		40
Marginal cost		280		385		424
Marginal Contribution		220		315		376
Fixed Cost						
Manufacturing	100		100		100	
Marketing	20		20		20	
Administrative	10	130	10	130	10	130
Net Income before tax		90		185		246
Tax at 50 percent		45		92.5		123
Net Income after tax		45		92.5		123

In this case, the two important variables in the budget are the volume of sales and the estimate of variable expenses. We may assign probabilities to the pessimistic, moderate and optimistic estimates on the basis of our past experience and future expectations.

Suppose, according to our judgment, the probabilities assigned to the pessimistic, moderate and optimistic sales estimates are 0.3, 0.5 and 0.2, respectively. Similarly, let us assume that the probabilities assigned to the pessimistic, moderate and optimistic estimates of variable costs are 0.2, 0.6 and 0.2, respectively. In the circumstances, we can have 3 further probable estimates of profits under each of the categories, pessimistic, moderate and optimistic, as indicated below :

(Rs.lakh)

1. Sales (@ Rs.10 each)		500			700			800	
		P=0.3			P=0.5			P=0.2	
2. Variable costs Manufacturing (Volume x Rs.5.10, Rs.5.00 or Rs.4.80)	255	250	240	357	350	336	408	400	384

	P= 0.2	P= 0.6	P= 0.2	P= 0.2	P= 0.6	P= 0.2	P= 0.2	P= 0.6	P= 0.2
3. Marketing	25	25	25	35	35	35	40	40	40
4. Marginal cost	280	275	265	392	385	371	448	440	424
5. Marginal contribution	220	225	235	308	315	329	352	360	376
6. Fixed costs	130	130	130	130	130	130	130	130	130
7. Net income before tax	90	95	105	178	185	199	222	230	246
8. Tax at 50 percent	45	47.5	52.5	89	92.5	99.5	111	115	123
9. Net income after tax	45	47.5	52.5	89	92.5	99.5	111	115	123
10. Joint probability	0.06	0.18	0.06	0.10	0.30	0.10	0.04	0.12	0.04
11. Net income after tax x joint probability (9 x 10)	2.70	8.55	3.15	8.90	27.75	9.95	4.44	13.80	4.92

Expected value of income after tax : Rs.84.16 lakh.

It may be observed that the absolute estimates incorporated in the budget give rise to a variation of the net income after tax from Rs.45 lakh to Rs.123 lakh and as such can provide us with an unstable base for future projections. A much better quantification of the future expected income after tax is possible if we incorporate probabilities of a few key variables in our analysis.

CHAPTER 11

PRODUCT PLANNING AND DEVELOPMENT

1. Meaning and Signifcance of Products; 2. Product Mix; 3. Product Life Cycle; 4. New Product Development; 5. Financial Evaluation of Brand 6. Product Elimination.

1. MEANING AND SIGNIFICANCE OF PRODUCTS

Product may be defined (following Prof.Kotler) as anything that can be offered to a market for attention, acquisition, use or consumption that might satisfy a want or need.

We are all familiar with physical products e.g. garments, utensils, cars, locks, etc. But the term "product" also includes :

Services	e.g.	repairing, beauty-parlour, consultancy
Idea	e.g.	family planning, conservation of energy
Place	e.g.	holiday in Nepal

Products are the most crucial factor in a company's marketing programmes and the bedrock of its marketing activities. The profile of product basket of the company affects advertising media, channels of distribution, physical distribution arrangement, marketing research programmes and other significant aspects of its marketing efforts. In fact, the entire edifice of the company's marketing rests on the foundation of its product-offerings.

To quote Levitt, "when we view the product as something far more than its generic content, we are immediately faced with the necessity of a new way to plan for its creation and a new way to manage the process by which we attract and hold customers. It means that products must be planned, not just designed. It means that the people charged with selling the product must participate in its creation at the outset nqt just after they get it from the manufacturing department." Thus marketeers have to be directly involved in designing the product to meet the diverse and specific requirements of the targeted customers.

In a systematic marketing, the main thrust will be to discover the needs - latent or patent - underlying every product. In other words, marketeers should sell benefits not features. In order to achieve this, it is essential to analyse the product on three or four different levels, as given below, using the example of a personal computer.:

Core product	what is the buyer really buying? (a cost-effective device for data entry, data storage, calculation and problem-solving)
Tangible product -	the needs of the buyer have to be converted to tangible products. Characteristics of tangible products are quality, performance, features, styling and brand name.
Augmented product -	covers installation, after sales service, user support service (e.g.softwares with manuals)
Expanded/broadened -	after new features are added or new product uses/applications established (e.g. expanding memory capacity, newly developed specialised softwares, etc.).

A product has two types of attributes, namely, physical or measurable attributes and psychological or perceived attributes. The physical attributes include its inherent quality, basic packaging and design parameters. Perceived attributes comprise individual's perceptions, likes and dislikes which in turn are influenced by brand name and would vary widely from person to person even for products or brands of identical physical attributes. The marketeers try to effectively exploit the perceived attributes, particularly for consumer products where buying decisions are generally impulsive. For instance, all the luxury toilet soaps use the same ingredients in about the same proportion and pass through the same manufacturing process. but the frills like the size, design, colour, perfume and packaging of one brand of soap cake are different from those of the others. The physical attributes being about the same, it is the psychological attributes that make all the difference at the market place. In case of industrial goods, however, the perceived attributes play a relatively less important role and physical attributes or performance parameters predominate the buying decision.

2. PRODUCT MIX

Multi-product situation rather than single product cases are common these days. Even the so called one-product situation may well involve actually a multi-product one, when we take into consideration the varied pack-sizes or different end-uses of the product.

When a marketing organisation handles a number of products or a product-basket, the question of product-mix arises, mainly to ascertain the relative importance or weightage of the different products along criteria like Sales, Gross Margin (GM), etc.

However, the generally loosely used concept of product-mix has to be understood in terms of different types and levels of mixes. This may be illustrated using the hypothetical situation of a fairly large pharmaceutical company, as below

Activities/products, etc.	Nature of Mix	Ratio or % of total Sale value / GM
i) Pharmaceuticals, Agrovet, Food Specialities	Business Lines Mix	60:10:30
ii) Under Pharmaceuticals: Chemicals and Formulations	Product Lines Mix	35 : 65 (of 60% of the total business)
iii) Under Formulations : Tablets, Liquids and Injections	Product-Range Mix	40:45:15
iv) Under Tablets: Antibiotics, Vitamins and others	Product Groups Mix	60:30:10
v) Under Antibiotic Tablets : Products : P1, P2, P3	Product -Mix	30:40:30
vi) Under Product P1 : Intensity-wise : 250mg, 500mg	Intra-Product Mix	30:70
vii) Under Product P1 250mg : Package-wise : Strip/Blister packages of 10's, Bottles of 25, Bottles of 100	Packaging Mix	35:40:25

Assuming a total sale value of Rs.1 Crore in a month, the estimated share of P1 250 mg in strip/blister packages of 10 will be:

0.35 x 0.3 x 0.3 x 0.6 x 0.4 x 0.65 x 0.6 x Rs.1 Cr.
= Rs. 29,484 say Rs. 30,000 only.

Manipulation of product-mix with an eye particularly on improving the overall profitability of operations is a very important area of marketing strategy and tactics. And to this end, need for relevant financial and cost data is evident.

3. PRODUCT LIFE CYCLE

Just as a human being or any animate being goes through different phases in the life cycle, a product too has similar phases. This is a useful concept in sales forecasting, planning and control as current company products cannot hold the market position indefinitely. In a product life cycle (PLC), four distinct stages can be observed :

I	- Introduction	-	The product is put on the market, awareness and acceptance are minimum.
II	Growth	-	Because of advertising, sales promotion and other introductory marketing strategies the product makes rapid sales again.
III	Maturity	-	Sales growth continues but at a diminishing rate.
IV	Decline	-	Sales reach a static position and then begin to fall because of introduction of better products and substitution.

A pre-natal i.e. "product conception" stage can precede the stage I given below; and between stages III and IV, "saturation" stage may also be added.

Relying rather heavily on Prof. Kotler's approach, we may summarise below the PLC Concept and its implications :

A. The PLC Curve

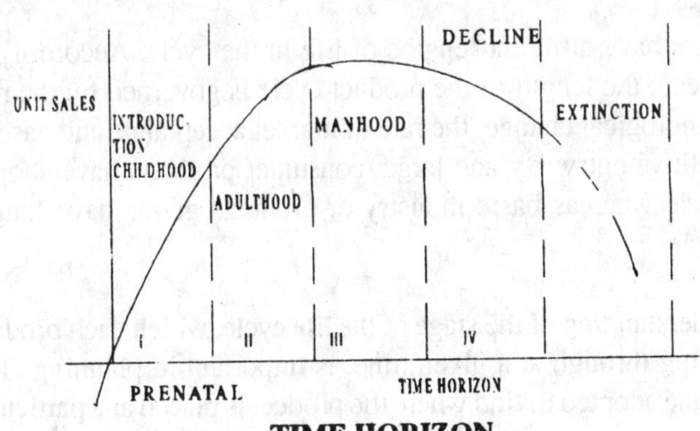

TIME HORIZON

B. Characteristics :

STAGES	I	II	III	IV
Sales	Low sales	Rising sales	Peak sales	Declining sales
Cost/Customer	High cost	Average cost	Low cost	Low cost
Profit	Negative	Rising profit	High profit	Declining profit
Customers	Innovators	Early	Middle adopters	Laggards Majority
Competitors	Few	Growing number	Stable number	Declining number

C. Marketing Objectives :

I	II	III	IV
Create product awareness and trial	Maximise Market share	Maximise profit and defend market share	Reduce expenditure

Products have different lengths of life in the cycle. According to Joel Dean, the length of the product cycle is governed by the rate of technological change, the rate of market acceptance and ease of competitive entry. By and large, consumer products have shorter life cycle whereas basic industry or products goods have longer life cycle.

An understanding of the stage of the life cycle, which each product is passing through at a given time, is important in planning. The technique adopted to find where the product is placed at a particular time in the life cycle path, is called diagnosis and prognosis technique. This technique consists in drawing six different curves and thereby following a few steps in a logical sequence. These are briefly explained below :

1. Sales revenue of the particular product for the last 5 years (or say for 5 units of time) of the particular firm.

2. Sales revenue for the same period as in 1 above, in respect of the same product but for the industry as a whole.

3. Direct cost of selling, in respect of the same product of the same firm and for the same period as in 1 above.

4. "Profit" which will be the difference between sales revenue (as per 1 above) and cost of selling (as per 3 above). (It is to be noted that this profit is not the same as the conventional profit which is arrived at by deducting all costs and expenses from the total revenue).

5. The Return On Investment (ROI), relating profit as per 4 above to the cost inputs or investment's as per 3 above. The ROI curve and comparison between the two curve as per 1 and 2 above will indicate adulthood or manhood or declining state of the product and will also suggest necessary corrective actions.

6. Action curve, indicating actions required to sustain adulthood or manhood and prevent decline. This could be in the form of more resource inputs, higher revenue through better pricing policy, etc.

The technique of diagnosis and prognosis should be adopted at regular intervals, say, every six months, in respect of consumer products and every two/three years in respect of industrial products.

Some marketing experts believe that product life cycle is actually brand life cycle. This is true in some cases where the importance of brand trends to gradually diminish. Product life cycle becomes very unpredictable in case of discovery of new uses, entry into totally new markets, emergence of new customers or addition of new features. Also PLC does not supply to classics category of products. Another oft referred view on the subject is that instead of "product life cycle" what really exists is "mismanagement cycle", as Robert Helfer has put it. There might be some truth in this.

In conclusion, the relevance of the PLC concept may be understood from the following :

	Product	**Length of PLC**
i)	Idea/Need fulfillment (e.g. storing the memory of an important event in life)	Virtually non-existent and almost irrelevant
ii)	Generic product(s) (e.g. Audio visual and video system)	Very long life cycle
iii)	Specific product(s) (e.g. cassette tape recorder, video camera)	Long life cycle
iv)	Specific brand(s)(e.g. Philips Two-in-one, National brand portable video camera)	Relatively short life cycle

4. NEW PRODUCT DEVELOPMENT

There are three broad aspects of product planning, viz.,

i) Exploring new uses of existing products
ii) Introduction of new products
iii) Pruning or phasing out weak products

Finding new uses for existing products could be simultaneously most thrilling and rewarding, though it is also a neglected area in marketing. Instances are of course there - both in industrial and consumer goods marketing - to demonstrate how success in such efforts could lead to substantial enlargement of the market, increase in turnover and improvement in profitability too. This also reduces product proliferation with its attendant benefits. The exercise, however, requires systems approach and demands creativity.

The second aspect is planning new products. The term "New Product" is highly flexible in import. Booz, Allen and Hamilton identified following types of new products with reference to newness to the company and to the market :

i) New to the world products - create an entirely new market.

ii) New Product lines - entering an established market for the first time.

iii) Addition to existing product lines - supplement company's existing product lines.

iv) Improvement in/revision to existing products - improved performance and greater perceived value.

v) Re-positionings - existing products targeted to new markets, new customers.

vi) Cost reductions - new products providing similar performance at reduced cost.

A company usually adopts a mix of these new products. New products in true sense (i.e. new to the world) involve the greatest risk - in terms of cost and market acceptability. The risk element tends to reduce progressively as one moves downward and becomes the least in case of (vi).

In the highly competitive environment, it is essential to identify new opportunities and take advantage of the situation by developing new products. This is all the more important because the existing product range will sooner or later be in a declining stage in their life cycle and the need for new products to bridge the sales gap would be urgently felt.

Criteria in New Product Decisions :

There are several criteria and considerations underlying new product decisions. Some of these are obvious (of course very important too) like fitting into the company's mission and objectives, state of competition, profitability, etc. Some other important criteria are summarised below :

(a) search for "synergy" i.e. to look for positively correlated products for example, fountain pen and ink. This covers :

i) Marketing synergy

ii) Suppliers synergy

iii) Customers synergy or "need package"

(iv) Technological synergy

(v) Equipment synergy

(vi) Manpower synergy

e.g. some companies are conscious of diversifying into products or activities in order to make use of unutilised capacities and productive facilities as well as manpower.

(b) search for "portfolio effect"— These are mostly negatively correlated products. Some examples are :

i) existing product versus possible replacement product (for example, fountain pen and ball-point pen),

ii) high-margin-low-volume product versus low-margin-high-volume product

iii) off-the shelf items versus made-to-order items.

(c) search for stability — highly fluctuating sale product versus stable business cycle product (for example, HMT manufacturing machine tools going into watches, tractors and presses, which are stable products)

(d) search for security — (for example, TISCO going in for vertical integration, both backward and forward)

(e) product life cycle consideration — this concept requires that investments should be made only in those products which are in the upward segment of their life cycle, not in the flat, horizontal or declining segment. That is, such products should be searched for, which represent either the introduction or the growth stage in the life cycle.

(f) Vertical specialisation — An example may again be cited from HMT. By moving from general purpose machines to special purpose machines, the Company introduced vertical specialisation.

(g) Segment movements — If a dairy firm moves on from the supply of milk at cheap price to supplying butter and other "value added" milk products to cater to different market segments, it would be an instance of segment movement.

New product planning thus involved what is called "product diversification" which can be broadly of three types viz.,

(a) Cost-push type — generally "old products in new markets"

(b) Demand-pull types — generally "new products in old markets".

(c) Conglomerate type — that is, "new product in new markets"

It is the conglomerate type of diversification that needs very careful consideration because the risk involved in this area tends to be the highest.

Different Stages Involved in New Product Development :

The different stages in new product planning and development may be briefly discussed ad seriatim below :

(i) *First information or ideas about products:* Such information or ideas would come from various sources, viz., market research, desk research, international journals, Government literature and publications, salesmen's reports and other sources like "brain storming sessions", group discussions, personal discussions, etc.

(ii) *Credibility Count :* A large number of new product information or ideas may come from the various sources listed above. Depending on the source of information, the various product ideas have to be given suitable credibility values. For example, a product idea coming from market research will have a low credibility value, since the function of market research is not to generate product ideas but to identify unfilled or potential need. Usually product ideas coming from salesmen's report will have a higher credibility value and next in the list would be perhaps the international journals. The credibility count as indicated here would straight away screen and thereby reduce the number of product ideas.

(iii) *Matching the objectives :* The product ideas remaining after stage (ii) should be subjected to a further scrutiny with reference to objectives or criteria listed earlier. This will enable a systematic ranking of various products. Obviously, this will eliminate some of the product ideas which do not fit in well with the company's philosophy, mission or objectives.

(iv) *Market Research* : The surviving product ideas (after stage iii) should now be subjected to a fairly in-depth market researches, including field surveys and a revised ranking of the product-ideas may be made on the basis of their demand and market-acceptability.

(v) *Technology Forecasting (T.F.)* : This should include a knowledge or understanding of the latest status of international researches in the relevant fields. Their absence may result in the unwise decision for high investment in an area where technology would be available at a price much cheaper than the cost of development through own R & D efforts. This would also reduce the chances of developing a technology through R & D which may eventually turn out to be obsolete.

(vi) *Technology Sourcing or R & D (Research and development)* : Depending upon T.F. findings either technology sourcing or R&D efforts should start with only very few product ideas available after the elimination tests under the above stages.

(vii) *First Financial Feasibility studies* : These should include broad financial exercises mostly on the basis of projections in respect of alliable alternatives. Another ranking based on relative financial attractiveness of the products should then be made.

(viii) *Filter* - This stage is meant to take stock of the situation and zero on with the alternatives left, that are apparently feasible - technically, commercially and financially, too.

(ix) *Pilot Stage :* This would include development of prototypes and technical testing of the product. Actual cost determination is also very important at this stage.

(x) *Second Financial Feasibility studies :* These would cover some further and more detailed financial exercises, mostly on actual basis, on the results obtained during the pilot stage.

(xi) *Test Marketing :* This should cross-check how far the earlier findings, say, through market research, are realistic and valid. This will also indicate whether a product stands a good chance of success at the market-place.

(xii) *Commercialisation of the product :* At this stage, marketing plan and programmes are to be finalised for exploiting market opportunities on a profitable basis.

There is an inherent danger of a product being killed at any of the above stages. This is particularly so because different people would be in charge of the various stages indicated above. To avoid any faulty judgment at any stage and to forge an effective co-ordination, there should be a new product manager who would be identified with the new products right from the beginning and put in charge of the entire process.

How many ideas should one generate for each idea that eventually culminates in a successful new product ? One study shows that out of every 58-odd ideas, about twelve products pass the initial screening test, which shows them to be compatible with the company objective and resources. Seven remain after a thorough evaluation of their potential. About three survive the product development stage, two survive the test marketing stage and only one is commercially successful. Thus about 58 new ideas are to be generated to find one good product. Another research finding in the USA indicates that it takes 16 apparently viable ideas to produce one successful product.

Under the modern conditions of competition, it is increasingly risky not to innovate since consumers expect a stream of new and improved products. It is at the same time extremely expensive and risky to innovate because (a) most product ideas that go into product development never reach the market; (b) many of the products that do reach the market are not successful; and (c) successful new products tend to have a shorter life than the existing ones. There are casualties in the innovation process because the company discovers belatedly that they are technically incapable or that they would have to incur too high costs to develop or that their market was over-estimated.

5. FINANCIAL EVALUATION OF BRAND

'Brand' for a firm is certainly a capital asset. Rather it is the only asset which may exist even when other forms of assets like machines, furniture, buildings etc. might disappear. The importance of brand until recently was assessed in qualitative terms only, like brand recall, awareness, positioning etc. The financial view of brand in terms of 'brand equity' is a recent phenomenon. We have seen a number of cases, from mid-eighties onwards, of mergers and acquisitions, both nationally and internationally, primarily with a view to getting hold of an established brand. The sum (merger/takeover bid) involved in each case far exceeds the intrinsic value of the firm being acquired as depicted by its balance sheet. It is now no longer rare to find offers at a multiple of more than 25 times of company assets or two to three times the market value of its shares.

This scenario has been triggered by a growing need of companies to gain a position of dominance by leveraging brand in a prospective market. As creating a brand from the scratch is often considered to be costly, time-consuming and risky, it is easier to invest in an existing and established brand. Apart from this, by getting hold of an existing successful brand as compared to creating altogether a new brand, a company restricts, to some extent, future competition. In this situation of multiple gains involved should we assume that the price paid for acquiring a company could wholly be attributed to its brand acquisition? The answer is only partly true. Theoretically, the acquisition cost less the value of tangible assets should be assigned to the brand. But practically, this also includes overbidding. Thus we can say that the acquisition price includes the value of tangible assets, price of the brand and the cost of preventing the brand from going into the competitors' hands.

The point to be considered now is how to treat this amount in the books of accounts. Different schools of thought have recommended different treatments for this, but all of them are open to controversies Some suggest that the value of brand should be shown as an asset in the balance sheet. This again can be depreciated year wise or left untouched. Others opine that this value should be completely written off against the available reserves and surplus balance in the balance sheet. Without going into respective merits and demerits of the various accounting treatments let us analyse the other issues involved. What happens to the valuation of internally created brands? Should it be shown in the company's balance sheet, if yes, when and how?

Our accounting system is by and large based on historical cost and thus there is no provision for assigning or imputing any value to internally created brands. Thus unable to show the values of its internally created brands in its balance sheet, a company allows itself to be undervalued and open to its predators (i.e. corporate raiders) as a prey. Its own shareholders are misinformed to this extent and are prone to sell their stocks to outsiders at a price which is truly not indicative of the company's real worth. At the same time, it has always been the endeavor of the Government authorities to keep the shareholders abreast of true and fair picture of a company. There lies a dichotomy.

If a company tries to assign monetary value to its brand, the whole exercise becomes highly subjective in nature, though it might reflect the true economic value of the company. A brand is created through several factors and many of these may not be exactly quantifiable. Even for factors which can be quantified, like advertisement expense, it is difficult to pinpoint as to how much of such expenses has gone towards brand building as distinct from those for achieving sales in the short-run.

How, for example, does one allocate out of total advertisement spent on Coca cola, the portion which has gone towards the brand creation. Since when? Again it will be difficult to say what part of the advertisement spending has been made with a long-term view, i.e. towards building a brand.

Brand valuation, in case of an acquisition, is a function of the ultimate purpose of the acquisition i.e. what use the acquirer will put the brand to would largely determine the price. If the purpose changes may be the value also will change. In case of internally created brands individual perceptions about the purpose might differ. Again evaluation from acquisition point of view and from accounting point of view will be very different. As for accounts one has to respect the time tested standards of valuation and recording the same. Furthermore, value once assigned is unlikely to remain static; it may have to be scaled up or down from time to time depending on various other factors. This will bring distortions in the annual reports on a year to year basis.

The people most likely to be the happiest with the onset of this kind of a process are the marketing professionals, for obvious reasons. This is going to give a concrete value to their own efforts and functioning. That is why, they will be more interested not in the final value but the process per se which necessitates a greater understanding of the concept of brand, how it operates and how their efforts towards creating it should be valued. On the contrary the accountants will be more interested in the final value and its treatment, keeping in tact the accounting principles and conventions that form the boundaries of their operations. This dichotomy further adds hurdles towards an effort to value a brand. Accountants should respect in particular the principle of prudence and in doing so they ought to recognize any major outlay of *funds* as an investment only where there is a likely, if not guaranteed, stream of future returns, however far-off it may be. This objectivity is not the case with brand valuation.

To conclude we can say that one cannot negate that brands have a value. While agreeing to it, the process of evaluation sets off a joint effort on the part of marketing and finance personnel who have to sit together and try to find out ways and means to reach a common objective, given various constraints. It also emphasizes that there is a paradigm shift towards what essentially constitutes a company's assets profile. We will agree that it is not only the land, machines, buildings etc. that form a company's assets, but its intangible assets such as brand, knowledge etc. and of course the human resource which truly form part of a company's assets, whether or not these are reflected in the company's balance sheet.

There are various methods available for brand valuation. Here is a summarized list of quantitative / semi-quantitative methods for brand valuation under different situations and parameters:

i) Valuation in Terms of costs
   a) Historic cost i.e. estimated actual cost of creation or acquisition of a brand.
   b) Replacement cost i.e estimated cost of replacing an existing brand by an identical new one through creation or acquisition.

ii) Valuation according to Market Price i.e. price to bid or pay for acquiring brand well established in the market.

iii) Valuation According to Potential Earnings i.e. price a company will be prepared to pay based on the future earning potential of a brand to be acquired. Formulas for calculating the Brand's Value:

a) Value of the brand $= \frac{\quad}{t\text{-}l} - \frac{N}{(l+r)t} + RBt \; \frac{\text{Residual value}}{(l+r)N}$

Where RBt = Anticipated revenue in year t, attributable to the brand

r = Discounting rate

Residual value beyond year N $= \frac{RB^{N}}{r} \quad \frac{RB^{x}}{r\text{-}g}$

g = Rate of revenue growth

b) The multiple method

When for a firm, P/E $= \frac{\text{Market Value of Equity}}{\text{Known Profits}}$

Brand Multiple $= \frac{\text{Brand Equity}}{\text{Brand Net Profits}}$

6. PRODUCT ELIMINATION

This is a very important and perhaps the most neglected area in product management. Most of the marketing organisations tend to overlook the importance of product elimination or phasing out sick and weak products, as compared to the attention paid towards developing new products. The reason could be :

i) It is always easier to add products than to eliminate.

ii) It is difficult to delist yesterday's good products since parting with old and tried friends is always a sad decision.

iii) Expectation that the weak product might do well in future with changes in the market conditions.

iv) Product elimination as well as its implementation decision requires some extra-ordinary and multi-faceted analysis, care and efforts.

Product proliferation, if unchecked, leads to a situation of having too many items under the varied types of products like, as per Peter Drucker's classification, yesterday's bread-winners, today's bread-winners, tomorrow's bread-winners, developing products, failures, unnecessary specialities, strategic products, investment in managerial ego and Cinderellas (sleepers).

Such product over-population involves substantial hidden costs, inefficiencies and losses like :

i) feeding too many product - mouths with limited resources resulting in waste of physical and financial resources that could be gainfully redeployed elsewhere.

ii) high unit cost of production due to short production run.

iii) a sizable part of the promotional expenses going waste.

iv) disproportionately higher costs of warehousing and distribution.

v) internal competition among products of the same company - sometimes even "product cannibalism".

vi) numerical increase in products leading to geometrical increase in the managerial problems - waste of valuable managerial time and attention.

vii) burdened with a large number of products and packs, little attention could be paid to further growth by seizing emerging market opportunities.

"Family Planning" for the products of a company should, therefore, be unavoidable. Occasionally euthanasia (mercy killing) is also necessary - one has to prune a product ruthlessly when it has outlived its necessity.

The basic question that arises at this stage is "How to identify the weak products or potential pruning candidates"? In Chapter - 25 of this book (Profitability Control) a few product performance evaluation models have been illustrated. These would be useful in this important task.

Apart from these, one can adopt a simple approach of ABC analysis. Using two bases, namely sales and contribution margin over the past three to five years, the entire product-basket of a company can be classified into : "A" (blue-chip products), "B" (good products) and "C" (weak products). This may be done at regular periodic intervals, say once a year.

Some more sophisticated methods are also available for product pruning decisions. We shall briefly discuss two of them. The first one is a product review based on the "Seven Scale Product Rating Form" adapted from "Phasing out Weak Products" by Prof Kotler.

The seven criteria are as follows :

i. What is the future market potential for the product?

ii. How much could be gained by product modifications ?

iii. How much could be gained by marketing strategy modification?

iv. How much useful executive time could be released by abandoning this product ?

v. How good are the firm's alternative opportunities?

vi. How much is the product's contribution beyond its direct cost?

vii. How much is the product contributing to the sale of other products ?

Against each criterion first some weightage factor should be given. Then a "Five Point Rating Scale" may be used across all the criteria. The maximum total "product retention index" would therefore be 35. The apparently weak products can be measured along the scale, albeit by subjective judgement or feel factor of the marketing executives and total weighted score obtained against each. A company may fix a minimum or cut-off rating score to justify the retention of the product, using this simple model.

Paul W. Hamelmon and Edward M. Mazze have, in their article "Improving Product Abandonment Decisions," presented a computer-aided model for product abandonment decisions called PRESS (Product Review and Evaluation Sub-System). The programme consists of four integrated parts, PRESS I through IV

PRESS I : Basic data - e.g. direct material cost, direct labour cost, variable overheads, sale price - all per unit and unit quantity sold, etc., with a provision for inter-product comparison so as to arrive at Selection Index Number (SIN) for each product.

PRESS II : Price volume relationship - examining the effect of a price change on the contribution margin of specific products and exploring the possibility of improving the margin.

PRESS III - Sales Trends - forming series of PRESS I ranking based on available historical data for each product and isolating the likely pruning candidates, that is those that keep appearing near the bottom of the list.

PRESS IV : Product Complementarity and Substitutability - calculating a new factor known as RESIN based on original SIN value for each product adjusted upward or downward for tie-in or replacement sales respectively. This is the final step and an automatic, stepwise product deletion alteration.

On a comparison between the two models, we may observe as follows:

a. Kotler's model takes the products one by one but PRESS takes up the whole lot and a continuous comparison is built into the model itself.

b. Kotler's model needs more subjective inputs from managers than the PRESS.

c. The PRESS model presents a more sophisticated and less expensive system compared to the Kotler's approach that needs substantial executive time.

d. The PRESS model, however, cannot be used unless there is a fully developed and updated standard marginal costing system, which very few companies in India really have. In the Indian context, therefore, the scope of its use is very limited, whilst Kotler's model has a wider scope of application.

CHAPTER 12

MARKETING ORGANISATION

1. Meaning and Significance of Organisation; 2. Major Considerations in Planning the Marketing Organisation; 3. Different Types of Marketing Organisation: 4. Attributes of an Effective Marketing Organisation;

1. MEANING AND SIGNIFICANCE OF ORGANISATION

Basically, an "organisation" is one of the important instruments for implementing the various plans and programmes of a corporation, and from this perspective, it should be looked upon as the instrumentality for achieving the corporate objectives. While it is customary to consider various physical, financial and human resources as inputs, organisation is seldom considered as such, although it is also a vital input and therefore, not something than can be just taken for granted. Another important point about organisation is that it is not a given, static, rigid, or frozen entity - it is the result of evolution - it is subject to changes over time - changes both in character and quality.

The structure of organisation is the anatomy while the process of organisation is the physiology. Structure indicates how an organisation is supposed to work, while the process shows how it actually works. The structure is the static "shell" and the process is the dynamic character of its contents. While structure indicates the levels and reporting relationships, process implies communication and coordination and closely related to these, decision-making and, therefore, information system. Any change in the structure would necessarily influence the process too.

Sometimes, an enterprise changes and consequently the organisation also changes without any conscious effort to effect such changes. These are unplanned changes which very often come either through adhoc decisions - decisions taken in isolation, or through the process of evolution over a relatively long period. However, nowadays, much more emphasis is placed on planned changes than unplanned ones.

Any conscious effort towards organisational planning and development requires that some basic factors, which generally effect changes in the organisation (both structure and process), have to be accorded adequate attention to. These are :

Size of the enterprise
Technology
Strategies (i.e.strategy structure hook-up or 'fit')
External environments, including state of competition apart from the emerging opportunities and threats in the environment.

2. MAJOR CONSIDERATIONS IN PLANNING THE MARKETING ORGANISATION

A marketing organisation should be geared in such way that it can anticipate changes and react to changes, instead of being overtaken by them. Any conscious effort towards developing a right marketing organisation should start with a proper diagnosis of the existing organisation to assess its capability to fulfil the present as well as future needs. The next step should be to develop alternatives, which is the basic step in any planning. There may be some alternatives which are desirable (i.e.logically acceptable), and some others which are feasible (i.e.can be worked out without "rocking the boat"). In organisational planning, there is always a gap between what is desirable and what is feasible. This has to be first established and then bridged, as far as possible. An effort should be made to develop a long-term direction showing the mode and time scale to reach the desired organisation structure. Another important point in organisational planning is that the people and the structure have to be logically separated. Structure may be modified thereafter, if necessary, carefully and consciously, to suit some people and only for some time; but not the other way round.

Let us now come to the concepts of "staff" and "line" in relation to marketing organisation. These concepts have been applied to marketing organisation for a pretty long time. Obviously the top marketing executive is looked upon as a line executive and under him the line identification is extended to those who direct the sales, e.g., the sales manager, regional and district manager,etc. It has been customary to treat advertising and sales promotion manager, distribution manager, sales training manager, product specialist, service managers, market research assistants, etc. as staff executives. The criterion usually applied to determine one as a "line" or "staff" in marketing, is whether one is "accountable" for sales, margin and/or profit. Those who are so "accountable" are "line" - others are "staff".

As in any other area, the important problem faced in marketing is how to get the two types of executives to work together as a team and how to minimise line-staff frictions at various levels. We are not going into details of these, except to point out that the organisation as a whole will be effective only when this team spirit is developed and line-staff friction is minimised, if not eliminated. Another important problem in this area is whether a product manager should be treated as a "line" or a "staff" executive. When the product management concept was first developed, the intention was to treat such managers as specialised staff executives and make them responsible for the total "health and well-being of the product", starting with the product conception and culminating in the product extinction. In course of time, however, product managers have been given additional responsibilities and many companies have made them directly accountable for sales, margin and profitability of the products under their control. Any attempt to broaden the job function of the product managers in this manner would obviously mean that they are treated more as "line" executives than "staff" specialists.

Many experts today consider the line and staff concepts in organisation to be generally obsolete, specially in marketing. This is by and large valid since there are well-developed tools and techniques available now to measure the effectiveness of the so -

called "staff" people and also make them accountable. For example, there is a new concept which considers the sales manager, advertising manager and product manager to be responsible in turn for selling, advertising and product effectiveness - their performances can be measured by such factors as share of market, share of customer's mind and product margins after deducting selling costs. Obviously, in a situation like this, none of the three managers can trace his success to himself alone; each one will be dependent on the others; and consequently, the conventional line-staff distinction will no longer remain valid.

Coming specifically to sales organisation, whether it should be market-oriented or product-oriented is a controversial issue. Many large companies in India have been making experiments in this area. Market oriented organisation is relatively an old and simple structure. But it often poses practical problems, especially when there are many product lines and the products are of highly specialised nature. It is difficult for the market-oriented salesman to be familiar with all products important to his market. As against this, product-oriented organisation has some distinct advantages, since the salesman would be a specialist in respect. But sometimes product-oriented organisation may not be the right answer when there are only a few markets, since this type of structure is costlier to maintain than the market-oriented type. In conclusion it may be stated that it is the market-oriented rather than the product-oriented sales organisation which fits in well with the marketing concepts.

3. DIFFERENT TYPES OF MARKETING ORGANISATION

Marketing organisation structure could be of various types. Some of these are as follows :

i) *Functional type :* This is a simple structure formed by grouping the various activities into basic function and placing an executive in charge of each such function. This structure is suitable for small organisations. But even in large organisations, this type of organisational structure is found to exist at the top level, comprising executives ultimately responsible for each basic marketing function, viz., direct selling, distribution, promotion and other marketing services.

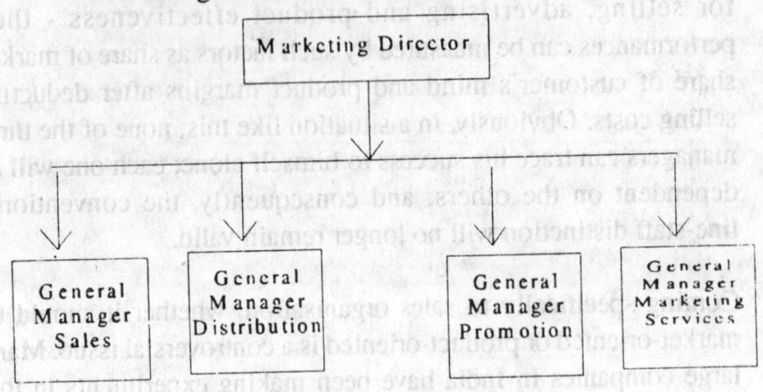

ii) *Territorial type :* This structure is formed after splitting the market into various sales territories, called districts, zones or regions and placing one executive in charge of each such territory. This is particularly suitable for direct selling functions in large companies.

iii) *Product division type :* This is another popular form of organisation structure in large companies. The various products handled by the company are put under the charge of several executives, each one of them being called product group manager, product manager, or brand manager. This type of structure is specially suited to provide better customer service and in marketing highly specialised products.

iv) *Customer division type :* This organisation structure is developed with an eye on the types of customers and consequently the type of specialisation required with respect to each type of customers.

v) *Combined type :* Usually a marketing organisation is not exclusively of any of the above four types, but rather a combination of two or more of them, which is again true for relatively large companies.

vi) *Matrix type* : Under this type sales activity as well as accountability is viewed from two mutually interdependent angles viz., product or product groups and geographical territory. Let us understand its implication from the simple table given below with hypothetical budget figures :

Product Group / Region	1	2	3	4	Total
East	100	80	50	70	300
South	35	50	40	25	150
West	140	30	100	80	350
North	25	40	70	65	200
Total	300	200	260	240	1,000

The manager PG 1 is responsible for achieving the budgeted sales of all regions in his product group. Similar will be the case for other managers of the different product groups. Likewise the manager of each region will be accountable for total sales in the respective command areas or territories. The mutual interdependence is quite clear. A regional manager cannot achieve his budget without the active support of all the product group managers, just as no product group manager can fulfil his all-India sales budget without adequate support from the regional managers.

It would be obvious that the two groups of managers will have different types of responsibility and therefore, the operational thrust. The regional manager's responsibility will be market penetration and thus achieving an extensive territorial coverage with respect to all the products. The responsibility of the product coverage duly backed by specialisation support, on all-India basis. Thus, the regional manager need not be a product specialist-he should rather be a product generalist but market specialist whereas a product manager should be a product specialist but market generalist. Marketing effectiveness can be optimised through well-coordinated efforts of these two groups of managers.

4. ATTRIBUTES OF AN EFFECTIVE MARKETING ORGANISATION

A marketing organisation can be considered as effective only when it exerts a positive influence on the work atmosphere and work relationship internally and is capable of responding to the stimuli emanating from the environment outside. These can be evaluated with reference to some important attributes of a good marketing organisation.

The first and foremost attribute of a good marketing organisation is "strategy-structure hook-up" that is, strategies are first determined and the structure is then designed such as would fit in well with the strategies, but not the other way round.

Next is the motivational aspect. Own performance is the single-most important motivator for a manager. But the organisational structure has to create a congenial atmosphere to this end. The emphasis should be to motivate as many managers as possible by entrepreneurial objectives as distinct from functional task performance objectives.

The third important aspect is proper staffing that needs to be based on a scientific assessment of workload and a rational distribution of the same covering all facets of marketing function. Productivity of human resources deployed as well optimisation of results would directly depend on these.

Next is the question of the number of levels and possible chain of command desirable in a marketing organisation. Organisational development experts all over the world have been increasingly emphasising the fact that the traditional hierarchical or pyramid structure is totally unsuitable under the present day complex marketing operations. The traditional organisational structure, based on the principles of span of control (an obsolete principle in management!), suffers from some basic limitations e.g.,

It pays the job, not the person;
Vital information gets diluted and distorted while travelling through various layers to reach the top person;

Communication problem arises mainly because of bureaucratic entanglements - many decisions are either hidden or lost in the morass of bureaucracy.

For effectively tackling these problems, marketing organisation structure should be a flat one, providing as few levels as possible - it should represent more a matrix, a team, than a pyramid. Also, the marketing organisation structure should be designed in such a way that the distance between the customers and the top management is reduced to the minimum. This will ensure lower reaction or response time.

The fifth criterion is directness and simplicity, the need for which in any organisational structure can hardly be over-emphasised. This includes decentralisation of centres of responsibility and delegation of authority to the responsible managers - both in a clearcut, strong and effective manner.

Lastly, succession planning should be a logical process built into the organisational structure. This would ensure suitable training and testing of the next generation of managers and equipping them with graded skills and experience to progressively shoulder increased responsibility.

SECTION IV

MARKETING DECISIONS

Keeping in view the fact that decision is a choice among alternatives, this section attempts to explain and illustrate the various tools and techniques useful in marketing decisions. The section starts with a discussion on the role and importance of cost analysis in marketing decisions (Chapter 13). The next Chapter illustrates a very common but effective set of decision-making techniques, viz., break-even analysis and cost volume profit analysis. Chapter 15 dealing with pricing policies and decisions attempts to explore, in a detailed manner, the various issues connected with pricing in the Indian context. Quite a few special pricing problems have been covered here, supported by suitable illustrations and cases, all drawn from real-life situations. The last Chapter in the section (Chapter 16) discusses and illustrates the important concepts and techniques of investment appraisal which form the bed-rock of investment decisions, again with special emphasis on their application to marketing sphere.

CHAPTER 13

COST ANALYSIS IN MARKETING DECISIONS

1. Decisional Phenomena of a Business; 2. Cost Analysis in Marketing; 3. A Few Marketing Decisional Problems involving Cost Analysis; 4. Strategic Cost Analysis.

1. DECISIONAL PHENOMENA OF A BUSINESS

While driving a car, if you suddenly find yourself in a blind alley, you have no alternative but to reverse. You cannot tell your wife or friend by your side that you are taking a 'dynamic decision' of reversing your car ! There is no question of taking a decision when there is only one alternative left, since in such a case it becomes an action. Question of taking a decision therefore arises only when there are two or more alternative courses available in tackling a certain problem or handling a particular situation.

Decisions have to be taken in an enterprise mainly with regard to planning and controlling its operations. Decision-making is a management prerogative. In fact, managements at different levels have to take a wide variety of deicisons. All such decisions may be grouped into two classes viz. (a) single-shot (or unprogrammed) decisions and (b) repetitive (or programmed) decisions. Each single-shot decision is a unique decision in respect of a unique problem. All capital expenditure decisions are of this type. Repetitive decisions are those that have to be taken at periodic intervals with reference to some repetitive problems or aspects of a business. Some examples of repetitive decisions are advertisement media selection and expense planning, decisions regarding inventory level norms, pricing decisions, decisions about optimum product and /or sales-mix, and so on.

Any decision, whatever be its nature and type, is essentially a leap in the dark. It involves some element of forecasting — an estimate of the future conditions and circumstances. According to Drucker, modern management should be interested not so much in present decisions as in the futurity of the present decisions. Though decisions are taken with an eye on the future, past is always a never-failing guide, especially in respect of repetitive decisions. A proper and systematic analysis of past data would definitely offer a good guide to the 'decision-maker'.

A right decision at right time cannot be taken simply on the basis of some quantitative data and information. There are non-financial or qualitative factors as well, which sometimes weigh more heavily than the financial or quantitative factors. In fact, a good decision-maker does not have always before him an array of both financial and non-financial factors relevant to a particular decision-making problem. The skill of the decision-maker lies primarily in his ability to analyse the interdependence and interaction of both these sets of factors, especially with regard to their futurity.

Barring a few 'balanced' executives, business houses abound in two types of decision-makers, viz. the Othello type (those who take decision without thinking and weighing the information) and the Hamlet type (those who always think but do not take decisions) — the hasty decision-makers and the prisoners of indecision. In order to convert these Othellos and Hamlets into balanced decision-makers they should be regularly fed with decision-based and purposeful information. And it is in this context that the concept of cost analysis is very important.

2. COST ANALYSIS IN MARKETING

The purpose of cost analysis is essentially to generate and provide financial and quantitative data to decision-makers to aid and improve the decision-making process. Cost analysis is made with reference to the data available from both financial accounting and cost accounting records and also various other statistical data. The types of cost analyses are varied and depend upon the decision problems for which the analyses are required. When cost analysis is to be used for control and decision purposes, the speed with which the cost data are provided is of greater importance than their accuracy. A proper analysis of marketing costs aids in the following :

* Determination of the marketing costs of each product so that when they are combined with production cost data, productwise profitability can be worked out.

* Control of marketing costs through establishment of budgets and evaluation of managers according to their cost responsibilities.

* Analysis of costs involved in serving different classes of customers and different areas to determine their relative profitability.

* Computation of such figures as cost per sales call, cost per order, cost to include a new customer on the books, etc.

* Decision - making in regard to sales such as selling through different channels of distribution, selling in different markets and regions, determining product profitability for differing levels of promotional expenses to choose the best possible method of sales promotion and, so on

Marketing cost analysis is carried out in two stages :

I The costs are initially reclassified from their accounting headings into functional cost groups in such a way that each cost group brings together all the costs associated with a particular activity in marketing the product.

II These functional cost groups are then allocated to control units (i.e. products, customer groups, channels of distribution) using reasonable bases.

The functional analysis of marketing costs may be follows :

i) Direct Selling cost — Salesmen's salary commission, travelling, entertainment, etc.

ii) Advertisement and sales promotion cost — media advertisement, catalogues and brochures

iii) Market research — cost of in-house research, cost of researches carried through outside agencies, etc.

iv) Distribution cost — Transportation, warehousing and storage, insurance, etc.

v) Credit and collection — cost of collection staff, bad debts, cash discount, etc.

vi) Financial and general administration — cost of sales invoicing, interest in working capital locked up in finished goods and receivables, etc.

As regards the second stage/type of cost analysis mentioned above, the following illustration should be useful :

A company produces a single product in three sizes A, B and C. The following expenses incurred on marketing are sought to be traced to the sizes using the indicated bases.

Expenses	Amount Rs.	Basis
Salesmen's salaries	10,000	Direct charge
Sales commission	6,000	Sales turnover

Sales office expenses	2,096	Number of orders
Advertising :General	5,000	Sales turnover
Advertising : Specific	22,000	Direct charge
Packing	3,000	Total volume in cft of products sold.
Delivery expenses	4,000	"
Warehouse expenses	1,000	"
Credit collection exp.	1,296	Number of orders
	54,392	

The following data are also available :

i No. of Salesmen (all paid same salary)	10	4	5	1
ii. Units sold	10,400	3,400	4,000	3,000
iii. No. of orders	1,600	700	800	100
iv. Percentages of specific advertising	100%	30%	40%	30%
v. Sales Turnover	2,00,000	58,000	80,000	62,000
vi. Volume of cft per unit of finished product		5	8	17

The following statement shows how the costs have been traced to the three sizes on the basis of information given. Also the analysis has been used to find out

* marketing costs per unit sold for each of the three sizes, and
* marketing costs as percentage of sales turnover.

ANALYSIS OF MARKETING COSTS

Expenses	Basis of Allocation	Total Rs.	Size A Rs.	Size B Rs.	Size C Rs.
Sales Salaries	Direct Charges (Ratio 4:5:1)	10,000	4,000	5,000	1,000
Sales Commssion	Sales Turnover (Ratio 29:40:31)	6,000	1,740	2,400	1,860
Sales Office Expenses	Number of Orders (Ratio 7:8:1)	2,096	917	1,048	131
Advertising General	Sales Turnover (Ration 29:40:31)	5,000	1,450	2,000	1,550
Advertising Specific	Direct Charge (Ratio 3:4:3)	22,000	6,600	8,800	6,600
Packing	Volume in cft. (Ratio 17:32:51)	3,000	510	960	1,530
Delivery Expenses	Volume in cft. (Ratio 17:32:51)	4,000	680	1,280	2,040
Warehouse Expenses	Volume in cft. (Ratio 17:32:51)	1,000	170	320	510
Credit Collection Exp.	Number of Orders (Ratio 7:8:1)	1,296	567	648	81
	Total	54,392	16,634	22,456	15,302
* Marketing cost per unit sold (Rs) (2)		—	4.89	5.61	5.10
** Marketing cost to Turnover (%) (3)		—	28.68	28.07	24.68

Note :

1. Volume in cft. for Size A — 5 x 3400 = 17,000
   Size B — 8 x 4000 = 32,000
   Size C —17 x 3000 = 51,000

2. Marketing costs per unit sold Size A 16,634/3,400
   Size B 22,456/4,000
   Size C 15,302/3,000

3. Marketing costs to Turnover Size A 16,634/58,000 x 100
   Size B 22,456/80,000 x 100
   Size C 15,302/62,000 x 100

Apart from the two types of marketing cost analysis covered so far, there are some alternative methods as well for analysis of marketing costs. Some of these are discussed with suitable examples :

i) Order Getting and Order Filling Costs - The order getting costs are all costs of obtaining orders through such activities as selling, advertising and sales promotion. Examples of order getting costs are market research expenses, advertisements, maintaining sales offices, salesmen's salaries and travelling expenses, sales promotion expenses, etc. These costs tend to vary with the changes in the level of sales.

Since sales volume will respond to the level of order getting costs, for a predicted level of sales the quantum of order getting costs to be incurred can be determined in advance. A peculiar feature of the order getting costs is that its relationship with the sales volume may not be linear. When a company's sales are declining, more amount may have to be spent on advertising and sales promotion to reverse the trend.

All costs incurred on physical distribution management activities can be classified as order filling costs. Examples of such costs are order processing costs, warehouse expenses, finished goods inventory carrying costs, transport costs, packing expenses, customer services expenses such as credit collection, repairs during warranty period and so on.

Order filling costs per unit of output will tend to increase with the increase in volume of sales as the company has to service customers living farther and farther away from its factories and warehouses. The level or order filling costs usually varies with:

* the bulk, weight and quantity of goods sold
* the nature of the goods and the packaging required
* the location of the customers
* means of transport employed (rail,ship,air or road)
* the degree of service expected by customers

It must be noted that the two categories viz. order getting and order-filling costs are mutually exclusive and all marketing costs can be classified into one or the other.

ii) Fixed and Variable Costs - Marketing costs can also be classified into fixed, variable and semi-variable costs. Usually, the behaviour of marketing costs in relation to the sales volume of a product is studied to classify them into fixed and variable. The advantage of classifying marketing costs into fixed and variable is that only variable costs that can be identified with the products will be allocated to the various products as product costs. The fixed costs will be collected for the firm and set off against the contribution earned by the various products. Examples of fixed marketing costs are sales manager's salary, salesmen's salary, sales office expenses, warehouse rent, etc. Examples of variable marketing costs are salemens' commission, packing and transportation expenses, etc. The general administration expenses incurred on marketing are usually semi-variable in nature.

iii) Cost Effectiveness Analysis - This is another popular technique intended to analyse the effectiveness (in financial or even non-financial terms) of a particular cost. Cost effectiveness has two important fields of application:

(a) One may be able to find the cheapest means of accomplishing a defined objective. For example, there may be a number of alternative modes of distribution, with varying cost estimates, of the same goods to reach the same customers.

Obviously, that alternative will be chosen which ensures the lowest cost.

(b) One may be interested in ensuring the maximum value out of a given expenditure in a situation where there is difficulty in exact quantification, in financial terms, of the value or the benefits. An example in view may be assessing the effectiveness of advertisement and promotional efforts given a number of alternative media, with the same amount of expenses involved.

Under both the approaches mentioned above, benefits cannot be quantified in strict monetary terms. But the point of difference between the two approaches is that, in the first case, the benefit is fixed but the costs are varied, while in the second case the cost is fixed but benefits are varied.

iv) Relevant Cost Analysis This is another technique used widely in decisional problems. Through a cost relevance study, an attempt is made to arrive that what is called the relevant cost, i.e., the cost (disregarding how much of it is variable and how much fixed) relevant to a particular decision. Relevant costing concept has wide application in the areas of introduction of new products, dropping a product or product line, changing the production process, introducing mechanisation to replace manual work, etc. For example, when we are considering a proposal to drop a product line, a part of the fixed cost in this connection might cease to exist after the line is dropped, while a part of it may still continue to be incurred and shared by other product lines. This fact should be considered in arriving at the cost relevant to that particular decisional problem.

v) Life Cycle Costing — The concept is very useful in pricing a new product that has a relatively short life but the market of which is highly competitive. This can be best understood with the help of the following illustration:

Traditional Costing

Period	Production (Units)	FC p.a. (Rs.)	VC @ Rs.2	Total Cost	Cost per Unit (Rs)
1.	10,000	50,000	20,000	70,000	7.00
2.	20,000	50,000	40,000	90,000	4.50
3.	1,00,000	50,000	2,00,000	2,50,000	2.50
4.	30,000	50,000	60,000	1,10,000	3.67
5.	5,000	50,000	10,000	60,000	12.00

Note: The pricing will be above Rs.7.00 per unit and the company is unlikely to get any foothold in the market.

Life Cycle Costing

Variable Cost	: 1,65,000 unit @ Rs.2/-	Rs.3,30,000
Fixed Cost	: Rs.50,000 x 5	2,50,000
Total Estimated Cost during product life		5,80,000
Estimated Total Production (Units)		1,65,000
Average Cost per unit (Rs.)		3.52

Note: The Pricing in the vicnity of Rs.4.00 per unit will help the company to enter into the market and make money too, taking into consideration the product's total life span of 5 years as a whole.

3. A FEW MARKETING DECISIONAL PROBLEMS INVOLVING COST ANALYSIS

(We discuss below the cost analysis involved in a number of decisional problems in marketing. The objective is to orient the reader to the task of generation of quantitative information pertinent to various marketing decisional problems).

A. Lease Out or Sell :

A marketer dealing in a high value industrial equipment, say, a material handling equipment, meets various customers — some of them being interested in outright purchases of the equipment and others on taking it on lease against monthly or annual rental. Similar situations arise in respect of various construction equipments, computers, automobiles, transportation trucks, etc. From the marketer's angle the crucial problem is to determine the rental charges and other terms and conditions of lease which would be attractive to the customers and at the same time, not favourable to the company, when compared to the sale of the equipment. And for the matter, all financial aspects involved in the two alternatives have to be thoroughly considered.

Since there are only two alternatives which are mutually exclusive in character, the cost analysis techniques to be adopted here is opportunity costing technique. If the leasing alternative is considered, the opportunity gained should be the rental charges less the depreciation of the equipment. As against this, the opportunity loss would be the contribution on sale value foregone. In case of sale alternative, however, it will be exactly the reverse — contribution on sale value being the opportunity gain but lease rental, the opportunity loss.

Both these opportunity gains and losses have to be worked out after taking into consideration the appropriate marketing expenses and other associated costs, which would be somewhat different under the two alternatives. On a comparison of leasing out as against selling if there be a net positive opportunity gain then the leasing alternative would be better. If this net opportunity gain is negative then selling would be better. An attempt is to be made at this stage, by trial and error method, to arrive at the net opportunity gain close to zero. This would mean that from the company's point of view it would have the same financial impact whether the customer chooses to take the equipment on lease or buy it outright.

If the time period for lease ranges for, say, 5 to 10 years, then discounted cash flow technique has to be adopted while working out the opportunity gains or losses.

B. Introduction of New Product :

Introduction of new products may take either of the two forms, viz. introduction of add-on products or line extension products and (b) launching of new products or a product line. The technique to assess the profitability of line extension products is the incremental contribution estimates. Usually, such incremental contribution is also the profit since there may be no addition to fixed overheads in such a case. The same technique of contribution analysis would be followed in assessing the profitability of a new product line.

In this case, however, the relatable fixed cost (i.e.the fixed cost arising directly out of the introduction of the new product line) would have to be deducted from the initial contribution to arrive at the net incremental contribution from the new product line. This contribution may again be taken to be an additional profit of the business since its other general fixed costs supposedly stand recovered through the sale of other existing products.

In any such analysis, forecasts of sales, variable costs and fixed costs have to be made realistically. Sales forecast would result from a market survey and market research. Variable costs should be forecast with reference to the existing cost structure and cost behaviour in respect of similar products in the company and/or other companies. The forecast of fixed costs is intimately linked up with the question of capacity proposed to be built up for production and marketing. Ordinarily, the fixed cost will contain two elements, viz. depreciation on the additional fixed assets to be installed and interest on additional working capital requirements.

C. Dropping a Product or Product Line

The same technique as in B above may be used here with slight modification. The objective should be to find the net gain or loss consequent upon the discontinuance of a product or product line. Such net gain or loss would result from the loss in contribution and saving in relatable fixed expenses on the one hand and the greater impact of general fixed expenses on the serving products, on the other.

A Comparative table showing side by side the status quo and the situation after the proposed discontinuance, like the one given below, would more telling :

(All figures in Rs.Lakhs)

	Status Quo				After Dropping C		
	A	B	C	Total	A	B	Total
Sales	50	60	40	150	50	60	110
Contribution	25	24	8	57	25	24	49
Direct relatable Fixed cost	4	5	3	12	4	5	9
General fixed cost (apportioned in the ratio of sales)	10	12	8	30	14	16	30
Profit	11	7	(3)	15	7	3	10

In a situation as above, the dropping of product C does not improve the overall profit position though apparently C is a loss-making product. The total profit in fact comes down by Rs.5 lakhs which is equal to the net contribution after relatable fixed sot, earned by C.

The decision rules in such a situation would be as follows :

(a) The product should not be dropped as long as the contribution earned by it is adequate to cover the direct fixed cost relatable to the product. Therefore, if the direct fixed cost is higher than the contribution, the product should be dropped

(b) General fixed costs and common expenses, which cannot be saved even after a particular product is dropped, have no role to play in the decision - the total amount involved should be segregated and considered to be the expenses of the company as a whole, whether the product is dropped or continued.

To conclude our decision we may highlight the significance of marketing cost analysis. With a proper analysis of marketing costs a firm can hope to set its marketing cost budgets at optimum levels - too high a budget may result in diminishing returns while too low a budget would not help in sales expansion. The mix of the various elements of marketing costs must be balance.

For example, if the nature of the product is such that the customer would require visits by salesmen to understand the technical details, a marketing budget that allocates more to general advertisements than to direct sales executives would be all wrong. A haphazard analysis of costs could also lead to sales efforts being directed towards products with very low contribution margin and neglect of more profitable products.

4. STRATEGIC COST ANALYSIS

The foregoing discussions on Cost Analysis with reference to Marketing relate mostly to the traditional approaches and some modern approaches too. Recently there has been a major development in West in this particular field. The discipline called Strategic Cost Management has created anew wave that has sweeping across both sides of the Atlantic. The important tenets or techniques in this area are Total Cost Management, Activity Based Costing (ABC) or Transaction Costing, Value Chain Analysis, etc.

A detailed discussion on all these is outside the purview of this book. However, it would be useful to throw some light on these, in the context of Marketing Cost Analysis particularly. According to Porter (Competitive Strategy) industry profitability is a function of the collective strength of five competitive forces : bargaining power of suppliers, bargaining power of buyers, the threat of substitutes, the entry of new competitors, and the rivalry among the existing competitors. These five factors determine industry profitability because they influence the prices, costs and required investment of firms in an industry. Cost Analysis oriented towards strategic advantages should therefore address of all these five areas.

Customers' Value Chain Analysis has been found to be extremely useful not only in cost reduction but also in providing a more rational basis of pricing - prices that the customers would be willing to pay, based on value addition at different stages.

Under ABC, volume-based overhead allocation is replaced by transaction-based overhead allocation and identification for this purpose of appropriate "cost drivers" for different types of common costs and expenses. This approach could make a significant difference in product costing in a situation where both standard products and non-standard or tailor-made products are manufactured using about the same manufacturing facilities.

Thus, the costs of non-standard products are actually much higher than those of the standard products and also that the extra price obtained through sales of non-standard products does not compensate for such extra cost. Hence, there is a need for striking a balance between the cost of diversity due to complexity in manufacturing operations on the one hand and the value of variety generated at the marketplace on the other.

CHAPTER 14

MARGINAL COSTING & BREAK-EVEN ANALYSIS

1. Marginal Costing — Basic Concepts; 2. Optimising Product mix; 3. The Break Even Concept; 4. The Break-Even Chart; 5. Cost Volume Profit Analysis; 6. Break Even Analysis in a Multi-Product Situation; 7. Conclusion.

1. MARGINAL COSTING - BASIC CONCEPTS

Marginal costing is the technique of segregating fixed and variable costs and thereafter arriving at the cost which would vary in proportion to the volume of production or sales. Total costing or absorption costing is the opposite of marginal costing. In the western countries, the expression direct costing and direct cost are treated to be synonymous with marginal costing and marginal cost, respectively. However, in the Indian context, this would not be correct. We should, therefore, consider only variable cost as the same as marginal cost is to isolate the cost that can be saved when one less unit is produced over a given level.

Fixed costs are costs that tend to be unaffected by variations in the volume of output. The important words here are 'tend to be unaffected' that is, fixed cost does not necessarily remain fixed for good. But it is assumed to be so under certain set of circumstances and within a particular range of activities and for a specified period.

Variable costs are those that tend to vary directly in relation to the volume of output. Usually direct materials, directly chargeable expenses and a part of the overheads constitute the total variable cost per unit. It is interesting to note here that, judged from the angle of a unit of product, fixed costs are the only variable costs and variable costs are the costs that remain fixed. This is because fixed costs are fixed in quantum but variable costs are fixed in rate per unit of product.

A distinction should be made between marginal or variable cost of production and marginal cost of sales — the latter should include the post-manufacturing variable costs, mainly for selling and distribution activities, while the former will obviously take into account the variable costs related to manufacturing operations only.

There is some controversy as regards treatment of direct labour in marginal costing. This is due to its general treatment in the western countries as variable cost and accordingly shown as such in the publications of these countries. While it may be correct from their point of view, it is erroneous in the context of developing countries like India, where direct labour, for that matter, all labour costs, are by and large fixed in nature.

Some exceptions are wages paid under piece work system (cases are rather few), part of the overtime pay, wages paid to purely casual workers engaged occasionally for handling extraordinary volume of work, etc. On a realistic assessment, the amounts involved in these are not significant; and these components of labour cost may be considered as variable. But the rest bulk of labour cost should be treated only as fixed cost, under the situations obtaining in the countries like India.

There are two more categories of costs, namely, semi-fixed and semi-variable costs. Semi-fixed costs increase in steps upto a certain extent, thereafter they remain fixed at that level. Examples are supervision, depreciation on shift operations, etc. Semi-variable costs are those that vary but not in proportion to production or sales - the variation may be at a lower rate or at a higher rate. Examples of such costs are power, telephone and telex charges, etc. For marginal costing, these semi-fixed and semi-variable costs should be subsequently segregated into fixed and variable elements, taking into account the degree of fixity and variability of such costs, so that ultimately we are left with only two categories of costs, fixed costs and variable costs.

Contribution is the difference between sales volume and marginal cost of sales (that is, total variable cost). This is called contribution.

because it represents the amount contributed towards fixed cost and profit. Thus profit is arrived at after deducting fixed cost from contribution.

Symbolically, C = SV - MC
(C = Contribution, SV = Sales Value and
MC = Marginal Cost)

OR, C + MC = SV

Also :

C = P + F (where P = Profit, F = Fixed Cost)
or, C - P = F or, C - F =P

The cost identification and profit build-up in Marginal Costing is illustrated below, under one product assumption and with hypothetical figures :

Cost & Profit under Marginal Costing

		Cost per unit (Rs.)
(i) Direct materials		40
(ii) Variable cost of Direct Labour		3
(iii) Direct Expenses (Variable)		3
(iv) Variable overheads :		
Factory	3	
Office & Administration	1	
Selling & Distribution	5	9
(v) Marginal cost of sales — (i) to (iv)		55
(vi) Selling Price		100
(vii) Contribution per unit — (vi) — (v)		45

	Rs. in lakh
Total contribution on 1 lakh units sold	45
Total Fixed Costs	25
Total Profit	20

The proponents of marginal costing technique strongly maintain that products do not earn profits — what they offer is only contribution. Fixed costs are not directly related to the products — they are only 'period costs' and should be related to the business as such. But the total fixed cost of the business has to be deducted from the total contribution earned by all the products and the result will be the total profit of the business. Marginal costing technique, therefore, precludes any apportionment of fixed costs among products - fixed costs as the period costs of the business are considered separately in arriving at profits of the business. Let us assume that Company X Ltd deals in three products, A,B and C. The hypothetical profit build-up would be as follows :

Illustration — (i)

	Month : M		
	A	B	C
Units sold (lakhs)	1	2	3
Contribution per unit (Rs)	45	20	30
Total Contribution (Rs.Lakhs)	45	40	90
Contribution fund of the business (Rs.Lakhs)			175
Total fixed cost of the business (Rs.Lakhs)			75
Total profit of the business (Rs.Lakhs)			100

Note : 'Contribution fund' is the total contribution earned by all the products.

Assume that the total production capacity (interchangeable between the products) is limited to 6 lakh units per month. It is interesting to examine how total profit of the business will change, merely because of a change in the sales-mix, whilst all other factors (viz. product-wise unit contribution an total fixed cost of the business) remain unchanged.

Illustration - (ii)

	A	Month : M B	C
Units sold (lakhs)	3	1	2
Contribution per unit (Rs)	45	20	30
Total Contribution fund of the Business	135	20	60 (Rs/Lakhs)
Total fixed cost of the business (Rs/lakhs)			215
Total profit of the business (Rs/lakhs)			75 140

Illustration —(iii)

	A	Month : M B	C
Units sold (lakhs)	1	4	1
Contribution per unit (Rs)	45	20	30
Total Contribution (Rs/lakhs)	45	80	30
'Contribution fund' of the business (Rs.Lakhs)			155
Total fixed cost of the business (Rs/Lakhs)			75
Total profit of the business (Rs/lakhs)			80

The total profit of the business improves from Rs.100 lakhs to Rs.140 lakhs because of a more favourable sales-mix in Illustration - (ii), then comes down to Rs.80 lakhs in Illustration — (iii) when sales-mix becomes relatively unfavourable. And for all such changes in overall profits, the total fixed cost of the business has no role to play whatsoever. This substantiates further why fixed cost is to be considered as a 'period cost' and not 'product cost', as emphasised under Marginal Costing technique.

We may now introduce the concept of Contribution to Sales ratio. This measured in terms of either unit or total, was earlier called P/V ratio, usually expressed as a percentage. The expanded form of P/V ratio is Profit Volume Ratio which is unfortunately confusing, perhaps a misnomer. The ratio is not profit to volume, but contribution to sales, therefore C/S ratio. Assuming sale price to be Rs.100 and contribution Rs.40, the C/S ratio would be :

Contribution/sales or 40/100 or 0.4 or 40 per cent

We may now introduce the C/S Ratios, (i.e.ratios of contribution to sales) respectively inventing some additional figures, in the above illustrations :

		(Rs/unit)	
	A	B	C
Sale Price	100	40	90
Marginal Cost	55	20	60
Contribution	45	20	30
C/S Ratio	45%	50%	33 1/3%

Product wise profitability and therefore, product preference from Sales-mix point of view may now be summarised as follows :

Criterion	Order of Preference		
i) Contribution per unit (when unit sale is a constraint)	A	C	B
ii) C/S Ratio (When sale price/value is a constraint)	B	A	C

2. OPTIMISING PRODUCT-MIX

According to management accounting principles, a product mix that maximises the total contribution earned would be the optimum one. Also, the key factor or limiting factor which imposes a constraint on the volume of output should be identified so that the contribution per unit of the limiting factor could be worked out for the various products. This would help in the ranking of the products, and the product which yields the highest contribution per unit of limiting factor would be produced, subject to other constraints, to the maximum and thus the profit maximised. Such ranking of the products, in addition to highlighting the most profitable product, would also ensure allocation of available resources in such a manner that a proper product-mix can be chosen, given a set of constraints.

Even when the firm may have the option of increasing prices of products to improve profits or may find that it would have to produce certain quantity of an unprofitable product as its demand is inter-related to that of some highly profitable product, or it may not be practicable for the firm to increase the costs on sales promotion, cost analysis techniques may be used to identify the more profitable alternatives so that a "what if" analysis can be made in respect of other options available and a proper product-mix chosen.

Let us envisage a situation where more than one product is manufactured by the same types of machines, using the same basic raw materials but yielding varying rates of contribution per unit. There may be constraints in one or more of the different machine-hours, availability of raw material and/or say, demand. The marginal costing techniques (for example, study of contribution per unit of limiting factor) can be brought to bear upon the problem of determining the optimum product-mix in such a situation.

Illustration :
The following particulars are extracted from the records of a company :

Details	Per Unit	
	Product A	Product B
Sales	Rs. 100	Rs. 120
Consumption of material	2 kg.	3 kg.
Material Cost	Rs. 10	Rs. 15
Direct wages cost (assumed to be variable)	Rs. 15	Rs. 10

Direct expenses	Rs. 5	Rs. 6
Machine hours used	3	2
Overhead expenses :		
-Fixed	Rs. 5	Rs. 10
Variable	Rs.15	Rs. 20

(A) Comment on profitability of each product (both use the same raw material) when -

* Total sales potential in units is limited
* Total sales potential in value is limited
* Raw material is in short supply
* Production capacity (in terms of machine hours) is the limiting factor

(B) Assuming raw material as the key factor, availability of which is 10,000 kg, and maximum sales potential of each product 3,500 units, find the product-mix which will yield the maximum profit.

Workings/Solutions

	Product A Rs.	Per Unit Product B Rs.
Direct materials	10	15
Direct wages	15	10
Direct expenses	5	6
Variable overhead	15	20
Marginal cost	45	51
Sales	100	120
Contribution	55	69
C/S Ratio	0.55	0.575
Contribution per kg.of material	Rs.27.50	Rs.23.00
Contribution per machine hour	Rs.18.33	Rs.34.50

Thus the profitability of each product will be determined on the basis of the principle: the higher the contribution per unit of limiting factor, the more profitable is the product. Accordingly, a statement of profitability under different conditions may be prepared :

Limiting factor	Ranking of Products	Ranking based on
i) Sales volume	BA	Unit contribution
ii) Sales value/Sale Price	BA	C/S ratio
iii) Raw material	AB	Contribution per kg. of material
iv) Production capacity (machine hours)	BA	Contribution per machine hour

Under the situation, in part (B), the product preference will be in the same order as (iii) above subject to the condition that maximum demand for each of the two products is 3,500 units. In other words, 3,500 units of more profitable product will be produced first. The balance of available raw materials will then be utilised for the production of the less profitable product. Thus, the optimum product-mix would be as follows :

Product	Units	Raw materials Per unit (Kg.)	Total raw materials required (Kg.)
A	3,500	2	7,000
B	1,000 *	3	3,000
			10,000

* (10,000 - 7,000)/3 kg = 1,000 units

The technique as illustrated above has, however, limited applicability. It can give us the desired result in all cases where the principal limiting factor or constraint is only one and in a few cases only where the constraints are two in number. And in many other cases of two constraints an in all cases where constraints are more than two (which is most akin to reality, needless to say) optimum product or sales-mix can be determined by the application of Linear Programming technique.

3. THE BREAK-EVEN CONCEPT

In marginal costing technique, contribution (C) is understood as contribution towards fixed cost (F) and profit (P). In other words, C = F + P or, C-F = P or C-P = F. Accordingly, if P=O then C must be equal to F only. This situation is called break-even point, which indicates a no-profit-no-loss situation. At this point, the total contribution (C) earned is equal to what would be necessary to meet only the total fixed expenses (F) of the business. Sales below break even point means incurring loss (a part of fixed expenses remaining unrecovered) and sales above this point would enable the business to earn profit. It is also important to note that once the break even point is reached, all earned (since total fixed cost stands already recovered at the break-even point itself).

The difference between the break-even sales or activity and actual (or projected) sales or activity is called margin of safety. The higher the margin of safety, the greater is the capacity of the enterprise to withstand fluctuations in actual activity due to internal or external reasons. It may be noted also that margin of safety and break-even point, related as proportions or percentages to sales, are complementary — both will together equal 1 or 100 per cent. If the margin of safety is 0.4 (40 per cent), then break even must be 0.6 (60 per cent),of the sale value and vice versa.

The break-even (BE) point may be worked out by different methods.

The simplest one is : $\dfrac{\text{Total fixed cost}}{\text{Unit contribution}}$

Assuming total fixed cost to be Rs.20 lakhs, the BE point at Rs.40 contribution per unit will be :

$$\frac{\text{Rs.20 lakhs}}{\text{Rs.40}} = 50{,}000 \text{ units}$$

With the help of C/S ratio also, the same result can be obtained in terms of sales value :

$$\text{B.E. sales value} = \frac{\text{Total fixed cost}}{\text{C/S ratio}} \text{ or } \frac{\text{Total fixed cost}}{1-\dfrac{\text{Variable cost}}{\text{Sales}}}$$

$$= \frac{\text{Rs.20 lakhs}}{40\%} = \frac{\text{Rs.20 lakhs}}{1\text{-}60/100}$$

$$= \text{Rs.50 lakhs} = \text{Rs.50 lakhs}$$

Let us take some illustrations at this stage :

1. Data

Period (quarter)	Sales Rs.Lakhs	Net Profit Rs.Lakhs
I	30	2
II	40	6

Required :

i) C S ratio

ii) Fixed cost per quarter

iii) B E sales value per quarter

iv) Margin of safety as on quarter II sales

v) Sales required in quarter III to earn a profit of Rs.10 lakhs

vi) Profit expected during quarter IV, given the sales forecast for the period, Rs.45 lakhs.

Workings

i) The crucial stage is to find the C/S ratio. It may be noted that, as per the given data, there have been net profits in both the quarters. This means that the total fixed cost per quarter has been covered fully in each of the two quarters. It may also be recalled that all post break-even constributions are actually net profits, fixed costs having been already covered at the break-even point itself.

Therefore, the additional net profit of Rs.4 lakhs (6-2) is actually the additional contribution earned on the additional sales of Rs.10 lakhs (40-30). Thus the C/S ratio would be 4/10 = 0.4 or 40%.

ii) Total contribution in quarter I = 40% of Rs.30 lakhs = Rs.12 lakhs

Therefore, fixed cost = Rs.12 lakhs-2 lakhs (net profit) Rs.10 lakhs

or

Total contribution in quarter II = 40% on 40 lakhs = Rs.16 lakhs

Therefore, fixed cost = Rs.16 lakhs - Rs.6 lakhs (net profit) Rs.10 lakhs

(Note : fixed cost per quarter has to be the same)

iii) B.E. sales value per quarter $= \dfrac{\text{Fixed cost per quarter}}{\text{C/S ratio}}$

$= \dfrac{\text{Rs.10 lakhs}}{40\%}$

= Rs.25 lakhs

iv) Quarter II sales	=	Rs.40 lakhs
B.E. sales	=	Rs.25 lakhs
Margin of safety (M/S)	=	Rs.15 lakhs

M/S as percentage of quarter II sales = 15 on 40 = 37.5%
(Therefore, B.E. = 62.5% of the sales)

v) Contribution required to earn a profit of Rs.10 lakhs = Rs.20 lakhs (fixed cost Rs.10 lakhs + profit Rs.10 lakhs)

Sales required $\dfrac{\text{Contribution required}}{\text{C.S.ratio}} = \dfrac{\text{Rs.20 lakhs}}{40\%}$

= Rs.50 lakhs

Alternatively, sales required = B.E.Sales + additional sales required for a contribution of Rs.10 lakhs

$$= \text{Rs.25 lakhs} + \frac{\text{Rs.10 lakhs}}{40\%} = \text{Rs.50 lakhs}$$

vi) contribution to be earned on Rs.45 lakhs sales = 40% of Rs.45 lakhs = Rs.18 lakhs. Therefore, net profit = Rs.18 lakhs - Rs.10 lakhs (fixed cost) = Rs. 8 lakhs.

2. Summarised Profit/Loss Account for the year ended on 31-12.19x8

	Rs. Lakhs
Sale (4 lakhs units @ Rs.100 each)	400
Variable cost of sales	300
Contribution margin	100
Total fixed cost	50
Profit before tax (PBT)	50
Tax @ 60%	30
Profit after tax (PAT)	20

For the year 19x9 (i.e.1-1-19x9 to 31-12-19x9) the company has projected its operations as follows :

i) Sales: 5 lakhs units @ Rs.100 each

ii) Proportion of variable cost of sales to sales : unchanged

iii) Total fixed expenses : to go up to Rs.55 lakhs

Required :

i) The break-even sales (units and value) for 19x8

ii) The break-even sales (units and value) for 19x9

iii) Why is there a difference in the break even sales between the two years ?

iv) What would the revised C/S ratio be if the company were to achieve in 19x9 a break even situation at the same break even sales value as 19x8

v) To achieve the revised C/S ratio as per (iv) above through price revision, what would be the revised price in 19x9 ?

vi) To achieve the revised C/S ratio as per (iv) above through changes in variable cost of sales, what would be the revised variable cost of sales per unit in 19x9 ?

Workings :

i) B.E. sales : 19 x 8 - Units : $\frac{\text{Rs.50 lakhs (total fixed cost)}}{\text{Rs.25 (contribution/unit)}}$

= 2 lakhs

$$\text{- Value : } \frac{\text{Rs.50 lakhs (total fixed cost)}}{\text{25\% (C/S ratio)}}$$

= Rs.200 lakhs

$$\text{ii) B.E. sales : 19 x 9 - Units : } \frac{\text{Rs.55 lakhs}}{\text{Rs.25}} = \text{2.2 lakhs}$$

$$\text{- Value : } \frac{\text{Rs.55 lakhs}}{\text{25\%}} = \text{Rs.220 lakhs}$$

iii) Since there is no change in C/S ratio, the only reason for the difference in the B.E. sales between the two years is the increase in total fixed expenses by Rs. 5 lakhs in 19x9 over that in 19x8.

$$\text{Check : } \frac{\text{Rs.5 lakhs}}{\text{Rs.25}} = \text{20,000 units}$$

$$\text{or } \frac{\text{Rs.5 lakhs}}{\text{25\%}} = \text{Rs.20 lakhs}$$

} Addition to original B.E. level

iv) To achieve B.E. at a sale of Rs.200 lakhs, with Rs.55 lakhs of total fixed expenses, the revised C/S ratio would be :

$$\frac{\text{Rs.55 lakhs}}{X} = \text{Rs.200 lakhs (X = C/S ratio)}$$

X = 27.5%

v) Let the revised price be P
then P - 75 = 27.5% of P
P = Rs.103.44 (app.)

vi) The revised variable cost of sales per unit would be
100 - 27.5 = Rs.72.5

4. THE BREAK EVEN CHART

There are various methods of drawing a break even chart to show C/S ratio, margin of safety, break-even point, profit, etc. The most popular and simple chart is given below :

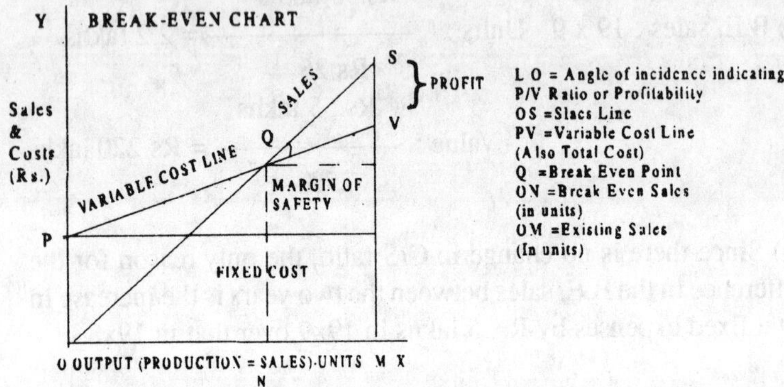

While drawing a break--even chart as above there are three input data required,

i) Fixed cost — this represented by a horizontal line

ii) Variable cost — the line starts from the point where it is drawn. The curve indicates both the variable cost 'slope' and also the total cost, at any point of the curve (measured along the Y-axis)

iii) Sales value — Sales units multiplied by sale price per unit (incidentally, under the break-even concept, quantity of production and sales are assumed to be the same)

After the break-even chart is drawn, there are four output results :

i) Break-even point — This is given by the intersection between the sales line and the variable cost line. The break-even point measured along the X-axis will indicate the break-even unit and along the Y-axis, the break even sales value.

ii) Margin of safety — This is the difference between the actual sales and the break-even sales — can also be measured both in units (X - axis) and in value (Y-axis)

iii) C/S Ratio — This is the trigonometrical measure of the angle of incidence created by the intersection of sales line and variable cost line. (The measurement being a little difficult, particularly for people not having a good mathematical background, it would be advisable to measure C/S ratio algebraically, as shown earlier).

iv) The absolute profit — This is measured along the Y-axis as the difference between the two points, the actual sales point and the point where variable cost line ends.

5. COST VOLUME PROFIT ANALYSIS

On an analysis of the break-even chart, the following facts would be clear :

Change		Impact/effect
i) In fixed cost :		
a) Increase	—	BE units — increase, C/S ratio — same, margin of safety — decrease,
b) Decrease	—	The reverse of above (in each case)
ii) In variable cost :		
a) Increase	—	BE units — increase C/S ratio — decrease, margin of safety — decrease profit — decrease
b) Decrease	—	The reverse of above (in each case)
iii) In sale price :		
a) Increase	—	BE units — decrease C/S ratio — increase, margin of safety — increase, profit — increase.
b) Decrease	—	Then reverse of above (in each case)
iv) In the sale units :		

a) Increase — Margin of safety and profit increase (others, no change)

b) Decrease — Margin of safety and profit decrease (others, no change)

Each of the above changes is considered in isolation and under the assumption of ceteris paribus (others remaining the same). However, it would not be difficult to envisage and reflect a number of factors, together, which is the situation obtaining in real life. For example, we may have to study the implication of the following changes at one and the same time, namely an increase in fixed cost and a decrease in variable cost (due to improved technology), a decrease in sale price (to market the increased output) and also higher unit sales (resulting from reduction in sales price). Such changes, whether one or many at a time, can be easily studied and understood with the help of break-even charts.

Cost Volume Profit (CVP) Analysis means any analysis to study the effect or impact on cost and profit of changes in volume, and vice versa (as indicated above). In fact Break-Even Analysis and CVP Analysis are rightly considered to be synonymous.

6. BREAK-EVEN ANALYSIS IN A MULTI-PRODUCT SITUATION

Let us take a simple illustration to show how the break-even sales for the business as a whole can be worked out in a multi-product situation.

		Sales (Rs. lakhs)		Contribution (Rs. lakhs)	
Product	C/S Ratio	Product-wise	Cumulative	Product-wise	Cumulative
A	50%	10	10	5	5
B	40%	20	30	8	13
C	20%	20	50	4	17

Composite C/S ratio = 17/50 = 34%

Total fixed cost of the business = Rs.8.5 lakhs (assumed)

Thus B.E. sales = 8.5 lakhs/34% = Rs. 25 lakhs

Following a similar approach, B.E. units also can be worked out by using the formula :

$$\text{B.E.units} = \frac{\text{Fixed cost}}{\text{Weighted average contribution per unit}}$$

If, for example, the unit sales in the above illustration are assumed to be 2 lakhs for A, 4 lakhs for B, and 4 lakhs for C, then the weighted average contribution would be Rs.1.70 worked out as follows :

	Unit Sales Lakhs	Total Sales Rs. Lakhs	Unit Price	Unit Contribution Rs.	Weighted Contribution Rs.
A	2	10	5	2.5	5
B	4	20	5	2.0	8
C	4	20	5	1.0	4
	10				17

$$\text{Weighted Average Contribution} = \frac{17}{10} = \text{Rs.1.70 per unit}$$

$$\text{Accordingly, the BE units will be} = \frac{\text{Rs.8.5 lakhs}}{\text{Rs.1.70}} = \text{5 lakhs}$$

(Check, BE sale value = Rs. 25 lakhs = 5 lakhs units x Rs. 5 per unit)

The concept of composite C/S ratio is based on a given sales-mix. Thus, if the sales mix changes, as it does happen in reality, the composite C/S ratio will change and consequently, the break-even sales too will change.

In the end, it must be noted that this method of working out the break-even sales of more than one product, can at best be a rough and ready approach — only to get a broad idea about the break even sales. And this is in fact one of the limitations of break-even analysis.

7. CONCLUSION

Break-even analysis is useful in studying incidence of cost at varying levels of output and sales. A break-even chart gives an indication of the situation the company is passing through and helps in chalking out its future path by highlighting inter alia the (a) margin of safety, (b) effects on profit of changes in price, variable costs, fixed costs and sales volume and (c) product mix and product selectivity.

Break-even analysis has several limitations too, namely over-simplification, inaccuracies, rigidity, etc. But despite all such limitations it has come to stay as a useful tool in Management. Because of its simplicity and effectiveness the techniques of Break-Even Analysis have a wide field of application and the horizon is still expanding.

Appendix

USES OF FORMULAE IN MARGINAL COSTING & B E ANALYSIS

1. C/S (Contribution to Sales ratio) =

$$\frac{S - V}{S} = \frac{C}{S} \times 100 \text{ (expressed as a percentage)}$$

2. B.E.U. = $\frac{\text{F.C.}}{\text{Contribution P.U.}}$

3. B.E.S. = $\frac{\text{FC}}{\text{C/S ratio}}$ OR C/S = $\frac{\text{FC}}{\text{BES}}$

4. FC = C/S x BES

5. Contribution = Sales –– V.Cost or, FC + Profit
   or, C/S x Sales

6 Margin of safety = Sales — BES = $\frac{\text{C - FC}}{\text{C/S}} = \frac{\text{Profit}}{\text{C/S}}$

7. Profit = C/S x MS

8. Sales = C/CS ratio

CHAPTER 15

PRICING POLICIES AND DECISIONS

1. Clearing the Ground; 2. Pricing based on Marketing Considerations; 3. Pricing based on cost considerations; 4. Development of Pricing Strategies; 5. Special Pricing Problems; 6. Concept of Fair Return; 7. Resale PriceMaintenance. 8. Conclusion. Case Studies.

1. CLEARING THE GROUND

Following pertinent propositions will facilitate our discussion on pricing :

i) Pricing is a crucial decision-making issue since this can make or mar an enterprise. (A statement of the obvious, but very important too).

ii) Pricing should be considered as an integral part of the marketing mix management, not divorced from the rest of the P's.

iii) Price, Cost and Volume are intricately inter-related with each other and all these affect Profit.

iv) As a corollary to the proposition (iii) above adhoc pricing might lead to either of the two types of vicious circles:

(a) high price - low volume of sales - high unit profit-low absolute profit-high price (to enhance profit level)

(b) low price-high volume sales-low unit profit-low absolute profit (due to high marketing and distribution costs) low price (to sell still higher volume and augment absolute profit).

One basic question is whether the price should be based on marketing or cost consideration. There are lots of arguments and counter-arguments between marketing and finance people in this regard. However, all agree that prices should be determined after striking a healthy balance between both marketing and cost considerations. But the relative importance between the two might change depending on several parameters as follows :

Parameter	Marketing consideration tends to be more important	Finance & cost consideration tends to be more important
1. Time-frame	Short & Medium-run	Medium & long run
2. Market condition	Buyers' market; intense competition	Sellers' market; competition not so intense.
3. Primary marketing objectives.	Market share	Profitability
4. Buying behaviour of customer	Erratic, impulsive, irrational	Stable, predictable, rational
5. Product characteristics mix of subjective & objective features (which again vary from person to person)	When subjective features are predominant -"perceived" attributes.	When objective features are predominant - "physical/measurable" attributes

It may be useful to present here in a nutshell the Economists' contention on pricing policy. Market condition, that has a significant bearing on a firm's pricing policy, has already been touched upon earlier.

"Two tools of elementary economic analysis must be understood before the pricing policy of the business can properly be discussed. These are : (1) the principles of supply and demand in the competitive markets: (2) the application of the marginal analysis to the profit maximising firm". (Savage and Small)

It is most frequently assumed in economic analysis that the firm is trying to maximise its total profits. And the proposition is that "no firm can be earning maximum profits unless its marginal cost and its marginal revenues are (at least approximately) equal, i.e. unless an additional unit of output will bring in as much money as it costs to produce, so that its marginal profitability is Zero". (Baumol)

It is very easy to see that this is so. Suppose a firm is producing 1000 units of some commodity, X, and that at the output level, T4 MR from X production is Rs.2.20 whereas its marginal cost is Rs.1.80. Additional units of X will, therefore, each bring the firm Rs.0.40 (Rs.3.30-Rs.1.80) more than they cost. Thus the firm cannot be maximising its profits by sticking to its 1000 production level. Similarly, if the MC of X exceeds its MR, the firm cannot be maximising its profits, for it is neglecitng the opportunity to save money-by reducing its output it would reduce its income, but it would reduce its costs by an even greater amount.

2. PRICING BASED ON MARKETING CONSIDERATIONS

Often, marketing considerations tend to dominate over others in determining prices of products or services. On that count, there could be reversal of marketing-based pricing approaches. Most important of these are briefly discussed below :

i) High-price — Low volume versus Low-price - High volume, depending on which approach will make marketing more effective.

ii) Going-rate pricing — In this method attempts are made to match the competitors' price without considering the demand and cost factors.

iii) Sealed Bid pricing — This method is used in tendering to win contracts. As such, the quoted price depends on expectations of how the competitors are likely to bid for the tender.

iv) Geographical Pricing — Where the customers are located over the country, the transportation costs need to be adjusted to base price. This is usually done in the following ways :

a. Uniform Delivery Price — In this method the buyers pay the same price irrespective of their locations. This is usually done by working out the average transport cost.

b. FOB Pricing — The buyer pays all charges of transportation, loading / unloading etc. in addition to the ex-base price.

c. Zone pricing — in this method, Zone-wise segmentations of customers are made and then principles of FOB pricing or uniform delivery price or a plausible combination of both is adopted.

v. Discount pricing — This method of pricing is very common and adopted for including prospective buyers to buy in bulk or for prompt payment or both. Discounts are offered on the base price and usually take place in terms of cash, quantity or seasonal discounts.

vi. Discriminatory pricing — In this method the same product is sold at different prices. The discrimination may be based on customers, place or time.

vii. Penetration price — The practice of deliberately keeping the price low in order to achieve a sizeable market.

viii. Skimming the cream — Starting with a relatively high price and coming down later, if necessary, rather than following the other way round.

ix. Snob value pricing — This is to fix a high price in order to give the product snob value it needs.

x. Pre-emptive pricing — A strategy to pre-empt competitors from adopting their own pricing decisions.

xi. Product life cycle pricing — In this method pricing strategy tends to be different even for the same product depending on the particular stage in the life cycle of the product.

xii. Price reductions — Usually takes the following sequential order:

  a. Price cutting - with the object of driving competitors out of the market as part of marketing stratcgics.

  b. Price warfare - as part of strategy to reduce the number of competitors.

  c. Formation of price cartel - this is fairly common in duopoly or oligopoly situations. Prices will bé determined and reviewed from time to time by "informal" cartels.

3. PRICING BASED ON COST CONSIDERATIONS

The methods and techniques discussed below are essentially cost-based and would range from the conventional to the more sophisticated approaches. The discussions here are not aimed at specific types of products and markets.

i) ***Full Cost Pricing :***

This appears to be most conventional and popular method of pricing, under which the final price of a product is determined after adding some mark-up to the full cost or total cost of the product. The indirect taxes and duties, forwarding expenses should be added to the price. The full cost recovery price represents the desired minimum long-run price.

The basic requirement for adopting this method of pricing is the availability of reliable cost data. The full cost approach to pricing is more relevant among firms whose products are clearly differentiated among companies manufacturing custom-made products and for new products, where an established market price does not exist. Even in highly competitive markets the full cost method is used to determine product profitability and related decisions. The principal advantage of this method is that it assures total cost recovery and planned profit margin.

Despite its popularity, the method has serious limitations:

a) It ignores elasticity of demand.

b) It fails to give consideration to competition.

c) It does not distinguish between fixed and variable costs. The impact on fixed cost due to change in volume sales or volume effect on cost is not given due consideration to.

d) A flat percentage is applied to product cost in order to provide for profit. This practice fails to recognise that all products cannot earn the same rate of profit.

ii) *Conversion Cost Method :*

Proponents of the conversion cost method of pricing maintain that profit should be based only on the value added by manufacturing i.e. cost of production less material or through-put costs. Conversion cost pricing is used most commonly in industries where the throughput cost elements of the different items produced vary to a considerable extent (e.g. printing industry and casting foundry) and also where the company manufactures on free issue materials.

iii) *Marginal Cost Pricing :*

Marginal (variable) costs are actually costs that can be directly associated with a particular product. The out-of-pocket recovery price i.e. total variable cost per unit is the minimum price below which a cash loss will be sustained.

Pricing under marginal costing is more flexible than full cost pricing. Under marginal costing, the decision-maker on price has to discover the price and volume that will maximise profit adopting marginal costing technique.

A basic knowledge of marginal costing is essential to adopt this method :

Marginal Cost = Direct Material + Variable Overhead (not Labour, in the Indian context at least)

Contribution = Sales minus Marginal Cost
= Fixed Cost + Profit

$$\text{Contribution/Sales (CS) Ratio} = \frac{\text{Contribution}}{\text{Sales}}$$

Price of a product/service =

a) Marginal Cost + Contribution (Fixed quantum)
b) Marginal Cost + Certain rate of contribution (C/S Ratio)

Pricing based on C/S ratio is very simple to work out and easy to apply. For example, if variable cost (V) is Rs.30 and expected P/V ratio is 40% then the selling price (s) would be Rs.50, worked out as follows :

$$C/S \text{ Ratio} = 1 - \frac{V}{S} \text{ or } 0.4 = 1 - \frac{30}{S} \text{ or } S = 50$$

Marginal cost based pricing (popularly known as pricing based on "Contribution Theory") is a short-run pricing for a particular purpose and should not be a long- run pricing stragey. Because of practical difficulties in allocating fixed cost to various products (Companies are by and large multi-product units), marginal costing technique using standard marginal cost is an essential tool for decision-making process in several areas apart from pricing like :

a) Assessing Product Profitability
b) Make or buy decision
c) Export pricing
d) Addition/Deletion of products.

Mention may be made that existence of idle capacity is a pre-condition in application of the Contribution Theory.

iv) *Return on Investment Pricing :*

Return on Investment (ROI) is the most important yardstick in measuring business efficiency. ROI-based pricing is of particular importance in multi-product firms where varying capital investments are required for different product. ROI is also applicable in working out proposed selling price of new products where no market price exists and also for desirability of producing a new item for which market price is already existing. A formula for establishing a sales price which will yield a desired ROI is :

$$P = \frac{(F + V.Sv + R.Fc)/Sv}{1 - R.Wc}$$

Legend:P = Selling price per annum
F = Fixed cost (total) per annum
V = Variable cost per unit
Fc = Capital investment in Fixed Assets
Wc = Working Capital expressed as percent of Sales value
Sv = Annual Sales Volume in units
R = Target Rate of Return on Capital Employed

4. DEVELOPMENT OF PRICING STRATEGIES

Development of appropriate pricing strategies, especially from a long term perspective is a must for the growth and even survival of an enterprise. This is of course not a simple task - it involves a host of considerations. We shall discuss below the more important considerations that gradually underlie formulation of pricing strategies.

First is the recognition and clear appreciation of two parallel streams, explained earlier, namely market-based and cost-based pricing decision, depending on the criteria vis-a-vis the situations obtaining. It needs to be underlined that pricing decisions cannot be exclusively market-based nor can these be entirely cost-based. But these two parallel streams should be made to converge at a certain time-frame in order to determine the right pricing strategies.

Second is an understanding of two divergent issues viz :

a) The price a buyer is willing or prepared to pay, and

b) Marketing objectives and their priorities that could influence the firm's proposed pricing plan.

The price a buyer is prepared to pay will depend on various factors like :

(i) value of goods to buyer — the buyer's need of the product and his ability to do with it — nearness to situation of the need ;

(ii) ability to deploy funds for the purpose — other demands on buyer's budget ; and

(iii) price charged by competitors — price charged for substitutes.

Coming to objectives, pricing can be a key to achieving for broader corporate objectives than those implied in the limited commercial concept of profit. Some of these objectives are : earning a target return on investment, achieving or substaining a certain level of market share, ensuring a planned level of economic production/ operations, achieving a specified rate of growth in turnover and/or profit, meeting or beating competitions, systematic product dilution and pruning and avoidance of government interference or restrictions.

These two apparently different aspect need to be matched in order to design pricing strategies for each product, for each market, segment and for different time-period i.e. short, medium and long-run.

Third is another delicate game of balancing, that is between multiple objectives mentioned above and expectations, plans and perceptions of multiple parties or key players. Although the firm's customers form the significant group while formulating pricing strategy, there are other parties who need to be considered. For example:

1) Intermediate customers	—	they are different from ultimate customers.
2) Competitors	—	Prices charged by competitors for the product or near-like products.
3) Suppliers	—	Suppliers of inputs, funds and labour.
4) Government	—	Various existing statutory acts like Re-sale Price Maintenance.
5) Company Executives	—	Different company executives viz. Sale Manager Production, Manager Advertising Manager and Finance Manager have their own views and varying perceptions of product pricing.

Our fourth point is a little elaboration of one of the key players mentioned above namely, competitors. Here again, one has to ensure a matching between outside-in and inside-out approaches. One of the primary aims of pricing should be to attain sustainable competitive advantage at the market place. If it is found that for a particular product the company cannot ensure this on a long-term basis, then the product will have to be either deleted or revamped with some features different from those offered by the competitors. pricing will follow such product differentiation exercise.

Our fifth observation is that in pricing strategy formulation, there should be some variation in such strategies by products or services types. In the consumer group field, for example, pricing is the most powerful weapon in the hands of the marketing manager. But in industrial marketing, pricing may not be so powerful tool. In the professional service sector, members usually do not knowingly compete with each other on professional charges - attempts should be made to improve upon the clients' financial results by other means, with of course each firm following a pricing strategy unique to itself.

Our next important suggestion, though useful primarily in consumer marketing but important in industrial marketing as well, is that pricing strategies should follow market positioning or product positioning in the market, not the other way round.

Closely related to this is our seventh point, that is determination of pricing strategies different for different market segments. For example, ITDC have four or five different tariff rates for their hotel rooms with identical facilities, applicable to so many different segments of the market e.g. Airlines personnel, company executives, foreign tourists, etc.

There are some important developments that have recently taken place particularly in the Western countries with respect to cost analysis methodology, oriented towards business strategy in general and pricing strategy in particular. These are Activity Based Costing (ABC), Transaction Costing and Customers' Value Chain Analysis. These techniques are of significant relevance to pricing of non-standard, specially products in particular. (Detailed discussions on these techniques are outside the purview of this book. But the enthusiastic reader may refer to relevant literature).

The ninth and the last but not the least point is that pricing strategy should be integrated with and not divorced from the rest of the elements of marketing mix management namely, products, promotion and placement or distribution. Therefore, a holistic view is strongly recommended in this regard.

4. SPECIAL PRICING PROBLEMS

i) New Product Pricing :

Depending on the nature of the new product, suitable pricing strategy has to be developed. If the product is only a new pack or even a line extension product, pricing can be based on marginal cost and incremental contribution approach. Once the product gets a good foothold in the market, its price may be progressively adjusted to bring it in line with the other products.

If the product is new to the company but not new to the country, an extensive market survey should be conducted not only to get a feel of its market but also to have an order -of-magnitude estimate of the proposed price. The final price may then be determined after considering the total cost as also the marginal cost, competitors' prices, etc.

In case the product is absolutely new to the customers and there is no precedent to guide the pricing policy, the only approach left is one of trial and error with the objective of ultimately arriving at the desired price after some time. But two factors are to be considered in such pricing decision. viz. recovery of search and development cost on the new products and encashing on the good brand image of the company by fixing up a relatively high price initially.

ii) *Pricing under Sale to Government :*

Selling to the Government very often poses special pricing problems. This may be due to various reasons, such as bulk purchase by the Govt., relatively less marketing expenses due to bulk orders, higher capacity utilisation resulting in reduction of unit fixed cost, likely new business to be triggered, etc. The most appropriate technique for this type of pricing situation is relevant cost analysis.

iii) *Pricing under Recession :*

While under normal situations optimisation of profits is the primary guiding objective in pricing decisions, under recessionary condition, the objectives should be minimisation of loss. During recession, an enterprise is confronted with the problem of staying in business until the recession is over and recovery starts. The entire effort should therefore be directed towards earning some positive contributions from the different products in order to sustain the fixed overheads. Marginal costing and contribution theory is, therefore, the only relevant technique for determining pricing strategy during recession.

iv) *Pricing in Joint Product Industries :*

Product costs computed in a joint product industry generally have very little value as a guide to price setting. The allocation methods adopted to produce such costs, while justifiable for purpose of income determination, are too arbitrary to be useful for pricing. Moreover, it is quite common in joint product industries to allocate total costs to individual products on the basis of their relative sales value. Selling price thus acts as a determinant of respective product costs instead of the reverse. Pricing of joint products and by products actually tends to be based on the company's overall profit expectation, state of competition and prevailing market prices of different products rather than on their so-called relationship to product costs. Thus it is judicious to play with the varying rates of contribution with an eye on maximisation of total revenue in framing pricing policy of joint products and by-products.

Spare Parts Pricing :

It is almost a general practice in industrial marketing to make up profit by selling spares of an equipment at very high prices. By persuading the customers to believe that only the original spare parts would keep the equipment running continuously, the industrial marketer often attempts a trade-off-between lower profit margin on equipment sales and higher profit on spare parts sales. Excepting the tendency to price them high as possible, following perhaps
v) the concept of "what the traffic can bear", there is no generally accepted principle of pricing spare parts. However, the following considerations may be kept in view while tackling this special pricing problem.

(a) Charging exorbitant prices for spare may be worthwhile for a short period when there is no competition and the parts under question are critical and short supply items.

(b) Besides the possibility of being priced out by competitors, very high prices may be also lead to a situation where spurious spares would flood the market.

(c) In case the equipment is of a general purpose in nature and therefore the user has several options, the pricing of spares should be reasonable.

(d) The principle of low-price-high-volume versus high-price-low volume will also supply in case of common parts meant for general purpose equipment.

(e) Prices should be kept on the higher side in case of uncommon, critical and insurance spares, near substitutes of which are not readily available.

(f) Pricing of spare parts and for that matter, any product or service, cannot remain divorced from cost for all time to come. It would, therefore, be necessary to establish and review from time to time the cost of sales of spare parts.

vi) Pricing of After-Sales Service :

A broad approach may be schematically presented below :

Pricing Methods :

	Components/Elements		Basis Of Charge
i)	Spare parts		List prices of different parts (to be reviewed and undated regularly).
ii)	Service Personnel	a)	Initial inspection charge (generally fixed).
		b)	Hourly or daily rates of service charges of different categories of maintenance & service Personnel (pro-rated salary plus overheads @ say, 100% or 200%)
		c)	Travelling & daily allowances (fixed in advanced or reimbursed at actuals)

NOTES ;

Estimates re: replacement of spare parts (free or chargeable) may be made on a statistical analysis of the failure of different spare parts in a number of identical equipment supplied during the immediate past. The results of such analysis could be useful also in improving the quality of products and this in turn will appreciably reduce the cost on this score.

vii) Price Discrimination :

It is a variation of demand-oriented pricing in which a particular product is sold at two or more prices. Price discrimination takes various forms e.g. discrimination on the basis of customers, the product version, place and the time. The application of price discrimination is successful if the following conditions are satisfied.

(a) Market is capable of division into distinct segments.

(b) Members of one segment are not informed of price variation operating in other segments of the market and hence, there is no possibility of resale.

(c) There should not be any chance of under-selling by the competitors in the segment where higher prices are charged due to price discrimination.

(d) The cost of market segmentation should not exceed the additional revenue generated from price discrimination.

viii) Export Pricing :

In general, export markets are highly competitive. The basic strategy for pricing will depend on the purpose of export, as stated below :

(a) The company is under specific commitment to the Government against the Industrial Licence for manufacture and export of a certain percentage of oputput for in-flow of foreign exchange. In a situation like this exports at a price even below marginal cost may be advisable if it is imperative for the company to meet its commitment.

(b) In case of 100 percent export oriented company, the very profitability of the company depends on how much remunerative price it succeeds in getting. Pricing in such case is no different from that for domestic sales.

(c) Exports may be necessary for utilising capacity which would otherwise remain unused, domestic market being limited.

(d) A company may like to get its products established in the overseas market for improving its brand image and enhance competitive edge in the domestic market itself (e.g. some competitive edge in the domestic market itself (e.g. some Indian manufacturers of TV sets, shaving blades, etc have been doing this for long).

As to pricing under situations (c) and (d) above, the following methodology may be suggested, in the exact sequence given here :

i) Marginal cost of sales for domestic operation - should be available readily.

ii) Marginal cost of sales "adjusted" for export operation (i.e. "Relevant" Marginal Cost) - adjustment being for "additions" and "substractions" to/from (i) above, as indicated below :

Cost Estimates (per Unit)

Additions	**Subtractions**
a) Extra quality & inspection costs.	a) Savings in variable selling & distribution expenses applicable to domestic sales.

b) Additional Packaging.	b) Savings in indirect taxes like excise duty, duty drawback, etc.
c) Out-of-pocket costs like port handling charges, insurance (if not borne by importers), etc.	c) Savings in the form of concesional rate of interest on working capital specific to the export order.
d) Overseas Professional expenses (only variable part like agent's commission, etc)	

iii) Rock Bottom FOB Price - to be arrived at after building easily quantifiable incentives into the adjusted (i.e. relevant to export marginal cost per (ii) above.

Illustration:

Incentives : 40 % on FOB (comprising say, cash compensatory support and premium on Import Replenishment Licence Exim Scrip or Rupee convertibility)

Adjusted Marginal Cost for Exports : Rs. 28 per unit (assumed)

Rock Bottom FOB (RB FOB) Price

$$= 28 - \left(\frac{40 \times 28}{140}\right) = \text{Rs. } 20 \text{ per unit.}$$

Notes : 1) RB FOB Price means the price below which export sales will involve actual cash drain.

2) Any price above this would generate some "contirbution" and that will be "profit" too, since the company's total fixed costs stand otherwise recovered fully from domestic sales.

3) The above analysis and the resultant figure of RB FOB price could be very useful in price negotiation for exports.

6. CONCEPT OF FAIR RETURN

It will be relevant to briefly discuss the concept of fair return and price in India. In case of Government administered pricing system, long-term marginal cost of products is being recommended to be the basis. But there is always the question of a fair return permitted by the Government authorities and subsequently built into the price. Fair return in turn is in most cases related to the concept of capital employed. The fair return on capital employed allowed by Government, authorities varies from time to time, from industry to industry and from authorities to authorities. Some of the common bases or norms generally adopted by the Bureau of Industrial Costs and Prices (BICP) are :

(a) 15 per cent on capital employed

(b) Profit before interest and tax at 16 per cent on total employed (that is, net fixed assets plus net working capital) or profit after tax at 8 per cent on the net worth (that is, equity share capital plus reserves)

(c) Post tax return of 12 per cent on net worth

Quite a few industries in India are some lacunae in administration of price control system in India. It is suggested that price control mechanism should be adequately flexible so that at least the following factors can be given due consideration to :

(i) Indirect taxes - Any significant change in excise duty, sales, tax, etc should automatically come to be regarded as an element of cost and suitable adjustments should be allowed in the final price.

(ii) Input costs change, especially in materials - There should be provision for regular periodic comparison of input costs so that any substantial price changes in these can be given effect to in adjusting selling prices. The same should be followed in respect of wages, interest and other major cost components.

7. RESALE PRICE MAINTENANCE

Resale price maintenance or RPM implies a situation where there is a stipulation by supplier that his distributors shall sell particular goods at prices fixed by him and not at lesser prices. RPM is therefore a policy of selling a product at the same price at all outlets. Such stipulation essentially involves a restrictive business practice. This may be adopted jointly by all the manufacturers or individually by one manufacturer. Once RPM gets firmly established in a trade, manufacturers always try to defend it. But RPM kills competitions and often keeps the prices for the ultimate consumer at a level higher than they would otherwise have been. Therefore, from social benefit angle RPM is to be discouraged. It has been established that RPM is prima facie harmful, detrimental to public interest and that discontinuance of RPM reduces the cost of living.

Considering the arguments in favour and against continuance of RPM many countries have enacted comprehensive legislation to restrict RPM. The Monopolies and Restrictive Trade Practices (MRTP) Act, 1969 provides for similar restrictions on the enforcement of RPM agreements in India. Section 33(f) (1) of the MRTP Act lays down that any agreement to sell goods on condition that the prices to be charged on resale by the purchaser shall be the prices stipulated by the seller shall be subject to registration unless it clearly stated that prices lower than those prices may be charged. More declaration of "maximum" prices without stating "that prices lower than those prices may be charged" may not meet that requirement of law. Section 39 prohibits the establishment of minimum price. Section 40 provides that no supplier shall withhold supplies of any goods to any wholesaler or retailer seeking to obtain them for resale in India on the ground that the wholesaler or retailer seeking to obtain them for resale in India on the ground that the wholesaler of retailer (a) has sold in India at a price below resale price, the goods obtained, either directly or indirectly, from that supplier : or (b) is likely, if the goods are supplied to him, to sell them in India at a price below that price or supply them after them either directly or indirectly to a third party who would be likely to do so.

Contravention of the provisions of Sections 39 and 40 has been made punishable under Section 51 with imprisonment for a term which may extend to three months or with fine which may extend to Rs.5000 or with both. If it therefore of utmost importance that those engaged in distribution should be careful about these provisions in their own interest and abandon the practice of RPM. Section 41, however, empowers the MRTP Commission to exempt certain classes of goods from the operation of Sections 39 and 40 under specific conditions. But the scope of such exemption is very narrow.

8. CONCLUSION

Pricing today is perhaps the most baffling problem modern management has to face. The problem has grown in magnitude and complexity recently because of quite a few external factors, mostly uncontrollable from the enterprise point of view. Such factors, to name but a few, are steady transition from sellers' market to buyers' market, government price regulations and price change and recent inflationary trends. It is all the more necessary today that an enterprise frames long-range pricing policy and also adopts suitable pricing strategies, depending on a given set of circumstances.

The question of pricing is intimately linked with the social obligations of a modern business enterprise. Very often, business houses are so much obsessed with the short-run profit earning objective that they fail to recognise the societal aspects involved - a situations not desirable from long -term point of view.

CASE STUDIES

I. RRB Ltd. - A CASE STUDY ON PRICING

This is the case of a one-product and one-customer plant of a particular company. The product manufactured by the plant being of national importance and the only customer being a public sector undertaking, the Government of India have introduced some control over profit through a suitable price control system.

The company has been offered by the Government two options regarding the 'fair return' or expected ROI. These are :

(a) Profit before interest and tax on total capital employed (total capital employed = Net fixed assets plus net working capital) - 16 per cent (maximum)

(b) Profit after tax on net worth (Net worth = equity share capital plus reserves)-9 per cent (maximum).

The total capital employed of the company is estimated at Rs.135 lakhs, comprising net fixed assets Rs.75 lakhs and net working capital (not the actual but based on Government Norms) Rs.60 lakhs. This total capital employed has been financed as own capital (equity plus reserves) Rs.45 lakhs and loan capital or borrowings Rs.90 lakhs.

The plant has got a licensed production capacity of 3000 units. The installed capacity being a little higher, depending on the needs of the customer, the actual production could be 3000 ±10 per cent units. At the optimum capacity utilisation of 3000 units the relevant cost figures are as follows :

	Rs. Lakhs
(i) Total variable cost	100
(ii) Total fixed cost (excluding interest)	80
(iii) Interest on borrowings (at 15.5 per cent approx.)	14
Total	194

We have to determine :

(a) Which of the two options, as regards the ROI, the company should choose?

(b) What should be the price per unit of the product under each of the two ROI norms allowed by the Government and under the assumption of three levels of capacity utilisation, viz. 3000, 3300, and 2700 units?

(Figures in Rs. Lakhs)

	R.O.I. Alternative I (Ebit = 16% on capital employed)	R.O.I. Alternative II (P.A.T. = 9% on net worth)
Profits (earnings) before interest & tax	22	
Less Interest	14	
Profit before tax:I	8	
Profit after tax		4
Profit before tax (assuming tax @ 60%) : II		10
A. Production/Sales 3000 units		
Variable cost	100	100
Fixed Cost	80	80
Interest	14	14
Profit	8	10
	202	204
Selling price per unit	Rs.6733	Rs.6800
B. Production/Sales 3300 units		
Selling price per unit	Rs.6424	Rs.6485
C. Production/Sales 2700 units		
Selling price per unit	Rs.7111	Rs.7185

The results under B and C have been arrived at following the method shown under A above. It is to be noted that, with changing volumes, only the variable cost will change proportionately - other elements (viz, fixed cost, interest and profit) will remain unchanged. It is evident that the ROI alternative II is the more attractive one, from the company's point of view.

2. VITAMIN PRODUCTS LIMITED

(A case study on pricing for selling to Government)

The Government of India have invited quotations from the manufacturers of pharmaceutical products for the supply of a product High potency Vitamin B complex tablets under their rate-contract scheme. V.P.Ltd., a leading manufacturer, finds that one of their products in the list confirms fully to the required specification. In fact, they have previously sold the same product to the Government of India.

Conditions for the Tender :

(i) Rate contract to be effective from 1.4.19x5 and to be renewed after one year, i.e. on 1.4.19x6.

(ii) Payment : 90 per cent against delivery. Balance 10 percent after 3 months, subject to no quality complaints

(iii) Approximate annual off-take 50,000 packs of 100s

(iv) Distribution only to major cities at suppliers' own expenses.

(v) Other things remaining the same, the order will go to the supplier quoting the lowest price.

The Marketing Services Department of the Company collects the following data in connection with the tender.

	Prices quoted			
A. Bidding history	19x1-x2	19x2-x3	19x3-x4	19x4-x5
V.P. Limited	90.00	92.50	93.00	94.50
Nearest competitor	92.00	91.50	95.00	95.00

B. Trade Price with excise duty of the pack of V.P.Ltd. (price 'frozen' as per D.P.C.O) Rs. 110.00

C. Cost escalation (primarily because of raw-material price rise) estimated during 19x5-x6 over 19x4-x5 by about 20 per cent.

D. Excise duty included in trade price Rs.10.00 proportionate refund of the duty available on price differential in case of sales to the Government.

E. V.P. Ltd's profitability of this product for 19x3-x4 (which is being broadly maintained in 19x4-x5) is as follows :

	Trade Sales	Govt.Sales
Unit Sales	30,000	40,000
Price Per Unit (Rs.)	110	93
Standard Cost (variable) including excise duty	75	75
Gross Contribution per unit	35	18
Variable Marketing expenses per unit (incl. distribution)	10	5
Net Contribution per unit	25	13
Total Net Contribution	Rs.7,50,000	Rs.5,20,000
P.V. ratio	22.7%	14.0%

Note : No excise duty refund was attempted in 19x3-x4 on sale of this product to Government of India.

F. The Marketing Services Department has got a separate Section for handling Government sales. The annual fixed expenses of this

Section vis-a-vis that of the total marketing services, as per 19x3-x4 figures, are as follows :

	Govt.Sales Section	Total for marketing Services
Turnover (Rs. Lakhs)	100	1,000
fixed expenses (Rs. Lakhs)	3	100

G. Total fixed expenses for the factory in 19x3-x4 : Rs.20 lakhs and that in General Administration and Accounts Department : Rs.10 Lakhs. The Total profit before tax Rs.1 Crore in 19x3-x4.

The Marketing Services Department likes to formulate a plan for approval of the top management before it goes to quote for the product.

The objectives are to get the order and to optimise profits under the situation.

Let us adopt a logical approach towards developing the price on behalf of the company under the facts and situations given above. It is be noted, however, that this is only one approach-there could be various other approaches in handling the same problem, as it should be in any case study.

1. Variable Cost of Sales (per unit) :		**Rs.**
Variable cost of product (as per last year)		75
Less excise duty		10
		65
Add escalation (@ 20%)		13
		78
Add Marketing exp. (variable)	5	
Excise duty	10	15
Projected variable cost of sales (with excise duty)		93

2. Rock Bottom or Break Even Price (With Excise Duty) :

x = 93 - 10% (20 - x)

or x = 91

Check, price:	91
Add E.D. refund	2
10% (110-91)	
Marginal cost	93

3. Price at the same profitability as last year's (i.e. P/V ratio: 14%)

$$\frac{x - 91}{x} = 14\% \qquad X = 106$$

Check Price	106
Less Rock Bottom Cost	91
Contribution	15

P/V ratio 14% (i.e.15 on 106)

4. Price at the same quantum of contribution as last year's :

$$\text{Unit contribution required} = \frac{\text{Rs.}5,20,000}{50,000}$$

= Rs. 10.40

Price = 91 + 10.40

= 101.40 say Rs.102.00

5. Price Expected to be quoted by the nearest competitior :

	Last Year	With 20% escalation	With 10% escalation
Price with E.D.	95.00		
Less E.D.	10.00		
	85.00	112.00	103.50
		(85 x 1.2 x 10)	(85 x 1.1 + 10)

6. Range of Pricing as per above :

(i) Rs.91 to Rs. 106 (Nos 2 ND 3 bove)

(ii) Rs.95 to Rs. 102 (Last Year's price and No.4 above)

Note : The range is shortened under (ii)

7. 'Expected Price' after assigning subjective probabilities to the various sale price alternatives within the range as per 6(ii) :

Figures Per Unit

(i) Sale Price (Rs.)	95.00	97.00	99.00	102.00
(ii) Probability	0.35	0.30	0.25	0.10
(iii) Value (i) x (ii)	33.25	29.10	24.75	10.20
(iv) Expected Value (total of iii)	Rs.97.30			
(v) Cost Of Sales (Rs.)	91.00	92.00	92.00	92.00
(vi) Contribution (Rs.) (i-v)	4.00	5.00	7.00	10.00
(vii) Expected total contribution	Rs.5.65			

Proposed price is therefore Rs. 97.30 or say, Rs. 98.00 per unit (with excise duty)

8. Other, including non-financial, features:

(i) The fact that through sales to Government there is likely to be a boost in trade sales, since a part of such sales are triggered off by hospitals and institutions ;

(ii) The fact of optimisation of revenue /contribution, as well as reduction in production costs, through better capacity utilisation in the plant;

(iii) Possibility of recovering a part of the fixed overhead - both in the Government sales section and also general fixed overhead;

(iv) Improvement in the overall profit position of the company if the order is secured as against the situation when the order is lost.

CHAPTER 16

INVESTMENT DECISIONS & CAPITAL BUDGETING

1. The Theory of Investment Analysis; 2. Evaluation of Financial Attractiveness of Projects; 3. Pay Back Period 4. Return on investment (ROI) 5. The Discounted Cash Flow (DCF) Techniques in General; 6. Net Present Value (NPV) Approach; 7. Internal Rate of Return (IRR) Approach; 8. NPV versus IRR 9. The DCF Techniques - Concluding Observations; 10. Risk Analysis; 11. Sensitivity Analysis; 12. Capital Expenditure Budgeting and Control; 13. Project Management and PERT/CPM.

1. THE THEORY OF INVESTMENT ANALYSIS

By investment we mean here any outlay on any extraordinary project or effort quite distinct from the normal expenditures connected with ordinary business operations. There are broadly three investment areas in a business from this stand-point. These are (a) capital expenditure, (b) new business venture, and (c) new marketing effort.

There may be various types of business needs giving rise to an investment proposal. To define an independent project and to recognise all feasible alternatives to it, identification of the specific need is important. Accordingly, need may be classified as follows:

1) Expansion
2) Cost reduction
3) Loss/cost avoidance
4) Replacement
5) Employee welfare
6) Improved manufacturing methods
7) Quality assurance and good manufacturing practice
8) Pollution control
9) Others (for example, penetration into new markets, improving the market share, etc.)

More often than not, a project would fulfil more than one of such needs.

After an investment proposal is made, it has to be thoroughly evaluated. Such evaluation requires collection, integration, quantification and analysis of all feasible alternative projects related to the particular course of action.

It is not difficult to envisage two important components of a project, the hardware and the software. In an area development project the software or the service aspects are more important. In the setting up of a factory, on the other hand, the hardware elements namely providing physical assets, are more important, though there would be some software elements also in the form of providing services and utilities.

Any project would require initially the deployment of some physical and financial resources which would provide the basis of the stream of costs. At a later stage will accrue a stream of benefits. There is a distinct time-lag between the stream of costs or investments and the stream of benefits or returns. Both these streams have to be identified in the form of cash flows - both outflows and inflows.

There are five general steps in the approach to most project analyses. These are:

1] problem/project definition;
2] recognition of all alternatives;
3] collection of all relevant data;
4] qualitative and quantitative analysis;
5] presentation of results to decision - makers.

To handle the above five steps, there are broadly three areas of responsibilities.

1] those closest to project - for collection of primary data initially and implementation of decision finally;

2] those responsible for data analysis and assembly of proposals;

3] those charged with approval/disapproval of the proposal

The management accountant or project analyst is in the second area of responsibility mentioned above.

There are various types of feasibility studies undertaken during a project analysis. These are:

1] technical feasibility or appraisal;
2] organisational set-up;
3] managerial competence;
4] economic analysis;
5] commercial aspects; and
6] financial feasibility.

Out of these, we will devote this chapter primarily to financial feasibility, since this is essential from the viewpoints of both the investors and the management - corporate as well as operating. Usually a project analyst will recommend to the decision - makers the acceptance or otherwise of an investment proposal as well as selection of a particular project to the exclusion of others on the basis of either financial justification or non-financial justification or both. For example, a substantial investment in the marketing area could be justified on non-financial grounds, namely marketing considerations alone. But more often than not, there will be a financial justification as well, besides various other aspects which are not amenable to quantification in strict financial terms. A project is said to be financially justified only when it can generate some net cash flow through higher sales, cost reduction, etc. A modern project analyst has a number of tools in his kit to evaluate the financial justification of an investment proposal.

2. EVALUATION OF FINANCIAL ATTRACTIVENESS OF PROJECTS

As in the case of an individual, in the case of a business also the means of finance are limited but the demands for investment prospects are numerous. Thus a situation may arise when a company has to choose one among a number of alternative projects. Profitability is generally the main criterion in such selection. But there may be other criteria as well; for example, need for getting back the money at the earliest possible time, creation of employment opportunities with emphasis more on the discharge of social responsibilities than on profits, building up a good image of the enterprise (which might in turn pay back in various ways in the future), and so on.

The tools and techniques used for financial evaluation of project attractiveness are somewhat different at micro level from those used at the macro level. For example, benefit cost ratio is the most common technique applied in the case of projects at the macro level. Under this technique all benefits and costs are amortised into annual benefits and costs, respectively, before the benefit cost ratio is computed. The higher the ratio, the greater will be the financial justification for the project.

There are various methods and techniques of assessing the financial justifiability of a project. These techniques can be broadly grouped under two sets, (a) undiscounted methods and (b) discounted methods.

Undiscounted methods include pay-back period calculation, benefit cost ratio approach, working out various return on investment (ROI) percentages, etc. The dominant feature of all these methods is that time value concept of money, on the interest element, is not considered at all under these methods.

Interest element or time value concept of money is taken into consideration in the discounted methods. The basic principle adopted here is the farther we move from the present, the lower will be the value at present.

There is thus the need for adjusting both investments and returns in respect of time. Discounted methods also have various approaches, discounted pay-back period, discounted benefit-cost ratio approach, net present value (NPV) approach, DCF rate of return or internal rate of return (IRR) approach, etc. The results arrived at under the discounted cash flow techniques can be further refined by adopting more sophisticated techniques like risk analysis and sensitivity studies. We shall now discuss and illustrate these methods and techniques.

3. PAY-BACK PERIOD

The pay-back period is defined as the period (number of years and months) at the end of which the net cash flow of a project is zero (0). In other words it is the period during which the original investment (cash outflow) is fully paid back by the returns (cash inflows). An example:

Year	Cash Flow Rs. Lakhs			
	Project A		Project B	
0	(50)	(Investment)	(60)	
1	5		20	
2	10		20	
3	15		20	® 0
4	20	® 0	20	
5	25		20	
6	30		20	

The pay-back period is four years in case of Project A and three years in case of Project B. Judged by this criterion, Project B is better than Project A. This is how the relative attractiveness of a number of competing projects is to be judged under the pay-back period approach.

The pay pack period is followed by those enterprises which are primarily interested in an early return of the original investment to reduce the risk factor or to put the same money to a better alternative use after a period of time which coincides with the pay-back period.

Besides this, the pay-back method has some distinct advantages:

1] It is simple to understand and easy to calculate.

2] It indicates at once an investment which is outright unacceptable (if the total investment is not paid back during the lifetime of the project).

3] In an industry which is experiencing rapid technological changes, The pay-back method ensures some protection against the danger of obsolescence (since investment decisions are based upon the lowest pay back period approach).

But the pay-back period approach suffers from some serious limitations:

1] It does not consider the interest factor or the time value concept of money.

2] It does not consider the staggering of the return during the pay back period. (Two projects may have the same pay back period, but the pattern of cash flow may be say 15+7+3 in one case and 5+7+13 in the other).

3] It does not take into account the post pay-back period returns which could be significant in some cases.

In sum, the pay-back period method happens to be the most popular method of project appraisal as revealed in some surveys recently conducted in the western countries. Unfortunately, for some unknown reasons, this method is yet to gain popularity in the Indian industrial enterprises, barring only a few houses.

4. RETURN ON INVESTMENT (ROI)

The return on investment method is a popular method of judging the acceptability of a project. To calculate the ROI both the investment and the returns are to be worked out with proper perspective.

Total investment usually means the net fixed assets (gross fixed assets less depreciation) plus net working capital (current assets less current liabilities) relatable to a particular project or an alternative. Returns may be either pre-tax or after-tax profit. Sometimes after-tax cash flows are taken to be the returns. This is of course not a healthy practice - ROI being basically an accounting concept, profit should be taken as the numerator, whatever be the way profit is defined. For example besides PBT or PAT, sometimes 'Ebit' (Earnings before interest and tax) is taken to be the returns for the purpose of ROI calculations.

An enterprise should have some minimum expectation in the form for ROI percentage. This minimum expectation is called the cut-off rate of investment. The projects showing ROI below the cut-off rate will automatically be excluded from consideration. And obviously, thhe one with the highest ROI rate, will be accepted when there are a number of projects competing for a limited or scarce investible fund.

There are various approaches towards working out the ROI even for the same project and, therefore, with the same set of data. Some of these methods are illustrated here, using the hypothetical example of Projects A and B given earlier (under the Pay Back Period), with some further assumptions as necessary :

Basis of calculating ROI	ROI Percentage		Assumption
	Project A	Project B	
1. Average Annual profit after Tax (PAT) on Investment	$\frac{105/6}{50/2}$ x 100 = 70 %	$\frac{20}{60/2}$ x 100 = 67 %	(i) Cash inflow figures assumed to be PAT here. (ii) No scrap value of fixed assets at the end
2. ---- do ---	$\frac{17.5}{\frac{50-10}{2}+10}$ x 100 = 58%	$\frac{20}{\frac{60-10}{2}+10}$ x 100 = 57%	(i) Same as 1(i) above (ii) Scrap value at end Rs. 10 lakhs for each project.
3. Average Annual PAT on original cost of investment	$\frac{17.5}{50}$ x 100 = 35%	$\frac{20}{60}$ x 100 = 33 %	Same as above
4. PAT in the year of optimum level of operations on original cost of investment	$\frac{20}{50}$ x 100 = 40 %	$\frac{20}{60}$ x 100 = 33 %	Year 4 is the year optimum level of operations for both the projects

Notes:

(i) In all calculations as above, Project A shows better ROI percentages than Project B.

(ii) In calculating average investment, it has been considered that the original investment on an asset diminishes from year to year along its life-span due to recovery of capital cost by way of depreciation charges. Thus, assuming the straight line method of charging depreciation, the average investment over the life of the project will be half the depreciable paprt plus the whole of the non-depreciable part of the cost of investment. The depreciable portion is divided by two because the initial outlay declines from the amount of original cost to zero at the end of the life of the asset.

Another illustration of ROI (with continuous/staggered investment; both for fixed assets and for working capital)

The cut-off rate of the company is 25 per cent in terms of average returns on PAT basis. Three projects X,Y,Z are under consideration. The investment pattern (assumed to be uniform for all the three projects) and the respective returns are given below. In the last columns are computed the average investment and average returns and the ROI percentages.

(Figures in Rs. lakhs)

Year	1	2	3	4	5	Average	
Investments (as at each year end)							
Fixed assets	10	10	15	15	15	13	
Working Capital	5	10	30	40	50	27	
Total	15	20	45	55	65	40	
Returns (PAT)							
ROI%							
Project X :	Nil	5	10	15	20	10	25%
Project Y :	5	10	10	10	5	5	20%
Project Z :	3	10	15	17	15	12	30%

Remarks :

(i) Project Y is to be summarised rejected since the ROI rate (20%) is below the 'cut-off rate' (25%) of the company.

(ii) Between X and Z, Project Z shows higher ROI rate (30%) and is, therefore the more attractive one.

Incidentally, fixing the cut-off rate at such a high level (25 per cent ROI on PAT basis) might involve some opportunity loss. If the company had enough funds, it could invest in Project Y also and earn a fairly good return. Under extreme capital raioning or scarcity of funds situation, of course, it makes sense to fix the cut-off rate a bit too high.

5. THE DISCOUNTED CASH FLOW (DCF) TECHNIQUES IN GENERAL

Discounted Cash Flow or time adjusted return is nothing but present value of different cash flows or returns in different future years; that is the future returns brought down to the equivalent present value level by applying suitable discount (or interest) rate. Discounting is nothing but the reverse of compounding.

Discounted cash flow technique is breakthrough in the area of project evaluation since, unlike all other conventional methods, this technique for the first time sought to recognise and introduce the time value concept of money or the interest factor. From the commonsense point of view, Rs.100 payable today is of greater value than Rs.100 payable say, after one year, because of the interest factor involved. Assuming a 10 per cent interest rate Rs.100 today is equivalent to Rs.110 after one year. Alternatively, Rs.100 after one year may be discounted to about Rs.90 (at 10 per cent rate), which is really the present value.

If we ignore the interest factor and add up all future cash flow in absolute monetary terms, it would be fallacy of aggregation since the addition of amounts would be from different frames of reference. Further, on the basis of this so-called total cash flows if we compare the profitability of different projects, that comparison will not be on an apples to apples basis, but between dissimilar things. Discounted cash flow technique solves these problems of aggregation and comparison. Therefore, the relative profitability of different projects assessed after the application of DCF technique is both correct and realistic.

As already indicated, there are various approaches in the application of the DCF technique. We will now illustrate these.

DISCOUNTED PAY-BACK PERIOD APPROACH

If we assume a discounting rate of interest rate of 10 per cent and rework the paya back period on the basis of the same set of data given earlier under Projects A and B, the position will be as follows :

CASH FLOW

(Rs. lakhs)

Year	Discounting factor	Project A absolute amount	Project A present value	Project B absolute amount	Project B present value
0	1	(50)	(50)	(60)	(60)
1	.91	5	4.55	20	18.20
2	.82	10	8.20	20	16.40
3	.75	15	11.25	20	15.00
					- 0
4	.68	20	13.60	20	13.60
					- 0
5	.62	25	15.50	20	12.40
6	.56	30	16.80	20	11.20

Notes on Working :

(i) Discounting factors available from discounting tables (or prest value tables).

(ii) P V in each case = amount of cash flow x the discounting factor

(iii) Cash flows assumed to accrue at the end of each year.

The pay-back period of the two projects as shown above are 4.8 years for A and 3.75 years for B. B is therefore better than A. It may be noted here that under the undiscounted pay back method also B is considered to be better than A. But on this basis the pay back is four year for A and three years for B.

DISCOUNTED BENEFIT-COST RATIO APPROACH

Following the same set of data as above, the Benefit Cost Ratio on an undiscounted basis would bee 105/50 = 2.1 for Project A and in case of Project B, 120/60 = 2. On this basis, therefore, Project A is considered to be better than Project B. But if we take the discounted benefit-cost ratio approach, the position is as follows :

$$\text{Discounted benefit-cost ratio} = \frac{\text{Total present value of returns}}{\text{Total investment at present value}}$$

$$\text{Project A} = \frac{69.9}{50} = 1.398$$

$$\text{Project B} = \frac{86.8}{60} = 1.447$$

On the basis, Project B is better than Project A. The results arrived at (1.398 and 1.447) are also called profitability indices or profitability factors of the respective projects.

6. NET PRESENT VALUE (NPV)

Under this approach, a suitable discounting rate is first decided upon. Usually, this rate is equal to more than the cost of borrowing or cost of capital for investment. Thereafter all the cash flows - both out (investment) and in (returns) - are converted into their respective present values applying the discounting rate. To faciliate the work, discounting tables are used (which show PV of Re 1 at different periods and under different discounting rates). The net total present value of all projects is then computed.

An illustration

Continuing the same example in respect of Projects A and B we may work out the NPV (assuming as before, a discounting rate of 10 per cent and cash flows accruing only towards the end of the respective years.)

	CASH FLOWS (in Rs. lakhs)	
	PROJECT A	PROJECT B
(i) PV of (investment)	(50)	(60)
(ii)PV of returns (total of all future returns, as calculated earlier)	69.90	86.80
(iii) Net present value (NPV)	19.00	26.80
Ratio of NPV to PV of investment	0.398	0.447
NPV as percentage of PV of investment	39.8%	44.7%

Let us now indicate the decision rules under NPV approach :

(i) A project showing negative NPV is to be sum marily rejected (since it does not recover the original investment).

(ii) Criterion of project selection is the absolute NPV amount if the PV. of investments of the competing projects are around the same.

(iii) Criterion of project selection is the ratio (or percentage) of NPV to the PV of investments for the respective projects in a situation where the PV of investments of the competing projects are significantly different.

Following the decision rule (iii) above, Project B is considered to be better than Project A.

7. INTERNAL RATE OF RETURN (IRR) APPROACH

One of the major problems of the NPV approach is that of deciding upon the correct discounting rate. Needless to say, any improper decision in this respect may vitiate the project profitability analysis, particularly in cases where different projects show widely different patterns of cash flows in different time periods.

This problem is obviated by a slightly more refined approach of the DCF technique. This is the DCF rate of return (also called time adjusted rate of return) approach or the IRR calculation. Under this approach, the NPV of each competing project is assumed to be zero and that unique discounting rate which would make NPV = 0 is to be arrived at separately for each project. The project showing the highest discounting or DCF rate or IRR is considered to be the best.

The methodology of arriving at the DCF rate is initially trial and error and then use of interpolation techniques, once the area of the rate is located after two or three trials.

An Illustration

Let us continue with the same set of data for clearer understanding. Assume the discounting rate of 10 per cent is not given. We have to find the unique discounting rate in respect of each of the projects, A and B, which would result in a zero NPV in either case.

It would be clear from the earlier workings that the DCF rate will be higher than 10 per cent in either case (since at 10 per cent is there are positive NPV's). Let us start with a higher rate in the first trial for each of the two projects and come down, if necessary, in subsequent trials. Incidentally, it may be noted that higher the rate of discount we choose,the lower will be the present value of returns. Our objective is to make it zero.

PROJECT A

Year	Cash Flow (Rs.lakhs)	Trial No 1		Trial No 2	
		Discount Rate 20%		Discount Rate 18%	
		factor	P.V. (Rs.lakhs)	factor	P.V. (Rs.lakhs)
0	(50)	1.00	(50.00)	1.00	(50.00)
1	5	0.83	4.15	0.85	4.25
2	10	0.69	6.90	0.72	7.20
3	15	0.58	8.70	0.61	9.15
4	20	0.48	9.60	0.52	10.40
5	25	0.40	10.00	0.44	11.00
6	30	0.35	10.50	0.37	11.10
N.P.V.			(0.15)		3.10

From the two trials, it is apparent that the DCF rate must lie somewhere between 18 per cent and 20 per cent. The rate may be arrived by interpolation as follows :

$$\text{DCF rate} = \text{Rate of low trial} + \frac{\text{NVP of low trial}}{\text{NPV of low trial + deficit in NPV of high trials}} \times \text{Diff.in rate between two trials}$$

$$= 18\% + \frac{3.10}{3.10 + 0.15} \times 2\%$$

$$= 18\% + 1.9\%$$

$$= 19.9\% \text{ (or approximately, 20\%)}$$

PROJECT B

Year	Cash Flow (Rs.lakhs)	Trial No.1 Discount Rate 25% factor	P.V. (Rs.lakhs)	Trial No.2 Discount Rate 23% factor	P.V. (Rs.lakhs)
0	(60)	1.00	(60.00)	1.00	(60.00)
1	20	0.80	16.00	0.81	16.20
2	20	0.64	12.80	0.66	13.20
3	20	0.51	10.20	0.54	10.80
4	20	0.41	8.20	0.44	8.80
5	20	0.33	6.60	0.36	7.20
6	20	0.26	5.20	0.29	5.80
N.P.V.			(1.00)		2.00

$$\text{DCF Rate} = 23\% + \frac{2.00}{2.00 + 1.00} \times 2\%$$

$$= 24.33\% \text{ (or approximately, 24\%)}$$

DCF rate or IRR being higher in case of Project B, this would be better than Project A. The fact that both umder undiscounted pay back method and under DCF rate, Project B in the example is more attractive, is more a coincidence than due to any specific reason. Take the following case, for example :

Year end	1	2	3	4	5	6	7....11
Cash Flow :							
Project X	(40)	10	10	10	10	10	5
Project Y	(40)	4	8	12	16	2	100

	PAY-BACK PERIOD	DCF RATE OF RETURN
Project X :	4 years	19%
Project Y :	4 years	25%

In spite of the same pay-back period, DCF rate differs significantly.

It would be to our advantage to tabulate and study all the results, obtained under various methods, in respect of Projects A and B.

Methods	Project A	Project B	Relative attractiveness
UNDISCOUNTED :			
1. Pay-back period	4 years	3 years	B
2. ROI	70%, 58%, 35%, & 40%	67%, 57%, 33% & 33%	A
3. Benefit cost ratio	2.1	2	A
DISCOUNTED :			
4. Benefit cost ratio (profitability factor)	1.398	1.447	B
5. Pay back period	4.8 years	3.75 years	B
6. Net present value (percentage on investment)	39.8%	44.7%	B
7. DCF rate (or IRR)	20%	24%	
B			

8. NPV VERSUS IRR

NPV indicates the excess of the total present value of future returns over the present value of investments. IRR (or DCF rate) indicates, on the other hand, the rate at which the cash flows (at present values), are generated in the business by a particular project.

Both NPV and IRR iron out the differences due to interest factor or, say, higher returns in earlier years vis-a-vis higher returns in later years (through the total returns in absolute terms may be around the same for several projects).

Between the two, IRR or DCF rate is the more sophisticated method - a popular method as well, since :

(a) IRR method obviates the mostly subjective decision regarding discounting rate.

(b) Whilst under NPV the main basis of comparision is between different NPV's of different projects, under IRR or DCF rate approach a number of bases is available, for example :

DCF rates vs. current rate of return (on normal operations)
DCF rates vs. cut-off rate of the company
DCF rates Vs. borrowing rate (or cost of capital)
DCF rates between different projects.
DCF rates of different projects vs. those of similar projects of other companies.
DCF rates of different projects vs. DCF rates of similar projects undertaken in the past.

(c) The results under DCF rate approach are simpler for the management to understand and appreciate.

We should, however, be very careful in applying the decision rules properly when NPV and IRR calculations show divergent results.

The rules are :

(a) NPV should be the basis of decision when :

(i) the projects are mutually exclusive in character; and

(ii) there is a capital rationing situation.

Illustration On (ii) Above

Assume there is a capital constraint of Rs.300 and there are 5 projects, the figures being as follows :

Project	Investment Rs.	First year and Cash Flow Rs.	NPV at 10% Rs	IRR %
F	100	120	9.08	20%
G	100	119	8.17	19%
H	100	112	1.81	12%
I	200	232	10.89	10%
J	300	354	21.79	18%

Under IRR approach, F, G and H will be selected (total investment required is Rs.300). But this would not be obviously correct. Project J should be the right selection in the case, based on NPV results. The criterion we are adopting here is maximising the total returns.

(b) IRR should be a better guide when there are plenty of project situations (as it is there in a big enterprice) and no major capital constraints (for example, in respect of macro-projects).

9. THE DCF TECHNIQUES - CONCLUDING OBSERVATIONS

Cash flows have to be calculated in accordance with the method explained earlier. To recapitulate, the simple formula to be followed is : estimated profit - tax + interest + book depreciation (the depreciation debited to P/L a/c whether it be the same as or different from the tax depreciation.

The discounting factors should be taken up to four or five places of decimals from the table (not two places as we have taken for convenience)

Timing of cash flow is important in any DCF calculation. Sometimes, investments may be staggered over a period that may have started in the past. In such cases, all past cash flows should be discounted forward by applying suitable discount factors to elevate them to the present value platform.

In all our illustrations worked out earlier, we have made a simplistic assumption that all cash flows arise only towards the end of the year. In reality, however, cash flows generate in most cases evenly during a year. Discounting tables are available for such even cash flows also. For example, 0.91 may be the discount factor at 10 per cent for Re.1 to be generated at the end of one year from now. If it is generated evenly throughout the year, the discounting factor at the same 10 per cent rate would be say, 0.955.

For DCF calculation, a project may be cut off after, say, five, eight or 10 years. If this is done for all the competing projects, the DCF rates will not be significantly affected, though they may have different life-spans and widely different patterns of return after that 10-year period.

Lastly we may indicate here a few limitations of the DFC technique, to be borne in mind always in its application:

(i) DCF takes care of the time value concept of money, but not the value of money as based on purchasing power. Inflation element is, therefore, to be considered separately (say, while estimating costs, revenues and cash flow).

(ii) IRR results would be valid provided there is scope for reinvestment of cash flow of returns all the time. The condition may not exist always.

(iii) Monitoring of actual cash flow on DCF basis (to ensure that actuals conform to earlier estimates) is almost impossible in real life business situations.

10. RISK ANALYSIS

Risk analysis is an attempt to reduce (if not eliminate) the element of risk involved in any investment decision which is basically and essentially a leap into the future.

The basic data of most of the investment analyses are the sales forecasts. The actual result may be widely different from the one anticipated if there is any error in sales forecasting and/or if reality does not conform to the situation envisaged. If instead of a deterministic forecast, we go by a probabilistic sales forecast, the risk element may be reduced to some extent. Needless to say, the probabilities would only be subjective probabilities given by responsible people closest to the proposed project. Let us consider the following situation:

PROJECT "P"

Sales forecast alternatives	Probability of success	DCF rate
A	0.05	30%
B	0.65	18%
C	0.30	9%
	1.00	

The weighted average DCF rate is 16 per cent (profitabilities being taken as the weight). This gives a better and more reliable rate than any one of the three given above.

Of course, it may be argued that if the worst comes ιo the worst, forecast 'C' may come true and we may net a meagre 9 per cent return. But some amount of calculated business risk must always be there, and more so in all investment decisions.

In risk analysis, the Bayesian decision model can also be used. This approach allows a flexible detailed model to be built for a specific decision problem and uses explicit probabilities to reflect uncertainty. Furthermore, it provides an estimate of the value of additional information in reducing the uncertainty.

11. SENSITIVITY ANALYSIS

Sensitivity analysis is a further refinement in project profitability appraisal. The purpose is to show:

(i) The profitabilities of alternative sets of estimates for a project; and

(ii) The effect on profitability of variations in the factors involved.

Let us assume that against the estimates of three major factors of a project, variable cost may go up or down by 10 per cent; sales forecast may differ by 20 per cent and fixed cost may be up or down by 5 per cent. Considering all such probable changes, a 'pay-off matrix' may be formed and the degree of sensitivity workedout.

Sensitivity analysis, in essence, seeks to highlight the extent to which the original decision will remain unchanged despite some changes in the factors involved. Assume that DCF rate of a project is calculated to be 25 per cent and cut-off rate of the company is 15 per cent. There being no other viable alternative, a go-decision is being considered. Now, it is also estimated that the sales forecast originally taken may go down by 20 per cent and in that case the DCF rate of return is also calculated to come down to, say, 15 per cent. The logical conclusion would be that the go-decision is unchanged up to 20 per cent reduction in anticipated sales and that it would probably be a 'no-go' decision if sales are apprehended to be down by more than 20 per cent over the forecast. Following the same approach, we may considered the effect on the DCF rate of return of increase or decrease in variable cost and also fixed cost. These have to be taken into account in sensitivity analysis and results suitably included in the project analysis report for presentation to the decision-makers.

12. CAPITAL EXPENDITURE BUDGETING AND CONTROL

The mode of control of capital expenditures should be significantly different from that of normal revenue expenditure since any capital expenditure :

(a) involves immediate cash outflow, sometimes of a significant amount, with little possibility of immediate returns; and

(b) it brings in its train a series of extra revenue expenditures (e.g. depreciation, maintenance, operators wages or salaries, general overhead expenses etc.) which are a drain on the revenue profit of the particular year and also of a few subsequent years.

Capital expenditures at the same time increase the profit earning capacity of the business. Hence, the importance of prudent investment on capital expenditure items needs hardly be emphasised.

While we are not going into a detailed and comprehensive control system for capital expenditures, we would like to mention here a few important considerations involved in it.

(i) All capital expenditures should be categorised as productive (say, plant and machinery) and service or support (office equipment, furniture, automobiles, etc). It has been found that capital expenditures have a greater tendency to increase in the second category (service or support). A more stringent system of control is therefore called for in this area.

Some multi - national corporations as well as progressive organisations are known to apply a thumb-rule such as allocation of the total capital expenditure budget for a year on a 50 : 50 basis between productive and support assets. The logic behind this may be that the additional contribution generated through the additional productive assets (consuming at least 50 per cent of the budget) should be able to take care of the full revenue backlash arising out of the entire capital expenditures pertaining to both productive and support assets.

(ii) All capital expenditures may be streamlined and centralised through a document, namely, Request for Capital Expenditure (RCE) in a standard form, preferably printed. The RCE will contain inter alia, the details of the asset to be purchased and the financial and non-financial justification for it.

(iii) For each of capital expenditure, an RCE should be initiated by the head of the department requiring the item. He should then pass it on to a responsible officer in the accounts department (say, the capital expenditure co-ordinator) for necessary verification and calculation of DCF returns (in case of high value items).

(iv) Before an item is purchased the relative RCE, duly verified, should be authorised by the appropriate approval authority The levels of such approval authorities have to be decided in advance, depending on the amount of capital expenditure involved. For example, a departmental head may approve any RCE's upto Rs. 1000. The general manager may approve upto Rs.2500 and beyond that all RCE's have to be authorised by the chief executive. Such limits should be determined with reference to the nature and volume of business and other pertinent factors.

(v) The RCE for every item must be included in the budget. For any unbudgeted item, special approval by the chief executive would be necessary, irrespective of the amount involved.

(vi) The capital expenditure budget or capital budget of the company should be complete in every detail in respect of items, departments requiring them, nature of requirement (replacement or new), purpose code (expansion, production support, employee welfare, pollution control etc.) estimated amount in each case, the timing of the cash flow, etc.

13. PROJECT MANAGEMENT AND PERT/CPM

Though not frequently, almost every company has to embark upon substantial expansion projects, diversification projects or any special project involving major capital or revenue expenditures. The efficient management of such a project specially during the construction and gestation period, is imperative in order to

(a) keep the total project cost within limits ;

(b) complete the project within the scheduled time limt, if not earlier ; and

(c) remove all bottlenecks and settle all exigencies and emergencies promptly and efficiently.

To ensure progress, systematically and as per schedule, facilitate prompt decisions and control costs, there should be a well-formulated project manual or control procedure, detailing inter-alia:

(i) the duties, functions and responsibilities of project management personnel;

(ii) the modus operandi of competitive bidding in connection with tender calls;

(iii) the project accounting systems and procedures (including progressive updating of cash flow plans); and

(iv) a suitable system of review and repoting.

The most popular and best known technique in project management is the Programme (or Project) Evaluation Review Technique or PERT which is basically a system of scientific scheduling. An important constituent of PERT is the use of networks to analyse all activities and events in respect of their interrelationships and determine therafter what is called the critical path.

The constituents of PERT emanate from a closely related methodology, the Critical Path Method or CPM

The advantages PERT/CPM in project planning and control may be summarised as follows :

(i) An orderly planning is possible through the use of a logical network diagram showing the sequence and interdependence of all activities and events, that is, which activities must be completed before others could start.

(ii) The network provides a framework for establishing time estimates for the completion of each activity.

(iii) It determines the critical path which controls the completion of the project, and facilitates concentration on corrective action on the activities lying along this path.

(iv) CPM once established may help project management even in crashing time for the earlier completion of a project.

(v) Periodic review of progress of a project is rendered easier through its PERT diagram.

SECTION V

MARKETING PERFORMANCE EVALUATION

Six Chapters included in this section attempt to explore the methods, quantitative as well as otherwise, available for evaluating the performance of the marketing function as a whole and also its various sub-functions. The discussion starts with an overview of marketing performance evaluation (Chapter 17). Then in the subsequent four chapters an attempt is made to explore the mode of evaluation of four important sub-functions of marketing, viz., selling, advertisement and promotion, distribution or placement and marketing research.

Performance evaluation has been construed as a necessary precondition or pre-requisite to the monitoring and control of operations. And these aspects of control form the subject-matter of the immediate next section.

A new addition to this section is a fairly detailed discussion on Marketing Audit (Chapter 22).

CHAPTER 17

MARKETING PERFORMANCE EVALUATION: AN OVERVIEW

1. Some General Concepts and Approaches; 2. Basic Criteria for Evaluating Overall Marketing Performance; 3. Some Other Evaluation criteria.

1. SOME GENERAL CONCEPTS AND APPROACHES

According to Peter Drucker, the justification for the existence of a business in society is two-old, viz., innovation and marketing. This contention may be valid in advanced economies but perhaps not in developing economies like India. However, the importance of marketing even in developing countries should not be under-estimated. With growing competition and steady transition from the sellers market to the buyers market even in developing countries, marketing has become an increasingly important function and perhaps the main reason for the existence of an enterprise. This has no doubt made marketing both challenging and exciting.

Quoting Drucker again "there is only one valid definition of business purpose: to create a customer". Any attempt towards the evaluation of marketing performance should therefore start with assessing how far the enterprise has been able to create, recreate, hold and attract the customer. Theodore Levitt describes the means by which this customer-creating-recreating-attracting activity can be performed. "People don't buy products: they buy expectation of benefits... A product is not just what the engineers say, but also what is implied by its design, its packaging, its channels of distribution, its price and the quality and activities of its salesmen. A product is therefore, a transaction between the seller and the buyer - a synthesis of what the seller intends and the buyer perceives".

Success in marketing through customer-creation is achieved by efficient management of the marketing-mix and consequently, all the P's (viz., product, price, promotion, placement people, etc.) that go to form the marketing-mix. To manage their affairs, marketers have at their command all the resources. And they are supposed to optimise the results by efficient management of such resources. Surplus or profit is produced by striking a balance scheme of evaluation should, therefore, highlight how and to what extent this balance, reflected through profit or surplus, has been achieved.

Performance evaluation should not, however, be confined to the measurement of results alone, though emphasis is always placed on the results or profits. It is necessary to appraise the strategies and tactics, too, not just the results obtained. Results might sometimes come accidentally, without any creative efforts.

Similarly, results may not be all the satisfactory despite the efforts and the right tactics adopted. Any evaluation scheme should do well to take care of this aspect and this is more important from the long range point of view.

According to Prof. Kotler, marketing is finding a product for the market and at its worst, a market for the product. That being so, marketers have a very important role to play in decision-making in all phases of management. They have to be deeply involved in designing the product to suit the diverse and specific requirements of the customers. This may apparently seem paradoxical in the age of the mass production. But when we see that no two cars of General Motors are exactly indential, we understand the need for meeting customers specific requirements even with the adoption of mass production technology. An evaluation of marketing performance should necessarily consider this aspect also viz., how far the marketers with a strong consumer orientation are helping product designs to meet customer's diverse requirements.

No scheme of marketing performance evaluation would have the right perspective unless it starts with the evaluation of the marketing objectives. Objectives are necessary whether or not the enterprise has formally accepted Management by Objectives (M.B.O.) as a style of management. Of course, under M.B.O., objectives will be more clearly spelt out and when there is no M.B.O., the objectives will be both covert and overt, partly explicit and implicit. An understanding of the objectives are framed, is a must. Sometimes, objectives are framed taking into consideration only what is capable of attainment but it is to be seen whether these objectives are desirable also. The capability-desirability-dichotomy is very common — what is desirable may not be attainable and vice-versa. Victor Buell states that in setting corporate objectives, the first effort must express what is desirable of attainment and only then must look at the concession required to bring them down to what is possible.

2. BASIC CRITERIA FOR EVALUATING OVERALL MARKETING PERFORMANCE

The most important criterion to measure the overall marketing performance is the share of the market. Market share should not be confused with volume, since volume may go up steadly with a market outstrips that of volume. Similarly, market share by price, besides various other facts. It is not difficult to envisage a situation when both the volume and rupee sales decline while the market share is increasing, just as it could happen that rupee sales increase, volume and market share remaining the same or even declining.

The primary reasons for using market share as the most important criterion of marketing objectives are as follows :

a) It reflects remarkably well the primary purpose of the business which is to create customers, recreate customers, and hold and attract customers.

b) It reflects the end result of all efforts in all marketing functions, both general and specific.

c) It segregates success and failure in sales due to external and mostly uncontrollable factors, including cyclical and seasonal fluctuations in the economy.

d) By ignoring volume of sales and the size of the market as such, and by looking only at the ratio, it measures in a real and meaningful manner, the position of the corporation in its market relative to others competing with it.

The chief criticism of market share as the prime corporate as well as marketing objective is that it is difficult to measure. On a closer scrutiny, however, it will be seen that the criticism is not valid. The concept of market share and its use as an objective are applicable to a competitive situation, not that of monopoly. In a monopoly situation, the extent of customer creation and customer satisfaction should be the criteria of performance evaluation.

There are, of course some situations when the determination of market share as well as the market size and its growth rate, even under competition, becomes extremely difficult. One such situation is that of very high growth, particularly when a product which is absolutely new to the country is introduced. Similarly, problems arise during the period of recession when the market itself is in a state of flux.

Then there is the situation when competition emerges. If it is a formidable competition, the existing suppliers will have to concede a certain part of their respective market shares would become extremely difficult in such a situation and a particular company might be considered to be faring well even when its market share has come down as long as this reduction is lower than the extent of concession that they should have made to competition.

Now, we come to the ways and means of measurement of the size of the market, the rate of growth of the market and the market share. The techniques are in some way different between consumers market and industrial market. The measures in either case will, however, be vitiated to some extent due to the existence of the unorganised sector, the necessary data of which is either not readily available or, if available, not highly reliable. This is particularly true in consumers market,although the problem exists even in industrial market,a part of which is catered by small and medium-sized enterprise. In determining the size of the market in all cases, an adhoc estimate should be made, on the basic of whatever data available, in order to demarcate the market size of the unorganised sector.

In respect of the organised sector, almost fully represented by joint stock companies, the measurement of the size of the market may be made in any or both of the two ways viz., a census of all customers and end-users of product and a study of the published accounts of the leading manufactures of the product. It may be noted that every company has to provide at the end of its balance sheet, by way of additional information, the quantitative data for the balance sheet year and the previous year, in respect of li censed capacity, installed capacity, actual production, sales etc., covering each of its major products. By collecting the data of all the competing companies of a particular product, and analysing the relative published accounts, it would be easy to establish the size of the market as well as the rate of growth of the same.

The estimates made as above should be supplemented by various other data and information collected from the literature and pamphlets published by Government authorities and various private research agencies. We may cite an example here in this regard. The Operations Research Group (O.R.G.) has developed highly sophisticated computerised system of market analysis on a monthly basis for the pharmaceutical industry and a few other consumer goods industries in India covering all major products and showing size of the market as well as market share of each company's products in each market segment.

Another very useful source of information could be the company's own sales staff. Vital and current information about the market can be obtained through a systematic periodic report from the sales staff. These data could be suitably analysed by the Market Research Department and the market size and market share established with a reasonable degree of accuracy.

If the market share is properly planned and the plan translated into reality, under ordinary circumstances, sales, income, expenses, ROI -all will take care of themselves, since all these are intimately interconnected with the market share. However, higher share need not necessarily reflect in higher profits or improved ROI. It is therefore necessary to have a second-level marketing objective should be expressed in terms of profits andmarketing ROI. It might be a corporate policy to achieve growth in market share or retain the existing share, even it this means low or nil profit in the short run. But the long-range corporate plan must show clearly how this will benefit in the long run and what additional future profit can be expected as a result of the current invested in achieving the market share objective.

3. SOME OTHER EVALUATION CRITERIA

In the subsequent Chapters, we will discuss in greater detail the criteria and techniques used for evaluation of major marketing functions, like direct selling promotion, placement and other marketing services. Here we will make only some general observations on two issues viz., the evaluation of marketing orgnisation and marketing information and control systems.

In evaluating the marketing organisation, the first and foremost thing to be seen is how far the organisation is geared to respond adequately and react quickly to the external stimuli. The changes that are continuosly taking place in the market place should be, through some sort of an automatic mechanism, related to the enterprise, which in turn should be able to develop, based on this information, suitable marketing strategies well in time to tackle the effects of changes. To this end, the organisation structure should be designed in such a way that the distance between customers and the top management is reduced to the minimum. The classical pyramid structure is mostly unsuitable in the present context of complex marketing operations. In order to avoid delays in decisions, there should be too many levels or layers and the organisation should be a flat one.

Similarly, there should be highly effective management information and control systems in the marketing area. We will discuss this in detail in the last section, i.e. Marketing Control. However, one very important observation may be made at this stage. Marketing information system should not be entirely statistics-oriented. Adequate importance should be attached to oral reports, personal observations and informal discussions, over and above statistical information. It is to be noted that creative marketing strategies and control actions emanate mostly from such oral reports and discussions. Of course, at the same time, there should be properly structured and regular information systems to suit the diverse needs of different levels and areas of marketing management.

CHAPTER 18

EVALUATION OF SALESMAN'S PERFORMANCE

1. Clearing the Ground; 2. Problems in Salesman's Performance Evaluation; 3. Evaluation Parameters and Criteria; 4. Salesman's Compensation and Incentive Schemes; 5. Concluding Observations.

1. CLEARING THE GROUND

Everyone of us in our own sphere is a salesman. Even as a child is born it has to adopt the selling technique may be by crying, to persuade its mother to give it food. Throughout our life wehave likewise to sell ourselves and therefore adopt selling techniques in different spheres and under different situations.Salesmanship, therefore, is not something uncommon or unusual. However, when we think of a salesman in a commercial orindustrial enterprise, this thought of ours is immediately associated with certain specific qualities, the qualities that go to make a salesman. More important among these are attitude,knowledge (of the product, market and people), habits and selling skills. Selling skills again are broadly determined by one'sability of aggressiveness or submissiveness depending upon the situation.

The purpose of this Chapter is to discuss broadly two important issues, one logically leading to the other,viz., evaluation ofsalesman's performance, and to develop a rational compensation package for the sales force. However, as an integral part ofthese two interrelated aspects, it will be necessary at theoutset to focus on the need for performance evaluation and thevarious problems that may be encountered, especially when aquantitative approach is attempted.

The need and purpose of designing and implementing an adequate method of measuring a salesman's performance in any marketing organisation can hardly be exaggerated. Broadly and essentially, this would help the marketing or sales manager to evaluate hissales force and improve its efficiency. It would help the manager in the task ōf creating, directing and stimulating a sales force to effectively respond to new challenges in the market situation.Besides this, in more specific terms, a good performance evaluation system could be very useful in.

a) Developing salesmanship as an inter-personal influence process.
b) Motivation of salesman and supervisory leadership.
c) Making decisions regarding selection, induction, training, award, promotion, transfer etc.
d) Identifying the need for continuous training and development of sales force.
e) Improving marketing marketing aids, strategies and tools, (e.g working documents, demonstration materials etc.)
f) Determining and restructuring salesman's territories and work assignments.
g) Improving sales planning, e.g. planning call cycles, routes and visits, job preparation, distribution centres etc.
h) Introducing sound compensation and incentive systems suporteby a rational evaluation scheme.

The concept of productivity of salesman is relevent in thiscontext. A salesman is considered to be productive only when the results achieved by him would not only offset the cost of efforts expended on him by the company but also leave some surplus thereafter, which would satisfy the company's predetermined norms of expectation from him. These norms could beexpressed in the form of certain productivity ratios, viz., sales per salesman, gross margin per salesman, contribution per salesman, net markting margin pėr saleman, etc. cost should be looked upon from two angles, viz., direct costs and indirect or associated costs. Direct costs are actually the compensation package including commission, if any, the company has to offer tothe salesman. The indirect or associated costs, mostly of a hidden nature, represent the costs that have to be incurred to equip the salesman to do his job, and to provide the necessary facilities and services to enable him to sell. Examples of such costs are travelling expenses entertainment expenses, promotional literature, samples, other selling aids used by the salesman,etc. It was estimated sometimes ago by a pharmaceutical company that it cost Rs.25,000/- per year to maintain even a newly appointed medical representative, though his basic salary would be only around Rs.500/- per month. This total cost ofRs.25,000/- takes care of both the direct and indirect elements. The question that necessarily follows is what should the company expect in monetary terms from the salesman before taking adecision to appoint him and commit itself to this cost of Rs.25,000/- and more importantly, what sort of checks and balances or evaluation and control systems the company should operate to achieve it.

2. PROBLEMS IN SALESMAN'S PERFORMANCE EVALUATION

Now, we come to certain problems that are inherent in any salesman's performance evaluation system, which might affect anddistort the results of quantitative evaluation. Some of these problems are enumerated below:

a) First is the problem arising out of evaluation based on qualitative judgement vis-a-vis quantitative data. Needless to say, in any qualitative evaluation ere is always the possibility of personal bias and subjective value judgement vitiating the evaluation. Similarly, if evaluation is based entirely on statistical data, the results may not be always correct, particularly because certain important qualities of a salesman can only assessed, not quantitatively established. These are broadly determined by one's ability to impress, influence or persuade people as well as an alternation between aggressiveness and submissiveness depending upon the situation.

b) Next is the problem of comparison between salesman based on the results of evaluation. Such comparison can never be on anapples to apples basis, since a great deal of human element is involved and different salesman have to work under different geographical and environmental pecularities and constraints, in addition to the differences in the features and problems of the different products they handle.

c) Third is the problem of determining standard or benchmarks. Evaluation should always be based on such predetermined standards of performance or norms. If the standards or norms are not realistically set, evaluation will be vitiated.

d) Fourth is the problem involved in determining the periodicity of evaluation. Evaluation based on very short-term results may be correct and it could sometimes be damaging in consequence. Similarly, evaluation based on very long-term results is not desirable because, if the results are not satisfactory, it will have a great impact on the operating results of the company for a longer period. Besides these, promotion, resignation, retirement, retirement, and transfer of salesman create several problems in deciding upon the periodicity of evaluation.

e) Somtimes saleman's perfomance evaluation based on quantitative data may throw up certain discoveries and, intriguing questions. for samples, all salemen in all other regions have surpassed their respective sales quota by 20 percent, but those in Region A have failed to reach 80 percent of the quota; sales volume for the company as a whole has increased by 20 percent but contribution falls short of the target by 5 percent and so on.

f) Next is the problem of comparing variation in sales activity of different groups in the sales force and comparing relevant parts of job for each salesman within each sales group.

g) The last problem in the list refers to the accounting system or the data base records are not adequate to provide precise comparison of salesman or sales-group performance. For example, difficulty will arise in evaluating an improvement in gross sales volume achieved by a group against the profitability of themix of products another group has sold. Similar would be the difficulty in comparing the performance of a man in one sales group with that of a man in another group when the make-up of the job is different in each group.

It can be appreciated that unless the issues stated above are properly analysed throughly, evaluation basd on primary results along might be not only erroneous but also misleading.The above problems also indicate the need for developing a scheme of evaluation with multiple measures criteria to make dissimilar data more comparable.

3. EVALUATION PARAMETERS AND CRITERIA

A brief survey of existing literature shows that efforts have not been wanting in developing suitable evaluation schemes to tackle such a multi-variate situation and provide a handy tool to thesales manager. The techniques developed so far range from the accounting system after introducing some necessary minor modifications.

A systematic and rather practicable approach has been suggested by James C. Cotham III and David Cravens*. According to them copying with dissimilar perfomance data is not a simlpe task, but by using the standard deviation personal selling influences are observed. The standard deviation adjusts seemin fly incomparable performance data so that measurement can be made against the same yardstick, thus allowing sales managers to make direct comparisons of dissimilar sales efforts. The technique, called a Z score or standard Score, can be utilised to place different measures of perfomance on the same scale. The formula for calculating the Z score is:

$$\text{Z Score} = \frac{P—M}{S.\ D}$$

Where P = A raw performance measure for a saleman;
M = Mean (average) raw performance for the sales group;
S.D = Standard deviation of raw performance measure for the sales group.

Consider a sales job with two performance measures, of volume and profitability. Assume that salesman Joseph produces Rs.2,000/- in volume in excess of his work target; the average for his sales group on the volume dimension is Rs.1,000/- and the standard deviation for the group is Rs.2,000/-. Joseph's Z score on the volume dimension is 2,000/- 1,000/- divided by 2,000/- which is equal to 0.50. If this Z score on the profitability dimension is 1.32 computed in the same fashion, then his composite performance (assuming equal importance of both dimensions) is 1.82 (0.50 plus 1.32).

After a performance score has been adjusted to a comman measuring scale using the Z score technique, it can be added to one or more additional standardised measure for a particular salesman to obtain a composite measure of his performance. This method provides a mode of examining salesman's performances of specific dimensions. It also furnishes sales managers a composite measurement of any number of combinations of quantitative and qualitive measures of performance for men in a sale group. Simultaneously,this technique eliminates the need for devising a single overall performance measure, which is generally difficult to deal with. Cotham and Cravens have extended their model to measure inter-group performance as well.

We will now discuss an alternative approach that can be more easily put into practice. The simple model delineated here has already been successfully tried in at least two companies, one engaged in consumer marketing and the other in industrial marketing. While applying this model, however, some suitable modifications would be needed, depending on the situations obtaining and specific purpose or purposes in view. At the outset, it should be stressed that our evaluation scheme like any other requires that the sales manager should,

a) organise sales activities into appropriate sales groups (such as industry, customer or product) and /or sales territories;

b) delineate the salesman's job in each group or territories;

c) set benchmarks or standards of performance for each part of the job; and

d) establish specific methods of evaluation and the criteria and techniques to be adopted to this end.

Our suggested approach provides, in the first place a check list of 20 paramenters or criteria that could be used for the purpose of evaluation of a salesman's performance. While the list is only indicative and by no means exhaustive, it is neither desirable nor practicable for any company to adopt all these criteria -only a few say, four to siw may be chosen. It is also important to assign suitable weightages to the criteria chosen, since all these may not be of equal importance. The criteria in the listare oriented towards an evaluation only of quantitative or financial nature. Now the list with a rational grouping, follows;

A Sales Achieved

1. Market Share

2. Sales Quantity

3. Sales Value

B Activity & Productivity

4. Number of calls

5. Number of orders

6. Value of orders booked

7. Value of orders per call (batting average)

8. Ratio of order value booked to the total value ("Hit Ratio")

C Financial Performance

9. Contribution and C/S Ratio

10. Direct selling expenses ratio

11. Direct Sales margin

D Working Capital Management

12. Average inventory

13. Average outstanding receivables

14. Average working capital locked up

E Vital Performance Index

15. Marketing Return on Investment (ROI)

F Others

16. New Product Performance
17. Number of accounts obtained

18. Number of accounts lost

19. Number of customer complaints

20. Information about competitors, plan and strategies.

In respect of each of the above criteria there should be some predetermined standards or norms expecting for those where such norms cannot be easily established (e.g. item nos. 19 and 20). Also the above criteria have to be adopted for evaluating the results of as a particular period, say a week, a fornight, amonth or a quarter; and this period should be used uniformly, regularly and without discrimination for all salesmen in the organisation.

Based on a hypothetical situation and data and using a few of the criteria chosen from the above list, a comparative evaluation of three salesman has been made and this is shown in Tables I and II.

4. SALESMAN'S COMPENSATION AND INCENTIVE SCHEME

It is almost an accepted practice that a salesman's compensation package should not be a fixed one, regardless of his performance or achievement. Incentive scheme in some form or the other should be initiated to provide his productivity and at the same time enable the organisation to share a part of the results arising outof the organised producting. The reverse is also true. If a salesman does not perform well, his total compensation package should get reduced to reflect, to some extent at least, the effect of his poor performance. The organisation also is not obliged to protect his pay packet as long as he does not pay back to it as per its norms. The provision of such negative incentive would also act as a positive motivation to all salesman. Accordingly, many companies have developed a scheme for compensating their salesman based on two broad elements viz. fixed remuneration (Salary, D.A. etc.) and incentive payments (commission, bonus awards, etc.).

As regards the fixed element of a salesman's compensation packet, it should be ensured that the amount is not too low for him to meet his basic requirements but should not be, at the same time, too high to dissuade him from putting in extra efforts required to earn some incentives, Coming to the second element of the compensation, viz., incentives, it is to be noted that there cannot be any straight-jacket scheme applicable to all companies or even to all salesman of a particular company marketing diverse, products and services. Every company has, therefore, to develop the scheme or schemes which suit it most. In developing a nature of the markets, area potential, seasonality in sales and a financial evaluation of the type of benefit-cost-analysis under various alternative situations that could be envisaged under the scheme.

In developing a suitable incentive scheme for salesman the parameters and criteria of performance evaluation indicated earlier, may be effectively made use of. In that case, it would be advisable to choose a few criteria, say only five or six of them, which are considered to be the most important to the company. In respect of each such criterion chosen, suitable norms or standards have to be established. Further, appropriate weightage should also be given to those criteria, since not all of them could be equally important. Again, in respect of each of the criteria so chosen, a suitable system of reward and penatly should be built into the incentive scheme to take care of the performance, higher or lower than the norm. To elaborate these points let us take the hypothetical illustration, as outlined in Tables I, II and III.

5. CONCLUDING OBSERVATIONS

Any scheme for the evaluation of salesman's performance and the financial incentives following from it, should have adquate provision for the following inter alia:

a) Experimentation with changes through lateral transfers should be encouraged. This is often useful since a particular salesman attached to a particular product or territory for a relatively long period might tend to take things for granted.

b) Personal evaluation through a good judgement system can never be replaced by quantitative analysis, however, detailed and scientific it may be. In fact, a judicious combination of personal evaluation and quantitative evaluation should be the right answer.

c) While evaluation based on short-term results are required to operate the schemes, similar analysis and evaluation for a longer term is also necessary to develop long-range marketing strategies.

d) Each sales manager has to develop his own method of performance evaluation and update it with changes over time.

e) Marketing information system has to be sufficiently geared to meet the requirements for developing and successfully operating the evaluation and compensation scheme. We will discuss this aspect in detail in the last section of the book, viz., Marketing control.

AN ILLUSTRATION OF A MULTIPLE-CRITERIA EVALUATION CUM COMPENSATION SCHEME

TABLE I THE PLAN

PRODUCT ____________

Sl. No.	Evaluation Criteria	Weightage	Norms	Basis of score: maximum 12 for each. (6 points for achieving norm + or - for deviation as shown below
1.	Market share	30	25%	+(-) 1 for increase (decrease) every 5% or part
2.	Value of orders	15	Rs.10 lakhs	-do- by every Rs.1 lakh or part.

3. Batting average	10	Rs.25,000	-do- by every Rs.5,000 or part.	
4. Sales Value	10	Rs.10 lakhs	-do- by every Rs.1 lakh or part.	
5. C/S Ratio	15	40%	-do- by every 5% or part	
6. Marketing ROI	20	20%	-do-	-do-
	100			

TABLE I **EVALUATION**

(Based on the Plan in Table I)

PRODUCT P ZONE Z

MONTH M DATE ____________

Sl. No.	Criteria	Salesman - A Figures *	Score	Weighted Score	Salesman - B Figures *	Score	Weighted Score
1.	Market Share	35%	8	240	20%	5	150
2.	Value of orders	Rs.8 lacs	4	60	Rs.11 lacs	7	105
3.	Batting average	Rs.27,000	7	70	Rs.22,000	5	50
4.	Sales value	Rs.9 lacs	5	50	Rs.10 lacs	6	60
5.	C/S Ratio	35%	5	75	30%	4	60
6.	Marketing	22%	7	140	12%	4	80
				635			505
Weighted Average Score (Max.12)				6.35			5.05

* HYPOTHETICAL

TABLE -III COMPENSATION PLAN

(Minimum Basic Salary Per Month Rs. 2,000 (ASSUMED)

Score	Basic Rs.	Incentive Rs.	Total Earning Rs.
Upto 6	2,000		2,000
6.1 to 6.5	2,000	500	2,500
6.6 to 7.0	2,000	1,000	3,000
7.1 to 7.5	2,000	1,500	3,500

Compensation	Basic Rs.	Incentive Rs.	Total Rs.
A	2,000	500	2,500
B	2,000		2,000

NOTE :

1. The award to a salesman for high scoring say, 10 or above in a month may be, in addition to the usual monetary award, a non-monetary one e.g. declaring him as an outstanding salesman of the month, giving a rolling trophy, awarding a merit certificate etc.

2. Payment of incentives may be effected only after 2/4 weeks from the end of the relative month, since some time is required for generating the basic data and working out the scores as per Table II. The basic pay, however, may be given at the end of each month in the usual manner.

The model illustrated above is based on hypothetical situations and data. But this being a simple one, any marketing organisation may adopt this with suitable modifications as may be required.

CHAPTER 19

EVALUATION OF ADVERTISEMENT

1. Backdrop; 2. Budgeting for Advertisement; 3. Measuring Advertising Effectiveness; 4. The Concept of Return on Promotional Investment (R O P I) ; 5. Concluding Observations.

1. BACKDROP

It is the marketplace where a marketing organisation will either earn its laurels or meet its waterloo. Notwithstanding all the attributes of good marketing e.g. quality, style, price, channels of distribution and the product itself, it may still fail at the marketplace because it has not been to the right people in the right time. Advertisement and persuasive communication to the buyers (sales promotion) are therefore a must for stimulating sales.

The basic difference between advertisement and selling is as follows:

> Advertising — The non-personal representation of goods and services by an identified seller through paid media. It is often described as "as above the line" advertising, and includes television, press, radio and posters.
>
> Selling — The personal representation of goods and services to potential customers as a means of obtaining orders or making sales.

Promotion is a broad term covering both personal and non-personal efforts. Thus, promotional activities include advertising, personal selling, sales promotion and publicity. Publicity is usually regarded as a part of public relation for keeping continuous contact with the press and the people. The main objective is to increase product awareness and develop favourable attitudes among the existing and prospective customers, Building up and projecting product-image as well as company image among the public is the primary purpose of publicity.

Advertising and sales promotion is the most dynamic function under marketing. In order to be successful in this area marketeers have to depend heavily upon various tools, techniques and concept in other disciplines. The purpose of advertising function is to present, promote, and sell goods, systems, services and ideas. Its primary aim is to sell at a profit. However, while advertising is the chief promotional tool for consumer goods, personal selling is a better mode for promotion of industrial goods. Yet industrial advertising has an important part to play by way of building awareness, comprehension and efficient way or reminding. The basic purpose of advertising is supposed to be achieved if it can "bring the buyer to water", but whether he 'drinks' depends upon the price, the packaging and other aspects of marketing process.

Often, a distinction is sought to be made between advertisement and sales promotion. Advertisement is effective product positioning through unique selling point or proposition (USP). It is, therefore, commonly associated with the mass media. The general role of sales promotion is persuasive communication and its basic task comprises stimulating customer buying and distribution effectiveness. However, to a large extent, advertising and sales promotion are complementary. For example, sales promotion is often used as a means of reinforcement for bringing a media campaign closer to the customers.

The term "media" describes the various channels available for carrying the advertising message to the target customers. The media normally used are magazines and periodicals, trade and technical journals, cinema slides, posters, radio, TV and press. Obviously, one medium will not carry out the message to target customers and a combination of media or a media-mix is often indispensable to cover the target group effectively. A

Managerial Accounting technique called Cost Effectiveness Analysis is increasingly being used with advantage in the area of media planning.

2. BUDGETING FOR ADVERTISEMENT

We would first refer to a controversial question, viz , "Does Advertising belongs in the Capital Budget" ? This was raised by Joel Dean in a paper published under the same title. Dean's thesis is as follows: "Most advertising is therefore a problem of investment economics. A new approach is required - economic and financial analysis of futurities. This approach focuses onfuture after tax cash flows and centres around the "profit productivity of capital", However, in known practice, no company puts advertising in its capital budget. Accountants usually treat this as revenue expenditure, as though its benefits areused up immediately. To this, Dean observes, It is just possible that the book-keeper's guide to top management thinking about advertising is wrong.

While not disputing the basic theme of Joel Dean, we would like to make two observations on this issue.

a. Under the accounting convention, there is a type of expenditure called deferred revenue expenditure which relates to expenditures which are strictly of a revenue nature but the benefits from which would accrue over a period long than one year. Advertising expenditure, especially major expenditure which satisfies this criterion of more than one year period benefit, can be treated as deferred revenue expenditure.

b. Although most advertisement expenditure cannot be considered as capital expenditure as such, there is no reason why this, especially major expenditure on specific and extraordinary advertisement campaigns, cannot be treated aninvestment. If so, one can always apply the economic and financial criteria of investment analysis to this, including the discounted cash flow approach.

FORMULATORS MARKETING LTD
(A Case History on Extraordinary Promotional Campaign)

The case deals with a problem regarding the promotional campaign for one of the products of a reputable pharmaceutical company.

As is well-known, pharmaceutical products are mostly subjected to 'ethical promotion', i.e., the medical representatives of the company concerned promote the products through personal contacts with doctors, known as 'doctors detailing'. The special featuresand merits of a product are explained to the medical practitioner and, if convinced of the efficacy of the drug, the doctor prescribes it to his patients. After detailing, the representatives also leave some free samples of the medicine forthe use of the medical practitioner. As per Government regulations, some drugs and medicines are specially earmarked forpromotion through ethical channel alone (i.e. in the above manner, However, there are some medicines for which, because of their nature, ethical promotion is not mandatory. The company has the option of promotion such medicines ether through usual ethical channel or directly to the customers through what is called O.T.C. (Over the Counter) campaign.

Formulators Marketing Ltd. had a product, viz., pediatric multivitamin syrup, which for a long time has been the marketleader. Some time in 1972-73, one of the major competitors to the product undertook a massive O.T.C, campaign. As a result, the company's share of the market started dwindling steadily. From the enviable position as the market leader, it came to a poor second (with only 30 per cent of the market share as against 60per cent enjoyed previously), in course of a year or so !

The Marketing Services Department of the company prepared an elaborate plan for an O.T.C. campaign for the product to meet competition effectively and get back the lost market share and also market leadership. The scheme, which was strongly recommended for approval, included the following:

1. A decision-tree or a schematic diagram to identify all the decision alternatives and their inter-relationship:

2. Sales forecasts under each alternative as per (I) ;

3. Net contribution (after deduction of both variable costs and related fixed expenses) under each alternative;

4. Return on promotional investment (R O P I) under each alternative ;

5. Finding the best pay-off alternative under (3) above.

When the above scheme was submitted to the top management for approval, it was found that the campaign would require over a period of four to five years a substantial financial out-lay, viz., about a crore of Rupees, to meet the costs of the O.T.C. set-up as well as media promotion, viz., radio, T.V., Cinema advertisements and liberal gifts and attractive quantity discounts to wholesalers and retailers, The Scheme, however, showed substantial profits and marketing advantages which would amply justify the massive investment on promotion. The scheme was indeed well-knit, comprehensive and presented in a very attractive manner to the top management. It was subsequently found that the Marketing Services Department had utilised theservices of a leading marketing consultant of the city, while preparing the scheme.

The Management Director, before taking a final decision in the matter, requested the Management Accountant of the Company to go through the scheme and submit his views and recommendation. The Management Accountant found that while the scheme was otherwise quite comprehensive, the following aspects/techniques had not been either considered or made use of:

i. Application of D.C.F. technique to find the N.P.V. or I.R.R. under each alternative, taking a uniform time horizon;

ii. Use of opportunity costing concept e.g., opportunity loss on money proposed to be tied up in promotional efforts;

iii. Risk analysis and sensitivity studies, especially in respects of the various sales forecasts included under the respective alternatives.

The Management Accountant accordingly developed the project further, making use of these refined techniques. Especially on D.C.F. basis,it was found that the project was not viable at allsince the I.R.R. was hardly 10 percent, while the company'spolicy all the time had been to adopt a cut-off rate of 15percent I.R.R. in respect of investment decisions. The primary reason for this low I.R.R. was that, while major investments would be made within the first two years, the major benefits, as per the project analysis, would accrue only in the 4th and 5th year and later. Incidentally, this involved a great deal of risk-especially, there was chance of a better product coming intothe market, perhaps with and O.T.C. campaign, and his analysis,the Management Accountant recommended a 'no-go' decision for the project.

A meeting was arranged by the Managing Director which was attended by the M.D. himself, the Marketing Services Department executives, the outside Consultants and the Management Accountant. The purpose was to consider the various view-points and discuss the viability of the project to help the Company takea right decision in the matter. Some of the more important issues raised at the meeting and contested by the Management Accountant were as follows:

Issue : The competitor being so successful in it O.T.C. campaign, how is it that the scheme is not financially attractive to this Company ?

Answer : What is right for one company may not also be right for another. This applies more to the area of major investment decisions.

Issue : Is not D.C.F. technique applicable only in case of capital expenditure decisions ?

Answer : No! D.C.F. technique is applicable to any investment decision. And investment, for this purpose, should mean any outlay on an extraordinary project or effort, quite distinct fromthe normal day-to-day expenditures connected with ordinary business operations. Substantial expenditure on a new marketing venture should also fall within the purview of investment.

Issue : Should we then allow the product to die a natural death?

Answer : Yes, it may be the desirable action. Particularly when we already have a more improved product, with added features, in our product list, any extraordinary investment on promotion of this product might be a waste, since the total market coming to the Company will mostly be shared between the product and its improved substitute.

The top management took a 'no-go decision' and accordingly the Company did not undertake the proposed O.T.C. campaign.

We may now come to the various bases for and methods of budgeting advertisement expenditures. Arranged in an order of the degree of sophistication (starting with the crudest one), these are :

Availability of Funds — This means what the firm can afford to spend. By emphasising unduly the immediate availability of finance, this method ignores the prospect of

a) future profits and therefore, fails to adopt a cost benefit approach.

b) Percentage of Sales — Estimating advertisement appropriation on the basis of percentage to sales, past or projected, is the simplest and most widely used method. This method is criticised on the issue that when the sales decline, that really is the situation where advertising expenses should be more and when the sales go up, it is a sheer wastage of money to spend more on advertising.

c) Fixed Rupee Unit Expenses — A fixed rupee expenditure on advertisement for each unit to be sold can becriticised, as were fixed percentages, for its ignoring the job that needs to be done.

d) Competitors' parity — while it would be not advisable for a company to base its advertisement budget on what the competitors spend, equally unwise would it be to ignore the competitors' advertisement expenses. Often in the case of competitive environment, special advertisement expenditure is needed to counter competitors' strategies and to protect the market.

e) Break-even approach — This is nothing but the application of the conventional break-even concept in determining the quantum of money to be spent on advertising of a product or group of products. The incremental contribution generated through expected additional sales should be the upper limit of incremental advertisement expenses (for getting the higher sales).

f) Profit Planning — This is perhaps a more scientific approach. This method focuses attention on the job to be done rather than on the resources that should be utilised. Also under this method, emphasis is on the products or product groups on the basis of which total advertisement budgets are built, instead of standing with the decision on the quantum of spending and then distributing the quantum among the products or product groups.

g. Task method — Here also the primary emphasis is on the job that needs to be done. This method is particularly useful while developing a marketing strategy under extraordinary situations like introducing new product, salvaging a product from declining stage in its life cycle, developing strategies for meeting the threats arising out of the emergency of a new and formidable competitor, to counter some special marketing strategies adopted by competitors, and so on. None of the methods suggested above is or should be used by itself. It would be advisable to have a judicious combination of all or some of these while developing the advertisement budget.

3. MEASURING ADVERTISING EFFECTIVENESS

There cannot be just one criterion for measuring the effectiveness of advertising, since advertising has various objectives calling for different techniques for testing the fulfillment of each. Also, because of a large of number of complex and interdependent variables,the results obtained by applying a specific technique to test the fulfillment or otherwise of a specific objective may not be reliable under all situations.

More often than not, sales is considered to be the most obvious test for measuring advertisement effectiveness. But such measurement may be vitiated by various factors, viz.,

i. Advertisement is only a part of the total marketing efforts, the result of which is reflected through sales. It i s therefore not possible to segregate advertisement efforts and its effect on sales.

ii. Similarly, it will be difficult to segregate the effect of advertising on sales, from the various other effects on it due to changing economic conditions including cyclical, seasonal and random fluctuations.

iii. The time-lag between advertisement and buyers' response to it is almost impossible to determine in many cases, leading to the perplexing problem of connecting cause with effect.

iv. Measurement of indirect effect of advertising is almost impossible. One example of such indirect effect would be the word of mouth communication from a buyer to a potential buyer that can influence the buyer decision of the latter.

v. The results of one particular company's advertising campaign might be nullified or enhanced, depending on the extent and skill of the competitors' marketing efforts.

Because of the problems stated above, the sales test cannot be considered an infallible guide to measure advertisement effectiveness. However, some broad ideas can be formed and approximate results arrived at by such a test, especially if some sort of controlled sales test is conducted.

We may give here a summary of several methods developed by HD Wolfe, JK Brown and GC Thompson, and published in their paper, "Measuring Advertising Results".

Measuring Awareness : This is the simplest and most Superficial of the various measurement methods. This is intended to assess knowledge without reference to sources. There are four ways ofdoing this, viz., Yes-No questions, open-end questions, checklist questions, and rating scales.

Measuring Recall : This measurement is intended to assess the knowledge relatable to advertising as a source and measure the extent to which the advertisers' messages are remembered. There are two basic ways for measuring recall, viz., unaided recall and aided recall.

Measuring Attitudes : Attitude tests are useful since they extendthe knowledge of consumer thinking when they are repeated overperiods of time, the various methods used in this respect aredirect questions, rating scales, checklists, semantic differential tests and partially structured interviews.

Psychological Measurement : An attempt is made to explore the preconscious and unconscious levels of mind, leaving out the conscious levels.The techniques used are in depth interviews and projective tests.

Sort-and-Court-Measurement : By requesting prospective buyers to ask for information, samples, and to make visits, the impact of advertisement can be analysed quickly and cheaply. However, only a few readers bother to make enquiries.

Measuring Usage : Usage can be measured by store audits indicating the movement of goods, by consumer interviews etc.

Although the methods given above have been deliberately described in brief, it is evident that these methods cannot be used to develop an acceptable basis of financial measurement of advertising effectiveness.

Clearly, advertising can be effective in various areas like image development, need recognition, customer awareness, etc. But there is no simple procedure to measure whether the money spent on advertisement as well as sales promotion has gone down the drain or given back some return to the company. This one of the reasons why decisions to spend substantial amounts on advertisement are being made on broadly subjective grounds. However, the problem can be tackled by attempting to answer such questions as :

i. Is there a credible relation between the expenditure proposed and the results expected?

ii. Are the results in line with those included in the marketing plans ?

iii. Are the results satisfactory, judged by past experiences?

iv. Are the expected results worth the money proposed to be spent?

4. THE CONCEPT OF RETURN ON PROMOTIONAL INVESTMENT (R O P I)

For all the developments in financial and marketing management sciences, measurement of advertising effectiveness in strict financial terms still remains a million-dollar question. Attempts are being made by various companies, as also by advertising experts, to develop some acceptable method orapproach, albeit a rough and ready one. These methods or approaches are usually not published but adopted for the own useof the companies concerned. As an example of this, we may cite the concept of Return on Promotional Investment (R O P I) developed and used successfully by a pharmaceutical company in India. The concept is very simple. An attempt is made to workout R O P I ratios on sales as also on net contribution,on totalas also on incremental basis. For the purpose of this concept,net contribution is defined as gross margin less directly allocable promotional expenses. We may discuss here the case of this particular company.

MODERN PHARMACEUTICALS LIMITED
(A Case study on Return on Promotional Investment
(R O P I/Analysis)

The Company has five product groups, All expenses in connection with advertisement and promotion are first divided into direct and indirect. All indirect expenses are excluded for the purpose of analysis. Only directly allocable promotional expenses are traced for each of the product groups.

The gross contribution or G.C. (Sales - variable cost of production), of Product Group 1 through Product 5 are 40 per cent, 50 per cent, 30 per cent and 45 per centrespectively. Net contribution is arrived at after deducting allocable promotional expenses from gross contribution in each case.

Exhibit I shows the allocable promotional expenses category-wise for all the Product Groups, for the year 19x7. The total figures for 1986 has also been shown.

Exhibit II shows R O P I analysis for 19 x7.

Exhibit III shows R O P I analysis on the incremental basis 19x7 over 19x6.

A critical examination of the above system is necessary to indicate (a) its uses, (b) its weakness, and (c) measures by which the system can be improved and refined.

EXHIBIT I
ALLOCABLE PROMOTIONAL EXPENSES
(Figures in Rs. Lakhs)

Product Groups	Advertise-ment (Dir-ect)	Samples (Direct)	Detailing Allocated ; Basis Detailing time	Total 19x7	Total 19x6
P.G. 1	4.00	10.00	14.00	28.00	20.00
P.G. 2	6.00	3.00	5.00	14.00	12.00
P.G. 3	3.00	4.00	16.00	23.00	13.00
P.G. 4	5.00	5.00	5.00	15.00	10.00
P.G. 5	7.00	8.00	5.00	20.00	15.00
TOTAL :	25.00	30.00	45.00	100.00	70.00

EXHIBIT II

R O P I ANALYSIS ; 19X7

(Figures in Rs. Lakhs)

G.C.	Product group	Net Sales	Allocable promotional expenses	Net Contribution	On Sales	On net contribution
40%	P.G. 1	350.00	28.00	112.00	12.5	4.0
50%	P.G. 2	225.00	14.00	98.50	16.1	7.0
60%	P.G. 3	150.00	23.00	67.00	5.5	2.9
30%	P.G. 4	175.00	15.00	37.50	11.7	2.5
45%	P.G. 5	100.00	20.00	25.00	5.0	1.3
TOTAL		1000.00	100.00	340.00	10.0	3.5

EXHIBIT III

INCREMENTAL R O P I ANALYSIS : 19X7 OVER 19X6

(Figures in Rs. Lakhs)

Product Group	Incremental sales	Incremental allocable promotional expenses	Incremental net contribution	On sales	On net contribution
P.G. 1	60.00	8.00	16.00	7.5	2.0
P.G. 2	20.00	2.00	8.00	10.0	4.0
P.G. 3	40.00	10.00	14.00	4.08	1.4
P.G. 4	45.00	5.00	8.50	9.08	1.7
P.G. 5	35.00	5.00	10.75	7.0	2.2
TOTAL	200.00	30.00	57.25	6.7	1.9

A. Uses of the Concept :

(i) Following the above approach, we may be able to rank the various Product Groups in terms of their market potential vis-a-vis investments on promotion. For example, Product Group 2 is the best in all respects, showing as it does a very high potential, Product Group 1 & 5 are also good in many respects, while Product Groups 3 and 4 are weak.

(ii) Allocation and budgeting of promotional expenses can be planned in a better manner accordingly. For example, the order of preference for such allocation should be Product Groups 2.5 and 1, respectively.

(iii) Some other areas of control action might also emanate from the R O P I Studies. For example, Product Group 3 shows a very poor R O P I in spite of high gross constitution percentage. This might be due to the fact that the Product Group has reached sales saturation or is perhaps in the declining segment of the life-cycle curve. Unless some strategic decisions are taken in this regard, allocation of additional promotional expenses will be mostly a waste. Product Group 4 also shows poor R O P I in terms of net contribution, although sales wise it is not so bad. Pricing of the products in this Group may be reviewed. If this does not help, perhaps the entire Group may have to be sent for a thorough medical check-up to diagnose the malady and initiate proper treatment.

(iv) The results for ROPI Analyses can be used in sales forecasting as well.

B. Its Weaknesses

(i) Increase in sales need nor necessarily be the result of promotional efforts - other factors contributing to this cannot be segregated under this concept.

(ii) Market sharp aspect is ignored by laying greater emphasis on absolute sales.

(iii) Varying gross contribution percentage between the Product Groups would affect R O P I

(iv) R O P I may be affected by external market conditions as well.

(v) The findings are rather inadequate to indicate control actions required for various Product Groups.

C. Measures for refinement :

(i) An attempt may be made to separate the impact of the respective components of promotional expenses.

(ii) Analysis of the indices for a number of periods with varying quantum or proportion of promotional investment would provide a better guide.

(iii) An attempt may be made to broadly establish the lead-lag relationship between promotional expenditures and returns, and suitably adjust the R O P I indices accordingly.

(iv) Norms in the form of minimum R O P I indices may be established to serve as control tools.

(v) A standard contribution rate application to all Product Group may be accepted as a norm for a more meaningful comparison instead of using actual contribution rates, which would always very between the various Product Groups.

If one is aware of the pitfalls of the approach and if some efforts are made towards its refinement, as suggested above, the R.O.P.I. concept may perhaps be given a fair trial by any marketing organisation to measure advertisement effectiveness. Even though the measures would only be broad and approximate, these could still prove to be very useful guides, particularly when precise measurements are just not available.

5. CONCLUDING OBSERVATIONS

Evaluation of advertising effectiveness is perhaps the most challenging task to any finance or marketing executive. For all the developments in financial and marketing management techniques, this still remains a million-dollar question. Results gained by advertising efforts defy any precise financial measurement. Notwithstanding this, however, some rough and ready approaches and approximate tools and techniques have been developed. One approach is to measure OTS (opportunity to see) and then link up financially. Another approach is DAGMAR which seeksto provide a linkage between "defining advertisement goals" (DAG)and "measuring advertisement results" (MAR). Some other financialtechniques could be made use of with advantage to establish, albeit on a rough basis, whether the promotional rupee is going down the drain or paying back. The guiding principle here should be, "It is better to be vaguely right than precisely wrong".

It is also to be borne in mind that the ultimate test of success in advertising lies in the result, the most important of which is market share. This result again is due to the coordinated and consolidated efforts of all marketing functions, not advertisingalong. Another test of success in advertising the development of brand loyalty of the buyers and, to this end, conversion of brand insistence, through successful promotional efforts. Finally, advertisement efforts would be considered to be highly successful when a corporate image is built up on a sound basis, improved over time and projected into society in proper perspective.

CHAPTER 20
EVALUATION OF DISTRIBUTION

1. Preview: 2. Different Channels of Distribution, 3. Planning the Distribution Channel; 3. Distribution Cost Analysis and Control; 5. Evaluation of Distribution Effectiveness; 6. Strategic Dimension; 7. A few Contentious Issues.

1. PREVIEW

Peter Drucker has described distribution as: "Industry's Dark Continent" implying thereby that the distribution system seldom receives the attention it deserves and there are lots of things yet to be explored in this area. This is intriguing when one considers the fact that distribution happens to be one of the first among the functions initially identified in Marketing. Distribution function includes all the activities in getting a product from the manufacturer to the ultimate consumer. Obviously there is a "gap" between manufacturer and consumer. It is the function of distribution to fill in the gap.

Distribution function broadly covers:
i. Transport services for timely and safe physical movement of goods.
ii. Warehousing facilities that irons out the market fluctuations and make the goods available to the customers when / where needed.
iii. Sorting / grading of goods thus facilitating customers' choice in selection of goods.

This chapter does not go into all these details, neither the logistics of distribution. Our emphasis, as evident from the above topic list, is the "management" of placement or distribution function, with an eye on cost effectiveness.

2. DIFFERENT CHANNELS OF DISTRIBUTION

The different types of distribution channels currently in India are:

Direct Selling/Direct Marketing

Manufacturer to ultimate customer e.g. manufacturer of machinery may directly contact the user firms, a detergent manufacturer employs sales girls to sell on door-to-door basis.

This is increasingly gaining popularity in India. So is also the closely related type called 'Telemarketing'.

Selling through Intermediaries (Middlemen)

A. Consumer Products:

a) Manufacturer - Broker or agent - Wholesaler - Retailer - Consumer (sometimes the product may flow direct from the agent to the retailer)
b) Manufacturer - Own stores - Consumer
c) Manufacturer - Mail order - Consumer. (Traditionally most popular form is VPP system. Of late 'sky shopping' is gaining acceptance)
d) Manufacturer - Wholesaler - Retailer - Consumer
e) Manufacturer - Own branches/Depots - Retailer - Consumer.

B. Industrial Products:

a) Manufacturer - Broker or agent - Distributor/Wholesaler - Industrial, Institutional or Commercial user.
b) Manufacturer. - Distributor/Wholesaler - Industrial, Institutional or Commercial user.
c) Manufacturer - Own branches/Depots - Industrial, Institutional or Commercial user.

A large organisation, or even a medium or small-sized organisation, engaged in whether consumer or industrial marketing, will generally have not just one channel of distribution but a number of channels i.e. a channel-mix.

3. PLANNING THE DISTRIBUTION CHANNEL

Channel Selection:

In channel selection, the overriding consideration will be maximum contribution to the profit performance and easy availability of company's products to ultimate users.

General factors influencing channel selection are summarized as under (following closely Prof. Kotler):

a) Determining channel objectives and constraints - This involves clear determination of target market and finding out the best channel to achieve this target. In other words, by using appropriate channel, the marketer wants to maximize revenue for a given distribution cost.

b) Customer Characteristics - This refers to geographical distribution, frequency of purchase, average quantity of purchase and number of prospective customers.

c) Product Characteristics - Such as perishability, bulk, colour, degree of standardization, unit value etc. These have important bearings in channel selection.

d) Middleman Characteristics - This involves certainty of availability, delivery service, technical support, financial strength, locations, size variation of middlemen and their strengths and weaknesses in selected area.

e) Competitive Characteristics - This involves collection of information regarding channels competitors use, since as a matter of policy, the producers would like to avoid the channels being used by their competitors.

f) Company Characteristics - This may include size, financial position, type of products and past channel experiences, etc. and all these factors have considerable impact on channel selection.

g) Environmental Characteristics - These include economic condition and the existing laws re: appointment of sole-selling agents.

h) Channel Compensation - This is the last but not least important criterion in channel selection. This involves cost-benefit analysis, sometimes intricate in nature, as discussed later in this chapter.

Planning the Channel-mix

Even small and medium sized units engaged in the distribution of consumer and industrial products have appreciated the need and importance of distribution channel-mix. This is because of availability of various alternatives with attendant advantages and disadvantages. The decision of channel selection is also a major determinant of distribution cost. The decision of channel-mix formulation is generally guided by the following broad factors :

a) Promptness and regularity in making the products available to the ultimate users
b) Cost of alternative modes of distribution
c) Extent of possible market segmentation and product differentiation and
d) Changes needed in the organisation e.g. setting up another Branch/Sales Depot.

The choice out of a few alternative distribution channels will involve a proper comparative assessment of different levels of capital investment, advertising and sales promotional expenses, working capital for inventory and forecast of sales and expenses - all over a future time-scale. After all in channel selection the overriding consideration should be maximum contribution to the profit performance and easy availability of company's products to ultimate users. However, only a few highly professionalised and well-managed marketing organisations in India have adopted till date sophisticated management tools and techniques in this important area i.e. planning the channel mix.

Illustration

Section of Distribution Channel

Alternatives

(Figures in Rs. Lakhs)

	I			II			III		
Year	**Sales**	**Expen-ses**	**Net Margin**	**Sales**	**Expen-ses**	**Net Margin**	**Sales**	**Expen-ses**	**Net Margil**
1	10	8	2	8	7	1	14	12	2
2	12	11	1	10	8	2	16	13	3
3	15	12	3	11	10	1	18	15	3
4	18	14	4	16	11	5	21	17	4

Note:

1) Sales expenses are estimated over the probable "Life" of the channels.
2) Expenses include deferred revenue items and variable expenses viz. discount, commission and finance charges.

Analysis and Decision-Criterion:

Since the Net Margin is spread over future periods, all the estimated net margins are to be brought down to their present values by using discount factors (i.e. using Discounted Cash Flow method). Then these have to be related to the present values of respective capital investments, also to be separately estimated for each alternative channel. The channel showing the maximum ratio or percentage of net margin at present value to capital investment should be selected.

PLACEMENT PRIVATE LTD

(A Case Study on Changeover in Distribution System)

The Company operates its own delivery vans to distribute its products in the metropolitan city where the factory is located. It is considering a changeover to agents who will collect their goods from the factory warehouse and deliver to the retailer. They will be paid a commission of 5 per cent from which they will pass on 1 per cent to the dealers. The Company will raise invoices on the agents on 30 days credit. Following are the other relevant data:

Particulars	Existing System	Proposed System
No of vans	5	
Original cost of the vans	Rs. 2,00,000	
Depreciation rate	20% of original value	
Drivers/delivery workers (number)	40	
Salaries/wages per month	Rs 25,000	
Maintenance and running expenses per van per month	Rs. 2,000	
Other overheads per month	Rs. 5,000	
Approx. Sales value of deliveries per month	Rs. 20,00,000	
Dealer's/agents commission	2%	5%
Terms	Cash	30 days' Credit
Sales may fluctuate	+/- 20%	

To arrive at the right choice, under the above situation, from the financial point of view the following aspects have to be considered:

(i) Total cost of operation per month under the existing system and the proposed system and in each case, under three alternative sales forecasts, viz, Rs. 20 Lakhs, Rs. 24 Lakhs and Rs 16 Lakhs, should be worked out.

(ii) For the purpose of (i) above, depreciation is to be

considered as an element of cost in the existing system Similarly, interest (at the marginal rate at which the Company will have to borrow money) on the working capital lock-up, because of the 30 day's credit to be allowed will have to be considered as a cost, under the proposed system

(iii) In case a changeover is to be made, the sunk cost, viz., unabsorbed depreciation on the delivery vans, and also the time required to recover the sunk cost after the change-over are to be worked out and considered while taking the decision.

Quite often a company would like to open its own branches or sales depots and change over from selling through distributors to selling through its own distribution set-up. While a similar financial evaluation on the lines suggested above would also be necessary in such a case, there may be a number of marketing and strategic considerations affecting such changeover. Here is an interesting real life case history highlighting the interaction between financial considerations and strategic factors in the decision making process and implementation of a decision.

BOMBAY PHARMACEUTICALS LIMITED

(A Case History on Opening a Sales-Depot)

The Company was selling its products in a particular semi-urban area through a distributor against an overriding commission of 10 per cent on sales. The annual set-up cost of a sales-depot in that area was estimated to be Rs.2 lakhs. If the distributor were to be eliminated there would also be an additional variable cost of 6 per cent on sales (due to additional transport charges, interest on working capital lock-up and other inventory carrying cost.)

Based on these data the management accountant of the company made a break-even study and suggested to the management that the break-even sales to justify a depot in the area was Rs. 50 lakhs

This was arrived at as follows:

$$\text{B.E. Sales value} = \frac{\text{Incremental Fixed Cost}}{\text{Incremental C/S Ratio}} = \frac{\text{Rs. 2 Lakhs}}{(10\text{-}6)\ \%}$$

$$= \frac{\text{Rs.2 Lakhs}}{4\%} = \text{Rs 50 Lakh}$$

To assist the management in similar decisions the management accountant also included in his report a simple table as follows

Rate of Overriding commission	Break-even sales value (Rs. Lakhs)
12%	33.33
11%	40.00
10%	50.00
9%	66.67
8%	100.00
7%	200.00

The above workings were based on the facts that.

1. the annual fixed set-up cost of a sales depot in any semi-urban area in India would be around the same Rs. 2 Lakhs,

2. the variable cost of 6 per cent would also remain unchanged and

3. the overriding commission rates varied from place to place, ranging from 8 per cent to 12 per cent.

On the basis of this analysis the top management came to the following conclusions:

(i) Based on the present turnover rate and immediate future growth in turnover, the company should open new sales depots in four places in India and thereby eliminate distributorship in those areas.

(ii) The decision to open a depot in one place which had been taken recently was wrong, since the turnover of that area was below the break even sales value to justify the setting up of a depot.

Accordingly, it was proposed by the top management to close down the depot where it was not justified and open four new depots on the basis of financial justification.

When the matter was referred to the marketing department, they raised a number of marketing and strategic factors, which would go against the proposed decisions and their implementation. Some of these were:

(i) Most of the distributors had been with the Company for a long period, say about 15 to 20 years, and they considered themselves very much a part of the Company and not just outside distributors. And the Company also had developed a good rapport with them. It would be unfair and unjust to sack them overnight on financial grounds alone.

(ii) The distributor in one area in which the decision was taken to open a depot was highly connected with hospitals and government authorities. The Company was, therefore, already on the verge of losing a big chunk of hospital business in that area.

(iii) Similar marketing and strategic consideration, as in (ii), also applied to other areas, chosen for the opening of new depots.

(iv) Simultaneous operation through depots as also distributors, suggested by some for a few areas, was neither financially justifiable nor practicable from the marketing angle.

Based on these considerations, the company took a decision: "Let us wait and watch. Let us lie low in the matter... Let us not rush and rock the boat". Apparently it was no decision - it was a commitment to a policy of drift. But this nonetheless illustrates how overriding marketing considerations might take precedence over the result of an impeccable financial analysis.

Channel compensation

Widely varying practices are prevalent in India in this aspect. The variations are primarily because of the industry nature, degree of dependence of the manufacturers on the intermediaries and the number of intermediaries involved. A broad picture covering a random assortment of different industry-types, based not on any specific research work but on our broad understanding of the market situations, may be presented here:

Range of channel compensation: 5% to 60% or 70%

Industry-type	Channel Compensation Rates [on Sale Value]
Engineering—Heavy Machinery & Equipment	5% - 10%
Light Engineering	10% - 20%
Industrial Consumables	10% - 30%
Consumer Durable (white goods)	15% - 30%
Drugs & Pharmaceuticals	20% - 30%
Consumer Soft / FHCG	40% - 60%
Publications (books etc)	45% - 50%
Textiles—Man-made Fabrics	45% 60%

Besides the predetermined rates of channel compensation as above, in order to motivate the dealers, manufacturers offer from time to time additional incentives which take different forms namely: quantity discount, incentive for prompt payment, bonus offer, best dealer/stockist award, special reward for fulfilling sales quota, which could vary from a cell-phone to an automobile or a free foreign trip.

Major Transportation Modes

The different transportation modes and the extent of their use in India currently may be summarised below:

Rail — The Railway system in India is very well developed. A large chunk of goods of all types are transported through the railways in India.

Road — Next to the railways are the roadways which are also used very extensively in India, for long distance transportation, transportation to places not having convenient rail heads and particularly for shorter distance and intra-city transportation of goods.

Water — Despite tremendous existing potential, inland water transport system is still in a nascent stage in India. Transportation of goods through water routes is hardly to be seen, excepting around the coastline areas, for connecting one port with another.

Air — Due to prohibitive freight charges, air transport is not popular in India. Airshipment of goods takes place only in cases of products having low weight, smaller dimension but very high value, emergency requirements and meeting deadlines when due to natural calamities or other reasons rail and road transport are not available or convenient.

4. DISTRIBUTION COST ANALYSIS AND CONTROL

The major elements of distribution cost, apart from channel compensation, are transportation, warehousing including storage insurance etc., material handling, credit & collection, finance & general administration (including invoicing, data processing, distribution personnel's compensation etc.) and interest on inventory carried at different selling points. The last element i.e. interest is quite sizable in India compared to the developed countries.

Distribution cost analysis is a fast growing and perhaps the most rewarding area in marketing cost analysis and control. Various methods and techniques have been developed in this area, ranging from the pure book-keeping approach of analysing the different heads of expenses, to the more sophisticated Operations Research (OR) models. Adoption of any tool or approach would depend upon the situation obtaining. However, attempts should always be made first to attack the obvious and achieve tangible cost savings. More sophisticated approaches may be adopted only after that.

Application of flexible budgeting concept for the purpose of distribution cost analysis has been found to be useful in practice. Distribution costs, for this purpose, may be classified as fixed (e.g salaries and benefits of distribution staff, warehouse rental and general charges etc.), semi-variable (e.g. traveling of staff, stationery, telephone charges, etc.) and variable (e.g. packaging, insurance, transportation, interest on inventories at selling points etc.). Budgets and norms should be established for each such major item of expense, under each category, and actual figures watched regularly, say on a monthly basis, to locate weak areas and initiate control actions. Potential use of computers could be very high in these areas.

A marketing organisation should be always aware of and willing to introduce technological improvements as well as the modern management tools that would contribute towards increase in efficiency at lower cost. Some of these are: material handling equipment in warehouses, mechanised invoicing system, inventory control methods and use of computers, including networking facilities, for close monitoring of inventory movements as well as for greater efficiency and speed in managing distribution function as a whole.

The overall distribution systems should be subjected to a thorough and objective review at regular periodic intervals. This review may throw up areas of inefficiencies as well as new ideas to reduce distribution cost in relation to volume, if not in absolute terms. Any significant change in the mode of distribution should be subjected to a detailed financial evaluation by cost benefit analysis, before any decision is taken in this regard. It has been seen that such evaluation would alter the distribution cost structure itself and in this case, the budgets and norms of various expenses would have to be reset.

Too much of mechanization or automation (e.g. like automated warehouse in Japan) may not be desirable in an overpopulated country like India, already reeling under the pressure of unemployment, even of the educated class of people.

5. EVALUATION OF DISTRIBUTION EFFECTIVENESS

Distribution costs are bound to go up not only with increase in the volume of sales but also with the efforts towards achieving higher market share through better coverage and penetration into new markets. The problem is not, therefore, to completely eliminate distribution costs, which is just not possible. The problem lies actually in eliminating inefficiencies and consequently preventing cost escalation on this score. Any measure of evaluation of distribution effectiveness should therefore be directed towards two things, viz., (a) how far is the distribution channels-mix adequate to enable the company to improve upon its market share and (b) whether the total cost of distribution is kept to the minimum. As regards the second aspect, viz., minimizing the cost of distribution, approaches discussed above would be useful to marketers. Further, an inter-firm comparison between competing firms could be made, if possible, to ensure how far this objective of minimizing distribution cost is being fulfilled in reality. This comparison should be made regularly on a periodic basis.

Dr. Donald R. G Cowan in his paper "Eleven Approaches to the problem of Distribution Costs" has presented. in a systematic and comprehensive manner, eleven tests for assessing distribution efficiency. These are briefly stated here:

1. **The Product Approach :** It is of prime importance to

ensure that the right product is being offered for sale. This is because the volume of sales and earnings depend upon a firm's distribution expenses besides salesmen's efficiency.

2 **The Product - Line Approach :** The distribution of a product-line rather than of a single product will frequently reduce marketing costs, when certain conditions are met. Briefly, products suitable for a line should be sold in the same market, and should be distributed through the same channels without involving different methods and problems.

3. **The Channels Approach :** Many alternative marketing channels are available, and the choice made will greatly affect distribution costs and efficiency. Moreover, as a firm's output grows, it is necessary to reconsider what channels can provide more efficient distribution and to revamp the structure of discounts and commissions.

4. **The Engineering Approach** : Distribution involves many physical activities in the moving and storing of goods to make them available at proper places and in proper quantities to cater to the ultimate buyers. This involves both transportation and space utilization between and within various establishments.

5. **The Accounting Approach :** The accounting approach is more familiar to sales executives, but has not been exploited fully in distribution. Typically, it involves the classification of a firm's distribution expenses, volume and earning's by salesman's territories, by a general line and special salesman, by departments and products, by activities performed, and the like. The resulting comparisons of expenses, volume and earnings are helpful in indicating the comparative profitability of the classified segment of distribution. Some firms have profit and loss statements for branches, individual salesmen, product

departments, and sales departments, and ask each responsible person to operate his unit as profitably as possible.

6. **The Operations Research Approach :** The operations research approach, recent and closely allied to engineering, offers many possibilities of alternatives in minimizing efforts and costs in accomplishing a given end.

7. **The Economic Approach :** The economic approach takes up where accounting leaves off. It is concerned with changing marketing conditions, sales potential of markets, areas and the application of selling, advertising and other such efforts under conditions of diminishing returns to the point of marginal balance between expenditure and income and further to the point of maximum total profit or minimum loss.

8. **The Personnel Approach :** The personnel approach to distribution efficiency is somewhat different from those already described. In the long run, the ability of its distribution employees is a powerful influence in aspects of distribution. Especially the customer selling function cannot be reduced to the impersonal and informal activities of a machine. Hence, the selection, training and compensation of distribution personnel, and the fitness of the employees to the task are important long term factors influencing distribution costs. Yet the opportunities for improvement are far from exhausted in a multitude of companies.

9. **The Organisational Approach** : The organizational approach is much wider than the personnel approach. To bring about a dynamic organisation there must be a clear perception and definition of the tasks to be performed at each level of management, both line and staff. Smooth working relationships and communication

between these tasks must be worked out, authority commensurate with responsibility must be delegated, procedures and inducements for stimulating maximum efforts must be applied and regular evaluation of performance must be undertaken at all levels to eliminate ineffective personnel or unprofitable activities.

10. **The Standardization Approach** : Distribution comprises a multitude of activities in which the human element looms large and in which, therefore, there is much variation in performance. The difficulties of bringing about standardization in case of human activities constitute the basic reason for lack of mechanization in many phases of distribution, especially in buying and selling. Nevertheless, there are important opportunities for increasing efficiency through standardization.

11. **The Management Approach** : The management approach includes and employs all the other approaches just outlined, but there is always that something extra, a priceless ingredient, which makes its contribution distinctive. It is not only management's comprehension of the various avenues of efficient and economical distribution, but also of new methods under conditions of continual changes in distribution. It must consider which alternative combinations of machines, personnel efforts, advertising channels, products, and the like, will yield the highest distributive return in the future.

6. STRATEGIC DIMENSION

Distribution could be a very effective tool of marketing strategy. In fact one of the primary reasons underlying the runaway success of consumer MNC's in India like Hindusthan Lever Ltd.(HLL), ITC, P & G as well as some relatively new Indian companies like Nirma is using distribution as a strategic weapon. Success in launching new products in the consumer soft category depends to a very great extent on having or creating an effective distribution set up. The industries in India are becoming more and more aware of the potential of strategic distribution, as evident from a few distribution strategy examples cited here :

i) Single versus multiple outlets - A premium brand gents' apparels manufacturer continues to have only one outlet (in Mumbai only) when several other competitors in the same market segment have been opting for multiple outlets in all major cities in India. The former is competing effectively with others, banking entirely on brand equity.

ii) Cutting down distribution channels - Several large textile mills (e.g. Reliance, Bombay Dyeing etc) have set up exclusive retail shops for their products in metro cities and even in mini-metros.

iii) Launching new products/brands - Developing an efficient distribution network for current products/brands would immensely facilitate new additions or product range extension, ensuring at the same time high cost- effectiveness too, for both old and add-on products / brands.

iv) Deeper penetration strategy - An example is greater emphasis on rural marketing by several large companies in order to take advantage of increasing purchasing power of the rural people, particularly big agriculturists, thanks to the fiscal and other pro-farmers policy of the Government of India.

v) Strategic Industrial Marketing Synergy - A private sector industrial marketing organisation succeeded in obtaining sole selling concessionaire for construction equipment manufactured by a leading public sector enterprise. The commission was very low, promotional expenses were shared equally by the two companies and the private sector organisation made use of their all India sales and service network to effectively distribute the product all over the country. The net margin earned by the private sector company by distributing this product was very low, rather negative.

But this helped the company substantially in getting greater mileage in sales of several other industrial products, mainly of their own manufacture including some important components and spare parts of the public sector company's product. This is an example of what we may call strategic industrial marketing synergy.

7. A FEW CONTENTIOUS ISSUES

What with some legal provisions or Government regulations and what with ethically questionable practices of the intermediaries, even manufacturers, often times some contentious issues arise like:

i) Exclusive dealership - This is prohibited under the MRTP Act, but manufacturers tend to bypass the relevant provision by camouflaging dealers as their respective own repair workshops (example, market leader in moulded luggage in India.)

ii) Conflict of interest - This may arise when the same dealer is handling two or more competing brands (examples, sale of TV sets, refrigerators, washing machines etc. in India). This is dealt with generally through a warfare of sorts in dealership commission and incentives. Since dealers in India are almost exclusively guided by profit motive, a dealer will provide the so-called guidance to an uninformed buyer, which is tantamount to misguiding, for selling a particular brand that gives the dealer himself highest compensation, irrespective of the quality or performance of the brand vis-a-vis that of other brands (example again, sale of white goods mentioned above)

iii) Provision re : MRP (Maximum Retail Price) - Although the spirit behind this provision is to ensure uniform Retail Price Maintenance (RPM) for mass consumption items all over the country, this is subverted by most of the retailers taking advantage of a loophole called 'local taxes extra'. Regulatory measures to tackle this issue have failed so far, due to varying indirect tax rates from one state to another.

iv) Terms of payments - Ensuring adherence to terms of payments is an endemic problem in dealing with the intermediaries in India. This is faced almost by all types of organisations, barring only mighty MNC's like HLL, ITC etc., who are privileged to enjoy a tremendous bargaining power over the dealers and stockists.

v) Unethical practices - Blatant unethicality on the part the dealers and stockists takes different forms e.g. creating artificial shortage of mass consumption items by hoarding, charging high prices, selling at normal prices inferior quality products (say, date-expired pharma and food products and 'seconds' or 'thirds' instead of good quality products), inadequate and/or ineffective after sales services, etc. Even though stringent laws are there to deal with such issues, at times the situation tends to become uncontrollable and regulatory mechanism appear to be ineffective. The personnel engaged in distribution function of different marketing organisations have a role to play in order to reduce the magnitude and intensity of such activities through close monitoring, particularly with respect to delinquent distributors.

CHAPTER 21

EVALUATION OF MARKETING RESEARCH

1. Market Research-Meaning and Significance; 2. Steps and Methodology in Market Reasearch; 3. Organising Market Research; 4. Cost Benefit Evaluation of Market Research; 5. Concluding Remarks.

1. MARKET RESEARCH-MEANING AND SIGNIFICANCE

Market research is defined by the American Marketing Association (AMA) as "the systematic gathering, recording and analyzing of data about problem relating to marketing of goods and services". Prof. Kolter has defined market research as "Systematic problem analysis , model building and fact finding for the purpose of improved decision making and control in the marketing of goods and services".

In the definition given by AMA two important functions viz. anlysis of the problem and improved decision-making and control (specially applicable to complicated marketing situations) are missing and in Prof. Kolter's definition this deficiency has been made up.

Market research is a broad term which includes all research activities related to all marketing problems. Apart from traditional function of fact finding relating to the marketing, its functions are given below:

1. Long and short-range sales forecasting,
2. Customers buying behaviour,
3. Competitors activities research,
4. Product testing and new product acceptance,
5. Packaging performance analysis,
6. Brand image evaluation,
7. Sales and distribution channel analysis,
8. Advertising and promotional effectiveness studies.

The above list is not exhaustive as market research is a relatively new but fastest growing field in Marketing. Consequently newer tools are still being developed.

A distinction is sometimes drawn between Market Research and Marketing Research. The former relates to the market profile,market conditions, demand gap-present and projected (for new projects) and all that, while the latter i.e. Marketing Research relates to the specific aspects of the Marketing-Mix management of a particular marketing organisation. For the purpose our discussions in this chapter, however, we shall treat these expressions, Market Research and Marketing Research as synonymous.

Generating information through market research can be compared to the functioning of antenna used in a telecommunication system, as mentioned earlier also (in Chapter 1). Market research collects the information that are already there on the market but of which we are not aware unless and until we make systematic use of certain tools and techniques.

Information is an essential element in planning and control of any operation. Information emanating from environment viz.customers reaction to our products, competitors strategy about market development, new products pricing strategy, etc. Effects the company's opportunities and performances. The availability of such information is ensured through market intelligence in a broad sense. The information which are difficult to obtain viz. marketing strategy of the competitors are made available through industrial espionage, a specialised facet of marketing intelligence function. Uses of intelligence reports are common in every crucial field like Govt. administration during both peace-time and war, matrimonial matters, games (e.g. during the World Cup Soccer tournament), VVIP security and of course in marketing.

2. STEPS AND METHODOLOGY IN MARKETING RESEARCH

Professional market researchers usually adopt the following sequential steps :

a) Setting the purpose or objective of the proposed market research and thence defining the problem — Unless the problem is clearly defined it is rather difficult for the market researchers to design effective research plan.

b) Determining the information needed and the source from which it could be collected i.e data collection— Data may be classified into primary and secondary data. The accepted ways of generating primary data are obsevation, experimentation and interviewing. Data that are already recorded and available are called secondary data e.g. various publications or research papers relevant to the problem including government publication. The secondary data should be critically tested as regards relevancy, accuracy and a completness for the purpose under reference. Market researchers should have a basic knowledge of the broad characteristics and limitations of the different ways of gathering data. All data collected through both primary and secondary sources should satisfy some basic conditions viz. impartiality or objectivity, validity, reliability and homegeneity.

c) Obtaining the relevant facts — This is usually done through a combination of several methods viz. observation, experimental and survery methods - both field survey and literature survey.

d) Analysis and interpreting the facts with refernce to the problem — Analyses of data require the use of several tools and techniques, some quantitative and some semi-quantitative, depending on the nature and volume of data.

Percentages and simple statistical tools like mean, median, standard deviation, variance, etc are commonly used. Sometimes involved statistical analysis may be necessary, like correlation, regression, paired comparison, rank correlation, chi-square tests,etc.

e) Prepgring the research reports incorporating the findings and presenting the inferences or recommendations — These have to be with specific reference to the purpose or objective spelt out beforehand. It needs also to be vital inputs for marketing planning and formulation of marketing strategies.

Marketing research,however efficiently carried out, can seldom provide answers to all marketing problems and can be no substitute to executive judgement in the decision making process. Marketing research findings may suffer from limitations mainly due to three factors :

i) Market — e.g. market sometimes being in a state of flux, market size growing or contracting at a very high rate.

ii) Technique — e.g. selection of sample, quality of questionnaires, choice of techniques, quality of interviewing, statistical errors in analysis of data, etc.

iii) Decision making — e.g. decision based on erroneous interpretation of the market research data.

3. ORGANISING MARKET RESEARCH

There is a saying about market research and market survey - "If the market research is very good it is just something ; if it is average, or even good, it is bad". This relates to the market research efforts as well as the results. There is much truth in the saying. It is therefore imperative that market research should be a well-organised activity. Unfortunately, most marketing organisations in India face a paradoxical situation in this regard.

If a full-fledged market research department is set up, with say management graduates majoring in marketing, the results of the market research would academically be very sound but mostly divorced from reality, since these people would not have first-hand knowledge of the market. If, on the other hand, the sales staff are entrusted with market research, they would not be able to devote much time and attention to do justice to this additional responsibility. Also their findings would not be cross-checked and intergrated with those of desk researches with the help of papers, pamphlets and publications which are very much a part of marketing research efforts.

Perhaps a judicious blend of external and internal expertise could provide the right answer, but such a modality is often found to be difficult to work out. One practical suggestion of ours is to create a small but effective marketing research cell should be entrusted with the on-going marketing research activities including necessary field work with respect to the existing business lines as well as range of products and any logical extension of the same.

We may sound a note of caution here : personnel in the market research cell should not only interact regularly with the sales personnel but should pay frequent fields visits in order to obtain a better feel of the market.

As regards market research for totally new projects, making use of external marketing consultants should be more appropriate. Here again there is a note of caution : any market research, to be effective, should endeavour consciously and systematically to establish the size of the market as well as the expected market share under varying levels of prices, keeping in mind that overheads, and even direct costs, will have increased, sometimes out of proportion by the time a product is ready for competitive marketing.

4. COST BENEFIT EVALUATION OF MARKET RESEARCH

Investment in marketing research is expected to produce additional revenues or reduce costs in much the same way as a new piece of equipment. Yet there are no widely accepted procedures for evaluating the returns, nor is there any standard set of criteria for evaluating the economic feasibility of proposed projects. R L Day in his paper, "Optimising Marketing Research through Cost Benefit Analysis" has outlined the main features of such analysis as follows :

i. Review objectives that are being sought.

ii. Establish criteria for use in evaluating the alternatives.

iii. Identify relevant alternatives with particular reference to assessment of the economic costs and benefits or gains associated with it.

iv. Recognise time pattern of benefits and costs.

v. Recognise uncertainty. Decide alternate strategy and outcomes. Apply probability criteria and come to the decision of better strategy.

vi. Develop a model to suit the analysis with the built-in probabilities to take care of uncertainities.

Costs of market research information are acquisition costs and operating costs, while its value is utility in terms of profitability, market share, etc.

We may now come to the basis of establishing the budget for market research. Before we go to indicate what it should be, let us first talk about what it is . The size of the budget is usually based on one or more of the following factors :

i) The "selling ability" of the marketing research head, instead of the value of the services rendered to the management ;

ii) Amount needed to meet or beat the typical level of expenditure incurred by competitors ;

iii) The amount that the company can afford to spend - obviously the budget gets expanded in good times and contracted when business conditions are tight; and

iv) Budgeting based on some fixed percentage of the total marketing cost budget, market research being largely a matter of habit.

It will be appreciated that none of these bases is acceptable. The literature on market and marketing research these days increasingly emphasise the fact that such research should be regarded as an investment and also that"research is used most efficiently if its budget is regarded as an investment rather than an expense".

In this article, "The Current Marketing Question", Twedt reported that a return on investment approach to past marketing research expenditures had been useful in appraising the value of marketing research at the Oscar Mayer Company. The formula used by Twedt is ;

$$\frac{\text{"Worth" or Value of Finding X Proportion of Crucial Cases}}{\text{Annual Marketing Research Budget}} = \text{Return on Investment}$$

Twedt reported that the return in investment computed in this way for his company was 351 per cent in the previous year. According to Twedt, this method "has turned out to be a matter of good personnel relations within the company, since it provides a reason for a mutually helpful annual review of the dollar value of the information supplied by the marketing research department". Although, according to us , Twedt's is a good approach to evaluate expenditure in market research on a historical basis, one limitation of his formula is that it does not provide a basis for setting a budget for a future period in which the anticipated circumstances may be quite different from those of the immediate past period.

From the financial angle, the most obvious question that arises is, what should marketing, of planning cost ? W.Dickerson Hogue in his article, "What should Marketing Planning Cost" has given a simple formula which is based on the assumption that any planning effort would require certain amounts and certain types of additional information and, consequently, there should be a cost benefit equation to examine this. The formula is :

$$C \text{ should be } \leq W_1 - W$$

$$\text{where , } W = P \times V - (P_1 \times F)$$

Definition of formula terms used :

C = the cost, after taxes, of obtaining information. Cost includes not only expenditure of money, but also opportunity cost, i.e. profits foregone either because manpower was used on this project rather than on other profitable projects or because the delay incurred by additional work on this project meant giving competitors an increased share of the future market.

"Should be $\leq$" = "should be limited by"or "should be less than or equal to".

W (the expected present value of a plan before additional information is collected) = (P X V) -(P_1 X F), where

P = the weighted average of a range of subjectively determined probabilities of "success"of a particular plan based on all the information now available.

V = the weighted average of a range of subjectively determined values of "success" of a particular plan based on all the information now available. The values are calculated as expected future earnings, after taxes, discounted to their present values.

P_1= 1.0 minus P

F = the weighted average of a range of subjectively determined cost (expected future losses, after taxes, discounted to their present values) of failure of a particular plan based on all information now available.

W_1 (the expected present value of the plan after alteration based on the additional information collected) is calculated in the same manner as W. The values of one or more of P, V, P_1 and F are changed because of alterations made in the previous plan.

This tool, according to Hogue, is used consciously or unconsciously by managers. It is obvious that the cost of additional information should not exceed the additional value of a plan based on the additional as well as earlier information. And this is exactly what the formula states. This can give some useful guidance in developing a cost benefit approach for marketing planning, both short term and long term.

5. CONCLUDING REMARKS

Market research is essesntially a staff function. Consequently, it is very difficult to establish accountability in this area and provide a basis for strict financial evaluation of results vis-a-vis costs. The problem is further aggravated by the fact that substantial part of expenses are "spending on the future" or investments.

There is a general tendency in companies which earn enough profits, to incur or commit substantial expenses in such area. Such expenses are incurred as a policy cost or as a status symbol. At the same time it is observed, executives develop a tendency to postpone any spending on the future. This is true of organisations which evaluate, reward and promote their executives on the basis of short-term results, mainly profits alone. It has also been seen that when, durng a not-so-good time, some sort of economy drive is actively thought of by an organisation, the axe falls heavily on all sorts of "un-productive" expenditure, which includes marketing research.

A balance has, therefore to be struck between what is necessary and what is unnecessary while arriving at a budget allocation in respect of all staff marketing functions in general and marketing research in particular.

Market research tools and techniques are increasingly being used in areas from or remotely related to marketing function, e.g. opinion polls before election, assessing reasonability of a political decision, assessing corporate or personal image, preparing intelligence reports and so on.

CHAPTER 22

MARKETING AUDIT

1. Preview. 2. Meaning and Significance of Marketing Audit. 3. Methodology . 4. Inferences and Recommendations. 5. Concluding Observations.

1. PREVIEW

In the foregoing chapter of this book conscious attempts have been made to highlight the salient features of marketing management process vis-a-vis the various factors and forces that are continuously at play in the market place. It has been stressed that the essence of marketing lies in "market orientation" as distinct from "product orientation", or any othher orientation. Market-oriented culture is a necessity in today's increasingly competitive world. In market-oriented environment a company gears the efforts needed to produce what the market demands. Market leadership is established by creating customer satisfaction through product innovation and customer service.

Marketing process is an amalgam of a host of variables, e.g.objectives, strategies, tactics,etc. and these are subject to rapid obsolescence in the fast changing marketing environment. Marketing executives being engaged in continuous analysis, planning and control can hardly find time to sit back and examine what they have been doing and how they could improve their effectiveness in the context of the only unchanging thing that is "change".

Marketing audit is an effective tools for assessing critically the need for such change and identifying key areas for enhancing the sectoral as well as overall marketing effectiveness.

2. MEANING AND SIGNIFICANCE OF MARKETING AUDIT

Marketing Audit is a sub-system or component part of Management Audit. While Management Audit has a very broad and all pervasive scope, Marketing Audit can stand on its own feet and may be conducted either as a part and parcel or independent of Management Audit.

"Marketing Audit is a comprehensive, systematic, independent and periodic examination of company's or business unit's marketing environment, objectives, strategies and activities with a view to determining problem areas and opportunities and recommending plan of action to improve the company's marketing performance."(Prof Kolter)

The above definition clearly spells out the following characteristics :

Comprehensiveness	-	covers all the mojor activities of the company.
Systematic	-	There should be structured audit programme to be followed in proper sequence for timely completion of the audit.
Independent	-	Marketing audit can be conducted by internal experts or by outside consultants. The second alternative is prefered for obvious reasons.
Periodic	-	Marketing audit should be conducted at regular periodic intervals.

Normal practice of conducting an audit takes a narrow view. In this connection, Prof.Shuchmen says : "The marketing audit is a tool that can be of tremendous value not only to the less successful, crisis-ridden company but also to the highly successful and profitable industry leader.

Even best can be made better. In fact, even the best must be better, for few if any marketing operations can remain successful over the years by maintaining status quo" It appears that marketing audit is more important in successful companies simply because they have a tendency to breed complacency.

Webster defines an audit as "a formal or official examination and verification of an account, a methodical examination and review". This is the concept of accounting audit which is carried out according to a fixed time table and under highly standardised procedures. In marketing audit there is no such clear-cut procedure. The accounting audit is directed towards the outsiders (shareholders, creditors, public etc.) whereas in marketing audit it is intended to deal with a specific marketing problem or assessment of component of marketing effectiveness, exclusively for internal uses.

In fact, the term "audit" assumes much broader connotation and import when used in the context of Management Audit as well as Marketing Audit.

3. METHODOLOGY

It is not possible to present a comrihensive list of all the tools and techniques that are generally used for conducting management audit as well as one of its most important components, marketing audit. This is particularly because the approach and methodology vary widely not only between one audit unit and another but also among different experts carrying out marketing audit even for the same or identical unit. We would briefly discuss here nevertheless some of the important and well-accepted tools and techniques that generally form part of the methodology. It needs to be emphasised that one has to adopt a judicious blend of these tools and techniques, having regard to the nature of the audit-unit and the purpose of the marketing audit.

i. Pre-Audit Briefing :

It is described that there should be a pre-audit discussion with the company officials to agree upon the broad audit areas such as:

a) Objective and purpose - general/specific,
b) Coverage,
c) Depth of study,
d) Time schedule, and
e) Expected specific outcome.

ii. Basic Instruments :

There are two accepted instruments for reviewing the overall marketing effectiveness :

a) Marketing effectiveness rating review, and
b) Marketing audit, as a sequel to (a).

a) Marketing Effectiveness Rating Review .

Structured questionnaires are prepared to cover the major attributes of marketing orientation namely, customer philosophy, marketing organisation, marketing information, strategic orientation and operational efficiency.

b) Marketing Audit :

The major components required attention of a marketing auditor are : Marketing Environment Audit, Marketing Strategy Audit, Marketing Organisation Audit, Marketing Systems Audit, Marketing Productivity Audit and Marketing Function Audit Typical questionnaires related to these areas have been given at the end.

iii. Swot Analysis:

Swot Analysis is an almost universally accepted tool for auditing marketing operation. Swot (as mentioned earlier also) is the abbreviated version of Strengths (S), Weaknesses (W), Opportunitites (O) and Threats (T) . The S & W parts of SWOT is actually Organisational Analysis (internal)and the O & T comprise Environment Scanning (external). SWOT analysis can be conducted through questionnaire technique or brain-storming sessions.

As an illustration, we are giving below only a few of the SWOT's listed during a brain-storming session of senior marketing executive of a leading instrumentation company, while a marketing audit was being carried out :

Strengths :

i. Wide range of products, thereby offering better business potential.
ii. Efficient after-sales service provided by the company.
iii. Availability of both indigenous and imported instrumentation equipment as alternatives; in some cases.

Weaknesses :

1. Poor Government liaison and public relation.
ii. Inadequate efforts on a continuing basis for development of new markets.
iii. Technological obsolescence in respect of some of the products manufactured and/or marketed by the company.

Opportunities :

i. Fast growing and varied markets offered by the Indian Economy for the products of the company.
ii. Increased' markets for the comapany's products arising out of Government legislations re:pollution control, stricter adherence to quality standards, etc.
iii. Scope for introduction of new products with latest technology and thus exploring market opportunities, due to the technology gap prevailing in India.

Threats :

i. Changing customer behaviour evident from unethical practices which the company is not willing to indulge into.
ii. Sociao-political instability in some regions causing retardation in industrial activities.

iii. Scarcity in foreign exchange leading to conservative import policy.

iv. Data Generation and Analysis :

Data collection is an integral part of the marketing audit and for statisfactory result, interfacing with company officials and file references are a pre-requisite. A cursory glance over the questionnaire given at the end will corroborate that apart from statistical data due emphasis is placed on the personal views obtained through interactions - both one to one basis and at times in groups. Because of this, an effective communication with all levels of management is needed.

For generating necessary data and information, different types of questionnaires may have to be designed and administered, depending again on the purpose and scope of the marketing audit. In course of conducting a fairly comprehensive marketing audit of a large engineering conglomerate (a multi-national unit with diversified product portfolio), as many as six questionnaires were designed and used respectively for: Company's Executives (middle-level marketing and sales), Company's Executives (senior-level-all functions), Customers (direct), Customers (indirect-agents etc.) Principals/Suppliers and Competitors.

v. Brain-Storming :

The expression was first coined by Alex Osborn. This involves collaboration of personnel to "storm" a problem. It is in fact a creative conference aiming to generate a host of ideas-good, bad or indifferent . In a brain storming exercise, quantitative and qualitative facts and figures are usually available to facilitate marketing audit, provided the brain-storming session comprises participants well-infomed in the reference subject.

4. INFERENCES AND RECOMMENDATIONS

This is the concluding part of marketing audit. The effectiveness of the audit is directly related to the auditors skill and professional expertise and of course objectivity with which the analyses of data (derived from pre-set questionnaires) are made,inferences are drawn from the analysed data (identifying for example areas where immediate corrective actions might be needed) and appropriate recommendations are incorporated in the audit report.

Much as the reader would like us to present some case studies on marketing audit in keeping with the age-old adage "Examples are better than precepts",it would not be practicable for us to do so here. We are nonetheless giving below a few interesting outcomes that were included in the respective marketing audit reports, by way of illustrations only :

i) Audit Unit — a large consumer products-based chemical company in a neighbouring country :

a. Immediate formation of a task force for expansion of the product-range by introducing at least ten new products in certain identified field like ....

b. Establishing appropriate methods for evaluation of promotion and advertisement activities with a view to ensuring cost effective promotion.

c. Conducting an attitude survey of marketing and sales personnel and simultaneously generating pertinent data re: their counterparts in the industry, in order to restructure their compensation and incentive package.

ii) Audit Unit — an old established foundry in the Eastern India:

a. The order - shipping -billing - cycle time (worked out at around 78 days for a new order and about 68 days for a repeat order) being very high, given the industry norms, needs to be cut down by the least 25% in each case within one year.

b. The present success rate against enquiries or "Hit Ratio" of 1 :8 can be improved to 2 : 8 or

1 : 4, given the proper organisation and support system in marketing operations, in order to double the capacity utilisation (from the meagre 20% at present) as well as the turnover level.

c. Taking a hard look at and revamping as necessary, the pricing policy and strategy of the company in order that demand and state of competion etc. are built into the pricing system, rather than allowing the same to be entirely cost-based as existing now.

d. Introducing an effective market-research function in the company not only for regular market share or hit ratio analysis but also for undertaking researches on the changing pattern of buying behaviour with respect to the company's products.

5. CONCLUDING OBSERVATIONS

It is the consensus opinion that the marketing audit should be conducted by outside consultants in order to have an independent look of the market orientation present and future - and to submit an unbiased report free from push and pull of various interested groups. After all outside experts would not have any axe to grind, score to settle or corporate ladder to climb !

The marketing auditor is to determine what is being done, appraise what is being done and recommend what should be done. It is essential that the audit should be conducted and completed within an agreed time frame so that the data forming the background of the audit do not become outdated and thus nullify some inferences and recommendations.

Also important is the auditor getting familiarised with the company's background including extent of professionalism, work culture, breadth of experience, result-orientation, cost - consciousness and recommendations.

The ultimate object of marketing audit is improving the marketing effectiveness and market-orientation and in no way should it be a tool of assessing individual competence. In other words, Marketing Audit should never be allowed to degenerate into a fault-finding or witchhunting exercise. Once these are ensured, progressive organisations will no longer shy away from getting marketing audits conducted. Thus, the prevailing apprehension or mistrust in this area could also be set at rest.

MARKETING AUDIT INSTRUMENT QUESTIONNAIRE

(Please indicate your rating by a ✓ mark against each criterion under the. *5 Point Rating Scale for I to V. Please put your observations briefly under VI)

I Marketing Enviroment :

The extent to which you are conversant with the changes in the environment — 1 2 3 4 5

A Macro Environment

- i) economic
- ii) financial and fiscal
- iii) social
- iv) political

B Task Environment

- i) market segments
- ii) customer
- iii) competitor
- iv) substitutes of products
- v) product/process technology

II Marketing Objectives and Goal :

- i) The degree of clarity of corporate objectives and how they lead logically to the marketing objectives.
- ii) The degree of clarity in the marketing objectives
- iii) Clarity in priority ranking between different marketing objectives (e.g.

market leadership, market shares, volume sales growth, rupee sales growth, marketing profitability etc.)

iv) The extent to which the marketing objectives are qualified

---

*1 = very Poor, 2 = Below Average, 3 = Average, 4 =- Good and 5 = Excellent.

III Marketing Organisation :

i) Degree of effectiveness in the existing marketing organisation structure. 1 2 3 4 5

ii) Degree of clarity of authority and responsibility of marketing executives

iii) Extent of smooth interaction between marketing and other departments

IV) Marketing Mix

Indicate your rating of effectiveness against each of the following elements of the Marketing Mix/functions

i) Product (range,packaging,performance, quality,after sales service, etc)

ii) Price (including financial terms)

iii) Promotion (mode, channels, media etc)

iv) Placement (distribution channels and network - both coverage and cost effectiveness)

V Marketing Systems :

Indicate your rating of effectiveness against each of the following areas under marketing systems

i) Marketing MIS (state of business monitoring and development)

ii) Marketing budgets and business plans

iii) Marketing long range plans

iv) Cash flow in marketing Operations

v) Product line profitability

vi) Marketing intelligence (including market researches and surveys)

vii) Sales analysis (from different angles)

viii) Market share analysis (overall as well as for different market segments)

ix) Sales force - recruitment and training

x) Marketing performance evaluation

VI Marketing Strategies :

i) Does your company have any long -range strategy in respect of your product group? If so, what methodology is adopted ?

ii) Is the long-range strategy supplemented by short range strategies and tactics ? If so, how are they linked and determined from each other ?

iii) What is your perception of the degree of clarity in communication of strategies developed or when strategies are changed ?

iv) What methodologies are adopted in monitoring the implementation of these strategies? What and to what is their effectiveness?

v) Does the Company have a contingency planning methodology for your product group ? If so, what and to whom extent ?

vi) Extent of use of sophisticated techniques (e.g. Product Life Cycle concept, Boston Consulting Group model etc.) that are adopted in developing marketing strategies.

[Note : Adequate space to be provided below each question]

Remarks or Additional Comments, if any

____

Name : ____________________ Signature : ________

Designation : _________________ Date : __________

Location : __________________________________

Responsibility Area : __________________________
(Business Centre/
Products/Territory, etc.). ________________________

SECTION VI

MARKETING CONTROL

This section, with a high practical bias, intends to equip marketing executives with the various tools and techniques available. ranging from the conventional to the more sophisticated ones, so that they are able to effectively control marketing operations in general and the various facets of the same in particular.

There are five Chapters here, The first two Chapters (23 & 24) discuss at length working capital management and control, covering inter alia working capital requirement forecasting, marketing inventory control and receivables management.

The next two Chapters (25 & 26) illustrate the techniques of selling and distribution cost analysis, various tools of profitability analysis and control, product line accounting and sales variance analysis.

The last Chapter (27) of this section, as well as of the book itself, devoted to management information and control system in marketing, should be looked upon not as quite different from all that have been discussed in the preceding twenty-six Chapters, but as one intended to present, in an integrated from, the message of the book. An attempt has also been made here to illustrate, through real life cases, the important areas of information and control of marketing operations through effective monitoring of the key result areas.

CHAPTER 23

WORKING CAPITAL MANAGEMENT & CONTROL

1. Meaning and Significance of Working Capital ; 2. Gross Versus Net Working Capital ; 3. Negative Working Capital ; 4. Fixed Versus Variable Working Capital; 5. Chief Determinants of Quantum of Working Capital ; 6. Working Capital Requirement Forecasting ; 7. Marketing Inventory Control 8. Working Capital Management-Important Issues ; 9. Some Case Histories on Working Capital Management.

1. MEANING AND SIGNIFICANCE OF WORKING CAPITAL

To recapitulate again, the requirement of finance for an enterprise arises mainly out of two factors : acquisition of fixed assets and provision for working funds or working capital (also called circulating capital). Fixed assets are land, building, plant machinary, equipment etc., meant for use in the business (for a period of time greater than one year), to earn profits through recurring production and sales. The working funds are necessary, on the other hand, to meet the day-to-day revenue expenses, like material purchase, wage payment, meeting overhead expenses, etc. Working Capital actually keeps the business going since physical assets like plant and machinery cannot effect any production or generate any sales unless these are adequately and regularly fed with materials and varied services. The finance required to buy such materials and pay for such services is really the working capital.

The significance of working capital lies in the fact that it enables an industrial unit to convert into actuality the potential of its fixed assets in terms of level of production and sales. Without working capital, fixed assets cannot be activated or made to generate business activities. This would mean also that, given a set of fixed assets, there should be an optimum level of working capital. Anything higher than this optimum level may not generate higher production or sales. Likewise, working capital below the optimum level would mean opportunity loss in terms of a part of fixed assets potential left unexploited.

From the accounting point of view, working capital is the money locked up in inventory, debtors and other current assets (like cash, advances made to suppliers,etc.) minus others' money locked up with the business in the form of sundry creditors, bills payable, etc. By definition, working capital is current assets minus current liabilities.

Such accounting viewpoint is, however not quite correct, judged from a broader perspective. Strictly speaking, working capital should comprise only the total of the current assets, and current liabilities should not be deducted from the same. This is because the latter is only a source of finance, albeit a 'free finance' generally. In case of fixed assets in the balance sheet we do not deduct the outside finance from the value of the assets. Why should therefore be a different approach with respect to the current assets ? The position will be clearer if we prepare a separate balace sheet, say 'Working Capital Blance Sheet' after extracting the relevant data from the main balance sheet. Incidentally this approach of viewing working capital as total of current assets is, besides being conceptually sound, extremely useful in operation of a management control system in this area.

2. GROSS VERSUS NET WORKING CAPITAL

When only the current assets consisting of inventory, debtors, cash, etc.,are considered as working capital, it is called gross working capital. If from the total of the current assets, current liabilities (creditors, bill payable, etc) are deducted, the result is net working capital. In business and other spheres, often these two expressions are not used and the general expression working capital is used to mean sometimes the gross and sometimes the net also. Very often, this creates confusion in understanding and interpretation.

After the publication of the report of the Study Group (headed by Prakash Tandon and therefore, called Tandon Committee Report), the expression Net Working Capital has been given a new meaning that is, the Gross Working Capital less Sundry Creditors and short-term bank borrowings also. Thus Net Working Capital means only that part of the working capital which is financed through internal resources and long-term borrowings.

The composition of working capital varies according to the nature of the business, particularly whether it is a purely trading business or a manufacturing-cum-marketing organisation. There are other factors too which cause variation, such as customary credit terms in the industry, in which business is engaged, general financial climate and conditions, and so on. For a purely trading or marketing organisation the composition or working capital would be as follows :

a) Inventory — finished goods only ....
b) Receivable — sundry debtors
bills receivable ....
c) Other current assets —cash,
sundry advances for value to
be received, etc. .... ——
Total (Current Liabilities)A ....
——
d) Sundry creditors, bills payable,
Advances to customers etc. ....
e) Outstanding liabilities (to
employees and outsiders) .... ——
Total (Current Liabilities)B ....
——
Working Capital (A - B) ....
——

For a manufacturing-cum-markeing organisation the inventory will include, besides finished goods, raw materials (of all types) and work-in-process.

3. NEGATIVE WORKING CAPITAL

Situation , though rare but not unreal, may arise when the net working capital of a business shows a negative figure because current liabilities are higher than current assets . The preponderance of current liabilities to an extent of more than offsetting the total current assets, leading to a situation of negative working capital, may enable us to arrive at either or the two diametrically opposite or extreme conclusions as follows :

> It may be that the business is going to collapse since it fails to meet the commitments to its suppliers and other creditors inspite of the fact that its outstandings are collected well and inventories are not very high. The cause may be overtrading by the business in general and/ or inefficient financial management. It may also be that the working capital position of the business is extremely good and also that the business enjoys some monopoly power to ask its customers for advances against the goods to be supplied at a future date.

4. FIXED VERSUS VARIABLE WORKING CAPITAL

In every enterprise, a part of the total working capital, usually a small part compared to the total, represents the fixed element and the balance, usually the major part, is variable. To identify such fixed and variable elements one has to be clear about the meaning and frame of reference of the concept of variability. A business operates within the range of a given activity level and during a time-period (say, a couple of years) this activity level does not change. Within this activity level the volume of operations of the enterprise keeps on changing from time to time due to seasonal factors, cyclical factors and random variations. But there must be a hard core element in working capital commensurate with the broad activity range within which the business operates. This part of working capital does not tend to change in response to change in activity from time to time. Such hard core element of working capital is called fixed working capital. There may be, on the contrary, changes in working capital position resulting from changes in actual activity from time to time . During the peak season, working capital requirement could be high and this may again drop down during the slack-season. This working capital which varies more or less in proportion to the actual activity (indicated by production and/or sales) may be called variable working capital.

5. CHIEF DETERMINANTS OF QUANTUM OF WORKING CAPITAL

There are various factors which generally afffect the quantum and composition of working capital required by a business unit. Some of these factors are mentioned below :

i) Technology — capital intensity, balancing of productive equipments etc.

ii) Size of scale — availability of economics of scale.

iii) Marketing conditions — credit conditions, demand pattern including seasonality, etc.

iv) Broad socioeconomic milieu.

v) Management attitude towards risk taking. This affects the quantum of inventory to be held.

vi) Optimal relationship between the sequence of production and sales.

vii) External constraints — import restrictions, credit squeeze, money market, etc.

6. WORKING CAPITAL REQUIREMENT FORECASTING

A forecast of the requirement of fixed capital depends primarily upon the capacity to be installed or expanded. This does not change too often. And it is rather easy to determine this from the technical feasibility study of the project. But working capital requirement forecasting is a little more complicated. The methods range from the crudest to the sophisticated. We shall first indicate the crude methods and then come to the more refined ones.

The crude methods of forecasting working capital requirement comprise mainly of establishing some broad percentage relationship between working capital and various parameters that would influence it. Some such bases commonly adopted are as follows :

i) Working capital as percentage of sales — This is simple and most commonly used. It can give some broad indication only if selling price is fixed and cost structure is stable.

ii) Working capital as percentage of cost of production — This is ordinarily a good method particularly when the cost relationship, if not the amount, remains unchanged.

iii) Working capital as percentage of cost of sales — The results may not be reliable because of the inclusion in cost of sales of selling and distribution costs which, besides including some policy costs, might vary widely and abruptly.

iv) Working capital as percentage of marginal cost of sales — This is perhaps the best among all these short-cut methods. Its strength lies in the fact that marginal cost, comprising only the variable elements in all costs, seldom changes except over a relatively long period and under extraordinary situations.

One of the more refined approaches would be to estimate working capital requirement after studying more systematically and quantifying as far as practicable the various parameters that would affect such a requirement . A host of factors have to be considered and relevant data collected before undertaking this excercise. For a manufacturing-cum-marketing organisation, the following factors should be considered :

i) How many weeks/months raw-materials should on an average be kept in store, always ready to be used in production.

ii) How many weeks/months sales requirement of finished goods should be kept on an average in stores.

iii) The average credit period to be allowed to debtors or creditors.

iv) The average credit period expected from suppliers.

v) The average production time.

In the case of purely trading concern, considerations (i) and (v) above would not arise, but all other factors, (ii) through (iv), have to be taken into account. In any case, however, to play safe, some extra amount (cash or unutilised overdraft) should be kept ready in banks and should be added to arrive at the actual net working capital requirement. Such extra amount is to be determined with reference to the nature and volume of the business and other pertinent factors, especially any upward variations in the average figures against the above-mentioned parameters during peak seasons or due to other reasons.

Let us take one illustration at this stage.

Working Capital Requirement Forecast Of A Purely Trading Concern

Projected annual sales	.... Rs. 65 lakh
per cent of net profit on sales	.... 20 per cent
Average credit period allowed to debtors	.... 10 weeks
Average credit period allowed by creditors	.... 4 weeks
Average stock holding (in terms of sales requirments)	.... 8 weeks

10 per cent to be added to computed figure to allow for contingencies in arriving at the forecast of working capital requirement.

WORKING CAPITAL REQUIREMENT FORECAST

	Period in weeks	Amount Rs. lakhs
Inventory	8	8
Debtors	10	10
Total	18	18
Less creditors	4	4
Net working capital	14	14
Add for contingency at 10 per cent		1.4
Working Capital		15.4

Notes and workings :

	Amount Rs.lakh	Per week Rs. lakh
I. Sales	65	1.25
Profit	13	0.25
Cost of sales	52	1.00

II. It has been assumed that creditors include those for both goods and expenses and that all such creditors allow one month credit on average .

III. The element of profit has been excluded from the working capital requirement forecast. This has been explained later.

Interpretation of the Results :

The amount of Rs.15.4 lakhs arrived at above is to be interpreted as the amount to be locked up in inventory and debtors (minus creditors) at any time during the period(year) in view, so that the anticipated activity (sales primarily) can go on smoothly. The amount is not for a period of time but for any point of time. It represents the average quantum of lock-up at any time during the relevant period.

Another refined method of forecasting working capital requirement is on the basis of the Concept of Operating Cycle. Operating cycle also called the working capital cycle, is defined as the time period required for the whole operation starting with cash and ending up with cash plus (assuming that the operations generate some profit). Operating cycle is therefore expressed in terms of months or weeks or days. The total period is broken up into various stages,like raw material waiting period, conversion period, finished stock period, debtors period, and creditors period in case of a manufaturing-cum-marketing organisation. In the case of a purely marketing organisation, however, the cycle would be relatively short, since it will comprise only the last three periods while the first two (namely raw material waiting period and conversion period) will not be of any relevance. It will be seen that the operating cycle concept is more or less akin to the projection based on parametres study which has been illustrated above. Under the illustration the operating cycle is 14 weeks comprising inventory of 8 weeks., minus credit enjoyed 4 weeks, plus credit allowed 10 weeks. Accordingly the working capital requirement can be straightaway arrived at as follows :

Rs.52 lakhs (cost of sales) Divided 52 weeks X 14 weeks = Rs 14 lakhs

When the operating cycle is known with a reasonable degree of accuracy it would be easy to project the working capital requirement for a given level of activity without the necessity of working out component-wise or element-wise details. When the operating cycle is not known this can be worked out by an analysis of the relevant figures, even those available from the published accounts of a company. The methodology is as follows :

Operating Cycle (OC) = R + W + F + D - C

Where R = raw materials and stores waiting period
W = work-in-process period
F = finished goods waitig period
D = debtors collection period and
C = creditors payment period.

the components of the OC may be calculated as follows :

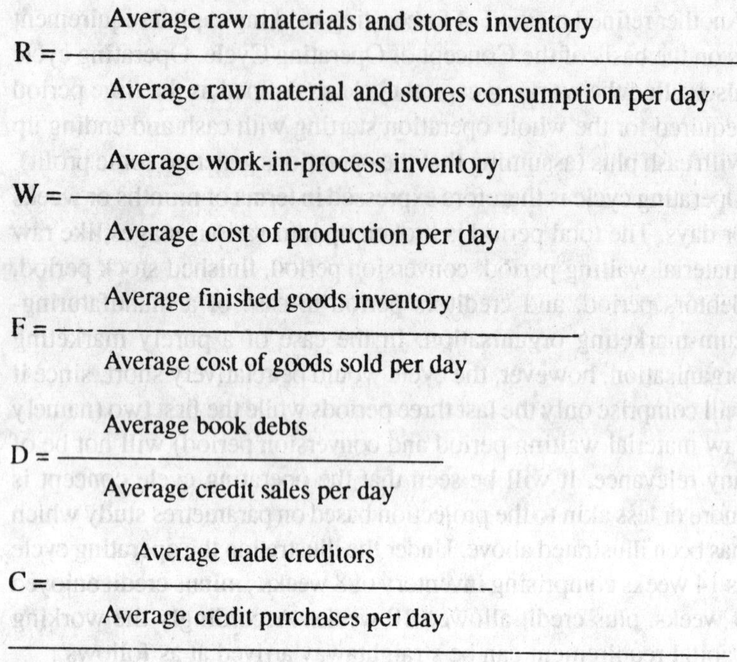

$$R = \frac{\text{Average raw materials and stores inventory}}{\text{Average raw material and stores consumption per day}}$$

$$W = \frac{\text{Average work-in-process inventory}}{\text{Average cost of production per day}}$$

$$F = \frac{\text{Average finished goods inventory}}{\text{Average cost of goods sold per day}}$$

$$D = \frac{\text{Average book debts}}{\text{Average credit sales per day}}$$

$$C = \frac{\text{Average trade creditors}}{\text{Average credit purchases per day}}$$

Note : All the results will be in the unit of time, that is days/weeks/ months.

It may also be emphasised in passing that the OC concept is very useful not only in forecasting working capital requirement, but also in controlling it.

There are various other sophisticated methods of projecting working capital requirement. Mention may be made of the ROI approach and financial ratio methods which are handy while projecting the working capital requirement on a long-term basis, say for the purpose of long-range planning.

Before concluding the discussion on working capital requirement forecasting, let us take a look at two more aspects of this system : profit vis-a-vis working capital and adoption of flexible budgeting concepts in forecasting.

As regards the nature and impact of operating profit on working capital we have to note the following three statements :

i) Profit does not form part of working capital requirement forecast.

ii) Profit generated over months eases the financing aspect of working capital, by reducing the amount needed to finance working capital.

iii) Working capital at any given point of time includes an element of profit.

To explain these three statements, let us study in detail the illustration given earlier. To keep the operation running the business has to spend Rs.1 lakh every week towards cost of sales (material,labour and overheads). This amount is to be eventually realised through collection sales. But at that time not only the cost of Rs.1 lakh is realised but an additional sum of Rs.0.25 lakh is also available. This is profit. No provision is necessary in working capital requirement forecast for such profit since it does not mean an expense to be incurred earlier. However, working capital at any point of time is defined as : Current assets (inventory, debtors and cash) less current liabilities. Thus the estimate of working capital in ex-post sense includes profits also through the inclusion of debtors at full value (sales value), although in the ex-ante sense (requirement forecast) profits are excluded. To summarise :

(i) Profit is an element in any estimate of actual working capital (ex- post sense).

(ii) Profit is not included in any forecast of working capital requirement (ex-ante sense).

There is the need for adopting a flexible approach while projecting working capital requirement for a certain activity-level. In the first place, activity itself might change up or down. Secondly level of efficiency in the management of working capital may also be different, better or worse, from what is envisaged initially. It would, therefore, be desirable, to develop a number of forecasts, instead of one, under the assumption of various, alternative levels of activity and efficiency-factors. Similarly, an attempt may be made to work out two forecasts against each alternative level - one for planning the availability of funds and the other for controlling the requirement of such funds through the imposition of adequate financial discipline.

7. MARKETING INVENTORY CONTROL

Many tools and techniques have been developed for inventory management and control. These are by and large applicable to all types of inventories, viz., raw material, work-in-process and finished stock. A successful adoption of such inventory control techniques would go a long way in putting inventory management on a sound footing and reducing thereby the working capital requirement on this score.

ABC analysis is an effective tool of inventory control. Through ABC analysis each item of inventory is catergorised as A, B, or C depending on its relative importance judged by its unit and/or transaction value during a period. Usually, very few items (say 10 per cent) come under category 'A' but these items may represent 70 per cent to 80 per cent of total inventory value. Similarly, some 20 per cent of items (grouped as 'B') might represent about 20 per cent of value. And balance 70 to 80 per cent of items are grouped as 'C' since they represent only about 10 per cent of total value. Such analysis immensely facilitates control of inventory by the 'principle of exception', since greater time and effort can be spent on a few items but with higher values. ABC analysis is in fact based on a sound and commonplace concept-one should concentrate on a few items or areas which influence the total result significantly. The famous Economic Law of Pareto also emphasizes the same thing - 15 per cent of the cause produces perhaps 85 per cent of the effect.

L ABC Analysis

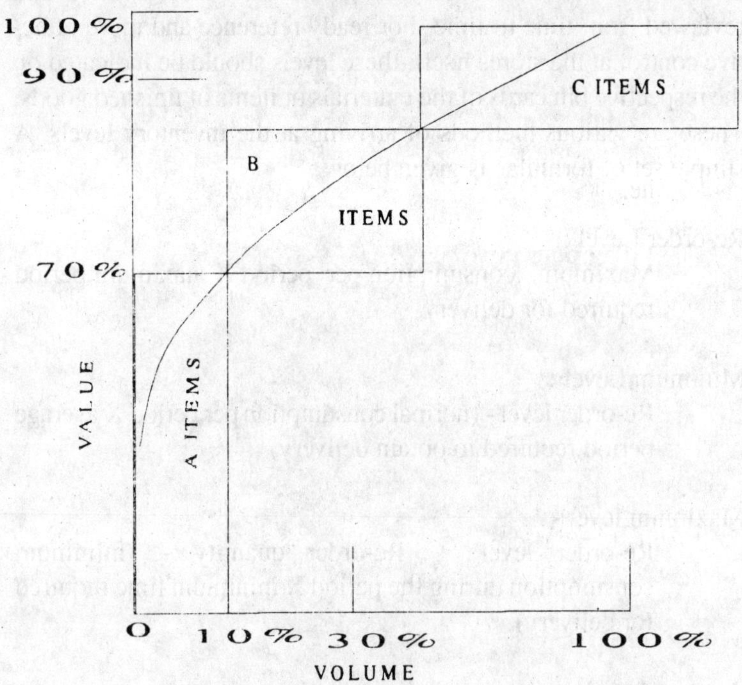

The next simple and effective set of techniques of inventory control is establishment of inventory level norms to watch closely and control the actual levels against such norms.

Inventory levels are mainly of four types viz.,

Maximum level	-	the level above which stock should not be allowed to rise.
Minimum level	-	the level below which stock should not be allowed to fall.
Re-order level	-	the level between maximum and minimum levels which indicates, and initiates action regarding placement of purchase requisition or processing of purchase order.
Average level	-	the average of the minimum and maximum levels.

In respect of each A item of inventory, and if possible each B item as well, the above inventory levels should be determined and reviewed from time to time. For ready reference and more effective control at the stores itself, these levels should be indicated on the respective bin cards of the materials or items of finished goods. These are various methods of arriving at the inventory levels. A simple set of formulae is given below :

Re-order Level :

Maximum consumption per period X maximum period required for delivery.

Minimum Level :

Re-order level - (normal consumption per period X average period required to obtain delivery) ;

Maximum level -

Re-order level + Re-order quantity - (minimum consumption during the period X minimum time required for delivery)

Average Level :

1/2(minimum stock level + maximum stock level)

(Note : Period may be in terms of days, weeks, months, etc.)

Illustration 1 : Inventory Level Norms

Data :

Re-order quality	600 units
Time required for delivery	2 to 4 months
(i.e. minimum 2 months, average 3 months; and maximum 4 months)	
Maximum consumption p.m.	125 units
Normal consumption p.m.	100 units
Minimum consumption p.m.	50 units

Workings :

(a) Re-order level :
125 X 4 = 500 units

(b) Minimum level :
500 - (100 X 3) = 200 units

(c) Maximum level :
500 = 600 - (50 X 2) = 600 units

(d) Average level :
1/2 (200 + 1000) =600 units

Next in the list of inventory control techniques is economic order quantity (E.O.Q). While re-order level indicates when to buy, E.O.Q should indicate how much to buy at time. E.O.Q. represents the most favourable quantity to be ordered each time fresh supplies are required. E.O.Q. may be arrived at with the help of a formula and also by tabulation method. Both these approaches are illustrated below:

Illustration 2 : Economic Order Quantity (E.O.Q.)

Data-Monthly usage 25 units; cost of placing and processing one order Rs 30; cost of materials per units Rs.25; cost of carrying 20 per cent p.a. of inventory value.
E.O.Q. with the help of formula :

$$E.O.Q = \sqrt{\frac{2\,QC}{1}}$$

Where Q = annual requirement in units C = cost of placing & processing one order

$$E.O.Q. = \sqrt{\frac{2 \times 300 \times 30}{5}}$$

I = annual carrying cost of one unit

$$= 60$$

Thus the E.O.Q. is 60 units (i.e. five orders per year at the rate of 60 units each time). The same results may be arrived at with the help of a table as shown below:

No. of orders per. yr	Units per order	Value per order at Rs. 25 per unit	Average Inventroy valie(1/2 of total value)	Inventory carrying cost at 20%	Order etc. cosat at Rs. 30	Total cost
		Rs.	Rs.	Rs.	Rs.	Rs.
1	300	7500	3750	750	30	780
2	150	3750	1875	375	60	435
3	100	2500	1250	250	90	340
4	75	1875	937	188	120	308
5	60	1500	750	150	150	300 (min)
6	50	1250	625	125	180	305
8	37.5	938	469	94	240	334
10	30	750	375	75	300	375

There are also some simple techniques of operations research being increasingly used in the area of inventory control. We may briefly indicate here two such techniques, viz., risk balancing and *exponential smoothening.*

Risk Balancing Technique : Very, often in determining the right inverntory level, one has to balance the risk and consequently the cost associated with holding high inventory level on theonehand and loss of contribution or profit due to stock-out in the event of holding lower inventory level, on the other. The simple riskbalancing technique may be adopted to determine the optimum inventory in such a situation. Let us take one illustration :

Illusration 3 : Risk Balancing Technique :

Data- Average sales per month 2400 units + 10% : order for the entire monthly requirement to be placed right at the beginning of the month; loss of contribution per unit due to stock out Rs.70

Inventory carrying cost p.m. Rs.10 per unit. We may determine the optimum order size (X) under the above situation with the hellp of an equation as follows:

70 (2640 - X) = 10 (X - 2160)

By solution, X = 2580.

This means that at 2580 units of order per month, the cost of holding inventory and stock out cost for not holding the same are balanced.

Exponential Smoothening : Sometimes it may be difficult to forecast monthly or periodic requirement of inventory for production or for sales.In such a situation this technique may be adopted.

The idea is to start with a set of estimates and put monthly actual figures and progressively update and refine the original estimates. That is, with the help of the actuals month to month, the estimates can be improved from time to time. To apply the technique a constant factor called K is to be determined and used for correction of the estimate. This requires some mathematical treatment. But even if K is assumed to be 0.3, broad forecasts on the basis of exponential smoothing may be possible. A simple illustration follows :

Illustration 4 : Exponential smoothening

We conclude our discussion on inventory control techniques by emphasising that all the simple techniques discussed and illustrated above are equally applicable to raw-materials of all types, tools and spares and also finished stock at all selling points. Only some minor modifications may be required at the time of application.

Sales units per month

	Original estimate	Actual figure	Estimate revised based on actual of previous month	Note
January	100	90		
February	100	100	100+K (90-100)	i) Assumed $K = 0.3$ ii) Revised estimate 107 arrived at before actual 100 is known
March	120	115	120+K (100-107)	Revised estimate 118 arrived at before actual 115 is known

8 WORKING CAPITAL MANAGEMENT — IMPORTANT ISSUES

Importance of Working Capital Management :

Let us first demonstrate the vital importance of working capital management in general. Working capital effects the Return on Investment (ROI) in two ways, the capital employed itself and also the return. Thus any improvement in the management working capital will affect ROI very favourably and the converse is also true. Let us study the following illustration.

Effects of Working Capital on ROI

(Figures hypothetical Rs. lakhs)

	Situation I	Situation II	Situation III
Fixed assets	100	100	100
Working Capital	100	50	200
Capital employed (A)	200	150	300
Earnings before interest and tax (Ebit)	55	55	55
Interest on WC Funds	15	7.5	30
Profit before tax (B)	40	47.5	25
ROI (B on A)	20%	31.7%	8.3%

Interpretation :

i) Situation I to II — Improvement in ROI is quite substantial due to (a) improved PBT through reduced interest and (b) reduction in capital employed itself. Both these factors are the result of improved efficiency in working capital management.

ii) Situation I to III — Fall in ROI percentage is quite drastic due to (a) reduced PBT and (b) increased capital employed. Both these are the result of inefficiency in working capital management.

Objective of Working Capital Management :

The objective of working capital management is to ensure its optimum utilisation for the overall profitability of a firm. An efficient manager would try to ensure that too much capital is not circulating in the business in the form of working capital. Nor will he allow the working capital to fall below a particular level. He will strike a balance between the two, possibly, by a careful study of movements of working capital in successive periods. Both the situations — too much working capital or too little working capital — will invite many dangers which may stand in the profitable working of a firm. G.L. Gole sets out the respective dangers in this way :

Dangers of too little working capital

1. Contributing factor to business failures.
2. Frustrates the enterprise objectives through lack of fund.
3. Reduces the rate of return on total investment.
4. Influences the credit rating adversely.
5. Prevents discounts being taken.
6. Prevents attractive opportunities from materialising.
7. Influences dividend policy adversely.
8. Influences management morale adversely.

Dangers of too much working capital :

1. Management efficiency may deteriorate through complacency.
2. Speculation may be encouraged.
3. Unjustifiable expansion may be stimulated.
4. Dividend may be too liberal.
5. Total investment may be working inefficiently.

The above points will justify the need for ensuring optimum utilisation of working capital in a firm. A mere fluctuation in the absolute figure of working capital does not necessarily indicate the degree of effective or otherwise utilisation of it. Therefore, it has to be related with volume which may be output or sales value. But sales being more subject to more fluctuation by outside factors, output seems to be a more appropriate measure. Accordingly, it can be stated that to ensure optimum utilisation of working capital, it should be minimum in relation to output and the requirement of working capital by a firm should increase at rate lower than that of increase in output. Even giving allowance for rise in price level, there should be such an acceleration of the flow of working capital that there is a constant economy in its use.

Management of working capital has two aspects, the requirement aspect and the finance aspect. The requirement aspect of management has to be studied from the point of view of the components of working capital. On the positive side such components are mainly inventory and debtors, and on the negative or neutralising side is the component of creditors. Working capital management in the requirement area thus boils down to the management of inventory, debtors and creditors. There are three financial ratios which are important and useful in keeping a constant watch on and controlling these parameters. These ratios are inventory turnover ratio, debtors turnover ratio and sundry creditors turnover ratio respectively. The next two chapters will deal with these three areas in greater details.

The finance aspect of working capital management essentially means controlling the cost of finance involved. Cost of finance varies according to the different sources of finance. Such costs have to be viewed from various angles namely real cost and opportunity cost direct cost and associated cost and implicit cost and explicide cost. Increase in the bank overdraft has some real (or monetary) cost which is the incremental interest. A decrease in credit period allowed by a supplier has an opportunity cost (the loss of interest on the money involved because of the shorter credit period). Again , the direct cost involved in bank overdraft is the interest, but there are some associated costs in the form of accounting and administration expenses in connection with such overdrafts. These associated costs are sometimes more than one or two percent annually of the overdraft. Interest on loans and overdrafts paid is the explicit cost. But since such interest is allowed as deduction for tax purposes, the implicit cost is much lower. Assuming a company is paying a tax at 60 per cent on an average and it borrows money from the bank at 15 per cent interest, then the explicit cost is 15 per cent per annum. But the implicit cost of financing working capital on this account would be only 40 percent of 15 percent, that in only 6 per cent (since the balance 9 per cent is actually borne by the government).

Of the problems that might arise in introducing and operating an effective control system in respect of working capital, mention may be made of the control of average working capital during a period, of say one year, as against deployment of working capital as at various points of time within the same period. Due primarily to operational reasons, sometimes working capital requirements might show seasonal peaks and throughs with a wide range of variations. If, in such a situation, control is sought to be exercised only on the basis of average working capital, then this would mostly be ineffective, if not even impracticable. But if the working capital requirement shows a steady and uniform pattern, without much of seasonal variations, control exercised on the basis of 'average working capital can be meaningful.

We may now come to the concept of effective working capital vis-a-vis actual working capital. Actual working capital means the working capital figure arrived at on the basis of the financial accounting records. The effective working capital employed in the business might be much less because of the preponderance of old, non-moving inventory, old and doubtful debts and also overdue creditors. Adjustments in these areas would be necessary to arrive at the effective working capital employed for initiating control actions to bridge the gap between the actual and effective figures.

The next important concept in working capital management is overtrading and the reverse situation, undertrading.

Overtrading is a situation which might develop in an enterprise when its responsibilities, orders and commitments come to be out of proportion to its available resources, specially the working capital position. Overtrading is basically a malady, a disease caused partly from ambitious business ventures and more from defective financial planning.

Undertrading is a situation just opposite to overtrading. The former is not so deadly a disease as the latter. Undertrading involves real and opportunity loss of income or profit. Undertrading may be due to internal factors (ultra-conservative attitude to risk-trading,etc) and also external factors (market constraint, etc). And discussion on working capital management would not be complete unless we say something about the effect of inflation on working capital. One such effect on inventory, more precisely, is valuation. Under the existing accounting and audit practices, valuation of inventory is undertaken at cost or market price whichever is lower. Under the inflationary conditions, the latest purchase price is always higher than the previous price of the materials and goods and this latest price is taken for the purpose of valuation of all items. The result is that an element of secret profit is built in the inventory value. But this secret profit is only monetary and that too, purely temporary more a myth than a reality.

Another important problem is that of internal generation of cash for financing increase in working capital needs during inflationary periods. Cash generation invariably tends to be lower than what is needed to support even the same activity level, let alone any increase in the same.

9. SOME CASE HISTORIES ON WORKING CAPITAL MANAGEMENT:

1. W.C. Ltd

(A Case Study on Effective Working Capital vis-a-vis Actual Working Capital)

The company is engaged in marketing its own manufacturing goods as also the agency items which are grouped as A & B : On an analysis of the past figures, discussions with marketing and production managers and other relevant facts, it has been established that the standards working capital requirement as percentage on sales should be.

40% for A (manufacturing and marketing)

15% for B (only agency items)

The actual working capital employed as on 1.1.19 X 0 is as follows:

(Rs. in lakhs)

	A	B	
Inventory	170	100	270
Debtors	270	120	390
	440	220	660
	240	120	360
	200	100	300

On scrutiny it is further revealed that the effective working capital employed should be different from the above because of the existence of old inventory, old debtors and overdue creditors the figures for which are as follows :

(Rs. in lakhs)

	A	B	Total
Old Inventory	15	10	25
Old debtors	50	20	70
	65	30	95
Overdue creditors	5	5	10
	60	25	85

The actual and Projected Sales for 19x0 & 19x1

	19x0	19x1
Own-manufacturing (A)	300	100
Agency items (B)	700	1100
	1000	1500

Under the situation stated above the company's working capital requirement for 19X1 sales should be based upon the effective working capital as at present for A & B which are 140 and 75 respectively. Now if financing for the additional amount becomes extremely difficult, control action for the company is to take up active measures for disposing of old inventory, collecting old debts and liquidating overdue creditors. This would bridge the gap at least to a great extent between the effective and actual working capital employed and probably ease the 19X1 financing problems.

2. C. G. Ltd
(A Case History on Inventory and Credit Policy Vis-a-vis Turnover Growth)

A group company engaged in diversified engineering trading activities had been following all along a tight inventory and credit policy. When the Study Group (Tandon Committee) recommendations were published it was found that the company had been operating with an average inventory and receivables much below the level recommended by the Tandon Committeee. The company had been also following all through a profit centre system on a full cost basis including the provision that the profit earned by a profit centre would be determined after charging interest on the company's funds used by the profit centre on the following:

> Month-end inventory - Prevailing rate of interest charged on bank overdrafts; Receivables up to 3 months — Same bank interest rate, Receivables between 3 and 6 months — Bank interest rate plus 3 per cent penal rate of interest ; Receivables beyond 6 months — Bank interest rate plus 6 per cent penal rate of interest.

Towards the end of 1975, some of the profit center heads maintained that it was difficult on their part to achieve the high growth rate in turnover, budgeted earlier, with the tight inventory and credit policy being followed by the company. They maintained that they were losing substantial business to competition since competitors could deliver the goods off the shelves and also since they were allowing credit to the customers for 60 days or even more.This company on the other hand could not deliver the goods on the spot nor could they allow that much credit to match competition. The executives, therefore, made a strong plea for liberalisation of inventory and credit policy in the interest of achieving higher sales turnover. They also maintained that they were prepared to bear financial charges on increased inventory and outstandings under the existing basis, since they were confident that with increased margin on higher sales they could generate higher profit even after charging such finance cost. The corporate management found some sense in their arguments. And obviously, before taking a decision in the matter the Finance Division was consulted.

According to the Finance Division, the fact that the company had been holding tight control on inventory and receivables had been instrumental to the company's growth with profitability, specially in the context of increasing cost of finance. Any liberalisation in the inventory and credit policy might bring in its train loose control and consequent lack of efficiency in operation. The finance people also maintained that as per the Tandon Committeee recommendations no company would be allowed to accumulate inventory or allow credit disproportionate to the operation as compared to the recent past. That is, a company which had been operating efficiently with certain inventory and receivables levels should be asked to maintain the same level and the banks would not encourage a significant rise in the levels. In fact additional bank finance would not be available under such circumstrances even though the company could establish that they would still be within the Tandon Committee norms with the increased inventory and receivables levels.

As regards profit centre heads, contention that they would bear the financial charges on account of increased inventory and receivables , the Finance Division observed that the financial charge was an internal charge levied for the purpose of performance evaluation and control in respect of various profit centres. But additional funds had to be generated to meet the increased working capital requirements. The fact that the executives were willing to bear the financial charges would not help in any way the generation of additional funds.

It was a crucial decisional problem for the management. A meeting was therefore arranged between the profit centre heads and the senior finance personnel. Some of the executive directors also attended the meeting. The decision taken in the meeting were all intended to strike a golden mean between the apparently conflicting and widely divergent issues. Some of the decisions were as follows :

1. The profit centre heads would exercise adequate discretion in the matter of inventory holdings as also granting of credit. Both these should be oriented towards higher sales and increased capital- turnover ratio.
2. Old, non-moving and slow-moving inventory would be identified and disposed of even at very low prices and the funds so released should be siphoned back to the growth sectors in the operations.
3. A collection drive would be instituted in respect of all old outstandings (beyond 6 months) and an attempt should be made to collect these even after offering attractive discounts to customers and the funds so released would also be channelised to the growth sectors in the operations.
4. The management information system of the company should be improved in respect of inventory and receivables so that both the finance people and the operating people could keep a continuos watch on the emerging trends in these areas, and accordingly undertake in time suitable control actions to ensure efficient operations on a continuous basis.

3. G D Ltd
(A Case History on Disposal or Holding of Non-moving Inventory)

A medium-sized engineering company operating as a unit of a highly diversified group company found itself saddled with a huge stock of forgings and castings which would no longer be required since there had been significant change in product-mix. The accumulation of these unusable inventory was essentially due to improper inventory planning and control at the unit level as also lack of co-ordination between marketing and non-moving raw materials was Rs.20 lakhs. Both the unit manager and the corporate management were deeply concerned as to how this inventory should be disposed of. Incidentally, the company was operating a profit centre system under which each manager was responsible for the net profit earned by the unit or activity under his control. This net profit was calculated on a full cost basis and after charging interest month to month on the company's funds used in operations, at the prevailing rate of interest charged on bank overdrafts.

It is common knowledge that in case of non-moving inventory like this there are broadly two types of costs involved, viz., visible cost and invisible cost. Visible cost is actually the inventory carrying cost is actually the opportunity loss which was around 20 percent per annumn in this case. Invisible cost is actually the opportunity loss which could be worked out on the basis of capital turnover ratio (found to be 4 times for the company as a whole) and the C/S ratio (estimated to be 20 percent for the company as a whole). Based on these the Management Accountant made a financial study. Assuming cost of inventory to be Rs.100, the break-even price for its disposal (Rs.X) was worked out to be Rs.45, with the following formula :

$$X == 100 — (20\% \text{ of } 4X + 20\% \text{ of } 100)$$

It was accordingly recommended that if the inventory was disposed of at any price higher than Rs.45 at the beginning of the year, that would be financially justified for the company as a whole, since the money so realised could be used in other operations during a full year in order to generate some additional contribution which would also be the additional profit (fixed cost being already recovered).

The manager of the unit, however, objected to the disposal of the stock at throw-away prices since that would mean about Rs.11 lakh loss (or somewhat less depending on the actual disposal value of the materials) for his unit in one single year. If this decision was not taken then his loss would be only Rs.4 lakhs (inventory carrying cost of 20 percent on Rs.20 lakhs) each year on this score.

The unit manager was correct in his viewpoint since the benefit out of the disposal of the stock would accrue to the other units within the group (depending on the group decision to utilise the money elsewhere) while his unit would stand to lose additionally by Rs.7 lakhs. It was essentially a problem of goal congruence — the unit goal and the corporate goal were working at cross purposes with each other.

The problem was, however, solved by taking a policy decision. The corporate management decided that the unit, for the purpose of performance evaluation, would be debited only with the amount of inventory carrying cost for one year while the unit which would utilise the sales proceeds should have to bear in the first year the estimated opportunity loss of Rs. 7 lakhs in lieu of the usual financial charges on the funds so used. Both these adjustments were to be notionally done only for the purpose of performance evaluation; and for obvious reasons, the statutory profit and loss account of the unit as also the group will reflect the actual monetary position based on the transactions.

CHAPTER 24

RECEIVABLES MANAGEMENT

1. Importance; 2. Basic Approaches; 3. Control System; 4. Float Analysis; 5. Factoring; 6. Criteria for Measuring Efficiency.

1. IMPORTANCE

In marketing operations receivables management assumes paramount importance due to two reasons :

a) No sale is complete until money is collected from the customer and responsibility for such collection should generally rest with the concerned sales personnel. Substantial delay or even non-collection of receivables invariably results in steady erosion of profits generated through sales.

b) If a large part of the company's working capital gets blocked up in the receivables outstanding then it would adversely affect the marketing margin (the numerator) because of higher interest charges and increase the level of marketing investment (the deminator), thus depressing the ROI significantly.

2. BASIC APPROACHES

While most companies have some norms in the matter of credit to be allowed to their customers, there is very often a wide divergence between such norms and actuals. It is important therefore not only to establish the norms but to keep a regular and close watch on the deviations between the norms and the actuals.

The next important issue in the management of credit allowable is evaluating the creditworthiness of the customers, again on a regular basis. There are three important methods used in evaluating creditworthiness of existing as well as potential customers. These are :

(i) examining the financial stability of the company using the published data and applying the tools of financial analysis, particularly the relevant ratios ;

(ii) confidential report from the company's bankers ; and

(iii) discreet enquiries from the market .

With respect to enterprises which are not public limited companies, item(i) may not be possible to adopt, but the other two may be made use of. Many progressive organisations continuously establish the creditworthiness of the parties along two lines, namely, the maximum credit period that may be allowed and the maximum amount of credit that may be granted to each party. While these are very important, it would be equally important to have a proper information system by which supplies can be stopped forthwith to a delinquent customer and efforts are initiated to recover the dues from him, immediately after the default is noted.

3. CONTROL SYSTEM

We may now come to the requirements underlying the installation and operation of an effective control system with regard to receivables/outstandings. These are:

(i) Development of a suitable credit policy, to be reviewed from time to time. This should include a clear definition of credit responsibilities and an adequate system for pinpointing the same against each credit sale.

(ii) A proper system for continuous credit appraisal and evaluation of creditworthiness of customers on the lines suggested above.

(iii) A provision for exception reporting especially in respect of old and overdue outstandings, so that sufficient and advance warning signal can be provided before these become bad debts or debts of doubtful recovery.

iv) A well-designed and well-oiled machinery for collection of receivables/outstandings. This should also be subjected to a periodic review to ensure its continued effectiveness.

Collection of Sales Tax Declaration (STD) forms from the customers is very important but mostly neglected area in receivables management. The onus lies on the selling companies to collect these forms or else bear the sales tax burden themselves. The financial implication of this is generally 6% to 8%. This means non-collection of STD forms would take away more than the profits earned in sales, in most cases !

4. FLOAT ANALYSIS

We may introduce at this stage a very effective tool for receivables control viz., the Float Analysis. This implies analysis of the period that affects cash as it moves through the different phases in the collection process. For a total number of nine activities, there are altogether eight floats as follows :

Activities	Floats
(1) Sales	(I) Billing float
(2) Sending invoice to customers	(II) Mailing float
(3) Receiving invoice to customer	(III) Net credit float
(4) Debtor sends cheque	(IV) Mailing fioat(ii)
(5) Receiving of cheque by the company's branch/operating office.	(V) Cheque processing float
(6) Cheque deposited into Bank	
(7) Cash available to branch/ operating office.	(VI) Bank float (i)
(8) Cash remitted to Head office (H.O)	(VII) Remittance float
(9) Remittance received and credited at HO bank	(VIII) Bank float (ii)

In order to apply the technique, one should first choose a particular period in the recent past, then a reasonable number of sample credit sales transactions during the period, work out, using relevant data from different records,all the above floats and present thereafter the figures on a suitably designed format. The choice of samples may be on a random basis, but stratified sampling approach should preferably be used. Different categories of customers with different credit terms may form different strata. Likewise, different geographical spread of the customers can be another way of stratification. However, the sample size should be such that it is by and large representative of the population.

After generating the basic float data as above, one may adopt simple statistical tools like range, mean and median, standard deviation,etc. in order to process the data. Analysis carried out on these lines by some companies in India beset with a nagging problem of receivables control, have invariably given a world of pertinent information and these have been used in exercising meaningful control over receivables.

Float numbers VI & VII, that is the two bank floats, are ordinarily considered to be outside the control of the company, while it is not fully so in case of the mailing floats. In western countries, particularly USA, bank floats are tackled successfullly by two methods - lock-box system (an arrangement with the post office) and concentration banking (having a number of bank accounts at different locations where customers are concentrated). Lock-box system is yet to be introduced in India. But concentration banking approach may be and is in fact being followed by many companies.

5. FACTORING

The next important subject of our discussion is factoring. Factoring is a financial service designed to help the firms in managing their receivables better. Factoring basically involves an outright sale of the receivables of a firm to a financial agency called the factor which specialises in the management of trade credit. Under a typical factoring arrangement, a factor collects the accounts on the due date, effects arrangement,a factor collects the accounts on the due dates, effects payments to the firm on these dates (irrespective of whether the customers have paid or not) and also assumes the credit risks associated with the collection of the accounts. For rendering these services, it charges a fee which is usually expressed as a percentage of the value of the receivables factored.

Factoring is therefore,nothing but an alternative to in-house management of receivables. Sometimes the factor provides an advance against the value of receivables taken over by it. In such cases,factoring also serves as a source of short-term finance for the firm.

Factoring is a popular form of financing and managing receivables in countries like USA and UK. But this concept is quite new to the Indian financial system. Recently, the commercial banks in India have evinced interest in promoting factoring companies. In the meanwhile, the Reserve Bank of India has constituted a committee to study the scope for setting up factoring organisations in the country and make recommendations for operationalising this service. These developments indicate that factoring is likely to emerge as an important financial service in the years to come.

6. CRITERIA FOR MEASURING EFFICIENCY

Finally we come to some efficiency criteria in receivables management. Two important ratios or relationships could be very useful.

a. Number of months (or days) sales outstandings, calculated as : either closing receivables divided by average monthly (daily) sales ;
or (preferably) relating month-end receivables backwardly to sales of the immediate preceding months (days).

b. Receivables outstandings as at end of a year or month as a percentage of total credit sales during the immediately preceding twelve months.

The first ratio can also be worked out on a different basis, namely Debtors Turnover Ratio (DTR). DTR actually expresses the rate of rotation of debtors in terms of months or days. The higher the DTR the better it is, since the number of months or days involved will be lesser when the DTR is higher, and *vice versa.*

Another important criterion is cost-benefit analysis with respect to allowance of credit to, and any change in credit terms for a particular customer or a category of customers. Risk is one factor which can be evaluated, partly by quantitative techniques and partly by qualitative approach. But even in a zero-risk situation, interest has to be taken into account in the cost-benefit analysis. This would be important even in case of allowing cash discount in order to get prompt payment or extend higher credit to customers.

We may include here a small illustrative situation for the reader to attempt a cost benefit analysis for decision on a credit policy.

X Company's present annual sales amount to Rs 30,00,000 at selling price of Rs 12 per unit. Variable costs are Rs 8 per unit and fixed costs amount to Rs 2,50,000 annually. The present credit period of one month is proposed to be extended to 2 or 3 months, whichever appears to be more profitable. It is estimated that in the event of extension of credit policy sales will increase by 10% and 15% respectively. The company requires a pre-tax return on investment of at least 25% for the level of risk involved. Evaluate the relative profitability of the proposals.

CHAPTER 25

PROFITABILITY CONTROL

1. Prologue; 2. Product Performance Evaluation; 3. Product-wise Profitability Analysis; 4. Profit Impact of Marketing Strategies (PIMS).

1. PROLOGUE

Profit is an absolute measure while profitability is relative- to sales, capital employed,etc. For every enterprise profit is an essential requirement, since it is nothing but the cost of being in business tomorrow. Yet a business enterprise should better frame its objectives not in terms of profit, but profitability. For any organisation Marketing ROI is by far the best measure of profitability of its marketing operations specifically.

This chapter of the book is devoted to measurement, comparison and control of profitability in marketing operations. Since at the end of the day it is the products that generate profits, the methodology used here have products as the main focus.

We have freely drawn from Management Accounting and allied disciplines appropriate tools and techniques for our purpose and have of course adapted these to suit marketing situations.

2. PRODUCT PERFORMANCE EVALUATION

We shall present and illustrate here some essentially finance-based tools for evaluating performance of products and product groups :

i) Product-Market Evaluation :

MARKET \ PRODUCT	NEW	OLD
NEW	1	3
OLD	2	4

N stands for New and O for Old. A cut-off period for both N and O should be adopted-we may suggest three years for consumer products and five years for an industrial marketing organisation. Thus for a cunsumer marketing company any product introduced or any new market developed within the last 3 years should be taken under N and the cases beyond 3 years as O. For this purpose, new use or application of an old product should be considered as new market and likewise a thoroughly revamped product may be deemed to be a new product.

Based on the above approach, all the products of the company may be analysed and put under the respective four blocks or quadrants. Thereafter for the products coming under each group percentages of total sales and of total gross margi earned may be determined separately. On a careful look at the figures some useful inferences may be drawn like :

a. If quadrant 1 shows a figure of at least 25% of the total sales and/or gross margin then it would be a satisfactory situation- below 25% would be rather poor and above 25% is encouraging. Every effort should be made to maintain and improve upon the figures appearing in this block.

b. If the quadrant 4 shows 80% and above in terms of sales and/or gross margin then the company might be heading towards sickness, if not sick already. This also indicates clearly poor marketing effectiveness. Effort should therefore be made to keep the figures as low as possible in quadrant-4 and should be never allowed to exceed.

c. Quadrants 2 and 3 representing new products in old markets and old products in new markets respectively indicate generally good marketing efforts - at least a sense of awareness as to marketing effectiveness.

ii) Returns - Margins Matrix :

		RETURN	
		HIGH	LOW
MARGIN	HIGH	1	3
	LOW	2	4

Hi stands for High and Lo for Low. Returns may be taken as Marketing ROI as explained earlier (Chapter-14). Margin may be gross margin or gross profit or contribution but preferably NMM (Net Marketing Margin). The cut-off rate for each may be fixed at the median of Marketing ROI and NMM respectively, taking all products or product-groups together.

Once the products or the product-groups are classified into the four squares, some interesting conclusions as well decision rules may be arrived at, as follows:

a. *Quadrant 1* - Statisfactory situation, therefore, retain the marketing mix.

b. *Quadrant 2* - Cut costs, adjust price (remember, however, that depending entirely on price for improving the situation is like skating on a very thin ice, hence not desirable).

c. *Quadrant 3* - Sell more, manage assets better - turn and earn.

d. *Quadrant 4* - The products need a thorough check-up. Some long-term solutions as a sequel may salvage the situation with respect to some of the products, others might have to be phased out.

A marketing organisation should try to have as many products as possible in block-1 and as few as possible in block-4. Too much concentration of products in block-4 be pointer to incipient sickness of the company.

iii) Product Life Cycle - Industry vis-a-vis Firm :

COMPANY \ INDUSTRY		
	INTRODUCTION	GROWTH
	MATURITY	DECLINE

The possible situations and corresponding inferences follow :

a. Industry launch, company launch - Very good because of the leadership status.

b. Industry growth, company launch - Good but watch and see.

c. Industry maturity, company launch - Be extremely careful, since the situation is fraught with danger.

d. Industry decline, company launch - Woe betide the company!

Incidentally, this is not strictly a financial too. All the same this is a useful guide in new product launching decisions.

iv). Boston Consulting Group (BCG) model :

The model is meant for product portfolio management. A balanced portgolio should always be aimed at, whether in personal investment decisions or in a company's resource allocation policies. From the marketing point of view also, it is necessary to have a balanced portfolio of products, some being highly profitable, some others profitable. Some making continuous losses and some others having temporary problems. At the same time, it is fact that the overall marketing profitability of a company depends to a very great extent on the mix of the various types of products in its portfolio. An interesting study has been made in this area by the Boston Consulting Group. Their simple model of product classification is as follows :

RELATIVE MARKET SHARE

ANNUAL MARKET GROWTH	HIGH	LOW
HIGH	*	?
LOW	CASH COWS	DOGS

"Stars" bring cash but consume more cash. "Cash cows" bring more cash but use less. A company's ultimate strategy should be to have more "cash cows" to milk! However, a significant part of the cash generated by these products has to be used for nursing the "problem children" and restore them back to health, the nursing programme will bring some of the "problem children" to the "stars" category and others to the "dogs". It is the "dogs" which take a lot of managment time and attention and also consume much of the financial and other resources of the company. Incidentally, the "dogs" include many of the products which need elimination. In passing, it may be mentioned that the Boston Consulting Group also found that the direct manufacturing costs would be relatively low in respect of those products which enjoy a larger market share (i.e. The stars and cash cows).

On a quick comparison of the four models given above, one might discover certain basic commonalities, particularly with respect to quadrant nos. 1 and 4.

The situation revealed in quadrant 1 in all the four models, albeit each from a different point of view, is highly satisfactory. The position indicated by quadrant 4 is of course extremely poor. It may well be that several products or product groups would keep appearing in quadrant 4 in all the cases. These are the most likely pruning candidates. Also too much concentration in this quadrant would unmistakably signify poor marketing effectiveness of the company and, as stated earlier, the company could be heading towards sickness. Incidentally signs of such sickness will become manifest through financial ratios etc. to banks and other outside financiers much later, while from the marketing angle, following the approaches given above, it should be possible to predict sickness much in advance and initiate corrective action well in time. Whether financial experts will agree or not, there is no denying the fact that, in a vast majority of cases, sickness starts at the market place, so does the recovery too ! Financial ratios can at best present only the effects not the causes of sickness particularly when these are latent and not patent.

3. PRODUCT-WISE PROFITABILITY ANALYSIS

The measurement of productwise profits can be attempted by comparing the sales revenues of each product with the costs associated with its production, selling and distribution. The productwise profitability analysis helps in :

* identifying the most profitable products so that more sales of that product could be encouraged,
* allocating funds available for future investment among the various product divisions, and
* maintaining a close control over cost. Knowledge of incidence of costs always helps in a better control of different costs.

Product-wise profitability analysis can be undertaken either through the contribution approach or through absorption costing approach. While contribution approach required the segregation of all costs into their fixed and variable components and variable components and tracing of only variable costs to the individual products, the absorption costing approach traces all costs, irrespective of whether they are fixed or variable, to the individaul products. Also, while the contribution approach judges the profitability of a product by the contribution earned,the absorption costing approach bases decisions on the profits measured as the difference between the sales value and total cost of sales of a product.

Between the two, the contribution approach presents a better picture of the profitability of a product as it does away with the need to arbitrarily apportion fixed costs to the various products.

It will be useful to give here two illustrations of the two approaches mentioned above - the first one on absorption costing or full cost approach and second one on marginal cost or contribution approach.

Illustration : 1 The MNF Ltd., decided to analyse its selling and distribution costs for products, A,B and C and arrive at product-wise profit or loss figures.

The income statement of the company for the past year is as follows :

		Rs.
Sales		5,20,000
Cost of goods sold		2,50,000
Gross profit on sales		2,70,000
Selling and distribution costs :	Rs.	
Salesmen's salaries	24,500	
Salesmen's commission	27,500	
Sales office expenses	14,800	
Advertising	65,000	
Warehouse	4,500	
Packing and shipping	5,600	
Transportation and delivery	8,400	

Credit and collection	4,100	
Bad debts	9,410	
Total	1,63,810	
General and administrative expenses	41,250	2,05,060
Net Profit		64,940

Additional Information :

	Product A	Product B	Product C
Sales (Rs.)	1,20,000	1,50,000	2,50,000
Cost of goods sold(Rs.)	55,000	70,000	1,25,000
Salesmen's salaries(Rs.)	8,000	7,000	9,500
Salesmen's commission(Rs.)	11,000	5,000	10,500
Advertising (%)	20	20	60
Warehouse space occupied	1/3	1/3	1/3
Invoice lines(Packing and shipping)	1,500	2,500	3,000
Transportation & delivery(Kg)	5,500	6,000	8,500
Average number of customers accounts outstanding	15,000	35,000	50,000
Accounts receivable uncollected	1.8%	1.5%	1.7%

Sales office expenses : Allocated in the same ratio as packing and shipping. General and administrative expenses : Allocated on the basis of sales.

Required : A comparative product-wise Profit and Loss Statement.

Solution :

COMPARATIVE PROFIT AND LOSS STATEMENT

Particulars	Basis of allocation	Total Rs.	Product A	B	C
1. Sales	Direct	5,20,000	1,20,000	1,50,000	2,50,000
2. Cost of goods sold	Direct	2,50,000	55,000	70,000	1,25,000
3. Gross profit on sales		2,70,000	65,000	80,000	1,25,000
4. (a) Selling & distribution cost :					
Salesmen's salaries	Actual	24,500	8,000	7,000	9,500
Salesmen's commission		27,500	11,000	6,000	10,500
Sales Office expenses	Invoice lines (15 : 25 : 30)	14,800	3,171	5,286	6,343
Advertising	1 : 1 : 1	65,000	13,000	13,000	39,000
Warehouse	Space occupied	4,500	1,500	1,500	1,500
Packing & Shipping	Invoice Lines (15 : 25 : 30)	5,600	1,200	2,000	2,400
Transportation & delivery	Weight (55 : 60 : 85)	8,400	2,310	2,520	3,570
Credit & collection	Accounts outstanding (15 : 35 : 50)	4,100	615	1,435	2,050
Bad debts	Accounts receivable uncollectable (1.8 : 1.5 : 1.7)	9,410	3,388	2,823	3,199
Total 4 (a)		1,63,810	44,184	41,564	78,062
(b) General and administrative expenses	Sales value (12 : 15 : 25)	41,250	9,519	11,899	19,832
Total (4)		2,05,060	53,703	53,463	97,894
5. Net Profit (3-4)		64,940	11,297	26,537	27,106

Illustration : 2 The Directors of Basak Chatterjee Industries have sought your help on costing and the type of information reporting system they should have in the following circumstances:

1) The company comprises a head office at Bhopal and two production centres, one in western India and the other in southern India. The head office expenses for the year ended 31st December 19X9 are as follows :

	Rs.
Marketing expenses (including advertising)	1,00,000
General administration and finance expenses	75,000
Production expenses(certain technical services)	10,000
	1,85,000

2) The western production centre makes two products. A (which is made only at the centre) and D (which is made also in southern India). Its results for the year ended 31st December 19X9 are as follows :

	Product A Rs.	Product D Rs.	Total Rs.
Sales	3,20,000	1,80,000	5,00,000
Standard cost of sales	1,50,000	1,20,000	2,70,000
Production cost variances (loss)	20,000	10,000	30,000
Production overheads (fixed)	—	—	60,000

3) The southern India production centre makes three products B, C (which are made only at the centre) and D (which is made also in western India). Its results for the same period are as follows :

	Product B	Product C	Prodcut D	Total
Sales	2,10,000	3,50,000	75,000	6,35,000
Standard cost of sales	1,80,000	2,50,000	55,000	4,85,000
Production cost variances (gain)	10,000	15,000	5,000	30,000
Production overheads(fixed)	-	-	-	1,00,000

You are required to prepare a statement of operation showing profitability by product for Basak Chatterjee Industries for the year ended 31st December 19X9, in the form which you condsider most informative for the Directors to enhance control (not for pricing purpose) and on the lines of which, for example, you recommend that monthly reports should be prepared. (vide the statement on the last page)

BASAK CHATTERJEE INDUSTRIES
OPERATING STATEMENT FOR THE YEAR ENDED 31ST DECEMBER 19X9

	Total		Southern India								Western India					
	All Products		All Products		Product B		Product C		Product D		All Products		Product A		Product D	
	Rs.000	%	Rs.000	%	Rs.000	%	Rs.000	%	Rs.000	%	Rs.000	%	Rs.000	%	Rs.000's	%
Sales	1135	100	635	100	210	100	350	100	75	100	500	100	320	100	180	100
Standard cost of sales	755	66.5	485	76.4	180	85.7	250	71.4	55	73.3	270	54.0	150	46.9	120	66.7
Standard contribution	380	33.5	150	23.6	30	14.3	100	28.6	20	26.7	230	46.0	170	53.1	60	33.3
Production variances profit / (loss)	--	--	30	4.7	10	4.7	15	4.3	5	6.6	(30)	(6.0)	(20)	(6.2)	(10)	(5.5)
Actual contribution*	380	33.5	180	28.3	40	19.0	115	32.9	25	33.3	200	40.0	150	46.9	50	27.8
Production overheads	160	14.1	100	15.7							60	12.0				
Net contribution	220	19.4	80	12.6							40	28.0				
Head Office expense:																
Marketing	100	8.8														
General administration and finance	75	6.6														
Technical services	10	0.9														
Total H.O. expenses	185	16.3														
Net profit before tax	35	3.1														

* This is the criterion to evaluate and compare profitability of different products (under Marginal Costing / Contribution Theory)

Profitability analysis division wise, product groupwise and productwise, whether under full cost approach or under marginal cost approach, is likely to be more complicated than in the illustration given above, particularly for large companies having diversified product range and operating through a large number of sales and distribution outlets. Computerised profitability analysis has therefore been gaining increasing popularity in India. In order to introduce this system an initial exercise comprising the following will be required.

i. Deciding upon the output format of profitability analysis as well as the periodic intervals for obtaining the same.

ii. Establishing pre-determined bases of allocation and apportionment of revenues and different heads of direct and indirect costs and expenses.

iii. Storing the budget figures in advance in line with the output requirements and broken-down according to pre-determined bases mentioned under (ii) above.

iv. Devising a system by which actuals (both revenues and costs) from month to month are obtained from the accounting and costing records (whether these are also computerised or not) and fed into the computerised profitability analysis scheme.

Before ending this topic, we would make a couple of pertinent observations regarding the uses and misuses of product profitability analysis. Such analysis can obviously help the management identify the growth sectors and the weak areas in the marketing operations and as a sequel deploy its resources for optimum results. Secondly, it is possible to improve the performance of weaker divisions or productlines through close monitoring when regular information is generated about their profitability. Thirdly, profitability analysis can help product rationalisation decisions that include product revamping, product range extension, product elimination and also new product introduction.

It is to be noted, however, that profitability analysis is not without its pitfalls. For one thing, any such analysis, however, scientifically done, cannot replace judgement, nor can it straightaway lead to the right decisions at the right time. This fact is often lost sight of. As a result profitability analyses are sometimes misused and wrong decisions taken based on the financial performance results alone,ignoring even some overriding strategic marketing considerations. In sum, therefore, product profitability statements should be used only, as a guide for obtaining useful information in planning appropriate measures for improving the performance of products.

4. PROFIT IMPACT OF MARKETING STRATEGIES (PIMS)

PIMS attempts to establish a link between strategic planning and profit performance. It is essentailly a computer based regression model (developed as a research project for General Electric at Harvard Business School in the early 1970's) for identifying the factors or variables that are related most strongly to the ROI marginally. The important questions which PIMS addressed are :

a. What factors explain differences in typical levels of ROI. and cash flows among various kinds of businesses ?

b. What rate of ROI and of cash flow is normal in a given type of business, under given conditions and using a given strategy?

c. How will ROI and other measures of performance,

in a specific business, be affected by a change in the strategy employed?

d. What are the promising directions to explore so as to improve performance of a given business?

Without going into the details of methodology of PIMS (comprising listing initially of a large number of factors or variables, tabulating them into several groups, developing a regression equation, working out co-efficient of determination etc.) we may present here the selected findings, as follows :

A. Determinants of ROI

1. *The impact of investment intensity*
   * As investment intensity rises ROI declines.
   * Large investment and high marketing intensity equal poor ROI.
   * Capacity utilization is vital when fixed capital intensity is high.
   * High capital intensity and small market share equal disaster.

2. *The Impact of Market Share*
   * ROI is closely related to relative market share.
   * Market share is most profitable in vertically integrated industries.
   * High R & D spending depresses ROI when market share is weak.
   * Capacity utilisation is most important for low share business.
   * Heavy marketing depresses ROI for low·share business.
   * Market share and quality are partial business substitutes for each oiher.

3. *The impact of growth rate*

* A rapid rate of new product introduction in fast growing markets depresses ROI.

* R & D is most profitable in mature, slow growth market.

4. *The impact of Life cycle stage*

* A narrow product line in early or middle stage of the cycle is less profitable than at the last stage.

5. *The impact of Marketing expenses to sales*

* High R & D plus high marketing expenses depresses ROI.

* High marketing expenditure depresses ROI especially when when quality is low.

B. Determinants of Cash Flow

1. The impact of relative Market Share on Cash Flows :

* High relative share improves cash flows ; high growth decreases it.

* High share and low investment intensity produce cash; low share and high investment intensity result in a cash drain

* High relative share produces cash - especially when marketing intensity is low.

c. The impact of investment intensity of cash flow

* Low or medium growth coupled with low investment intensity produces cash; high growth coupled with high investment intensity is a cash drain.

* Harvesting share when investment intensity is low produces cash; building share when investment intensity is high is a cash drain.

* Investments plus marketing intensity result in cash drain.

* Few new product introductions coupled with low investment intensity produces cash.

PIMS has been proved to be a very effective tool since it identifies a set of underlying principles of successful business strategy, or "laws of the market place", based on empirical research. Its data bank contains information based on the strategic experiences of over 3000 business units. PIMS reseaches had shown that three quarters of the variability in business profitability could be explained by around 30 strategic variables and their interactions. A number of concepts has been developed from this, such as PAR (expected value for returns for a business unit, given its strategic position and market/industry situation) and strategic peers (a group of business units in the PIMS data base that "look alike" a client's business unit).

CHAPTER 26

PRODUCT LINE ACCOUNTING & VARIANCE ANALYSIS

1. Introduction; 2. Product Line Accounting; 3. Division-wise and Product-wise Profitability Analysis; 4. Uses and Misuses of Profitability Analysis; 5. Sales Variance Analysis; 6. Uses and Misuses of Sales Variance Analysis.

1. INTRODUCTION

Profitability analysis is of different types. Since net profit is the simplest and the most easily understood criterion of performance, often it is necessary to arrive at, through preparation of comparative profit and loss statements, product or product line-wise, territory-wise, or even salesman-wise net profit figures. In preparing such statements management accounting tools and technique are being increasingly used. Specially, the technique of analysis of selling and distribution costs is of great use in any such profitability analysis.

Profitability analysis of divisions or product lines or products is relatively simple in case of small or medium sized marketing organisations handling a few divisions and operating through a few selling establishments. But in case of a multi-product,multi-market marketing organisation with highly diversified product range and operating through multiple selling and distribution establishments, division-wise and product-wise profitability analysis becomes a very complicated exercise. And in such cases, computer is often made use of. This requires a detailed systems study and suitable programming to get realistic performance results in the form of profits.

Through various illustrations we will explain in this chapter such varied types of profitability analysis.

* [Different methods of Sales Variance Analysis are also covered in this chapter.]

2. PRODUCT LINE ACCOUNTING

We are giving here three ilustrations of varied types to show cost and profit analysis under product line accounting with a view to meeting diverse purposes.

Illustration 1

A company manufactures and markets radios, electric fans, and electric heaters, which are distributed in three main territories- Calcutta, Bombay, and Madras. The sales in Delhi region are controlled by the Calcutta head office. The analysis of sales for the month of June 19X8 is as follows :

Line of Products	Territory 1 Calcutta Rs.	Territory 2 Bombay Rs.	Territory 3 Madras Rs.	Total Rs.
Radios	120,000	200,000	50,000	370,000
Fans	60,000	40,000	20,000	120,000
Heaters	20,000	10,000	5,000	35,000
Total	200,000	250,000	75,000	525,000

The gross profit based on analysis of pricing is estimated to be 25 per cent of sales for radios, 40 per cent of sales for fans and 30 per cent of sales for heaters.

The direct selling costs during the month are tabulated as under

Selling costs directly Chargeable	Territory 1			Territory 2			Territory 3		
	Radio	Fans	Heaters	Radio	Fans.	Heaters	Radio	Fans	Heaters
	Rs.	Rs.	Rs.	Rs.	Rs.	Rs.	Rs.	Rs.	Rs.
Advertising through paper	5000	1000	2000	10000	4000	2000	5000	1000	1000
Advertising through cinema	2000	500	500	2000	1000	1000	500	200	200
Salesmen's commission	6000	3000	1000	10000	2000	500	2500	1000	250
Telephone	300	100	100	500	100	100	100	100	150
Entertainment	4000	1000	2000	5000	1000	1500	1000	500	500
	16300	5600	5600	27500	8100	5100	9100	2800	2100

Indirect selling costs		**Basis of distribution**
Executive office Rs.	12,000)	Equally among territories
Service Dept cost	15,000)	and lines of product
Other sales promotion expenses	25,000	Ratio of actual sales

Required :

Comparative Profit and Loss Statements for each territory and for each line of product.

1 DIRECT SELLING COST ANALYSIS

Product	T_1 Rs.	T_2 Rs.	T_3 Rs.	Total Rs.
Radios	16,300	27,500	9,100	52,900
Fans	5,600	8,100	2,800	16,500
Heaters	5,600	5,100	2,100	12,800
Total	27,500	40,700	14,000	82,200

II INDIRECT SELLING COST ANALYSIS

Territories	T_1 Rs.	T_2 Rs.	T_3 Rs.	Total Rs.
Executive office and service dept. costs	9,000	9,000	9,000	27,000
Other sales promotion expenses:				
Radios				17,630
Fans				5,710
Heaters				1,660
	9,500	11,920	3,580	25,000
Total	18,500	20,920	12,580	52,000

Notes : (i) indirect selling costs to be assigned equally among territories and lines of products Rs. 12,000

15,000

27,000

(ii) The indirect sales promotion expenses of each product in each territory are not calculated, since, in the problem, only totals are required.

III. TERRITORYWISE PROFIT & LOSS STATEMENT

	Territory 1 Rs.	Territory 2 Rs.	Territory 3 Rs.	Total Rs.
Sales	2,00,000	2,50,000	75,000	92,500
Gross Profit :				
25% on radios	50,000	50,000	12,500	92,500
40% on fans	24,000	16,000	8,000	48,000

80% on heaters	6,000	3,000	1,500	10,500
Total	80,000	69,000	22,000	1,51,000
Less direct selling cost	27,500	40,700	14,000	82,200
Less direct selling cost	18,500	20,920	12,580	52,000
Net Profit (loss)	14,000	7,380	(4,580)	16,800

IV PRODUCTWISE PROFIT & LOSS STATEMENT

	Radios Rs.	Fans Rs.	Heaters Rs.	Total Rs.
Sales	3,70,000	1,20,000	35,000	5,52,000
Gross Profit	92,500	48,000	10,500	1,51,000
Less direct selling costs	52,900	16,500	12,800	82,200
Less indirect selling cost	26,630	14,710	10,660	52,000
Net Profit (loss)	12,970	16,790	(12,960)	16,800

Illustration 2 :

A decision is to be taken relating to the possible introduction of a new product. There are three basic design versions of this product, aimed at different sections of the cusumer market.

The relevant figures are as follows :

Variable cost (per unit):	Model I Rs.	Model II Rs.	Model III Rs.
Materials	1.54	1.22	0.86
Labour	1.06	0.95	0.58
Variable overheads	0.40	0.33	0.31
	3.00	2.50	1.75
Selling price (per unit)	4.25	3.50	2.50

Expected sales volume Per months (units)	800	200	4000
Capital expenditure before production can commence (financed by bank overdraft @ 15% interest per annum)	Rs.800	Rs.3000	Rs. 4000
Fixed overheads per month attributable to new models including depreciation in capital expenditure, but excluding interest	Rs.280	Rs.850	Rs.1100

You are required to prepare a Schedule of relative profitability showing, for each model, the figures making up expected total cost per unit, the expected net profit per unit, and the percentage of net profit to selling price at the expected sales volume.

Solutions :

PROFITABILITY STATEMENT

Expected Monthly sales volume	MODEL I		MODEL II		MODEL III	
	800 Units		2,000 Units		4,000 Units	
Expenses	Total	Cost per unit	Total	Cost per unit	Total	Cost per unit
	Rs.	Rs.	Rs.	Rs.	Rs.	Rs.
Variable costs						
Materials	1232	1.54	2440	1.22	3440	0.86
Labour	848	1.06	1900	0.95	23220	0.58
Variable overheads	320	0.40	660	0.33	1240	0.31
Total variable cost	2400	3.00	5000	1.50	7000	1.75
Sales	3400	4.25	7000	3.50	10000	2.50
Contribution to fixed overheads	1000	1.25	2000	2.00	3000	0.75

Fixed overheads	280	0.35	850	0.42	1100	0.27
Interest on Bank overdraft	120	0.05	450	0.07	600	0.05
Total fixed overhead	400	0.40	1300	0.49	1700	0.32
Net profit	600	0.85	700	1.51	1300	0.43
Percentage of net profit to selling price (per cent margin sale)	17.6 %		10.0%		13.0%	

Illustration 3 :

A warehousing concern proposes to purchase electric high-lift trucks and auxiliary equipment to replace hand trucks used now. The new trucks would necessitate additional capital expenditure for buildings and fitting. The following appeared in last year's Profit and Loss Account.

	Rs.		*Rs.*
Management and clerical costs	32,000	Space rentals	2,50,000
Warehouse wages cost	1,04,000		
Rates and licence cost	18,000		
Power, light and water cost	15,000		
Insurance cost	7,000		
Maintenance cost	3,000		
Depreciation :			
Building	10,000		
Hand trucks (final)	2,000		
	1,91,000		2,50,000

Proposed new expenditures :

Trucks etc Rs 60,000 life 10 years, residual value Rs 10,000.

Building and fittings, Rs.50,000 to be written off over 20 years.

Estimated increased operating cost :

Management and clerical : estimated increase 10 per cent

Warehouse wages : estimated increase 25 per cent

Power .. Rs. 3,000

Insurance .. Rs. 2,000

Maintenance .. Rs. 500

Rental income : increase of available facilities for renting 50 per cent.

It is estimated that an overall reduction of charges of 50 per cent will be possible.

From the above infrormation, present a forecast comparing the present profit and loss with the projected profit and loss account when the scheme is in full working.

Comparative Profit and Loss Account

Details	Present Rs.	Projected Rs.	Details	Present Rs.	Projected Rs.
Managament and clerical cost	32,000	35,200	Space rental	2,50,000	3,75,000 (A)
Warehouse cost	1,04,000	1,30,000			
Rates & licence cost	15,000	18,000			
Power, light and water cost	15,00	18,000			
Insurance cost	7,000	9,000			
Maintenance cost	3,000	3,500			
Depreciation buildings	10,000	12,500 (B)			
Hand truck (final)	2,000				
Electric high lift truck		5,000 (C)			
Profit	59,000	1,43,800			

Workings (A) : $(2,50,000 \times \frac{50}{100}) + 2,50,000$

$= 1,25,000 + 2,50,000 =$ Rs. 3,75,0000

(B) $\frac{50,000}{20} = 2,500;\ 10,000 + 2500 = 12,500$

(C) 60,000

$\frac{10,000}{50,000} \quad \frac{50,000}{10} = 5,000$

3. DIVISION-WISE AND PRODUCT-WISE AND PROFITABILITY ANALYSIS

As stated earlier division-wise and product-wise profitability analysis would be more complicated than in the illustrations given above for large companies having diversified product range and operating through a large number of sales and distribution set-ups.

We will discuss here a real life case dealing with the introduction of a computerised division-wise and product-wise profitability analysis in case of one such big company.

MULTI-PRODUCT MULTI-MARKET LTD.

(A Case Study on Computerised Profitability Analysis)

Brief background of the company: The comapany has 12 marketing divisions which handle a wide range of industrial products and services. Division Nos.1 to 7 market their products through 4 regional headquarters situated in Bombay, Delhi, Calcutta and Madras, which in turn have under their control 21 branches (4 to 5 branches under each region),scattered through-out India. For a pretty long time the regions were considered as profit centres. But recently the primary profit centres have been shifted from regions to divisions and each division has been under the charge of a general manager who operates from the headquarters, aat Bombay. However, the regional and branch set-ups are still being used to ensure prompt and efficient sales and services. In addition, to watch the geographical growth prospects and problems, the company continues to treat the regions as secondary profit centres (primary profit centresm as already started, being shifted to the divisions). Since the company has so long been treating the regions as main profit centres, the entire accounting structure continues to be region-oriented and to avoid unnecessary increase in accounting costs, this system is allowed to continue instead of a change over to divisional accounting.

The other 5 divisions (Nos. 8 to 12) have been since the beginning, operating as centralised all-India trading divisions. Since the nature of the products and services they handle do not require a regional and branch set-up, there has been no change in the mode of operation of these divisions. In respect of these divisions, some crude methods of divisional accounting have been in existence for quite some time.

The scheme of profitability analysis : The management accounting department of the company has recently developed and introduced a çomprehensive scheme of division-wise and product-wise profitability analysis. Given below are :

(i) Exhibit 1 : Extracts from the outline of the scheme as submitted to the Directors (This shows a phased implementation with time-schedule).

(ii) Exhibit 2 : Bases of allocation and apportionment (variòus expenses to be adopted in Phase 1.)

(iii) Exhibit 3 : A blank format of computerised profitability statement.

Exhibit 1

OUTLINE OF THE COMPUTERISED PROFITABILITY SCHEME

(1) The total scheme is intended to be taken up and completed in three phases, as follows :

Phase I : (6 months from inception

(i) Bases as shown in the Exhibit 2.
(ii) Restricted to regional operations

of systems study)	as well as the 7 Divisions operating through the regions.
Phase II : (3 months from implementation of Phase I)	(iii) Bases as shown in the Exhibit 2 with some refinements by way of division -wise actuals in respect of the following five items under the direct and variable expense group: (a) Advertising (b) Motor vehicle expenses (c) Godown and forwarding expenses (d) Stamps and bank charges (product - wise allocation will continue to be on percentage basis). (ii) Extension of the scheme to the 5 centralised all - India trading divisions.
Phase III : (3 months from implementation of Phase II)	(i) Same as reached under phase II (ii) Provision for budget actual comparison in the profitability statement, in all casess

(2) Indirect, (managerial, accounting, ect.) expenses forming part of the items 3 to 11 in the direct and variable expenses are to be segregated as regional/branch overheads and clubbed under item 7, viz., 'indirect and fixed expenses' and distributed among division and products based on the percentages applicable to this head (indirect and fixed expenses).

(3) The profitability statements under the new scheme will be prepared regularly every month upto the contribution (after financial charges) stage (i.e. A to F in Exhibit 3). P/V ratio calculations will also be shown on the basis of both (a) contribution before financial charges, on sales and (b) contribution after financial charges, on

sales. In addition to this , after every 6 months, profitability statements will be prepared on a 'full cost' basis, that is, upto net profit/loss stage (A to I in Exhibit 3). In these statements R.O.I. calculations will also be shown on the basis of both (a) net profit before financial charges on average capital employed and (b) net profit after financial charges on average capital employed.

(4) An attempt has been made to develop the first set of percentages on a realistic basis. However, it is intended that these percentages are to be reviewed every year or every six months (but not more frequently)

(5) Phase I of the scheme which has already been implemented takes adequate care to avoid any distortion or dislocation in the existing coding structure and in the mode of preparation of both input and output statements under statutory accounting framework. The present exercise is, therefore, purely statistical in nature.

(6) The new scheme of profitability analysis is not the ideal, nor the ultimate. It is obvious that we have to make some compromise knowing full well that this might render the analyses somewhat inaccurate. But such compromises have been made only after striking a balance between the cost involved due to huge workload at regional/branch office and at the E.D.P. department on the one hand and the benefits of greater degree of accuracy that may accrue, on the other.

(7) During the first two/three months, until the programme gets stabilized, our statements might show some errors/inaccuracies. We would request the users to bear with us and also point out to us such deficiencies. In course of the next six months or so we hope to be able to produce statements which would be both accurate and realistic as far as possible, under the scheme outlined here.

Exhibit 2

BASES OF ALLOCATION AND APPORTIONMENT

Details	Basis for Divisional profitability	Basis for product wise profitability
A. Net Sales	Actual (as per computerised sales statistics)	Actual (as per computerised sales statistics)
B. Gross Income	-do-	-do-
C. Direct and Variable Expenses 1.Sal.direct staff 2.-do-fringe benefits 3. Travelling	Actual - based on staff attached to each division Actual	ASM's percentages (approved by RM) as to product-wise allocation of staff attached to each Division) ASM's percentages (approved by R.M.)
4. Advertising	RM's percentage based on adv.budget	-do-
5. Motor veh.exp.	RM's percentage	-do-
6. Godown & forwarding exp.	-do-	-do-
7. Entertainment	Actual	-do-
8. Printing & stationery	RM's percentages	-do-

9. Postage & telegrams	-do-	-do-
10. Telephone & Telex	-do-	-do-
11. Stamp & bank charges	-do-	-do
Total (C)	Resultant figure	Resultant figure
D. Contribution (before fin.charges) (B-C.)	Resultant figure	Resultant figure
E. Financial Charges	Actual - based on average inventory and net receivables	Actual - based on average inventory and net receivables
F. Contribution (after fin.charges)	Resultant figure	Resultant figure
G. Indirect & Fixed Expenses	RM's percentages	ASM's percentages (approved byRM)
H. Head Office Expenses	Net expenses ratio	Net expenses ratio
L. Net Profit/Loss (F-G-H)	Resultant figure	Resultant figure

Notes : (i) RM = Regional manager; ASM = Area sales manager

(ii) Net expenses ratio = 'net expenses' for his purpose defined as the total of direct variable expenses (C) and indirect & fixed expenses (G)

Exhibit 3

PROFITABILITY ANALYSIS FOR THE PERIOD ENDING

Page

Region Division Product Amount in lacs

Detail Variance	Current			Year to date			Year to date	
	Bud.	Act	Pre. Yr	Bud.	Act	Pre. Yr. Amount	Bud.	Pre Yr. Amount
A.Net sales								
B.Gross income								
C. Direct & Variable Expenses								
1. Sal. direct staff								
2. Fringe benefits								
3. Travelling								
4. Advertising								
5. Motor vehicle exp.								
6. Godown & ford.exp.excl. godown rent								
7. Entertainment								
8. Printing & stationery								
9. Postage & telegrams								
10. Telephone & telex								
11. Stamps & bank charges								
Total of C-1 to 11								
D. Contibn. before fin. chrg. B-C-D								
-do-% to net sales -A-								
E. Financial charges								
F. Contribn. after fin. chrg. D-E								
G. Indirect & fixed expenses								
H. Head office expenses								

I. Net profit/loss F-G-H-I
-do-% to net sales -A-

J. Return on cap. employed (ROI)

4. USES AND MISUSES OF PROFITABILITY ANALYSIS

A well-desinged and systematic profitability analysis can be used for diverse purposes. In the first place, profitability analysis can help the management in identifying the growth sectors and the weak areas in its marketing operations. This in turn might lead to various decisions for better planning and control of operations. These decisions could be sometimes of strategic nature, sometimes of operational types and at other times involve tactical shifts. For example, some strategic decisions from long-term point of view, could be made while allocating limited investible funds among a number of competing divisions. Ordinarily, a sizeable proportion of the fuinds will be diverted towards the divisions showing higher profitability and relatively lesser proportion to those showing higher profitability and relatively lesser proportion to those showing lower profitability. Similarly, various tactical and operational decisions could be taken and suitable control actions initiated to arrest the downward trend in profitability shown by some divisions. These may help substantially in improving the performance of the weaker divisions and consequently, the company as a whole. Further, a scientifically designed profitability analysis could be used in projecting for the future period division-wise profitability on a realistic basis, both for meeting short-term purposes as well as in developing long-range plans of the company.

One other important use of product profitability analysis, as a sequel to the foregoing observations, is product rationalisation decisions using profitability analysis as a tool. Product rationalisation includes, product revamping, product range extension, product elimination and also new product introduction.

It is to be noted, however, that profitability analysis is not without its pitfalls. For one thing, any such analysis, however scientifically done, cannot replace judgement, nor can it straight-away lead to the right decisions at the right time. This fact is often lost sight of. As a result profitability analysis are sometimes misused in taking wrong decisions based on the results alone.

The most important thing to be kept in view while using profitability statements is that these are nothing but accounting statements which can only present some figures and not the facts that lie hidden behind the figures. These facts and operational aspects have to be analysed in propert perspective while interpreting the results presented in these statements. And only through such analysis of the operational reasons can right decisions be taken and this is how the figures of the statements can be effectively used.

5. SALES VARIANCE ANALYSIS

The technique of variance analysis of standards costing can be used very effectively for the purpose of sales variance analysis which in turn could be used to locate precisely the reasons for divergence between budgeted or expected results and actual results. Proper analysis of such reasons will help initiate suitable control actions as well.

Sales variances can be calculated in two ways, viz.,

A. The value method : This will show the variances in terms of sales value. Total sales value variance may first be analysed into price variance and volume variance and then *volume variance* may be further analysed into quantity variance and *mix variance.*

B. The proft method : Under this method, variances are shown in terms of their effect on profit (or gross margin or contribution). This is a more improved method than the former. These variances are also called *margin variances* and the model of their calculation and analysis would be the same as under (A) above, with the only difference that here sales value would be replaced by profit in each case.

Let us take two illustrations to explain sales variance analysis under both these methods.

Illustration 1 - Sales variance Analysis - The value Method

The budgeted and actual sales of DCP Ltd, For the next year 19X1 are as follows:

Product	Budget Quantity	Budget Price Rs.	Budget Amount Rs.	Actual Quantity	Actual Price Rs.	Actual Amount Rs.
D	1,000	1,000	10,00,000	1,200	980	11,76,000
C	600	5,000	30,00,000	500	5,100	25,50,000
P	1,250	800	10,00,000	1,000	800	8,00,000
	2,850		50,00,000	2,700		45,26,000

Required : Detailed analysis of sales variances :

(i) Sales value variance : (i.e. Total sales variance)

50,00,000 ~ 45,26,000 = 4,74,000 (A)

(ii) Sales price variance : Act Qnty. X (std. Price Act Price)

D : 1200 (1000 ~ 980) = 24,000 (A)

C : 500 (5000 ~ 5100) = 50,000(F)

P : 1000 (1250 ~ 1000) =

Rs. 26,0000(F)

(iii) Sales volume variance : Std. Price X (Std. Qty.Act. Qty.)

D : 1000 (1000 ~ 1200) = 2,00,000 (F)

C : 5000 (600 ~ 500) = 5,00,000 (A)

P : 800 (1250 ~ 1000) = 2,00,000 (A)

Rs. 5,00,000(A)

check (ii) + (iii) = Rs. 4,75,000 (A) = (i)

(iii/a) Sales mix variance : std. Price X (Std.Act Qnty.Act.Qnty)

Standard actual quantity =

$$\text{Std Qnty X} \frac{\text{Act Total Sales (Units)}}{\text{Std. Total Sales (Units)}}$$

$$D: \quad 1000 \text{ X } \frac{2700}{2850} = 950$$

$$C: \quad 600 \text{ X } \frac{2700}{2850} = 570$$

$$P: \quad 1250 \text{ X } \frac{2700}{2850} = 1180$$

D : 1000 (950 ~ 1200) = 2,50,000 (F)
C : 5000 (570 ~ 500) = 3,50,000 (A)
P : 800 (1180 ~ 1000) = 1,44,000 (A)

Total 2,44,000 (A)

(iii/b) Sales quantity variance :

Std. price X (Std.Act.Quty. ~ Std. Quty.)
D : 1000 (950 ~ 1000) = 50,000 (A)
C : 5000 (570 ~ 600) = 1,50,000(A)
P : 800 (1180 ~ 1250) = .56,000 (A)

Total 2,56,000 (A)

Check (ii/a + (iii/b) = (iii)
2,44,000 (A) + 2,56,000 (A) = 5,00,000 (A)

Illustration 2-Sales Variance Analysis - The Profit Method

Household Product Ltd. had budgeted the following Sales for March 19X8.

Product A	900 units @ Rs.	50 per unit.
Product B	650 units @ Rs.	100 per unit.
Product C	1,200 units @ Rs.	75 per unit.

As against this, the actual sales were :

Product A	1,000 units @ Rs.	55 per unit.
Product B	700 units @ Rs.	95 per unit.
Product C	1,100 units @ Rs.	78 per unit.

The marginal cost of sales per unit of A, B and C was Rs. 45, Rs.85 and Rs. 65 respectively.

We have to compute the different variances to explain the difference between the budgeted and actual profit.

To start with, the following figures are necessary :

1. Budgeted contribution
2. Actual contribution
3. Standard contribution
4. Revised standard contribution

	A	B	C
Budgeted selling price (Rs.)	50	100	75
Budgeted marginal cost (Rs.)	45	85	65
Contribution per unit	5	15	10
Per cent contribution	10%	15%	13 1/3%
Actual selling price (Rs.)	55	95	78
Budgeted cost (Rs.)	45	85	65
Actual Contribution per unit	10	10	13

Standard and revised standard contribution can be arrived at by applying the budgeted contribution percentage on standard and revised standard sales. Hence, it is necessary to ascertain these two:

SALES ANALYSIS

Product	Unit	Budgeted Sales Price Rs.	Value Rs.	Ratio %
A	900	50	45,000	22.5
B	650	100	65,000	32.5
C	1,200	75	90,000	45.0
Total	2,750		2,00,000	100.0

	Standard Sales			Revised Standard Sales		
Product	Actual Qty.	Standard price Rs.	Value Rs.	Standard Sales (Total) Rs.	Budgeted ratio %	Revised Standard sales Rs.
A	1,000	50	50,000	2,02,500	22.5	45,562
B	700	100	70,000		32.5	65,813
C	1,100	75	82,500		45.0	91,125
	2,800		2,02,500			2,02,500

Statement of Comparative Contribution

Product	Budget Rs.	Actual Rs.	Standard Rs.	Revised standard
A	4,500	10,000	5,000	4,556
B	9,750	7,000	10,500	9,872
C	12,000	14,300	11,000	12,150
Total	26,250	31,300	26,500	26,578

Calculation (Product A)

1. Budgeted contribution :	10% of budgeted sales. 10% of Rs. 45,000 = Rs.4,500
2. Actual contribution :	Actual Quantity x Actual Profit per unit. 1,000 x Rs. 10 = Rs.10,000
3. Standard contribution :	10% of standard sales 10% of Rs. 50,000 = Rs. 5,000
4. Revised standard contribution :	10% of revised standard sales 10% of Rs. 45,562 = Rs. 4,556 (Approx.)

Similar calculations are made for B and C.

Calculation of Variances

1. Total sales margin variance : Actual contribution ~ Budgeted contribution.

	Rs.		Rs.		Rs.
A	10,000	~	4,500	=	5,500 (F)
B	7,000	~	9,750	=	2,750 (A)
C	14,300	~	12,000	=	2,300 (F)
Total	31,300	~	26,250	=	5,050 (F)

(a) Sales margin variance due to selling price : Actual contribution ~ standard contribution .

	Rs.		Rs.		Rs.
A	10,000	~	5,000	=	5,000 (F)
B	7,000	~	10,500	=	3,500 (A)
C	14,300	~	11,000	=	3,300 (F)
Total	31,300		26,500	=	4,800 (F)

(b) Sales margin variance due to volume : Standard contribution~Budgeted contribution.

	Rs.		Rs.		Rs.
A	5,000	~	4,500	=	500 (F)
B	10,500	~	9,750	=	750 (F)
C	11,000	~	12,000	=	1,000 (A)
Total	26,500	~	26,250	=	250 (F)

Sales margin variance due to volume, as per (b) above can be further analysis as follows :

(i) Sales margin variance due to quantity : (Revised standard contribution ~ Budgeted contribution)

	Rs.	Rs.		Rs.
A	4,556	~ 4,500	=	56(F)
B	9,872	~ 9,750	=	122(F)
C	12,150	~12,000	=	150(F)
Total	26,578	~ 26,250	=	328 (F)

(ii) Sales margin variance due to sales quantities (mixture) : Standard Contribution ~ (Revised standard contribution)

	Rs.	Rs.		Rs.
A	5,000	~ 5,556	=	444 (F)
B	10,500	~ 9,872	=	628 (F)
C	11,000	~ 12,150	=	1,150(A)
Total	26,500	~ 26,578	=	78 (A)

Profit and Loss Statement

	A Rs.	B Rs.	C Rs.	Total Rs.
1. Budgeted sales	45,000	65,000	90,000	2,00,000
Less: Budgeted marginal cost of sales	40,500	55,250	78,000	1,73,750
2. Budgeted contribution	4,500	9,750	12,000	26,250
3. Variances				
Sales quantity	56	122	150	328
Sales mix	444	628	(1,150)	(78)

	500	750	(1,000)	250
4. Standard contribution on sales (2 + 3)	5,000	10,500	11,000	26,500
5. Sales price variance	5,000	(3,500)	3,300	4,800
6. Actual contribution	10,000	7,000	14,300	31,300

Note : indicates unfavourable or adverse variances

6. USES AND MISUSES OF SALES VARIANCE ANALYSIS

The following observations may be made in this connection :

(i) Sales variance analysis of, for that matter, any variance analysis, should not be considered as an end in itself - this is only the means to achieve certain ends. This important aspect is often unfortunately lost sight of.

(ii) Sales variance analysis is to some extent a mechanical exercise and should be done either by or with the help of the accounting to be precise, management accounting staff. But what follows at the next stage is much more important than the mechanical exercise and should be done by the operating people, the marketing and selling staff. This is what we may call analysis of the reasons of variance, especially the unfavourable ones. Unless this is done, the mechanical variance analysis will be just a wasteful exercise.

(iii) While analysing the reasons for variances an attempt should be made to classify all the reasons into controllable and uncontrollable categories. Thereafter, an attempt should be made to quantify each reason, at least the major ones, under each category. In this exercise of quantification, it may be necessary to make use of the expertise of the management accounting staff.

(iv) Only after such quantification of the various reasons of sales variances is made can suitable control actions be initiated. Such control actions should primarily be aimed at attacking the controllable variances. But the uncontrollable variances should not be completely ignored, since their adverse effect on a long-term basis will have to be eliminated, as far as practicable, by tactical and strategic action plans.

(v) Executives- and marketing and sales executives are no exceptions-are found to be a little sensitive to variances, specially adverse variances. An atmosphere of mutual faith and confidence has to be created whereby executives will look upon variances not as means of fault finding but as divergence between actual and expected performances, so that genuine efforts in a co-ordinated manner can be initiated to correct any adverse divergence. Any variance analysis should have as its focal point not the man but his performance. Such analysis should be always objective-never to be vitiated by personal equation or subjective value judgement.

CHAPTER 27

MANAGEMENT INFORMATION AND CONTROL SYSTEMS IN MARKETING

1. Basic Concepts of MIS ; 2. Marketing Management and Information System; 3. The Concept of Management Control ; 4. The Process of Management Control ; 5. An Integrated Framework of Management Information, Control and Reporting Systems ; 6. A Few Case Studies. 7. Salesman's Report.

1. BASIC CONCEPTS OF MIS

Meaning and Implications of MIS :

Management Information System has three components, viz., management, information and system. Management essentially means planning and controlling operations, but such planning and controlling presuppose making decisions about planning and controlling. Information has to be distinguished from data. For example, customers invoices are data only, while the inventory analysis, sales analysis, etc., are information (after the same data are converted). System essentially implies a systems approach to turn data into information and integrate all systems of a business.

Thus, MIS may be defined as a set of integrated, well-knit and scientifically designed systems whereby raw data get converted into decision-based and control-oriented information and continuously and regularly flow from one end to another. A sound MIS ensures, inter alia, the following :

(i) Right information at right time to right person and in right manner;

(ii) Regularly in the periodicity of information-flow;

(iii) Information geared toward aiding managerial decisions for planning the control ;

(iv) Screening of all information at the point of transmission to select the relevant and reject all irrelevant details, keeping an eye on the diverse needs of the different levels of management; and

(v) A built-in system of link and follow-up.

There are three key elements in any information-flow ,viz., timing, degree of accuracy and nature of details.

Timing of information is perhaps of greatest importance in any MIS since it is an accepted fact that information delayed is information denied. Closely linked up with timing is the degree of accuracy which should be determined with reference to the purpose of and the decision that might emanate from the proposed information. Nature of details to be provided or the volume of information is also an important factor in MIS. Inadequate information and more than adequate information may both be worse than no information.

What is information (finished product) to one may be data (raw materials) to another — it all depends upon the levels and functional areas of management. For example, a detailed customer-wise outstandings analysis is an information to the line management but only data to the top management. From these data may be prepared division-wise working capital locked up in respect of outstandings and this may become an information to the top management.

The philosophy underlying the principle of cost of costing should form the bedrock of MIS so that the desire for more and more information is tempered with a proper cost-benefit analysis. It is to be noted that information industry is the most expensive industry today. Some companies have started treating MIS functions a profit centre. This would reduce the cost of information substantially since the MIS department will appropriately charge the user department in respect of all information provided.

Last but not the least, MIS should be more future-oriented than just an extrapolation of past data. Unfortunately, futuristic element is absent from most information today. Taking decisions based on past data alone is the same as driving a vehicle with eyes fixed on the rear view mirror — the vehicle can never achieve even reasonalbe speed and reach the destination in time.

Need for MIS :

The need for MIS is felt more in its absence than in its presence. Very often, in an organisation some failure symptoms become apparent necessitating the introduction or revamping of MIS. Such failure symptoms could be :

(i) Organisation unable to meet its commitments ;
(ii) Increased overtime in respect of clerical and other staff ;
(iii) Huge backlogs in executive workload ;
(iv) Delayed decisions, indecision and wrong decisions;
(v) Non-availability of timely and relevant information;
(vi) Maintenance of pocket and/or desk information by executives;
(vii) Loose control resulting in wastages, losses and inefficiencies and
(viii) Duplication of work and disjointed efforts.

The increased incidence of heart ailments, ulcers, blood pressures, etc., among today's executives may be largely ascribed to the absence of MIS which in turn generates more tension at work. Similarly, inability of executives to regularly avail themselves of annual leave or executives going for their own marriage with casual leave (as if marriage is a casual affair !) are also due to absence of proper MIS.

A Few Myths about M.I.S. :

One myth is that the study of management information system is about the use of computers. In a subsequent topic we will discuss this aspect. Another myth is that more data in reports mean more information for managers. Closely related to this is another myth that more frequent reporting means more useful information! It is also a myth that the accountant aims to keep the cost of information to the minimum. Almost similar is the myth that the accuracy in reporting is of vital importance.

One of the largest myths, particularly about MIS in Indian industry, is the managers information needs can be determined by professional system study. Line managers seldom do any home-work to identify their information needs and consequently depend heavily upon the MIS man or systems man to do this job theirs. Obviously good MIS cannot be evolved with this type of attitude of line managers. Staff managers in charge of MIS may at best assist them or even guide the line managers in identifying their information needs. But nothing more than that is either desirable or practicable.

The supreme myth about MIS is that "we understand what management information is"! Yes; we claim to understand. May be, we understand the technical aspects involved. But the managers hardly understand the human element and more particularly the decision process of an organisation and the interface between the MIS and such decision process. To prevent MIS from degenerating into a mechanical exercise (as it is today in about 99 per cent of the cases), the understanding of human factor as also the decision process is vitally important both for the line managers and for the MIS staff.

MIS and Computers :

The following are the requirements of data processing under MIS:

(i) Large volume

(ii) Provision for systematic storing of the data,

(iii) Convenience of access to and easy retrieval of the data.

(iv) Continuous up-dating of the data base.

(v) Manipulation of the data according to fixed as well as variabel decision rules.

(vi) Processing the data inappropriate time-frame.

(vii) Ensuring acceptable level of accuracy (arithmetical) and reliability (of inputs) and

(viii) Processing data economically.

If we could meet all the above requirements or even most of them manually, through well-designed systems and procedures,then there is no need for computer in the area of MIS in fact it is so in case of small or some medium-size organisations. It is therefore to be noted that, contrary to the popular belief, computer is not synonymous with MIS. But it may be an ideal vehicle of MIS — ideal- but not ultimate, nor indispensable. Even in large organisations computer-manual combination,based on suitable cost-benefit analysis,might provide the right type of MIS and this is what should be attempted.

Impact of MIS on Management :

The result of installation of a sound MIS is improved management. This benefit cannot be quantified in strict monetary terms, but the all-pervasive impact may be felt quite well. For one thing, a sound MIS should explode the myth that a particular executive, is indispensable.

The first major impact of MIS on an organisation is that decisions are based on facts and rationale, rather than on bureaucratic procedures and subjective factors. Secondly MIS would flatten the universal pyramid structure of an organisation. In a typical pyramid organisation people run on hunch and history and get lost in the labyrinthian intricacies of the bureaucratic system — the inevitable results are indecision or delayed decision and emphasis on procedures rather than on results, obsession with inputs rather than with inputs.In the new organisation brought about by MIS would facilitate delegation, since the problem of what to delegate is effectively solved by MIS. According to the conventional principle of span of control, too many people reporting to one is considered to be bad. But this reporting of too many to one is, what a sound MIS seeks to achieve. Lastly, MIS replaces'management by activity' by 'management by results' and substitutes 'management by technocrats' for 'management by generalists' — generalists who can plan, organise and control in any functional area, backed by sound MIS. To sum up, MIS improves a manager's responsibility by enlarging his job scope and result-orientation.

2. MARKETING MANAGEMENT AND INFORMATION SYSTEM

The first basic implication of a scientific information system for management in general and marketing management in particular is to replace traditional approach by systems approach. Let us examine what this really implies.

The traditional organisation structure, based on the span of control and specialisation concepts, suffers from two basic limitations :

(i) It pays the job, not the man ;

(ii) Communication problem arises because of bureaucratic entanglement — many a decision is either hidden or lost in the morass of bureaucracy.

These problems can be effectively taken care of under the systems approach, where organisation is more a team than a pyramid.

The traditional control also suffers from a serious limitation in that it is more historical in nature. Often it is too late to do anything about it. Further, whatever control there is, more an 'accounting control' (through budgets) than ' managerial control'. Under the systems approach control becomes really managerial control and

Decision-making is required for planning and controlling operations. Decision, by definition, is a choice out of two or more alternatives. Under tradional method, programmed decisions are based on procedures and the non-programmed ones, on hunch, intuition and judgement. Under systmes approach, both types of decisions will be based upon MIS by providing better information to the decision-maker ensures that he can take a better decision and can also check for himself continuously whether the decision-making process is being improved or not.

The starting point of planning under an integrated MIS effort should be profit planning. The Table given below may be useful.

Elements	Plan	Control
1. Sales	Sales Plan	Sales Quota
2. Cost of Sales		
i) Materials	Material Plan	Unit usage
ii) Labour	Labour budget	Functional
iii)Overheads	Overhead budget	relationship between different items of activity
iv) Selling and distribution	Budget	—do—
3. General and administrative expenses	Budget	—do—
4. Profit	Profit Plan	R.O.I.

3. THE CONCEPT OF MANAGEMENT CONTROL

Since these days we talk more of control system, rather than control per se, it would be useful if we start with the implication of systems approach. Systems usually are defined as whole structures organised by the inter-relationshiops of their parts or elements, called sub-systems. In management science there are many advocates of the Systems approach as an attempt to analyse the parts in relation to the whole under complex situations. Under systmes approach there is an emphatic interest in systems designs, corresponding with their aims to ensure the systems functioning. Control is one managerial process where systems approach has been found to be highly effective.

The meaning and significance of the term control is somewhat different in management from what it is in ordinary usage. Control is an important element of management functions, the others being planning, decision-making etc. Control in management essentially means monitoring and taking remedial action when necessary. The purpose of control is to maintain a desired state or condition. Managerial control exercised systematically should have four basic elements :

i) Selector—A device representing what should be happening so that it can be compared to what is happening. (What should be happening is actually the objective, goal, expectation, standard, norm, or any such thing used as bench-mark).
ii) Detector — A measuring device which detects what is happening.
iii) Effecter — A device for effecting change in what is happening, to bring this in line with what should be happening. (Sometimes the effecter might provide an acceptable and scientific basis for changing or restating what should be happening).
iv) Information — A means of communicating information among the three elements mentioned above.

These elements are universal in any control system. Therefore, they can also be applied to an organisation. However, in order to apply these to an organisation, the selector, that is, what should be happening, has to be determined through a conscious management process, called planning. This is how the planning process and control systems in any organisation are closely interlinked. However, there are some types of planning which are not so closely related to control.

The planning and control responsibilities differ according to the various levels of management. From this standpoint, planning and control activities may be classified into three categories,strategic planning, management control and operational control. We may first define these three expressions, quoting from Anthony and Dearden (Management Control Systems; Text and Cases).

> Strategic planning is the process of deciding on the goals of the organisation, on changes in these goals, on the resources added to attain these goals, and on the policies that are to govern the acquisition, use and disposition of these resources.
>
> Management control is the process by which managers assure that resources are obtained and used effectively and efficiently in the accomplishment of the organisation's goals.
>
> Operational control is the process of assuring that specific tasks are carried out effectively and efficiently.

Closely following Anthony and Dearden again , we have shown in a tabular form, some points of distinction between these three concepts.

DISTINCTION BETWEEN STRATEGIC PLANNING, MANAGEMENT CONTROL AND OPERATIONAL CONTROL

Characteristics	Strategic Planning	Management Control	Operational Control
1) Level of Management	Corporate management(board level)	Executive mangement (middle level and above)	Operating management (lower level)
2) Persons involved	Staff and top management	Line and top management	Supervisors
3) Focus of activity	Whole operation	One aspect at a time	Single task

4) Mental activity	Creative,analytical	Administrative, pursuasive	Following directions
5) Source discipline	Economics	Social Psychology	Physical sciences economics
6) Planning and control	Planning dominant but some control	Emphasis on both planning & control	Emphasis on control
7) Time Horizon	Long	Short	Very short (day-to-day)
8) End results	Policies and strategies	Implementation of policies strategies	Fulfilling each task
9) Nature of information	Tailor made, external, predictive, less accurate	Integrated, internal, future and historical more accurate	Tailor-made to the operation, often non-financial, precise
10) Degree of structure	Unstructured and irregular	Reasonably structured	Highly structured
11) Complexities	Many variables	Less complex	Very few variables
12) Appraisal	Extremely difficult	Much less difficult	Very easy
13) Judgement	Highly subjective	Relatively subjective	very - little subjectivity
14) Types of costs	Committed and discretionary	Only discretionary	Engineered

As will be evident from this table, planning, and control responsibilities would vary at different levels of management. Corporate management, represented by the board and the heads of various functions who are not members of the board, should formulate strategic plans (including setting out long-range objectives) and also plans for translating the srategic plans into short-term quantified targets of achievement. They will also approve short-term targets for example, profit plans,contingency plans and also action programmes framed by the executive management. The control role of the corporate management comprises reviewing the performance of the organisation in relation to components (say, monthly targets) of annual profit plan and also taking remedial actions by way of periodic policy review and tactical policy shifts necessary to achieve the long-term objectives as well as the short term targets set out in the profit plan.

The executive management representing product group heads, operational heads or profit centre heads, in their planning role, will formulate profit plans, contingency plans and action programmes and will also approve annual plans for product lines, functions,etc., contingency plans and action programmes developed by the operating management. The control role of the executive management lies in reviewing, perforamance of profit centres or functions in relation to components of annual profit plan and also taking remedial actions for achieving organisational targets. The operating management comprises product-line managers, production supervisors, etc. They have to formulate profit plan or programmes or operational plans for their respective product lines, production units, etc., also contingency plans and action programmes in such areas. The control function of operating management is to review performance of each area at short periodic intervals with a view to taking remedial action relating to shortfalls in performance.

From this discussion, it may be noted that the need and intensity of planning are the highest at the corporate management level and progressively comes down to the lowest at the operating management level. The reverse is true of the control role — the intensity of control is the highest at the operating management level and progressively comes down as one goes up higher. At the corporate management level, control is only overall, emphasis being place more on achieving the long-term objectives than fulfilling the short-term targets.

4. THE PROCESS OF MANAGEMENT CONTROL

There are five basic steps or components in the process of management control. These are :

i) Determination of standards or norms to be used in measuring actual results ;

ii) Measurement of actual results vis-a-vis planned results on the same lines and in the same areas as per standards and norms set earlier;

iii) Identification and analysis of the gap between the expected and actual results, specially the operations which show unfavourable results or shortfalls;

iv) Initiating remedial action either to correct the shortfall or to provide an acceptable basis for revising the norms themselves. (these actions could take the form of a contingency plan framed earlier, developing new policies, prodecures and programmes, redeployment of resources and efforts etc.);

v) Recycling the information relating to the actual performance for its use in developing future plans.

There are three important considerations in the installation of an effective control systems. These are :

i) Development of a number of smaller units, groups or subunits which may be called, responsibility centres;

ii) Identification of critical variables, that constitute critical success factors in the overall performance of the organisation, to be able to bring these into sharper focus; and

iii) An effective information system and mode of reporting to aid suitable remedial actions preceded by problem analysis and followed by appropriate decisions.

Item number (i) and (iii) above have already been dealt with in detail. We will, therefore, make a few observations here only on the second one, critical variables.

Critical variables are also called key variables. This expression is somewhat akin in import to a few other expressions used in budgetary control, namely key factor, principal budget factor, limiting factor and governing factor. For the purpose of control system, we have to recognise those important aspects of the organisation's operations that are critical to its success and considered crucial to the process of managment control. We may cite a few examples of critical variables : Occupancy rates and repeat customers in hotel industry and also in hospitals, yield percentage of base chemicals in fermentation process, waste ratios in spinning and damages in weaving in taxtile industry and measures of performance indices in industrial equipments including say, construction, mining, drilling etc. We may, therefore, define critical variables as those aspects or operation which , if ineffectively carried out, would jeopardise the realisation of planned outcomes, however efficiently other operations in the organisation are performed.

5. AN INTEGRATED FRAMEWORK OF MANAGEMENT INFORMATION, CONTROL AND REPORTING SYSTEMS

A Schematic Presentation of an Integrated Approach

This is presented here for providing the reader a broad perspective view of the entire gamut of management information, control and reporting system (MICRS). The presentation being self-explanatory in nature, there is no need to add any further observations in this regard.

Decision Support System :

It is both interesting and perhaps a bit intriguing to note that MIS is steadily being replaced by Decision Support System or DSS in the advanced countries, particiularly as a sequel to the recent computer revolution all over. This phenomenon reminds one of a similar situation when Data Processing of the 60's was replaced in the early 70's by MIS. Although a detailed discussion on DSS is outside the purview of this book, it may be useful to mention here some important points of difference between MIS and DSS. First, DSS is entirely computer-based while MIS need not necessarily be so. Second, while MIS implies periodic reporting (say, on a weekly or monthly basis) DSS is an on going , on-line and interactive exercise with the use of computer terminals as and when needed. Thus reporting at regular periodic intervals is not involved. Third, under DSS, models with basic parameters are stored in the computer for each specific area involving decisions. And at any point of time a decision-maker can change some variable/s and get guidance from the computer on the most optimum and feasible solution under the given set of circumstances or variables. In areas like inventory control, cash management, product-mix management, project analysis and implementation monitoring etc., DSS has been found to be highly effective. Obviously, MIS cannot provide this kind of flexibility as well as effectiveness mainly because a decision-maker has to wait for the information and might have to lose during this waiting period some opportunity due to right decision not being taken at right time.

Some Concluding Remarks :

Information has two important roles in management — information for decision-making and information for control. Information for decision-making needs to be essentially futuristic in nature. Information for control,on the other hand, should be basically of the feed-back type, with some futuristic element built into the same. It is unfortunate that most of the enterprises in India, both in the public and the private sectors, are yet to appreciate the real potential of MIS, not to speak of DSS. Consequently, in India, MIS has by and large degenerated itself into not only an extension of the accounting systems but a mechanistic ritual, and management reporting;in many cases a lack-lustre formality rather than an instrument to serve some specific decision-making purpose. It is, therefore, important that the top management as well as management at all levels should be oriented towards the real significance of MIS and how this can be designed and installed in an organisation effectively.

An Integrated Managment Information, Control Planning and Control Function

Level in the Organisation	Planning		Control	
	Responsibility	Tools	Responsibility	Tools
CORPORATE (TOP)	Strategic Planning	Corporate Planning & Strategy	Overall Control	i) Management By Objectives (MBO) ii) Profit Centre System iii) Responsibility Accounting
EXECUTIVE (MIDDLE)	Medium range Business Plan	Budgeting	Management Control	i) Budgetary Control ii) Performance Budgeting iii) Zero Base Budgeting
OPERATING (SUPERVISOR	Short Range Planning & day-to-day scheduling	Budgets (broken down into short periods)	Operational Control	Productivity Techniques

Framework of
& Reporting System (MICRS)

MIS for planning and control

Nature of MIS			Nature of Report	
Contents	**Source of Data**	**Uses**	**Format**	**Frequency**
1) Environment and end-user information. Regyulatory Policies and Supply of inputs 2) Market shre, competitive activity and market trends 3) Aggregate financial results for the organisation which highlight;	Qualitative Environmental data, Competitive data, Financial Accounting System	Overal Orginasi-tional perform-nce analysis. Trend analysis, Identification of strategic & tactical shifts	Lesser Degree of Structuring	Monthly / Quartely / Half-yearly /
(i) Growth in sale, (ii) Product Gorss Margin, (iii) Profit bef. & After tax. (iv) _ Return on investment. (v) Receivables, (vi) Inventories, (viii) Liquidity.				
1) Financial Perfo-mance ; (i) Order bookings, (ii) Capacity utilisation, (iii) Sales, costs, margin, over-head, profit before tax (for each product & region), (iv) Working Capital -- Inventories, Receivables, (v) cash Flow, (vi) Rejections & Complaints.	Financial Acco-unting system. Production & Marketing records	Product Group & Regional perfo-rmance analysis, Identification of remedial action for making up shortfall in tar-gets, Identifica-tion of operatio-nal and functio-nal policy changes.	Structured	Fortnightly / Monthly
1) Operational Perfor-mance for each produ-ction unit & product line (i) production quantity & value, (ii) Inventroy -- Raw material, stores * Supplies, (iv) Product-vity -- labour, machne overtime, (v) sales volume & price realis-ation, (vi) field efficie-ncy, (viii) Rejection. 2) Financial informa-tion; Product cost, material, supplies, labour, utilities, marketing costs.	Departmental operational records, Cost accounting system	Chane in pricing & product mix, mix, Product promotion decisions, Production scheduling change, Technical adjustments and changes.	Highly structured	Daily/ Weekly/ Fortnightly/

Change is the only unchanging thing in this changing world. The management information and reporting system once developed cannot serve the purpose and need of all time to come, particularly when situations change, as they do — sometimes widely and abruptly. Every MIS as well as reporting system should, therefore, contain some built-in flexibility in order to adapt to changes from time to time.

6. A FEW CASE STUDIES

1. ENGINEERS AND MERCHANTS LIMITED
(A Case Study on Profit Centre Systems)

Engineers and Merchants Limited initiated about 5 years ago, phased implementation of the profit centre system. To start with, they established 4 geographical profit centres viz., Western Region, Northern Region, Eastern Region and Southern Region. Simultaneously, the 100-odd major products the Company was dealing in (both their own manufactured products and agency products) were conveniently grouped into 6 product groups coded as 100,200,300,400,500 and 600.

Only about an year earlier, the Company had also started establishing profit centres in respect of each of these product groups, while maintaining the regional profit centres established earlier which were found to be working satisfactorily.

There is an elaborately detailed system of regular analysis and reporting of performance in respect of the regional profit centres. However, in case of product group profit centre, the reporting is at present, restricted to only sales and gross margin stages, since the accounting system is not yet geared to provide further details, of product group performance.

Besides the same products covered under the profit centre system, (both regional and product group-wise), the Company has several other lines of activities which have been left out of the profit centre system.

Last year, the management accounting department of the company introduced a more rational classification and grouping of expenses so that the profit centre performance could be judged at different levels and under various bases. The brief details of such classification of expenses are given below :

1. **Variable Selling and distribution expenses :** Salaries and fringe benefits of the direct staff, advertising, traveling, godown and forwarding expenses, entertainment etc.

2. **Fixed expenses subject to regional control :** Salaries and fringe benefits of clerical staff, staff welfare, godown rent, conveyance and motor vehicle expenses and sundry expenses. (This also includes financial charges as per 4 below).

3. **Fixed expenses not subject to regional control :** Salaries and fringe benefits of officers and executives, rent rates and taxes, insurance,, maintenance and depreciation.

4. **Financial charges :** This is levied on the profit centres on the basis of the Company funds utilised by them for their operations. The rates are different for stocks and outstandings. For stocks, the prevailing bank borrowing rate is applied each month. For outstandings, however, besides the prevailing bank borrowing rate applicable to outstandings upto 3 months, there is a provision for levying penal rate of interest at 3% for outstandings between 3 to 6 months and at 6% for outstandings more than 6 months old. (Financial charges, after calculation in the above manner, are included under the fixed expenses subject to regional control, for the purpose of reporting).

Exhibit I

BUDGET ACTUAL COMPARISON
REGIONAL OPERATION — 19x5

(Figures in Rs. lakhs)

Details	4 Region Total		Western Region		Northern Region		Eastern Region		Southern Region	
	Budget	Actual	Budget	Actual	Budget	Actual	Budget	Actual	Budget	Actual
Sales	3967	4061	1261	1357	1020	906	716	655	970	1143
G.M	585.92	662.37	164.98	199.36	155.98	147.25	131.50	136.48	133.46	179.28
% of Sales	14.8	16.3	13.1	14.7	15.3	16.3	18.4	20.8	13.8	15.7
Net Expenses	268.53	277.78	76.62	82.20	66.71	66.56	69.36	71.47	55.84	57.55
% of Sales	6.6	6.7	5.8	5.9	6.5	7.3	9.3	10.8	5.7	4.9
H.O. Expenses	61.82	69.07	20.88	23.08	13.73	14.76	16.02	17.10	11.19	14.13
'Ebit'	255.57	315.52	67.48	94.08	75.54	65.93	46.12	47.91	66.42	107.60
% of Sales	6.4	7.8	5.4	6.9	7.4	7.3	6.4	7.3	6 8	9.4
Financial Charges	89.59	83 04	22.94	24.04	22.46	22.53	28.77	23.33	15.42	13.14
Net Profit/Loss	165.98	232.48	44.54	70.04	53.08	43.40	17.35	24.58	51.01	94.46
% of Sales	4.2	5.7	3.5	5.2	5.2	4.8	2.4	3.8	5.3	8.3

Exhibit II

PROFIT CENTRE PERFORMANCE ANALYSIS
4 Regions

Details	Annual Total		W.R.		N.R.		E.R.		S.R.	
	Amt.	%	Amt.	%	Amt.	%	Amt.	%	Amt.	%
1. Sales	4061		1357		906		655		1143	
2. Gross margin	662	16.3	199	14.7	147	16.2	137	20.9	179	15.7
3. Variable selling expenses	105	2.5	28	2.1	28	3.1	25	3.8	24	2.1
4. Contribution margin (2—3)	557	13.7	171	12.6	119	13.1	112	17.1	155	13.6
5. Fixed exp. subject to regn. control	118	2.9	34	2.5	32	3.5	35	5.3	17	1.5
6. Performance margin (4—5)	439	10.8	137	10.1	87	9.6	77	11.7	138	12.1
7. Fixed exp. not subject to Regn. control	152	3.7	51	3.8	31	3.4	38	5.8	32	2.8
8. Regional margin (6—7)	287	7.1	86	6.3	56	6.2	39	5.9	106	9.3
9. Head office expenses	55	1.4	16	1.2	13	1.4	14	2.1	12	1.0
10. Operfg. profit loss (8—9)	232	5.7	70	5.2	43	4 7	25	3.8	94	8.2

Exhibit III

RATIO ANALYSIS

Detail	Western Region	Northern Region	Eastern Region	Southern Region	4 Region Total
1. G.M.ratio(%)	14.7	16.2	20.9	15.7	16.3
2. P.V.ratio (Contribution to sales) (%)	12.6	13.1	17.1	13.6	13.7
3. Performance margin (%)	10.1	9.6	11.7	12.1	10.8
4. Regional margin (%)	6.3	6.2	5.9	9.3	7.1
Avg. working capital employed (Rs.lakhs)					
a. Inventory	73	66	74	51	264
b. Net outstandings	83	103	55	35	276
c. Avg.monthly expenses	12	10	11	8	41
TOTAL	168	179	140	94	581
5. Contribution on avg. working capital (%)	102	67	80	166	96
6. Net profit on avg. working capital (R.O.I)	42	24	18	100	40
7. Components of R.O.I.					
i. Margin ratio (net profit to sales) (%)	5.2	4.7	3.8	8.2	5.7
ii. Cap. turnover (times)	8.1	5.1	4.7	12.2	7.0

Exhibit IV

PRODUCT GROUPWISE PERFORMANCE ANALYSIS

(Figure in Rs.lakhs)

	Budget			Actual		
Product group	Turnover	G.M.	G.M. percentage	Turnover	G.M.	G.M. percentage
100	1322	162.0	12.2	1527	230.6	15.1
200	948	63.0	6.6	1010	62.5	6.2
300	1103	181.4	16.4	994	202.8	20.4
400	63	5.8	9.2	27	1.8	6.6
500	151	40.4	26.7	162	27.2	16.7
600	380	133.2	35.0	341	137.5	40.3
TOTAL	3967	585.8	14.8	4061	662.4	16.3

5. Head office expenses : About 80 per cent of this is distributed among profit centres in the ratio of their net expenses which include 1, 2, and 3 above. The balance 20 per cent or so is apportioned on some other suitable basis.

There are 4 exhibits showing analysis of performance for the full year 19X5, as follows

Exhibit I - Budget actual comparision of regional operations.

Exhibit II - Profit centre performance analysis.

Exhibit III - Ratio analysis.

Exhibit IV - Product group-wise budget actual comparison.

2. INDUSTRIAL MARKETING LIMITED

(A Case Study of Comparative Analysis of Performance)

The Company is engaged in distribution and sales of about a hundred products rationally grouped into five product groups, viz., PG1,PG2,PG3,PG4 AND PG5. The marketing setup of the company is as follows :

The entire sales territory is divided into four geographic regions, viz South, West, North ans East. The number of branches under each such region is 2,4 1 and 3, respectively. There are four regional headquarters controlling the respective branches under each region. The head office of the company is located centrally and this offiee effects all purchases and organises all dispatch goods to the regional headquarters from time to time.

Given below are only a few Tables containing figures relative to the month M, extracted and analysed by the management accountant of the company at the head office. The contents of each table are as follows :

Table I : Regional figures and the total figures for the company as a whole.

Table IA : Details in respect of the branches under eastern region only.

Table II : Details in respect of only product group I analysed as to each region.

Problems : Appraisal of performance based on these Tables, highlighting inter alia the various control areas and control points emanating therefrom.

(The reader should be able to make such an appraisal after filling in the banks)

PERFORMANCE APPRAISAL : MARKETING CONTROL
MONTH : M : 19X

Table I

Figures : Rs. Lakhs

Details	South	West	North	East	Total	Company norm
1. Sales : Budgeted	20	50	20	30	120	

Actual	15	40	10	35	100
2. G.C. * : Budgeted (25%)	4	12.5	5	7.5	30
Actual	3	10	3	7	23
3. G.C. as percentage of sales (Actual)					25%
4. Branches set - up cost	1	3	1	2	7
5. Branches contribution	2	7	2	5	16
6. Branches contribution as percentage of sales					15 %
7. Regional set-up cost	1	3	0.5	2	6.5
8. Regional contribution	1	4	1.5	3	9.5
9. Regional contribution as percentage of sales					10 %
No. of salesmen	5	12	5	8	30
G.C. per salesman					0.80
Average branch contribution per salesman					
Average regional contribution per salesman					
Average working capital (W/C) employed	5	30	15	20	70
Reg. contribution as percentage of (W/C) employed					15%

* G.C. menas gross contribution
(= Sales - variable cost of sales)

AMAR MARKETING ENTERPRISE LTD.

(A Case Study on Control of Marketing Operations)

The Company is engaged in marketing of highly diversified engineering products through their all-India marketing set-up. To effectively monitor and control the marketing operations of the Company *vis-a-vis* the budget, a system has been recently introduced which covers:

Exhibit I: A format on Progressive Budget Actual Comparison in *key result areas.*

Exhibit II: Procedure of filling in/using the format as per Exhibit-I.

Exhibit—II

PROCEDURE OF FILLING IN/USING THE FORMAT

1. Two pages of the same format will make one complete set. In the right hand top corner of the format, please put page 1 (of 2) on the first page and page 2 (of 2) on the second page. Once a set is made up. This set will show monthly figures for the complete accounting year—first 6 months' figures will appear on the first page and figures for the next 6 months will appear on the second page. Previous year overall figures shown under 'details' column will provide additional information for the year as a whole, for ready reference.

2. One set of format will be maintained and used for the whole year by each of the following:

(i) Product-oriented engineers in all the branches—in respect of each product they are handling. (A sales engineer may have to use more than one set depending on the number of products he is handling).

(ii) Product-oriented engineers at the regional headquarters—same as (i) above.

(iii) Divison heads attached to the regions—in respect of each division after appropriate consolidation of statements as per (i) and (ii) above.

(iv) Executive responsible for all-India sales operation—in respect of each product and each product-group they handle.

Table I-A

REGION : EASTERN — Figures : Rs. Lakhs

Details	B1	B2	B3	Total
1. Sales: Budgeted	12	11	7	
Actual	13	12	10	
2. G.C: Budgeted (25%)	3	2.5	1.75	
Actual	3.25	1.85	1.90	
3. G.C. as percentage on else (Actual)				20%
4. Branches set-up cost	1.00	0.50	0.50	
5. Branches contribution	2.25	1.35	1.40	
6. Branches contribution as percentage of sales				14%
7. Number of salesmen	3	3	2	8%
8. G.C. per salesman				0.88
9. Average branch contribution per salesman				0.63

Table II — Figures : Rs. Lakhs

Details	PG1	PG2	PG3	PG4	PG5	Total	Company norms
1. Sales:							
Budgeted	40	30	20	20	10	120	
Actual	35	20	25	10	10	100	
2. G.C.:							
Budgeted	12 (30%)	7.5 (25%)	4 (20%)	4 (25%)	2.5 (25%)	30 (25%)	
Actual	9	6	4	2	2	23	
3. G.C. as percentage of sales actual						25%	25%
4. No. of salesmen	10	6	5	5	4	30	

5. G.C. per salesman						0.77	0.88
6. Average working capital employed	25	15	20	5	5	70	
7. Do as percentage of sales						70%	50%
8. G.C. as percentage of working capital						33%	40%

Table III

Figures : Rs. in lakhs

Details	S	W	N	E	Total	Company norms
1. Sales: Budgeted	8	15	5	12	40	
Actual	5	14	6	10	35	
2. G.C.: Budgeted	2.4	4.5	1.5	3.6	12	
Actual	2.0	2.8	1.6	2.7	9	
					25.7%	30%
3. No. of salesmen	2	3	1	2	8	
4. Average W/C employed	5	12	5	8	30	
5. G.C. as percentage of sales					86%	50%
6. G.C. as percentage of W/C						40%

Exhibit 1

PROGRESSIVE COMPARISON IN KEY RESULT AREAS

Region ——————————
Division ——————————
Branch ——————————
Product ——————————

DETAILS			QUARTER		
			MTH Budget	Actual	
I. ORDER BOOKING	CURRENT	T.O.			
		G.M.			
(Total for the previous year ——————)	YTD Cur Yr.	T.O.			
		G.M.			
	YTD Prv. Yr.	T.O.			
		G.M.			
II. BILLING	CURRENT	T.O.			
		G.M.			
(Total for the previous year ——————)	YTD Cur Yr.	T.O.			
		G.M.			
	YTD Prv. Yr.	T.O.			
		G.M.			
III. RECEIVABLES (Month end)		Open Credit			
		Upto 3 Months			
(Previous Year ——		Betw. 3-6 Months			
Average : Gross ——		Over 6 Months			
		Total Gross			
Net ——————)		Net Book Debts			
IV. Stocks (Month end)	YTD	Current			
(Previous Year Average ———)		PRV. YR.			
V. Expenses	YTD	Current			
(Total for the Previous Year ——————)		PRV. YR.			

Figures in Rs. Lakhs with 2 decimals correct

Exhibit I

PROGRESSIVE BUDGET-ACTUA

KEY RESULTS

Year ________ (Page of — 2)

Region ____________

Division ____________

Branch ____________

Product ____________

DETAILS			QUARTER			QUARTER		
			MTH Budget Actual	MTH Budget Actual	MTH Budget Actual	MTH Budget Actual	MTH Budget Actual	MTH Budget
I. OREDER BOOKING	CURRENT	T.O.						
		G.M.						
(Total for the previous year ———)	YTD Cur Yr.	T.O.						
		G.M.						
	YTD Prv. Yr.	T.O.						
		G.M.						
II. BILLING	CURRENT	T.O.						
		G.M.						
(Total for the previous year ———)	YTD Cur Yr.	T.O.						
		G.M.						
	YTD Prv. Yr.	T.O.						
		G.M.						
III. RECEIVABLES (Month end)	Open Credit							
	Upto 3 Months							
(Previous Year ——	Betw. 3-6 Months							
Average : Gross ————	Over 6 Months							
	Total Gross							
Net ————)	Net Book Debts							
IV. Stocks (Month-end)	Current							
(Previous Year Average ———)	YTD	PRV. YR.						
V. Expenses	Current							
(Total for the Previous Year ———)	YTD	PRV. YR.						

Figures in Rs. Lakhs with 2 decimals correct

Exhibit - II

PROCEDURE OF FILLING IN USING THE FORMAT

1. Two pages of the same format will make one complete set. In the right hand top corner of the format, please put page 1 (of 2) on the first page and page 2 (of 2) on the second page, once a set is made up. This set will show monthly figures for the complete accounting year-first 6 months figures will appear on the first page and figures for the next 6 months will appear on the second page. Previous year overall figures shown under 'detail' column will provide additional information for the year as a whole, for ready reference.

2. One set of format will be maintained and used for the whole year by each of the following :

(i) Product-oriented engineers in all the branches-in respect of each product they are handling (A sales engineer may have to use more than one set depending on the number of products he is handling)

(ii) Product-oriented engineers at the regional head-quarters same as (i) above.

(iii) Division heads attached to the regions-in respect of each division after appropriate consolidation of statements as per (i) and (ii) above.

(iv) Executives responsible for all-India sales operation in respect of each product and each product-group they handle. After appropriate consolidation of the statements as per (iii) above, wherever applicable.

(v) Branch Managers - in respect of their respective branches (overall position).

(vi) Regional Managers - in respect of their respective region (overall position)

(vii) General Managers - in respect of product-groups or Divisions they are in charge of.

(3) At the outset, the respective figures for the previous year under the details column should be filled in. Then, all figures against "YTD Prv.Yr." (i.e. year to date - previous year) should be filled n against items Nos. 1,2,4, & 5. Similarly, as soon as the budgets are finalised, all figures against budget columns (on both the pages - i.e.for the complete year) should be straightaway filled in. Incidentally, it may be noted that quarterly budgets will have to be allocated pro rata (i.e.putting one-third against each month)to arrive at the monthly budget gifures. It is also to be noted that all formats should be complete in all respects and should be maintained always up to date.

(4) Source of all data for filling in and maintaining the control format is the accounts department of the office which the executive is attached to.

(5) It is absolutely essential that each executive in charge of sales in any capacity, should maintain an updated set of format for himself. At any time should any of his senior call him for review of performance, this updated format will form the basis of the discussion/review. Similarly, when directors or general managers go to visit regions and want to review the performance in some specific areas (or even want to review the same at head office itself) the updated format should form the basis of discussion. In case more details are required, such details could also be provided after calling for the same format in respect of specific product or product-groups under a particular region/branches.

7. SALESMAN'S REPORT

We would end this chapter with a mundane but very important and down-to-earth topic like this.

A report may be defined as a written document through which are transmitted factual information that the executive must have as a basis for future plans and decisions. Sales reports form the basis of personal contact between sales force and management. However, if the salesmen is required to write over-elaborate reports he will regard his employers as impractical whereas if the reports do not generate any action he will feel frustrated. Whereever possible emphasis should be given to informal reporting i.e.personal discussions with salesmen and supervisors. This informal reporting system, because of personal contact, is always more informative, clarifying and thus more effective than written reports.

There are various channels for obtaining information about salesman's activities of which salesman's periodic report is most important.

Salesman's report may cover :

a) Work Plan - Plan for future activities, and
b) Performance - Write-ups on completed activities.

Several forms are used by salesmen to present their completed activities and achievements but the most important one is Call Report indicating inter alia dealing with customer, best time for calling, resistance from customer etc.

Let us start with a Salesman's Performance Report on the lines suggested below:

SPECIMEN OF PERFORMANCE REPORT

Salesmen's Name ——————Area ———— Month ——————

PRODUCT	BUDGET				ACTUAL					
	TM		YTD		TM		YTD		YTDLY	
	VOL	VAL	VOL	VAL	VOL	VAL	VOL	VAL	VOL	VAL

X
Y
Z

TOTAL

Legends :	VOL	=	Volume in MT/KG/Number
	VAL	=	Value in Rs.000's /Rs.Lakhs
	TM	=	This Month
	YTD	=	Year-to-date
	YTDLY	=	Year-to-date last year

Additional reports may cover :

a) Report on new business secured or potential new business
b) Report on lost business,
c) Report on local business activity including state of competition.

Sales information may be compiled in respect of :

a) Product-model, pack-size,
b) Zone/Area,
c) Physical/financial terms,
d) Channels of distribution,
e) Daily record of sales, production and inventory in physical terms.

Daily sales reports of salesmen contain wealth of information. However, the company's senior executives should not be burdened with all the detailed information and such the information should be filtered and summarised to suit various levels of management.

Given below a specimen of Sales Call Report with special reference to industrial marketing. (It has already been in successful operation in some companies):

SALES CALL REPORT

NAME OF CUSTOMER ________________ CODE ________

ADDRESS ________________ TEL/PHONE/FAX ________

____

A) DETAILS RE : VISIT

1. DATE OF VISIT ________ DATE OF PREV.VISIT ________

2. PERSON(S) NAME (S) ________________

CONDUCTED : DESGN (S) ________________

3. IMPETUS/REASON OF THE VISIT ________________

____

B) OBJECTIVES & OUTCOMES OF THE VISIT :

AREAS	OBJECTIVE	OUTCOMES
1. Order Booking	VOL — VAL —	VOL — VAL —
2. Collection	________	________
3. Technical Service/ Complaints Handling	________	________
4. General/others (indicate briefly here)	________	________
5. Follow-up Action	________________	
(incl.further visit)	________________	

C) MARKET RESEARCH DATA :

1. PURCHASE BY THE CUSTOMER
(OF PRODUCTS WITHIN OUR PRODUCT-WISE)

PRODUCT	YEAR - VOL VAL	YEAR -1 VOL VAL	YEAR - 0 VOL VAL	YEAR + 1 VOL VAL	YEAR + 2 VOL VAL
________					
________					
________					
________					

TOTAL VALUE
OF PURCHASES
(ALL PRODUCTS)

2. OUR COMPANY VIS-A-VIS COMPETITORS
(As perceived by the costomer) :

CRITERIA OUR CO. ——— ——— ———

QUALITY
COST
DELIVERY
SERVICE

USES CODES
A : VERY GOOD
B : GOOD
C : AVERAGE
D : POOR
E : VERY POOR

3. GROWTH POTENTIAL DURING NEXT 5 YEARS
(PLAN TO INCREASE CAPACITY/MODERNISATION ETC)

(To be filled in only during the first visit and updated once a year).

NAME ———— SIGNATURE ———— DATE ————

OTHERS

The first thing included here is a Questions Bank, segregated into principles and concepts first and then problems and cases. All the questions, in each of these two categories, have been included in a classified form following the sequence of sections, as well as the sequence of Chapters in each section(s), of the book. The Questions Bank will, it is hoped, enable the reader to test his knowledge and understanding through a self-examination process and also to the teachers/faculty in management courses on the relevant subjects.

D C F (Discounted Cash Flow) tables have been included since this will be relevant to the chapter dealing with investment decisions.

Finally, a list of suggested reading, with particular reference to the topics covered in this treatise, has been given at the end.

ANNEXURE 2

QUESTIONS BANK

PART A - PRINCIPLES AND CONCEPTS

General Introduction

1. Examine critically three oft-quoted definitions of Marketing.
2. Discuss what according to you should be the purpose and role of marketing in a developing economy like India.
3. Attempt short explanatory notes on :
   (a) Market Profile
   (b) Consumers Market vs. Industrial Market
   (c) Market Segmentation
   (d) Market Growth and Market Share
   (e) Fads, Fashions and Classics
   (f) New Products
   (g) Product Life Cycle concept
   (h) Test Marketing
4. Indicate and explain briefly the various general marketing functions and specific marketing functions.
5. Explain briefly the methods usually followed in :
   (a) Sales forecasting
   (b) Developing distribution channel-mix
   (c) Improving brand loyalty
6. Examine the role of an Accountant in a modern business organisation.
7. Enumerate the basic principles and concepts of Accounting.
8. Examine how Capital-Revenue allocation is the inevitable extension of the Accounting Period concept.
9. Illustrate with hypothetical data how strict adherence to the principle of conservatism may lead to gross understatement of profits of a business.
10. Write short notes on the different branches of Accounting.
11. Indicate and explain briefly the various functions that usually come under the Accounting and Finance department of an organisation.

12. Bring out the areas of independence and inter-dependence between Marketing and Finance. What are your suggestions towards achieving more effective co-ordination between these two functions?

13. Explain with examples how the Principle of Dual Aspect in Accounting is the foundation of Double Entry System.

14. Mention four advantages and three alleged disadvantages of the Double Entry System

15. List all relevant steps under Double Entry System in a logical sequence.

16. What are the two sets of Books? What are the purposes served by each of them ?

17. Distinguish between :

    (a) Subsidiary Books and Cash Book

    (b) Subsidiary books and Journal Proper

18. Explain why cash Book is called both a Journal and a Ledger.

19. "If the Trial Balance does not agree there must be mistake in the Ledger. If the Trial Balance agrees there may still be mistakes in the Ledger Trial Balance is therefore useless". Examine the statement.

20. Why is it that a Balance Sheet is prepared as on a particular date whilst the relevant P/L A/C is for a particular period ending on the same date ?

21. Explain with illustrations why a Trial Balance and also a Balance Sheet must agree in total.

22. As an objective of published accounts which of these two would you consider to be the better expression ?

    (i) To present a true and correct view .....

    (ii) To present a true and fair view ...

    Give reasons with hypothetical figures, if necessary.

23. Explain with imaginary figures the distinction between window dressing and secret reserves.

24. Explain with illustrations the limitations of Published Accounts from the viewpoint of Management. Can you suggest some measures to overcome such limitations ?

25. As a financier what safeguards would you ensure in assessing the credit- worthiness of a company from its Published Accounts.
26. Examine the importance of financial ratio analysis in the interpretation of financial statements.
27. Indicate the controversies in the computation of Gross Profit Ratio. Debt Equity Ratio, Inventory Turnover Ratio and Debtor Turnover Ratio.
28. Explain with imaginary figures the concept and different interpretations of Return on Capital Employed, with Special Reference to marketing operation.
29 The Red Company Ltd., earns 8% on Sales and has an asset (investment) turnover of 3.25 per annum.

    The Blue Company Ltd,earns 6.5% on sales, but has an asset turnover of 4.75 per annum.

    Which Company shows the higher rate of return on Investment?

    What deficiencies do you see in using rate of return to compare the performance of these two Companies ?
30. Explain with examples how and to what extent the preparation of funds flow statement can facilitate interpretation of published accounts.
31. Show with hypothetical figures when depreciation is a source of funds and when it is not.
32. Discuss the purposes and objectives of Cost Accounting.
33. "Cost is a fact, estimate an opinion and price a policy" - Elucidate and examine the statement.
34. State whether each of other following statements is True or False. Give brief reasons (in one sentence) for your answer, in each case:

    (i) The only function of the Cost Accountant is ascertainment of Cost.

    (ii) There cannot be anything called True Cost.

    (iii) Ascertainment of historical cost is unnecessary under Standard Costing System.

    (iv) Works Cost is an alias of works overhead.

    (v) All material costs are included in Prime Cost.

(vi) Office and Administrative overhead is a part of Total Cost (vii) Total Cost is something different from Cost of Sales.

(viii) Indirect material costs are not considered in arriving at the cost of a product or job.

(ix) Decisions as to Direct Cost and Indirect Cost are in all cases a matter of policy.

(x) Over or Under-Absorption of Overheads arises only due to errors in fixing the overhead recovery rates.

(xi) Service Department Costs should be fully absorbed by the products of the Production Departments.

(xii) Selling Overhead does not included Advertisement expenses.

(xiii) Analysis of Selling and Distribution Overheads is necessary only for collection of cost and expenses.

35. All the methods of Costing have got either 'product' emphasis or 'period' emphasis - Explain with examples.

36. Distinguish between Absorption Costing and Marginal Costing.

37 Enumerate the more important techniques of costing and give one example of the specific area of application of each such technique.

38. Explain with examples what special advantages accrue from the introduction of Standard Costing System in a company where a system of Budgetary Control is already under successful operation.

39. Enumerate the important considerations involved in the establishment of Standard Cost.

40. Write short explanatory notes on :

(i) Principal Budget Factor

(ii) Budget Manual

(iii) Budget Committee

(iv) Responsibility Accounting

41. Distinguish (with example) between Estimate, Forecast, Target and Budget.

42. Illustrate the method of calculating the average due date.

43. As a result of shrinking market and high cost, the market

for one of the consumable durable products of a large marketing organisation is shrinking. In order to boost the market for this product, the Marketing Manager is contemplating sale of the product on Hire Purchase basis Critically analyse the financial implications of the proposal with your recommendation for making the scheme a success.

44. Explain with examples the impact of Sales Tax and Excise Duty on the final price of a product when some discount is offered to the customers.

45. Indicate some important areas of Tax Planning in respect of Sales Tax and Excise duty.

Marketing Planning :

46. Discuss briefly the process of Corporate Planning indicating specially the major steps involved in developing a Corporate Plan.

47. "Marketing Planning is the forerunner of any Corporate Planning" Examine the statement and discuss the important points to be considered in developing the Marketing Long-Range Plan.

48. Discuss some of the basic issues which are to be sorted out before developing the Marketing Budgets. Examine also the mode of integration between the annual marketing budgets and the Marketing L.R.P.

49. What are the uses of Sales Forecast? Discuss factors that should be considered in a Sales Forecast.

50. Outline the budgeting process for a marketing organisation. What are its uses and its limitations.

51. Explain with examples how flexible budgeting system can be used for both budgeting and controlling marketing expenses.

52. How does profit planning differ from budgeting ? Discuss the important aspects to be considered in profit planning.

53. What are the various criteria in new product planning ? Discuss also the various stages involved in such planning.

54. Explain with hypothetical facts and figures how you would determine the phase in the life-cycle which a particular product is passing through. Examine also the utility of this knowledge in product planning
55. Explain briefly the need for and the mode of organisational planning in the area of marketing operations.

Marketing Decisions :

56. Examine the importance of Cost Analysis in Marketing Decisions.
57. Write short explanatory notes on :
    (a) Differential Cost and Incremental Revenue Analysis.
    (b) Relevant Cost Analysis.
    (c) Cost Effectiveness Analysis.
    (d) Opportunity Costing Analysis.
    (e) Benefit Cost Analysis.
    (f) Engineered Cost, Committed Costs and Managed Costs.
58. Discuss the utility and limitations of Break-Even Analysis.
59. Explain with the help of Break Even Charts the effects of (a) 10% increase in variable cost and (b) 10% increase in Selling Price.
60. You have been asked by the top management to review and report upon the existing product pricing policies and strategies. How will you draw up a well-knit plan before you actually begin your assignment ?
61. While fixing prices, the Marketing Director prefers to add profit margin at a standard rate to the total cost of sales while the Finance Director likes to add contribution at a standard rate to the variable costs. Discuss the pros and cons or the two methods with suitable illustration to highlight the points.
62. Discuss briefly how you would approach to tackle the following special pricing problems :
    (a) New Product Pricing.
    (b) Export Pricing
    (c) Pricing of Spare Parts
    (d) Pricing for after sales service.

63. What are the various incentives and assistance provided to entrepreneurs who go in for export marketing ? Suggest chnges to make such assistance more effective.
64. Discuss how you would introduce an effective system of taking product elimination decisions and implementing such decisions in a large marketing organisation.
65. Explain the Product Review and Evaluation Sub-system (PRESS) What is the role of Cost Accounting in the operation of PRESS?
66. Discuss the principles and steps in investments analysis .
67. Examine the relative merits and limitations of Pay Back Method and Return on Investment Method for evaluation of project attractiveness.
68. Mention the special cases where the following methods of investment appraisal should be adopted with reasons in each case.

    (a) Pay-Back Period

    (b) Return on Investment

    (c) Net Present Value approach.

    (d) D.C.F. Rate of return.

Marketing Performance Evaluation

69. "There is only one valid definition of business purpose to create a customer".(Drucker)- Examine critically this statement and indicate how this can be used as the basis for evaluating the overall marketing performance of an organisation.
70. Discuss the rationale and pitfalls of using market share as the primary criterion to measure the overall marketing performance.
71. Develop a conceptual framework for conducting Marketing Audit
72. Outline an approach for measuring the social value of marketing.
73. Two district sales managers are discussing evaluation methods. One states, "I always evaluate on the basis of efforts which can be counted, such as the number of calls

made. Then no one can complaint about subjective bias." The second states, "To me a good judgment system is the best, because each man works under different conditions which make direct comparision of number of calls and other such statistics of little value." Discuss the relative merits of these two approaches.

74. If you were a Sales Manager, what would you do upon discovering each of the following in an evaluation programme :
(a) All salesmen surpassed their sales quotas by 20% or more
(b) All salesmen in District A failed to reach 80% of their sales quotas while the salesmen in all other districts met their quotas almost exactly.
(c) Sales volume for the company as a whole increased by 20% but profit contribution dropped by 25%.
(d) Sales volume increased by 10% but market share declined by 5%.

75. Enumerate and rank in order of preference ten various criteria that could be used for evaluating salesmen's performance. Add brief justifications for your ranking. Based on the criteria and the ranking so made, discuss how you would develop a salesman's Compensation-cum-Commission Scheme for a newly set-up marketing organisation.

76. Develop a conceptual model for evaluating sales territory performance.

77. Does advertising belong in the capital budget? Examine critically. Discuss also the various bases adopted for budgeting advertisement expenditures.

78. Discuss some of the criteria for measuring advertisement effectiveness.

79. You have been asked to use distribution cost analysis to audit sales performance. Specifically what would you do ?

80. Discuss how you would develop a quantitative model for use in the selection of the most profitable alternative out of a number of modes of distribution.

81. How would you evaluate the effectiveness of distribution.
82. Discuss some recent approaches for evaluating the effectiveness of Marketing Planning and Marketing Research.

Marketing Control

83. Bring out the points of distinction between Strategic Planning, Management Control and Operational Control.
84. Examine the merits and pitfalls of a performance evaluation system against pre-determined norms.
85. Discuss the significance, advantages and disadvantages of profit Centres as a major tool of performance control.
86. Explain the principle of Management by Exception in the light of the various methods of appraisal of performance in the marketing area.
87. There is a current trend-towards more emphasis on marketing profitability analysis as compared with marketing cost analysis. What difference do you see between the two? Which do you think would be more useful for the purpose of control devices ? Why ? What kinds of additional complexity are introduced by profitability analysis ?
88. State briefly three uses which each of the following analysis of sales may have in contributing to the provision of planning and control information for Management.

    Analysis by

    (a) Salesman.

    (b) Territory.

    (c) Product.

    (d) Unit Price.

    Suggest two additions to this list mentioning similarly three uses of each.
89. A large Durg Company follows the practice of making an economic study of each of its product lines every three years. As a member of a committee assigned to accomplish this objective what type of quantitative data do you think would be appropriate.
90. "A cynic is one who knows the cost of everything and the value of nothing" (Bernard Shaw) - Examine this statement and indicate the philosophy and concept of a modern cost reduction programme.

91. What are the main difficulties likely to be encountered in the control and evaluation of Marketing Costs? Give reasoned opinion as to the relative importance of the control of expenditure on Marketing as distinct from manufacturing costs.
92. Write short notes on :
    (a) Working Capital Gap.
    (b) Negative working capital.
    (c) Fixed and variable working capital.
    (d) Operating cycle concept.
    (e) Inclusion of profit in working capital forecasting.
93. Discuss the various sources of financing working capital.
94. Give an example with hypothetical figures how overtrading can develop in a company. What measures would you suggest to combat overtrading.
95. Discuss briefly some of the important areas in working capital managment with special reference to the control of working capital requirement in marketing system .
96 Accounts Receivables and Inventory form a significant part of Marketing Cost. Discuss ways of controlling them.
97. What do you mean by M.I.S. ? Is it altogether a different system from Budgeting and Performance Evaluation ?
98. Discuss the conditions precedent to a sound M.I.S. for a medium size organisation engaged in manufacturing-cum-marketing.
99. Write a note on the role of computer in M.I.S. in a reasonably big typical Indian company engaged in manufacture cum marketing operations.
100. Outline a framework for developing an integrated marketing information system for industrial products.
101. Assume that your company 'Meal Product Ltd.' has just established a new product business of steel windows, locks and other steel products for the building industry. This new product division has decentralised engineering, production, marketing and staff services into a relatively autonomous 'profit centre'. You have been named Sales Manager, reporting to the Manager, Marketing. What kind of data, what kind of reports and with what frequency do you think you would request from the Account Department and field sales force for control purposes ?

QUESTIONS BANK

PART B - PROBLEMS AND CASES

Marketing Finance and Costs

1. State with brief reasons whether each of the following items should be treated as Capital, Revenue or Deffered Revenue
   - (i) Repairs of chairs and benches in a school for Rs. 10,000.
   - (ii) An amount of Rs.1 lakh paid to some management consultants to advise on the capital structure planning of AB Company Ltd. which is considering major structural changes.
   - (iii) Purchase of machinery Rs. 50,000 by Mr. X who is a dealer in machinery and equipment.
   - (iv) Mr. Y is a furniture manufacturer and dealer in furniture. He transfers Rs. 12,000 worth of furniture from his factory to his office for the purpose of office use.
   - (v) Alternation expenses of Rs.10,000 to widen the canteen space of the factory of Mr. Z engaged in the manufacture and sale of pharmaceutical products.
   - (vi) Loss of sale of old furniture Rs. 5,000 incurred by PQ Ltd.
   - (vii) Preliminary expenses incurred by XY Ltd. Rs. 10 lakhs in connection with initial issue of shares.
2. Classify each of the following Accounts and state whether it is usually debited or credited :
   - (i) Government of India (customers) A/c.
   - (ii) Nowhere Ltd. (suppliers) A/c.
   - (iii) Bills Receivable A/c
   - (iv) Salaries A/c
   - (v) Commission (received on sales) A/c.
   - (vi) Interest (paid on loans) A/c
   - (vii) Office Equipment A/c.

   Also state in which sub-division of the ledger you would expect each of the 7 accounts to exist.

3. Following transactions occurred in the business of the Book Keeping Ltd in the month of January 19XX. State the *two Accounts* involved in each case and also the *Account* to be debited and the Account to be credited under each transaction with *brief reasons.*

   1. Purchased furniture from ABC for cash Rs. 10,000
   2. Sold goods for cash Rs. 27,000
   3. Purchased goods from PQR Rs. 20,000
   4. Sold old furniture to MON Rs.3,000
   5. Sales made to DEF Rs, 13,000
   6. Purchase in cash Rs. 9,000
   7. Paid wages to workers Rs. 4,500
   8. Received interest on Bank deposits Rs.375
   9. Goods returned to PQR Rs.4,400
   10. Purchased from GHR Rs. 8,000
   11. Paid carriage inward charges on purchases on 10th Rs.1,200
   12. Deposited money into Bank from Cash Rs.20,000
   13. Received from DEF against Sales on 5th Rs. 10,000
   14. Goods distributed as samples Rs.5,000 and as charity Rs.7,000

4. Consider the Q. No.3 above. Prepare from the information given:

   Purchase Book
   Sales Book
   Returns Inward Book
   & Returns Outward Book

   (Complete 'rulings' should be provided in each case)

5. Show how you would make the Ledger postings in respects of the transactions recorded in the Subsidiary Books as per Q. No. 4 above.

6. Assume you are starting a trading business. Imagine ten different types of transactions during the first week of your business. Write down those transactions. Then show entries of each of these in the Journal (with complete ruling and narrations)

7. Mohendra Jalan started his business in the name of M.Jalan

& Co.with cash Rs. 50,000, furniture worth Rs. 5,000 and goods worth Rs. 15,000 on 1st January 19X6. His other transactions for the month of January were as follows :

19X6 Jan		Rs.
	1.Purchased an office space	15,000
	3. Purchased a Typewriter	500
	Purchased goods for cash	8,000
	5. Purchased goods from Agarwala & Co.	3,000
	6. Deposited into Bank	20,000
	7. Sold goods for cash	6,000
	8. Deposited into bank	5,000
	9. Paid Agarwala & Co.by cheque	3,000
	10. Purchased goods from Kalu Khan	4,000
	13. Paid to Kalu Khan	3,900
	Discount allowed by him	100
	15. Drew from Bank for personal use	1,000
	16. Purchased an Almirah	300
	17. Sold goods for cash	1,500
	18. Deposited into Bank	1,000
	19. Purchased from Dutta Brothers	1,000
	23. Paid for stationery purchased	100
	(*Indicating dates in the month of Jan.)	
	27. Paid wages	70
	29. Paid taxes	50
	30. Paid salaries	200

Journalise the above transactions in the books of the firm.

8. Journalise the following transactions in the books of TDH Ltd.

Jan .
19X6 :

1. Computer Services Bill for Rs.1,00,000 received from Datam Corporation and Rs. 30,000 is paid by cheque to them.
2. An old boiler (book value Rs. 10,000) is traded in at Rs.18,000 to purchase a new one from Boiler Manufacturers India Ltd. at Rs. 1,00,000 the difference being paid by cheque.

3. A Credit Note for Rs. 10,000 received from CPM Ltd., in respect of our purchases from them to correct some errors in their invoices to us.
4. RSP Ltd. settled their Account with us by paying Rs. 12,500 only. A Credit Note of Rs. 2,520 is issued to them in this connection. They had purchased from us goods worth Rs. 35,000 in April 19X5, paying 50% of the amount in advance at the time.

9. Show all relevant Ledger Accounts (all operations involved) under Q.No.8 above.

10. Prepare B. Banerjee's account from the following transactions :

19X8

Jan.

	Rs.
1. Sold goods to B Banerjee	1,200
4. Received from him	700
8. Purchased goods from him	600
11. Paid to him	200
15. Sold goods to him	500
17. Goods returned by him	75
30. Received from him cash and allowed him discount	25

11. On 1st October, 19X86 Sri D.Gupta started his business with Rs. 17,500 as his capital (Rs. 15,000 deposited in an account with the Central Bank of India, and the balance in hand)

His other transactions during the next three months were as follows :

19X6

October

		Rs.
3.	Paid for the purchase of stationery goods	200
5.	Purchased furniture on credit form Calcutta Timber Co.	1,200
9.	Bought goods on credit from Maganlal & Co.	3,000
17.	Sold goods on credit to Goenka & Co.	4,900
28.	Purchased goods for cash from Shri Ramsaran.	1,750

Nov.		
5.	Received cash from Goenka & CO.	1,500
15.	Paid by a cheque to Maganlal & Co.	2,000
22.	Withdrawn by the Proprietor from Bank for own use	250
29.	Received a cheque from Goenka & Co. cheque + sent to Bank.	2,500
Dec.		
3.	Goenka Co's cheque returned dishonoured by the Bank	2,500
13.	Paid to Calcutta Timber Co. by a cheque	1,200
20.	Sundry sale of goods for cash	2,300
21.	Deposited into Bank from office cash	2,500
25.	Paid for printing charges and stationery	300
30.	Paid for priniting charges office rent	600

Record all the above transactions in proper Ledger Accounts and prepared a Trial Balance as at 31st December, 19X6.

12. The undermentioned balanced were extracted from the books of Shri N Kundu as on 31st March 19X6. You are asked to prepare there , from a Trial Balance as on that date :

	Rs.
Capital	78,000
Stock on 1-4-19X5	5,000
Leasehold Premises	46,000
Furniture and Fixtures	13,500
Plant & Machinery	35,000
Purchases	78,900
Sales	1,30,620
Discount Received	470
Discount Allowed	540
Carriage Outwards	120
Carriage Inwards	230
Returns Inwards	1,500
Returns Outwards	380
Wages & Salaries	17,680

Rates and Taxes	1,370
Rent Recoverable	530
Sundry Expenses	1,660
Trade Creditors	22,760
Book Debts	34,000
Drawings	3,000
Bills Payable	1,140
Cash in hand	1,200
Bank Loan	5,800
Closing Stock	3,900

13. Correct the following Trial Balanace drawn up by a novice, giving reasons for your corrections :

	Dr. Rs.	Cr. Rs.
Capital		20,000
Furniture & Fixture		2,000
Deposit with Bank	15,000	
Interest Received from Bank	750	
Miscellaneous Receipts	1,500	
Sundry Creditors		2,500
Sundry Debtors	7,000	
Discount Allowed		500
Discount Received	400	
Purchased	60,000	
Sales		80,000
Returns Inward	1,000	
Returns Outward		1,500
Carriage Inwards		1,500
Carriage Outwards		1,000
Salaries and Wages	5,000	
Miscellaneous Expenses		2,000
Cash in hand	250	
Opening Stock	11,400	
Closing stock	5,700	
	Rs.1,09,500	1,09,500

14. Frame a problem on Double Column Cash Book (no solution is required) to assess the knowledge in this subject of a student who has just learnt it. Add short comments at the end giving down briefly the ideas you have in mind while setting the problem.

15. Write up a Cash Book with Cash and Bank columns (cheque paid into Bank daily). Also post the items into ledger.

19X6.
March

		Rs.
1.	Cash at Bank	1,420
	Cash at hand	270
2..	Paid railway freight	30
3.	Received cheque from Goenka	310
4.	Paid to M.Majumder by cheque	86
5.	Cash sales	180
6.	Paid taxes by cheque	15
10.	Bought postage stamps for cash	5
14.	N.Naskar paid on account by cheque	200
18.	S.Singh paid his dues by cash	350
23.	Sold goods for cash	400
27.	Bought goods by cheque	500
31.	Withdrew for private expenses	200
	Paid wages in cash	150

16. Enter the following transactions in a Cash Book with Cash, Bank Discount Columns. Also balance the Cash Book and bring down the balance.

19X6
March

		Rs.
1.	Cash Balance	370
	Bank Balance	2,450
3.	Cash received from sale of shares	4,000
	Paid M.Lahiri by cheque	750
	Discount allowed by him	25

4.	Paid into Bank	3,150
	Paid wages by cash	50
5.	Brought goods for cash	1,000
6.	Sold goods for cash	510
7.	Paid for stationery in cash	50
	Received from R.Mitra, cheque	360
	Allowed him discount	10
8.	Paid R.Mitra's cheque in Bank	360
9.	Paid office salaries by cash	450
	Cash withdrawn for personal expenses	200
10.	Drew cheque for office use	500
12.	Paid cheque for office rent	50
16.	Paid into Bank	500
22.	Received chheque from S.Adhikari and paid the same into Bank	400
25.	Paid cheque for cash purchase	350
27.	Received cheque from N.Ghosh	1,250
	Allowed him discount	60
30.	Sold goods for cash	250

17. From the following Trial Balance of D.Sen prepare Trading and Profit and Loss Account and the Balance Sheet as on 31st December 19X6.

	Dr. Rs.	Cr. Rs.
Capital		10,000
Opening Stock	3,000	
Purchases	15,000	
Carriage Inwards		500
Wages	1,750	
Returns Inwards		1,250
Sales		32,000
Returns Outwards		1,000
Salaries	2,000	
Postage & Stationery	100	
Furniture	1,800	
General Expenses	3,000	

Sundry Debtors	2,600	
Cash in hand	300	
Cash at Bank	12,400	
Drawings	2,400	
Sundry creditors		3,100
	46,100	46,100

Closing Stock	Rs.2,700
Outstanding Wages	Rs. 150
Depreciation of furniture at	5%

18. From the following Trial Balance of Jamnalal, prepare Trading and Profit & Loss Account for the year ended 31st March 19X7 and a Balance Sheet as on that date.

		Debits	Credits
Plant & Machinery	:	39,440	
Fixtures & Fittings	:	18,960	
Freehold Works	:	50,000	
Goodwill	:	60,000	
Sundry Debtors	:	156,280	
Horses & Carts	:	10,330	
Cash at Bank	:	15,080	
Cash in hand	:	290	
Jamnalal's Capital Account	:		2,40,000
Sundry creditors	:		1,08,320
Bank Loan	:		20,000
Provision for Bad & Doubtful Debts	:		4,000
Purchase Returns	:		2,280
Sales	:		4,13,700
Stock, 1st April, 19X6	:	68,340	
Purchases	:	1,94,330	
Manufacturing Wages	:	69,930	
Carriage inwards	:	3,960	
Manufacturing expenses	:	18,910	
Factory Fuel & Power	:	2,552	

Factory Lighting	:	1,972	
Salaries	:	31,930	
Carriage Inwards	:	4,300	
Insurance & Taxes	:	8,350	
General Expenses	:	16,284	
Distribution Expenses	:	4,946	
Sales Return	:	6,340	
import Duty	:	1,856	
Bad Debts	:	2,970	
Interest & Bank Charges	:	950	
Total		Rs. 7,88,300	Rs.7,88,300

Adjustment :

(i)	Stock as on 31st March19X7		Rs. 79,260
(ii)	Depreciation	- Plant & Machinery	10%
		Fixtures & Fittings	5%
		Horses & Carts	Rs. 2,000

(iii) Bring up Provision for Bad & Doubtful Debts to 5%

(iv) Unexpired Insurance Rs.600/- and Taxes Rs.380/-

(v) A Commission of one percent on Gross Profit to be provided for Works Manager.

(vi) A Commission of 5% of Net Profit (after such commission) to be credited to the General Manager.

Make the calculations to the nearest rupee.

19. The PL A/c of Liquidity Ltd for the year ended 31.12.19X3 shows a Net Profit of Rs. 10 Lakhs. The tax is estimated at Rs 6 Lakhs out of which Rs. 45 lakh has already been paid in three quarterly instalments. The company finds it extremely difficult to :
    (i) Pay the balance tax.
    (ii) Pay bonus to staff for the said year (estimated amount : Rs. 1 lakh already 'provided' in Accounts).
    (iii) Pay a dividend @ 10% declared on its equity capital of Rs.30 lakhs.

Besides the difficulty in these payments the company is running very well during the year 19x4.

Invent all other relevant facts and figures and then explain why the company cannot meet these obligations in spite of good business and good profits in general.

20. Data: current ratio 2.5, Liquid Ratio 1.75, Proprietory Ratio (Fixed Assets to Proprietors Fund) 0.80, capital Gearing Ratio (Equity share capital to Preference Share Capital) 6, Working Capital Rs .75,000, Reserves & Surplus Rs. 25,000, Bank Overdraft Rs.20,000. Required : A summarised Balance Sheet.

21. On the basis of information given below, fill in the blanks on the Balance Sheet.

Sales (all credit)	..	1,00,00,000
Cost of Goods Sold	..	60,00,000
Gross Margin	..	40,00,000
Expenses	..	20,00,000
Taxes	..	10,00,000
Net Profit		10,00,000
Net Profit/Net Worth	..	25%
Funded Debt to Net Worth	..	1:2
Inventory Turnover	..	4 Times Per Year 72 days Collection period (use 360 days years)
Current Ratio	..	2 1/2 :1
Turnover of Total Assets	..	1 1/4 Times a Year
Rate of Return in Total Assets	..	12.5% After Taxes

Balance Sheet as at 31.12.19X3

Liabilities :	Assets:
Total Current Liabilities	Cash.....................
Long Term Debt (Debentures)	Accounts Receivable .....
Net Worth..	Inventories ....
	Total Current Assets.......
Total Liabilities & Net Worth	Fixed Assets..............
	Total Assets ....

22. Critically examine the operating efficiency of the three companies as revealed by the following ratios and rank the companies in the order of merit. Give reasons for you answer :

	A		B		C	
	19X6	19X7	19X6	19X7	19X6	19X7
Net Profit before tax as percentage of sales	5	6	7	6	3	4
Current Ratio	2.1	2.2	2.8	3.0	2.0	1.8
Quick Ratio	0.9	1.1	1.2	1.4	1.2	1.0
Inventory Turnover Ratio	14.0	16.0	12.0	15.0	16.0	18.0
Price Earning Ratio	18.0	15.0	8.0	20.0	3.0	8.0
Debtors as a % of a sales	5.0	3.0	4.2	4.8	2.5	3.5

23. A friend of yours desires to invest in the equity shares of either X Ltd. or Y Ltd. both belonging to the same industry. He has approached you to advise him on which company he should invest in. He has given you the published accounts of the two companies for the last four years and also the trend of market prices of the shares of each company during the same period. To advise your friend properly what are the accounting ratios you will compute? State briefly how each of these ratios will be useful for your purpose.

24. Both A Ltd. and B Ltd. have shown R.O.I. of 20% in 19X6/19X7. In case of A Ltd. the R.O.I. is made up of 10% net Profit Ratio and only 2 times Capital Turnover. In case of B Ltd. the Net Proit Ratio is only 2% but Capital Turnover is 10 times. What conclusions would you draw

from these data about the nature and relative operational efficiency of the two companies.

25. **Set of information : Published Accounts (in each case)**

situations : (a) On behalf of a banker you have to examine whether a proposal for increased overdraft may be accepted in favour of X Ltd.

(b) On behalf of a friend of yours (a prospective investor) you have to examine whether investment in Y Ltd. would be advisable.

(c) On behalf of a prospective supplier you have to assess the credit worthiness of Z Ltd.

(i) State briefly how you would approach in each situation.

(ii) Mention the accounting ratios you would compute under each situation and explain how each of these ratios is going to help you fulfil your purposes,

(Invent any facts and figures you deem necessary)

26. The Balance Sheets of Financial Analysis Ltd., are given below.

(Figures in Rs. lakhs)

	As on 31-3-19X2	As on 31-3-19X3		As on 31-3-19X2	As on 31-3-19X3
Share Capital			Goodwill :	6	4
Equity	30	45	Other Fixed Assets	30	40
6% Preference	15	15	Investments	4	4
Share Premium		3	Advertisement		
Gen. Reserves	4	10	Suspense		2
Long-term loans	6	7	Current Assets		
Current Liability	20	30	Debtors	10	12
			Stock	15	30

		Bank	8	14
		Cash	2	4
75	110		75	110

Depreciation written off fixed Assets (other than goodwill) for the year 19X2-X3 is Rs.2 lakhs. Assume accumulated Depreciation till 31.3.X2. to be nil.

Required :

(i) A Statement of Increase or Decrease in Working Capital between the two years.

(ii) A Statement of Sources and Uses of Funds for the year 19X2-X3.

(iii) An Analysis of financial trend with the aid of relevant Accounting Ratios.

27. Draft the Balance Sheet of a company with imaginary figures.

    Then explain clearly with the help of this Balance Sheet how you would :

    (a) Estimate the Working Capital of the business.

    (b) Prepare a Statement of Proprietory Funds.

    (c) Determine the Capital Employed in the Business.

    (d) Find out the Own Capital and The Loan Capital.

28. From the following balances at 1st January and 31st December, prepare (i) Funds Flow Statement and (ii) Statement of Increase or Decrease in Working Capital.

	1st January	31st December
	Rs.	Rs.
Equity Share Capital	1,00,000	1,20,000
Share Capital	—	10,000
General Reserves	6,000	11,000
Profit & Loss Account	7,500	20,800
5% Debenture	—	26,000
Sundry Creditor	33,500	36,400
Provision for Taxation	9,800	10,900

Proposed Dividend	10,000	12,000
	1,66,800	2,47,100
Land & Building	55,400	1,13,200
Machinery	35,600	51,300
Furniture & Fitting	2,400	1,500
Stock	36,500	39,100
Sundry Debtors	32,100	38,000
Bank	4,800	4,000
	1,66,800	2,47,100

Depreciation writtten off during the year :

Machinery	Rs. 12,800
Furniture & Fittings	400
Land & Building	Nil.

29. From the data of Zenet Steel Pumps Ltd., given below, prepare a Funds Flow Statement for the period 19X6 / 19X7 making such of the adjustments as may be necessary.

(Amount Rs. in lakhs)

Liabilities	19X7	19X6	Assets	19X7	19X6
Sundry Creditors	214	61	Cash Balance	4	2
Cash-Credit, over-draft etc.	482	291	Loans & Advances	192	41
Provision for Income Tax	8	45	Accounts & Receivables	180	99
Other Current Liabilities	11	9	Inventories	719	417
Deposits from the Public	3	3	Gross Fixed Assets	406	327
			Preliminary		

Long-term loans	57	8	expenses and		
Equity Capital	252	104	Deferred revenue		
Reserves and			expenditure		1
Surplus	352	223			
Accumulated depreciation	122	107			
	1,501	887		1,501	887

Notes :

1. Bonus equity shares of the value of Rs.112 lacs were issued during the period.

2. A loss of Rs.0.5 lacs was incurred on sales of fixed assets disposed of during the period whose gross book value was Rs.4 lacs the accumulated depreciation on such assets was Rs.0.5 lacs.

30. The Crown Electricals Ltd., has the following balance sheet

BALANCE SHEET AAS ON DECEMBER 31

(Rs. in lakhs)

Liabilities	19X5	19X4	Assets	19X5	19X4
	Rs.	Rs.		Rs.	Rs.
Current Liabilities	105	30	Current Assets:		
Long term loans	150	—	Cash	2	10
			Sundry debtors	60	30
Equity and surplus	207	160	Inventories	100	50
				162	90
			Fixed Assets (Net)	300	100
Total Liabilities	462	190	Total Assets	462	190

Net profit for the year 19X5 was Rs. 54 lakhs. Dividends paid were Rs. 7 lakhs. Depreciation was Rs.20 lakhs. Fixed assets purchased during the year for 200 lakhs.

Beni Prasad Agarwal, the Managing Director of the Company was a superb operating executive. He was an imaginative, aggressive marketing man and an ingenious, creative production man. But he had little patience with financial matters. After examining the above most recent balance sheet and the income statement, he muttered, "We have enjoyed ten years of steady growth; 19X5 was our most profitable year. Despite such profitability, we are in the worst cash position in our history. Just look at those current liabilities in relation to our available cash. This whole picture of the more you make, the poorer you get just does not make sense."

1. Prepare a Fund Flow Statement.

2. Using the Fund Flow Statement and other information, write a short note to Mr. Agarwal explaining why there is such squeeze on cash.

31. The following are the summarised Trial Balance of a Limited Company as at 31st March 19X3 and 19X4

	19X3		19X4	
	Dr. Rs.	Cr. Rs.	Dr. Rs.	Cr. Rs.
Fixed Assets	23,36,960	24,60,500		
Current Assets	9,60,540	7,91,800		
Debenture Discount	30,000		25,000	
Issued Capiital				
Equity		15,00,000		15,00,000
Preference		3,00,000		4,00,000
Share Premium Account		30,000		40,000
Debentures		5,00,000		5,00,000
Current Liabilities		6,20,000		4,40,000
Provision for Depreciation		1,80,000		1,95,000

Provision for doubtful debts		6,000		5,000
Dividend for 19X2-X3		15,00,000		
Balance of P.L.A/c.from previous year		24,400		1,91,500
Net profit for the year		1,67,100		1,55,800
	33,27,500	33,27,500	34,27,300	34,27,300

(a) During the year ended 31st March 19X4, Machinery costing Rs. 2,00,000 (accumulated provision for depreciation Rs 60,000) was sold for Rs.1,50,000

(b) Rs.1,00,000 preference share capital was issued during 19X3/X4 at a premium of Rs.10,000

(c) The net profit for 19X3-X4 has been arrived at after taking credit for the profit on sale of machinery, reduction in the provision for doubtful debts and writing-off the discount on issue of debentures. You are required to prepare :

(1) A statement showing the net increase in working capital during the year 19X3/X4.

(2) A statement showing the sources of the increase in the working capital and application thereof during the year.

32. Job Order Ltd. have the following cost data for the year 19X3.

	Rs.		Rs.
Direct Material	6,00,000	Administrative overheads	2,80.000
Direct Wages	5,00,000	Selling & Distribution Overheads	3,50,000
Factory Overhead	3,00,000	Profit	5,07,000

In 19X4 the Company receives an order which would require Materials Rs.80,000 and Direct Wages Rs.50,000 for completion. What would be the price for the job if the company intends to earn the same rate of profit on sales as in 19X3, assuming that,

(i) Selling & Distribution overheads have gone up by 10% in 19X4.

(ii) The bases of overhead recovery are : Factory Overheads as percentage of direct wages and Administrative, Selling & Distribution Overheads as percentage of Works Cost.

33. A manufacturing company with spare capacity proposes to increase its range of products to utilise its resources more fully. The fixed costs, which amount to Rs.57,500, are unlikely to be affected by the contemplated increase in output. Budgeted sales, now running at Rs. 2,45,000 per month, are to be increased so that the budgeted total will be Rs.3,67,500 per month.

Expected figures for variable overhead per month are as follows:

	Production	Selling	Administrative & distribution
	Rs.	Rs.	Rs.
Present Scale of Manufacture	25,000	23,700	17,500
Proposed future scale of manufacture	37,500	60,000	25,000

The direct material cost per month is expected to rise from a total of Rs.27,500 to Rs. 42,500 and direct wages per month from a total of Rs. 42,500 to Rs.75,000.

Using marginal costing technique, tabulate these data in the form in which you would present it to management to give assistance in reaching a decision upon the proposal. Add your recommendation to management.

Marketing Planning

34. From the following information prepare a flexible budget to show levels of activity of 80%, 90% and 100%.

1. Sales, based on normal level of activity of 80%, are 80,000 units at Rs.20 per unit. If output is increased to 90%, it is thought that the selling

price should be reduced by 2 1/2 and if output reaches 100% it would be necessary to reduce the original selling price by a further 2 1/2 in order to reach a wider market.

2. Prime Costs are :

	Per unit Rs.
Direct Material	2.00
Direct Labour	2.00
Direct Expense	1.00
	6.00

If output reaches a 90% level of activity as above, quantity discount will be received and this will lead to reduction of purchase price of raw material by 5%.

3. Variable Overheads : Salesman's commission is 5% on sale value.

4. Semi-variable overheads at normal level of activity are :

	Rs.
Supervision	80,000
Power	70,000
Heat and Light	40,000
Maintenance	50,000
Indirect Labour	1,00,000
Salesmen's expenses	60,000
Transport	2,00,000
	6,00,000

Semi-variable overheads are expected to increase by 5% if output reaches a level of activity of 90%, and by a further 5% if it reaches the 100% level.

5. Fixed Overheads are :

	Rs.
Rent and Rates	10,000
Depreciation	40,000
Administration	75,000
Sales Department	20,000

Advertising	50,000
General	5,000
	2,00,000

35. The following is the summarised picture of the 3 years' results of Home Delivery Traders Limited.

(Rupees in Lakhs)

	19X4	19X3	19X2
	Rs.	Rs.	Rs.
1. Sales	230.00	180.00	150.00
2. Cost of Sales	195.00	149.00	120.00
3. Gross Profit	35.00	31.00	30.00
4. Selling and Distribution Expenses	22.00	18.00	15.00
5. Administration Expenses	10.00	9.00	8.00
6. Net Profit	3.00	4.00	7.00
7. Capital Employed	45.00	40.00	35.00

The management of the Company is at a loss to know why despite substantial growth in its sales, the profitability of the Company has been deteriorating year. Analyse the reasons for the deteriorating profitability of the Company and suggest ways and means of improving it.

36. The Bina Bakery sells two very popular speciality cakes, a butter cream delight and a chocolate layer cake. Both are baked in the same oven, which will accommodate 15 cakes at one time and can be operated for a maximum of 60 hours per week.

The demand for both cakes is so great that the bakery could sell the maximum output of the oven in any combination of the two cakes including all of one or all of the other. The only direct costs of these cakes are their respective ingredient costs. A comparison of the prices, ingredient costs and oven time of the two cakes are as follows ;

	Butter Cream Rs.	Chocolate Layer Rs.
Price	2.00	1.66
Ingredient Cost	0.80	0.75
Oventime	30 minutes	20 minutes

What would be the most profitable sales mix of these two cakes.

Marketing Decision

37. The sales turnover and profit during two quarters were as under.

Quarter - April to June 19X9	Sales Rs. 20 lakhs
	Profit Rs. 2 lakhs
Quarter - July to sept. 19X9	Sales Rs. 30 lakhs
	Profit Rs. 4 lakhs

Calculate :

(i) Fixed Cost
(ii) Break-Even point
(iii) Sales required to earn a profit of Rs. 5 lakhs

38. Period	Sales Rs.lakhs	Net Profit (Loss) Rs.lakhs
Jan - March	15	(1)
April - June	20	1

A. Based on the above data find out

(i) Ratio
(ii) Fixed Cost per quarter
(iii) B.E. Sales Value per quarter
(iv) Margin of Safety as percentage on April - June Sales
(v) Sales required in the third quarter to earn a profit of Rs.5 lakhs.

(vi) Profit expected during the last quarter, given the sales forecast for the period, Rs.35 lakhs.

B. Present in break-even charts the actual position of the first and second quarters and also the expectations during the third and forth quarters.

Hints : The Contribution on the incremental sale of Rs.5 lakhs (Rs.15 lakhs - Rs. 10 lakhs) is Rs. 2 lakhs (Rs.1 lakh profit after recovering Rs.1 lakh loss).

39. The Kitchen Tools Company has developed a new model gadget which the Management plans to market. Through survey of the Company's distributors. Management has determined that the market for the new model is :

(a) 1000 per year at a price of Rs.20/- each
(b) 1200 per year at a price of Rs.18/- each
(c) 1500 per year at a price of Rs.15/- each

Since the Company has excess production capacity, the only additional costs to produce the new model will be:

Overhead :	Labour ..	Rs.5,000 per year
	Other ...	Rs.1,000 per year
Direct Labour Cost	..	Rs. 4 per unit
Direct Material Cost	...	Rs. 3 per unit

The Company depreciates machinery on the basis of Units of Production at Re. 1 per unit.

1. Disregarding all other Costs except those listed above, construct Break Even chart for this project at each price level.

2. From the standpoint of maximizing profits alone, at what price should the Company sell this new model.

40. (a) From the following particulars draw a break even chart and find out the break-even point. Rs.

Variable cost per unit	15
Fixed expenses	54,000
Selling price per unit	20

(b) What should be the selling price per unit, if the break-even point should be brought down to 6,000 units ?

41. From the following data draw a single break-even chart.

Selling price per unit	Rs. 10.00
Trade discount @.5 per cent	
Direct material cost per unit	3.00
Direct labour cost per unit	2.00
Fixed Overheads	10,000

Variable Overheads 100% on direct labour cost. If sales are 10% and 15% above the break-even volume, determine the net profit.

42. Sales of a product amount to Rs.200 units per month at Rs.10 per unit. Fixed overhead is Rs. 400 per month and variable cost Rs.6 per cent. There is a proposal to reduce prices by 10 per cent. Calculate, present and future ratio and find, by applying ratio, how many units must be sold to maintain total profit.

43. Summarised figures from a manufacturer's budgets are as follows :

	Quantity Units	Unit Price Rs.	Total Rs.
Sales	17,500	180	31,50,000
Marginal costs			
Material		50	8,75,000
Wages		45	7,87,500
Variable overheads		36	6,30,000
		131	22,92,500

Assuming that the period costs, which are Rs.5,00,000 remain unaffected calcuate:

(a) Unit margin;

(b) total margin;

(c) profit/volume percentage;

(d) total contribution;

(e) effect on profit of making and selling, a further 2,500 units, and

(f) additional sales required to produce the same profit with unit sales reduced to Rs.162 each.

What is break-even point ?

44. (a) Alcos Ltd. manufacture and sell four types of products under the brand names A, B,C and D. The sales mix in value comprises of 331/3%, 41 2/3%, 16 2/3% and 8 1/3% for A,B,C and D respectively. The total budgeted sales (100%) are Rs.60,000 per month. Operating costs are :

Variable posts -

Product	
	A 60% of selling price
	B 68% of selling price
	C 80% of selling price
	D 40% of selling price

Fixed cost - Rs. 14,700 per month

Calculate the break - even point for the products on an overall basis.

(b) It has been proposed to change the sales-tax as follows, the total sales per month remaining Rs.60,000

Product	
	A 25%
	B 40%
	C 30%
	D 5%

Assuming that the proposal is implemented, calculate the break-even point.

45. Three Advertising men, Mathew, Mani and Mishra, have formed an agency in which they are to be equal partners. The new agency advises its customers on the

media for their advertisements and submits copy, layout and rough design for approval. The agency charges the stanadard 15 percent of media billings for their services. For example, an advertisement that is billed by Times of India for Rs. 10,000 would be subject to a 15 percent agency commission . The agency would be billed by *Times of India* for Rs. 8,500 and they in turn would bill the client for the full 10,000. Total charges to customers include :

Billings (Media cost including 15% Agency Commission)		XXX
Production charges (work done outside the agency) :		
Finished at work	XX	
Type setting	XX	
Engraving	XX	XXX
	—	—
Total Charges		XXX

To serve the number of customers who have followed the owners from their previous employments, two accounts executives are hired. The two, George and Jacob, are each paid Rs. 12,000 per year plus three-fourths of 1 per cent of all the agency's media billings. George,Jacob and the three partners entertain the agency's clients at a beach resort maintained for that purpose at an annual cost of Rs. 10,000. In addition, the agency pays Rs.4,200 annually for membership in clubs where clients are entertained. Other annual costs are :

	Rs.
Office Rent	48,000
Subscription to Readership, Surveys and service publication	1,500
Clerical and Administrative Expenses	42,500
Production Chief's Salary	26,200
Copywriters Salary (2 X 18,000)	36,000
Property Tax and Insurance	1,500
Salaries of Partners	1,80,000

Required :

1. What media billings are needed to break-even ?
2. The partners believe that they can expand their services and profits if they set up their own art department. To begin with the artists will be paid on an hourly basis. The art department would use a converted storage room adjacent to the offices. Rent would be Rs. 250 per month and insurance and tax would be another Rs. 250 per annum . A messenger service to carry the art work from the agency to the clients and back would cost Rs 5,000. Materials are expected to cost 1 percent of art work charges. The partners agree to charge Rs. 20 per hour for work done in the art department.

   (a) Mani estimates that the art break-even point is billing of Rs. 43,200. How much per hour does he plan to pay the artists?

   (b) Mishra has determined that art work billings of Rs. 77,000 will yield a profit of Rs. 9,100 with a department contribution margin ratio of 12%. How much per hour does Mishra plan to pay their artists?

46. The management of a concern, manufacturing two products, X and Y have the following independent possibilities before them :

   (a) To produce and sell 16,000 additional units of Y but only if the production of X is reduced by 20,000 units.

   (b) To reduce the price of X by Rs. 0.20 per unit. This will result in a 25% increase in the sale of X without any changes in the activity of Y.

   (c) To produce and sell 55,000 units of X and 1,05,000 units of Y.

		Product X	Product Y	Total
Sales (in units)		50,000	1,00,000	
Sales (value)	Rs.	2,50,000	8,50,000	

Cost of sales		1,50,000	6,00,000	
Gross Margin	Rs.	1,00,000	2,50,000	3,50,000
Selling and Distribution expenses	Rs.	60,000	1,50,000	
Net Margin		40,000	1,00,000	1,40,000

Direct costs included in total costs amount to Rs. 1,20,000 for Product X and Rs. 3,40,000 for Product Y.

Present the information to the management in a suitable form, giving your recommendation.

47. A company currently operating at 80% capacity, has the following profit and loss account.

	Rs.	Rs.
Sales		6,40,000
Costs		
Direct material	2,00,000	
Direct Labour	80,000	
Variable Overheads	40,000	
Fixed Overheads	2,60,000	5,80,000
Profit		60,000

It has just received an offer of an overseas order that would require the use of half the factory's capacity. The order, which must be taken in full or rejected completely must be supplied at prices 10% below current home prices. The following alternatives are available to the management.

(i) Reject the order and carry on with home sales only as currently:

ii) Accept the order, split capacity equally between overseas and home sales, and turn away excess home demand : or

(iii) Increase factory capacity to accept the export order and maintain the present home sales level by :

(a) buying machine that will increase factory capacity by 10% and fixed costs by Rs. 20,000 and

(b) work overtime at time and a half to meet balance of required capacity.

Which one is the most profitable alternative ?

48. In the face of the trade recession, M/s. Modern Engineering Ltd. is having a difficult period due to lack of Government orders and is operating below 60% of its normal capacity. This is however considered to be a temporary phase and the management has taken a decision not to retrench labour. An enquiry has been received for 10,000 units of a product which could be manufactured by the company under the existing capacity and the costing data are as follows :

Direct labour - Re. 1 per unit
Time required - 1 hour per unit
Direct Material - Rs.2 per unit
Variable O.H. - 400 per cent of direct labour
Fixed O.H. - 600 per cent of direct labour
Cost of special tools - Rs. 25,000

What is the minimum price you would recommend and why ?

49. The capacity of your factory is to manufacture 10,000 units of a product. The actual production is 50% of the capacity and the entire production is sold in India. The demand in the home market is unable to absorb any more of production. The price cum cost structure is detailed below :

Price		Rs. 60 per unit
cost-Material	Rs. 20 per unit	
Wages (50% variable)	20 per unit	
Other overheads (fixed)	10 per unit	
		50 per unit
	Profit	Rs. 10 per unit

An offer has been received for exporting 5,000 units of the product, after meeting the demand in the home market, at an F.O.B. price of Rs 25 per unit. The export order will call for additional expenses on export promotion estimated at Rs.60,000 (This will qualify for the export market development allowance @ 33 1/3% of the actual expense in terms of Sec. 35B of the Income Tax Act. 1961). The export will provide for the following further benefits:

(a) A cash subsidy at 10% on the F.O.B. value of exports to be received from the Government of India.

(b) The Government of India will also issue import licence for an amount equal to 30% of the F.O.B.value of export.

The import licence may be sold at a premium of 100% or as an alternative, the imported raw materials may be used in the manufacture of Rs.5,000 units of a completely new product. The expected sales price and further costs particular to this new product will be :

Selling Price	Rs.	60 per unit
Indigenous raw materials to be used (In addition to imported raw materials)	Rs.	60,000
Additional wages to be paid		1,00,000
other expenses specific to the new product		40,000

The effective rate of taxation for your company is 50%

You are required to suggest, with detailed working, if the export order should be accepted and if so, the manner in which the import licence should be utilised.

50. A firm purchases 10,000 units p.a. of a spare part from an outside source @ 6.00 per unit. There is a proposal that the spare be produced in the factory itself. For the purpose a machine costing Rs. 1,00,000 with annual capacity of 15,000 units and life of 10years, will be required. A foreman

with a salary of Rs.800 per month will have to be engaged. Materials required will be Rs. 120 per unit and wages 90 paise per unit. Variable overheads are 150% of direct labour and other fixed expenses are recovered at 200% of direct wages. The firm can easily raise funds at 15% per annum. Advise the firm whether the proposal should be accepted.

51. Following are the operating results of Departmental Store Ltd. during 19X1.

(Figures in Rs. Lakhs)

	Total	Stationery Dept.	Ready made Garments dept.	Musical Instruments dept.
Sales	100	40	50	10
Gross Profit	37	15	20	2
Expenses (apportioned in the ratio of sales)	30	12	15	3
Net Profit	7	3	5	(1)

Since the Musical Instruments Dept. is running at a loss, the company is thinking of closing the Dept.

(i) State whether it would be financially justified to close the Dept.

(ii) Mention the factors/conditions which would make your advice as per (i) wrong.

(iii) Would your advice as per (i) be the same if a new Department (Restaurant) is opened in place of Musical Dept. with an estimated Sales and Gross Profit of 10 lakhs and 40% respectively? Invent any facts and figures you require.

52. Janata Bazar which did not keep any departmental accounts till the year ended 31st December, 19X3, decided to

introduce departmental accounting with effect from 1st January 19X4. At the end of 19X4, it was found that; although the business as a whole earned a gross margin of approximately 15% and net Profit of 1.8% on sales of over Rs. 25 lakhs, the Ready-made Garments Department showed a net loss. The income statement for this department was as follows :

	Rs.	Rs.
1. Sales		4,16,000
2. Cost of Sales		3,75,000
3. Gross Margin		41,000
4. Expenses :		
(i) Salaries of departmental staff	21,000	
(ii) Salesmen's commission	6,000	
(iii) Rent (charged on the basis of the area occupied by the departmental in the Stores rented building)	13,000	
(iv) Insurance of inventories and equipments of the department	1,000	
(v) Depreciation on the air-conditioning plant of the stores (charged on the basis of the Cu. ft. area of the department)	2,000	
(vi) General Administration Expenses (allocated on the basis of the departmental sales)	13,000	
(vii) Interest on capital employed (chharged notionally at 9% per annum; the Stores had no outside borrowings for working capital)	3,000	59,000
5. Net Loss		18,000

The management of the Bazar was very happy that the introduction of departmental accounting had brought to light the fact that the readymade garments department was making loss which was in the past disguised in the overall profits of the Bazar. It was, therefore, considered whether this deparment should be closed down. However, it is decided to consult, you as an expert before taking a final decision. What action would you recommend ?

53. Protex Ltd. want to establish one of their products in the highly competitive export market. The domestic marginal cost of sales of the product is Rs. 95 per unit. If export is made, this cost will increase by Rs. 9 per unit due to more attractive packaging, freight and more stringent quality control. There will, however, be a saving of Rs. 4 per unit on account of variable selling expenses. Calculate the Rock Bottom F.O.B. price per unit of the product which the company can quote against a global tender, after transferring to the prospective importer the benefits from :

(a) Cash subsidy + 25% on F.O.B. value

(b) Import Licence + 25% on F.O.B value, which licence has got a premium value of 100%.

54. Mr. Confectioner manufactures three types of sweets, viz, S1, S2 and S3, demand for each of which exists. In January 19X3 he sold Rs. 20,000, Rs.30,000 and Rs.40,000 worth of these products respectively, and the relative contribution earned was Rs.6,000, Rs.6,000 and Rs.10,000. The ratio of consumption of sugar by S1, S2, and S3 was 3:4:2 during the month.

Effective February 19X3, sugar is controlled and the quota for Mr. Confectioner was fixed at 20% below the consumption level of January. Investing any relevant facts and figures, advise Mr. Confectioner on the most profitable production sales mix from February onwards.

55. The consumer goods of a particular category attract excise duty at 10% on the ex-factory value which is calculated by deducting from the list price the trade discount - if the

rate is uniform for all dealers - and the actual freight cost, if charged separately. From the following data, compute the excise duty and advice your Marketing Director about the pricing structure you would like bim to adopt.

Product X Rs. Per Kg.	'A' Co. Metropolitan Cities	'A' Co. Rest of India	'B' Co. Metropolitan Cities	'B' Co. Rest of India
List Price	5.00	6.00	5.50	7.00
Commission/ Discount	1.2% (depending on order size)	1.2%	10%	10%
Freight&Delivery	nil	Actual	nil	nil
Excise duty (on ex-factory value)	10%	10%	10%	10%
Sales Tax	9%	10%	9%	10%
Despatch/delivery terms	Free Delivery	Freight to pay	Free Delivery	F.O.R. Destination

56. The Home Product Company manufactures plastic jugs. At the current operative level, which is below full capacity of 1,00,000 units per year, the following results are expected :

	Rs.	Rs.	Per unit
Sales 80,000 Units @ Re. 1/-		80,000	1.00
Manufacturing costs :			
Variable,80,000 Units @ 50 paise		40,000	0.50
Fixed		25,000	0.3125
Total Manufacturing cost		65,000	0.8125
Gross Margin		15,000	0.1875
Variable Selling Expenses	4,000		0.0500
Fixed Selling Expenses	8,000		0.1000
Total Selling Expenses		12,000	0.1500
Total Expenses		77,000	0.9625
Net Operating Income		3,000	0.375

A department store offers to buy 20,000 Units @ 75 paise. The buyer will pay for the transport expenses. Should the order be accepted ? Discuss the factors which you have considered relevant for the decision.

57. Following are the details of two alternative projects.

		(Rs.000)	
Project		X	Y
Cash Flow : Present (Ivestment)		(200)	(150)
Year-end	1	30	—
	2	60	20
	3	90	40
	4	90	60
	5	90	90
	6	—	50
Realisable value of assets at the end of respective project-life		30	40

Assess the relative profitability of the projects on the basis of

(i) Pay Back Period

(ii) Return on Investment

(iii) N.P.V.

(iv) D.C.F. Rate of Return

Assume for the purpose of N.P.V. a discount rate of 10%.

58. A toy manufacturer who specialises in making fancy items has just developed a Rs. 50,000 moulding machine for automatically producing a special toy. The machine has been used to produce one unit. The machine will be depreciated evenly over four years after which time the production of the toy will be stopped.

Suddenly, a machine salesman appears. He has a new machine which is ideally suited for producing this toy. His automatic machine is destinctly superior. It reduces the cost of materials by 10% and produces twice as many units per hour. It will cost Rs. 44,000 and will have zero disposale value at the end of four years.

Production and sales would continue to be at the rate of 25,000 per year for fou r years; annual sales will be Rs.90,000. The scrap value of the toy company's machine is now Rs. 5,000 and will be Rs. 2,600 four years from now. Both machines will be useless after the 1,00,000 unit total market potential is exhausted. With its present equipment, the Company's annual expenses will be :

	Rs.
Direct Material	10,000
Direct Labour	20,000
Variable Factory Overheads	15,000

Allocated fixed factory overhead, exclusive of depreciation, is Rs. 7,500 annually and allocated fixed selling and administrative expenses are Rs.12,000 annually. The company pays tax at 60%.

Required :

Assume that expected minimum rate of return is 18% after tax. Using discounted cash flow technique, show whether the new equipment should be purchased. What is the role of the book value of the old equipment ? What is the payback period for the new equipment?

59. Kerala Fishing Industries Private Limited is contemplating the purchase of a machine costing Rs. 60,000. In order to assess the profitability of the proposed investment, the following data are given :

(1)	Estimated life	6 years
(2)	Estimated Scrap value	Rs. 6,000
(3)	Net Cash benefits before depreciation and tax —	
	Year 1 to 3	Rs. 25,000 per yr.
	Year 4 to 6	Rs. 35,000 per yr.
(4)	Assume that the whole asset can be depreciated fully in 6 year period for tax purpose	
(5)	Tax rate	50%

Required :

Discuss the profitability of the proposed investment under the following methods:

(a) Pay back method

(b) Discounted Cash Flow method.

60. KL Ltd. is considering the purchase of a machine to provide additional output. Details of two alternative machines with estimated Costs and value of Sales are shown below:

	Machine A	Machine B
	Rs.	Rs.
Capital Cost	60,000	60,000
Sales (full Production at Standard Price)	1,00,000	80,000
Costs		
Direct Labour	10,000	6,000
Direct Material	8,000	10,000
Factory Overheads	12,000	10,000
Administration Cost	4,000	2,000
Selling & Distribution Cost	2,000	2,000
Serviceable Life	2 yers	3 yers.

Sales are expected to continue at the rates shown above for the full life of the machine. The costs shown relate to the annual expenditure resulting from each machine.

Income tax is payable at 50% of net earnings. It may be assumed that for Sales and Costs all amounts are received and paid out in the years shown. For the purpose of calculation, these cash receipts and payments may be taken to be settled on the last day of each year. Interest on capital is to be ignored.
Show the most profitable investment on the facts given, by the following method.

1. Payback method
2. Return on Investment Method.

61. Your factory's product range includes product 'A' which sells at a loss. detailed as under :

Sales price per unit		Rs.4,000
Cost - Variable	Rs.3,000	
Fixed - Specific to Product 'A'	1,200	
Fixed General	800	5,000
Loss per unit		Rs.1,000

The fixed costs specific to the product 'A' will be annually Rs.3,00,000 for the next three years after which they will be discontinued with the termination of the production. The sales forecast for the next three years are as follows :

19X1	Rs.12,00,000
19X2	8,00,000
19X3	2,50,000 - thereafter nil

Existing finished stocks at book value (variable cost), amounts to Rs. 8,00,000. There is also a stock of service spares amounting to Rs.18,00,000 (at variable cost i.e. sales less 50%). Forecast sales are at Rs.4,20,000 for each of the next three years and Rs.1,80,000 for each of the following three years. After this, the business will fade away.

Your competitor has offered to take over the manufacture and sale of Product 'A' including that of service spares. The terms offered are as under :

(a) Rs.2,00,000 to be paid for the manufacturing rights,

(b) A royalty at 5% on total sales, including spares sales for the next three years — payable at the end of each year.

(c) Finish stock to be taken over at the book values and paid for immediately and Rs.10,00,000 to be paid for spares on take over.

The cost of finance to your Company is at 8% per annum. You have been asked by your directors to suggest with reasons, if this offer should be accepted.

Present value of Re.1 assuming that the Re.1 is received in a single payment on the last day of each year, regard being given to interest at 8%, is as under.

After 1 year	.93
" 2 years	.86
" 3 years	.79
" 4 years	.74
" 5 years	.68
" 6 years	.63

62. The old fleet of cars of your company require immediate replacement. The company is paying 15% interest on overdraft and the possibility of getting additional finance for purchase of cars is ruled out. There are two alternatives.

(a) Purchase of 8 cars required by the company at Rs.80,000 each draining out the necessary finance from, working capital.

(b) Take on hire 8 cars at Rs. 2,000 p.m. each as hire charges. The running and other expenses are the same for either of the alternatives. Additional information available :

(i) The working capital turnover ratio is 1:3 and the contribution on sales is 20%.

(ii) Expected working life of a car is 5 years and after that period an owned car has a resale value of Rs.30,000.

(iii) Depreciation at 25% and hire charges (full) are tax deductible (No Capital Gains Tax on resale profit on car).

(iv) The earning on working capital accrue and payment of hire charges are made annually, towards the end of each year.

Advice your management as to which of the two alterna - tives is financially beneficial.

63. Few Product Ltd. produced three products in 19X6 - sales and costs are given below.

COST and SALES of PRODUCT A,B & C in 19X6

	Product A		Product B		Product C		Company
Revenues		2,50,000		3,20,000		1,70,000	7,40,000
Direct wages	40,000		1,20,000		20,000		
Direct Matreial	1,20,000		1,20,000		30,000		
Variable Overheads	20,000		30,000		25,000		
Fixed Overheads	15,000		90,000		30,000		
Total Cost		1,95000		3,60,000		1,02,000	6,60,000
Profit							
(Loss)		55,0000		(40,0000)		65,000	
Aggregate Profit							80,000

You may assume that the above is a 'fair' allocation of all costs. Variable overheads have been found to vary in direct proportion to the production of each product in the long run. In the short period (in this case 6 months to a year), however, 1/3 of variable overheads is inescapable, due to large stocks of spare parts.

The Marketing Manager of Few Product Ltd. was appalled when he saw this statement at the end of 19X6. He suggested that Product B should be summarily cut from the 19X7 product range. "Even if we achieve the same level of sales, our profit would be Rs.1,20,000," he said.

Required :

Assuming there is no hope of introducing a replacement product in the coming year :

(i) tabulate the effect of the Marketing Manager's suggestion at constant unit sales, prices and costs;

(ii) give your judgement of his suggestions with your reasoned arguments; and

(iii) consider the feasible alternative strategies.

Marketing Performance Evaluation

64. Apollo Corporation manufactures industrial products which are sold to industrial users. Its market is divided into 10 territories. The sales volume of the territories are given in Exhibit 1. With a view to improve sales performance you have taken up for appraisal four of the territories, viz Calcutta, Madras, Banglore and Madurai, those of salesmen Ahmed, Bose, Chopa and Desai respectively.

    Exhibit 2 gives the details of sales performance of these four salesmen Scrutinise the data and make whatever recommendations to management you think might be appropriate. Briefly explain the significance of the tools used by you for salesmen appraisal.

Exhibit 1

VOLUME OF SALES BY TERRITORY

Territory	Per cent of Company Total Potential	Sales volume Rs. (.000)	Per cent of Company Total sales	*TPI
Bombay	21	1,780	28.03	134
Ahmedabad	8	375	5.96	74
Poona	6	345	5.43	91
Delhi	11	750	11.81	107
Kanpur	7	480	7.56	108
Punjab	8	425	6.68	84
Calcutta	12	810	12.75	106
Madras	10	515	8.11	81
Bangalore	9	405	6.37	71
Madurai	8	465	7.31	91
	100	6,350	100.00	

* TPI is the Territorial Performance Index

Exhibit 2

SALESMAN AND TERRITORY ANALYSIS

s.	*1 Sales Volume	2 Salesmen's Compensation	3 Slaes Expenses	4 Total Direct Sales Costs	5 Days Worled	6 Orders Written	7 Prospect Cells	8 Customers cell	9 Total Calls	10 New Accts.	11 Lost Accts.	12 Slaes nes ccts	
	Rs. (.000)	Rs.	Rs.								Rs.		
Ahmed	800	24000		7000	32000	220	900	80	1120	1200	20	5	16000
Bose	500	15000		5000	20000	250	700	100	1000	1100	30	10	20000
Chopra	400	12000		5000	18000	240	750	200	1200	1400	40	50	36000
Desai	500	14000		6000	20000	210	600	60	840	900	10	0	18000
Total	2200	65000		23000	90000	920	2950	440	4160	4600	100	65	90000

65. A company has three branches and their summarised accounting particulars for a period are given below :

Branches	Bombay Rs.	Calcutta Rs.	Madras Rs.
Sales	4,50,000	4,00,000	7,00,000
Branch expenses :			
Salaries, commissions and travelling expenses	41,000	40,000	60,000
Advertisement	9,000	10,000	11,000
Other expenses	10,000	11,000	12,000

Central Office expenses :
Rs. 1,55,000 apportioned to branches on the basis of sales. 25 per cent of sales is taken as Gross Profit.

Based on the above information, prepare a comparitive Profit and Loss Statement for the different branches. Offer your views on the contemplated closure of the branch which shows a loss assuming that in the event of closure of a branch, central office expenses :

(a) will remain unaffected ;

(b) can be reduced by 30%

66. Mr. Reddy, Sales Manager of the Red Star Engineering Company, has been asked by his superior what seemed to be a relatively simple question: 'Who is the Company's best salesmen"?

He replied off handedly tha t Kashyap was his top sales producer. However, the more he got to thinking about the question, the more be wondered if Kashyap really was his best salesman; after all Kashyap did have the Bombay territory.

Mr. Reddy decided to ask one of his assistants to make an evaluation of best performer. A week later Mr. Reddy's assistant submitted the follwoing information :

	Kashyap (Bombay)	Hari (Madras)	Basu (Calcutta)	Singh (Delhi)
Sales, 000 Rs.	1250	840	720	380
Order Nos.	340	280	320	275
Call Nos.	430	520	405	310
Days Worked	210	205	260	270
New Accounts	86	53	45	21
Accounts Lost	15	26	11	20
Expenses, 000 Rs.	48	22	50	42
Area Potential, 000 Rs.	14,000	8,000	5,000	2,600

67. A district sales manager collects the following information about his five salesmen to help him select his best salesmen to receive a company awared :

	Salesman					Total
	Ravi	Bharat	Krishnan	Naik	George	District
Territorial Sales						
Potential	Rs. 250000	300000	325000	225000	200000	1300000
Sales	Rs. 170000	190000	195000	180000	160000	895000
Number of orders	200	250	275	190	350	1265
Batting Average	.667	.750	.3755	.500	.875	
Total Compensation	Rs. 9200	10000	10200	9600	8800	47800
Sales Expense Ratio	3.4%	4.2%	4.5%	3.8%	4.2%	
Customer Complaints	22	14	7	21	12	76
Personal Evaluation of Supervisor (best=100)	82	76	86	85	90	

From this informaation, devise an evaluation plan using only what you think is pertinent for the purpose indicated. Which salesman should receive the award? Indicated how you arrived at your decision, and state any assumptions you felt were necessay.

Evaluate the relative performance of the four salesmen. If you were Mr. Reddy, what advice would you give to each of the salesmen?

68. A one-product Company shows the following operating performance during 19X0.

Sales 1,00,000 units @	Rs.	100 each
Variable cost per unit	Rs.	60
Fixed Cost (Total)	Rs.	25 lakhs

The Company intends to increase selling price by 20% in 19X1. It is expected that unit sales will come down by 5% and to prevent it from further coming down a substantial amount has to be spent on advertisement during the first year (19X1). It is also estimated that fixed cost will rise by 10% and variable cost will increase by 2% in 19X1.

Estimate the amount the company can afford to spend in 19X1 on advertisement, maintaining the profit at the same quantum as in 19X0.

69. The Porter Manufacturing Company has been accused of discriminating against its small-order customers(25 to 30 cases) in Territory 1 as compared with the same class of customers in Territories 2, 3, and 4 The Company has broken down its selling and distribution cost by territories, and now desires to pro-rate the territorial costs between classes of customers with each inventorial costs between classes of customers with each territory. The following is a tabulation of the average selling and distribution costs per year in Territory I.

Expenses	Amount
Advertising	Rs.
Direct-to-customer	3,600
Radio and newspapers	9,800

Salesmen's Salaries	36,000
Salesmen's Commissions	48,000
Delivery Expenses	28,000
Travelling cost of salesmen	10,800
	1,36,200

The cost department has tabulated the following information to assist in pro-rating costs in Territory I between small-order, medium-order and large-order customers :

	Small Order	Medium Order	Large Order
Net Sales (Rs.)	1,50,000	2,00,000	3,50,000
No.of sales order taken	2,500	2,000	1,500
Number of cases of + product sold	1,00,000	1,50,000	2,50,000
Relative Shipping cost (per order) Rs.	1	2	3
Number of customer	1,500	1,500	2,000
Relative number of miles travelled per day	4	10	16
Number of salesmen	13	6	5

All salesmen are paid the same salary; each salesman works within a single class of customer.

Prepare a statement showing the pro-ration of the selling and distribution costs of Territory 1 to the classes of customers. Indicate the base or bases on which you made each pro-ration.

70. A company is supplying its products to the ultimate consumers through the wholesalers to retailers. The Managing Director thinks that if they sell through the retailers or to the consumer direct, they can increase their sales, earn better prices and make profit. As a Cost Accountant of the company you are required to advise the Managing Director in selecting the channels of distribution from the following information :

Channels of distribution	I TO Consumer direct	II To Retailer direct	III To Wholesaler
Sales price per unit(Rs)	9.50	8.50	7.25
Estimated sales per year (Nos.)	6,00,000	5,70,000	5,40,000
Selling and distribution cost per unit (Rs.)	3.00	1.60	0.90
Cost of production :			
Variable cost @ Rs.4 per unit			
Fixed Cost Rs. 5,00,000			

In selecting the channels of distribution what factors besides cost would you consider?

Marketing Control

71. Following are the relevant sales data of AB Ltd. for June 19X0.

	Budget			Actual		
Product	Units	Price Rs.	Amount Rs.	Units	Price Rs.	Amount Rs.
A	100	50	5,000	120	60	7,200
B	50	120	6,000	60	110	6,600
Total	150		11,000	180		13,800

Required : A detailed analysis of Sales Variances.

72. As a part of the annual review of the year's trading, your company is studying its sales prices and costs. Your part of this work is to tabulate actual sales and selling prices and compare these with standards set at the beginning of the year. Your assistant has produced the following table:

	Standard			Actual		
Products	Quantity sold in units	Selling price (Rs.)	Revenue (Rs)	Quantity sold in units	Selling price (Rs.)	Revenue (Rs.)
Product A	900	3.20	2,880	1,000	3.20	
Product B	1,200	2.60	3,120	1,200	2.40	
Product C	400	10.00	4,000	500	12.00	

Required :

(i) Compute the value of variance of each product and analyse their causes; and

(ii) For each product, briefly outline the likely events that led to these variances.

73. The following statement is an analysis of the expected cost structure of the sales budget for the year to 31st December, 19X5.

		%
Direct Material		30
Direct Wages		26
Works Overheads :	Variable	16
	Fixed	12
Administrative and sales expenses		
	Variable	4
	Fixed	6
	Profit	6
		100

After four months, it is evident that the sales target is over optimistic and it is now estimated that the full year's sales will total Rs.6,30,000 representing 75% of the volume provided for in the budget. Calculate the Break-Even point (Value) - both as per original budget and as revised.

74. A company has five salesmen working in its Bombay branch. The following information is available in thè Branck office record for the month of December 19X0. In assessing the performance of each salesman, Branch office costs of Rs. 60,000 are apportioned as a percentage of cost of goods sold. The result of salesmen B and E are considered unsatisfactory and their discharge is recommende. Do you consider the method of apportionment equitable and support the recommendation? Prepare comparative salesmen's profit and loss statement showing contribution margin and net profit.

Salesmen	Net Sales	Cost of goods sold	Travelling expense and contingencies
	Rs.	Rs.	Rs.
A	80,000	60,000	2,800
B	1,60,000	1,48,000	2,400
C	40,000	24,000	1,600
D	1,20,000	96,000	2,000
E	80,000	72,000	2,400

75. ABC Co. Ltd, manufacture three products X,Y, and Z and sell them direct through their salesmen in three Zones — A, B, and C. The overall còntrol of distribution and sales is done centrally at head-quarters which is also resposible for sales promotion. The analysis of sales, cost of sales and selling and distribution expenses for a year are as follows :

	Sales	Selling and Distribution expenses allocated direct.
	Rs.	Rs.
Zone A : Product X	75,000	5,190
Product Y	50,000	5,300
Product Z	25,000	2,660
	1,50,000	13,150

Zone B :	Product X	1,00,000	7,110
	Product Y	1,00,000	1,685
	Product Z	50,000	5,240
		2,50,000	21,735
Zone C :	Product X	25,000	2,100
	Product Y	20,000	1,685
	Product Z	55,000	7,375
		1,00,000	11,160

Selling and distribution expenses at headquarters are as follows:

Office expenses	Rs. 10,500
Advertisement	Rs. 15,000
Other Expenses	Rs. 13,500

Advertisement costs are allocated to zones and products on the basis of sales,

The other two items of expenses are apportioned equally to the zones or the products while computing the profit or loss for the zones or the product, as the case may be.
Cost of sales are :

Product X	85% of sales
Product Y	80% of sales
Product Z	75% of sales

Tabulate the above information to present comparative profit or loss statements for each zone and for each zone and for each product and offer your recommendations.

76. Excellent Industries shows the following results for the year 19X5.

Sales	Rs. 1,000,000	100.0%
Manufacturing costs of goods sold ·	Rs. 675,000	67.5%

Selling and Advertising	220,000	22.0%
Administrative (all nonvariable)	35,000	3.5%
Total expenses	Rs. 930,000	93.0%
Net income before income taxes	70,000	7.0%

* All nonvariable, except for Rs.40,000 freight-out cost.

The sales manager has asked you to prepare statements that will help him assess the company efforts by product line and territories. You have gathered the following information.

	Product			Territory		
	A	B	C	North	Central	Eastern
*Sales**	25%	40%	35%			
				50%	20%	30%
Product A				15%	70%	15%
Product B				14/35	8/35	13/35
Variable manufacturing and packaging cost**	68%	55%	60%			

	Product			Territory		
	A	B	C	North	Central	Eastern
Non-variable						
Separate costs:						
Manufacturing	Rs. 15000	14000	21000	(Not allocated)		
Selling and Advertising	40000	18000	42000	28000	32000	40000
Freight out	(not allocated)			13000	9000	18000

* Percent of company sales

** Percent of product sales

Note : All items not directly allocated were considered joint or common costs.

Prepare a product-line income statement, showing the results for the company as a whole and the results for the three products and the three territories. Comment on the performance of each product and each territory.

77. From the following data :

(a) prepare a Working Capital requirement forecast showing component wise details.

(b) Interpret the results as per (a)

Cost & Selling price	Rs.	Projected sales during the year
Materials	7	6 lakh unit @ Rs. 20 each
Labour	3	
Overheads	5	
Cost	15	
Profit	5	
Selling price	20	

Other information :

(i) Average credit allowed 3 months

(ii) " " enjoyed 2 months

(iii) Raw materials in stores 2 months

(iv) Finished stock in stores 3 months

(v) Processing time 1 month

(vi) Lag in payment of wages 1 month

(vii) Money always to be kept in Bank for contingencies Rs.10,000 Assume uniform production and sale month to month during the year.

78. Following is the summarised Balance Sheet of Financial Management Ltd. as at 31.3.X3 and 31.3.X4.

(Figures in Rs.lakhs)

	31.3. 19X3	31.3 19X4		31.3 19X3	31.3. 19X4
Equity Share Capital (Rs. 100 each fully paid up)	20	30	Goodwill	6	4
			Other Fixed Assets	15	20
6% preference	10	10	Investments @ 6% (Nominal Value 3)	2	2
Share Premium	—	1			
Reserves and Surplus	4	10	Advertisement Suspense	3	2
10% Public Deposits (Short term)	8	6	Current Assets:		
			Stock	17	29
			Debtors	10	12
Current Liability	21	30	Bank	8	14
			Cash	2	4
	63	87		63	87

Required :

1. A Funds Flow Statement for the period 19X3-X4.

2. A short note on working capital position as at end of the two accounting years.

3. A note on profitability and financial stability of the company.

4. A critical comment on the policy pursued by the company for financing its operation during 19X3-X4.

5. A note on the working capital Management of the Company during 19X3-X4.

79. From the following information, prepare a Cash Budget by quarters for the year ending 31st December, 19X8.

As at 31.12.19X7	Rs. (000's)
Cash in hand and at the Bank	70
Stock	130
Debtors	100
Creditors	80

Budgeted Profit Statement (fig. in Rs.000's) 19X8

	Quarter			
	1st	2nd	3rd	4th
Sales	300	270	330	300
Cost of sales	204	188	220	204
Gross Profit	96	82	110	96
Administration, Selling & Distribution expenses	46	42	50	46
Net Profit	50	40	60	50

Budgeted balances at the end of each quarter :

Stock	130	150	120	130
Debtors	120	90	130	110
Creditors	100	80	110	96

Dividends amounting to Rs. 80,000 will be paid during the first quarter. Income-tax amounting to Rs.85,000 will be paid during the third quarter. Capital expenditure amounting to Rs.90,000 is expected to be incurred during the fourth quarter and will be partly financed by a further issue of debentures amounting to Rs.25,000 and the proceeds of the sale of investment Rs.10,000 (market value Rs.12,000).

Depreciation amounting to Rs.10,000 is included in the cost of sales for each quarter.

80. The Sales Manager of the Janardhan & Co. Ltd. has made the following sales estimate for the next five months :

	Rs.
January 19X8	6,00,000
February 19X8	7,00,000
March 19X8	8,00,000
April 19X8	10,00,000
May 19X8	10,00,000

The sales during the preceding 3 months were as follows ;

December 19X7	5,00,000
November 19X7	4,00,000
October 19X7	3,00,000

All sales of the company are made out on credit, 75% of Accounts receivable are collected in the month of sale, 20% the month after the sale and the remainder in the third month.

Purchase orders for materials will have to be placed one month before the desired date of delivery, along with 25% of the value as advance payment, the balance being payable within one month from the date of receipt of goods. All goods are manufactured in the month of sale and that factory wages and expenses are paid in the month in which the goods are manufactured.

Cost of goods sold (excluding depreciation) is estimated to be 75% of sales. Material cost is 20% of sales. Selling and administrative expenses are forecast as follows .

January 19X8	1,25,000
February 19X8	1,40,000
March 19X8	1,50,000
April 19X8	1,60,000

Annual depreciation is Rs.45,000

As of end of December 19X7, the company has a cash balance of Rs.80,000 and an inventory of materials of Rs.1,20,000 the minimum inventory required to be maintained being 20% of the next months estimated sales subject to a minimum of Rs.1,00,000. The minimum cash balance required is Rs.1,00,000. The company has tax liability of Rs. 1,65,000, which amount is payable in the month if March 19X8.

Under the cash-credit arrangement with its bankers, the company borrows up to 50% of the value of inventories and accounts receivables. As of December 31, 19X7 the company has the following :

	Rs.
Net Fixed assets	4,90,000
Term Loan	2,00,000
Capital	2,00,000
Reserves	1,20,000
Short term loan outstanding	60,000

An interim dividend of Rs.20,000 is payable in January. Capital expenditure scheduled for January - Rs.10,000, March - Rs.15,000 Miscellaneous income by way of rents etc. expected to be received in the month of March - Rs.5,000. An instalment of Rs.50,000 of the term loan is payable in the month of April.

Required :

(a) Prepare a cash budget for the company for the next 4 months.

(b) Prepare Proforma P & L Statement for the 4 month period and Proforma Balance Sheet as on April30, 19X8,

(c) Discuss how the financial needs of the company may be met.

D.C.F. TABLE
Table 1
Present value of Re. 1 payable or receivable at the end of each year

Future Year	4%	5%	6%	7%	8%	9%	10%	11%	12%	13%	14%	15%	16%
1	.9615	.9524	.9434	.9346	.9259	.9174	.9091	.9009	.8929	.8850	.8772	.8696	.8621
2	.9246	.9070	.8900	.8734	.8573	.8417	.8264	.8116	.7972	.7831	.7695	.7561	.7432
3	.8890	.8638	.8396	.8163	.7938	.7722	.7513	.7312	.7118	.6931	.3750	.6575	.6407
4	.8548	.8227	.7921	.7629	.7350	.7084	.6830	.6587	.6355	.6133	.5921	.5718	.5523
5	.8219	.7835	.7473	.7130	.6806	.6499	.6209	.5935	.5674	.5428	.5194	.4972	.4761
6	.7903	.7462	.7050	.6663	.6302	.5963	.5645	.5346	.5066	.4803	4556	.4323	.4104
7	.7599	.7107	.6651	.6227	.5835	.5470	.5132	.4817	.4523	.4251	3996	.3759	.3538
8	.7307	.6768	.6274	.5820	.5403	.5019	.4665	.4339	.4039	.3762	.3506	.3269	.3050
9	.7026	.6446	.5919	.5439	.5002	.4604	.4241	.3909	.3606	.3329	.3075	.2843	.2630
10	.6756	.6139	.5584	.5083	.4632	.4224	.3855	.3522	.3220	.2679	.2697	.2472	.2267
11	.6496	.5847	.5268	.4751	.4289	.3875	.3505	.3173	.2875	.2607	.2366	.2149	.1954
12	.6246	.5568	.4970	.4440	.3971	.3555	.3186	.2858	.2567	.2307	.2076	.1869	.1685
13	.6006	.5303	.4688	.4150	.3677	.3262	.2897	.2575	.2292	.2042	.1821	.1625	.1452
14	.5775	.5051	.4423	.3878	.3405	2992	.2633	.2320	.2046	.1807	.1597	.1413	.1252
15	.5533	.4810	.4173	.3624	3152	.2745	.2394	.2090	.1827	.1599	.1401	.1229	.1079
16	.5339	.4581	.3937	.3387	.2919	.2519	.2176	.1883	.1631	.1415	.1229	.1069	.0930
17	.5134	.4363	.3714	.3166	.2703	.2311	.1978	.1696	.1456	.1252	.1078	.0929	.0802
18	.4936	.4155	.3503	.2959	.2503	.2120	.1799	.1528	.1300	.1108	.0946	.0808	.0691
19	.4746	.3957	.3305	.2765	.2317	.1945	.1635	.1377	.1161	.0981	.0830	.0703	.0596
20	.4564	.3769	.3818	.2584	.2146	.1784	.1486	.1240	.1037	.0868	.0728	.0611	.0514
21	.4388	.3589	.2942	.2415	.1987	.1637	.1351	.1117	.0626	.0768	.0638	.0531	.0443
22	.4220	.3419	.2775	.2257	.1839	.1502	.1229	.1007	.0826	.0680	.0560	.0462	.0382
23	.4057	.3256	.2618	.2110	.1703	.1378	.1117	.0907	.0738	.0601	.0491	.0402	.0329
24	.3901	.3101	.2470	.1972	.1577	.1264	.1015	.0817	.0659	.0532	.0431	.0350	.0284
25	.3751	.2953	.2330	.1843	.1460	.1160	.0923	.0736	.0588	.0471	.0378	.0304	.0245

TABLE 1 (Contd.)
Present value of Re.1 payable or receivable at the end of each year

Future Years	17%	18%	19%	20%	21%	22%	23%	24%	25%	26%	27%	28%	29%	30%
1	.8547	.8475	.8403	.8333	.8264	.8197	.8130	.8065	.8000	.7937	.7874	.7813	.7752	.7692
2	.7305	.7181	.7062	.6944	.6830	.6719	.6610	.6504	.6400	.6299	.6200	.6104	.6009	.5917
3	.6244	.6089	.5934	.5787	.5645	.5507	.5374	.5245	.5120	.4999	.4882	.4768	.4658	.4552
4	.5337	.5158	.4987	.4823	.4665	.4514	.4369	.4230	.4096	.3968	.3844	.3725	.3611	.3505
5	.4561	.4371	.4190	.4019	.3855	.3700	.3552	.3411	.3277	.3149	.3027	.2910	.2799	.2693
6	.3898	.3704	.3521	.3349	.3186	.3033	.2888	.2751	.2621	.2499	.2383	.2274	.2170	.2072
7	.3332	.3139	.2959	.2791	.2633	.2486	.2348	.2218	.2097	.1983	.1877	.1776	.1682	.1594
8	.2848	.2660	.2487	.2326	.2176	.2038	.1909	.1789	.1678	.1574	.1478	1388	.1304	.1226
9	.2434	.2255	.2090	.1938	.1799	.1670	.1552	.1443	.1342	.1249	.1164	.1084	.1011	.0943
10	.2080	.1911	.1756	.1615	.1486	.1369	.1262	.1164	.1074	.0992	.0916	.0847	.0784	.0725
11	.1778	.1619	.1476	.1346	.1228	.1122	.1026	.0938	.0859	.0717	.0721	.0662	.0608	.0558
12	.1520	.1372	.1240	.1122	.1015	.0920	.0834	.0757	.0687	.0625	.0568	.0517	.0471	.0429
13	.1299	.1163	.1342	.0935	.0339	.0754	.0678	.0610	.0550	.0496	.0447	.0404	.0365	.0330
14	.1110	.0985	.0876	.0779	.0693	.0618	.0551	.0492	.0440	.0393	.0277	.0316	.0203	.0254
15	.0949	.0835	.0736	.0649	.0573	.0507	.0448	.0397	.0352	.0312	.0277	.0247	.0219	.0195
16	.0811	.0708	.0618	.0514	.0474	.0415	.0364	.0320	.0282	.0248	.0218	.0193	.0170	.0150
17	.0693	.0600	.0520	.0451	.0391	.0340	.0296	.0258	.0225	.0197	.0172	.0151	.0132	.0116
18	.0593	.0508	.0437	.0376	.0324	.0279	.0241	.0208	.0180	.0156	.0135	.0116	.0102	.0089
19	.0506	.0431	.0367	.0313	.0267	.0229	.0196	.0168	.0144	.0124	.0107	.0092	.0080	.0058
20	.0433	.0365	.0308	.0261	.0221	.0187	.0159	.0135	.0115	.0098	.0084	.0072	.0061	.0053
21	.0370	.0309	.0260	.0217	.0183	.0154	.0129	.0109	.0092	.0078	.0066	.0056	.0048	.0041
22	.0316	.0262	.0218	.0181	.0151	.0126	.0105	.0080	.0074	.0062	.0052	.0044	.0037	.0031
23	.0270	.0222	.0183	.0151	.0125	.0103	.0086	.0071	.0059	.0049	.0041	.0034	.0029	.0024
24	.0231	.0188	.0154	.0126	.0103	.0085	.0070	.0057	.0047	.0039	.0032	.0027	.0022	.0018
25	.0197	.0160	.0129	.0105	.0085	.0069	.0057	.0046	.0038	.0031	.0025	.0021	.0017	.0014

TABLE 2

Present value of Re.1 payable or receivable annually for N.years

Year	1%	2%	3%	4%	5%	6%	7%	8%	9%	10%	Year
1	0.9901	0.9804	0.9709	0.9615	0.9524	0.9434	0.9346	0.9259	0.9174	0.9091	1
2	1.9704	1.9416	1.9135	1.8861	1.8594	1.8334	1.8080	1.7833	1.7591	1.7355	2
3	2.9410	2.8839	2.8286	2.7751	2.7237	2.6730	2.3243	2.5771	2.5313	2.4868	3
4	3.9020	3.8077	3.7171	3.6299	3.5459	3.4651	3.3872	3.3121	3.2397	3.7908	4
5	4.8535	4.7134	4.5797	4.4518	4.3295	4.2123	4.1002	3.9927	3.8896	3.7908	5
6	5.7955	5.6014	5.4172	5.2421	5.0757	4.9173	4.7665	4.6229	4.4859	4.3553	6
7	6.7282	6.4720	6.2302	6.0020	5.7863	5.5824	5.3893	5.2064	5.0329	4.8985	7
8	7.6517	7.3254	7.0196	6.7327	6.4632	6.2098	5.9713	5.7466	5.5348	5.5349	8
9	8.5661	8.1622	7.7861	7.4353	7.1078	6.8017	6.5152	6.2469	5.9852	5.7590	9
10	9.4715	8.9825	8.5302	8.1109	7.7217	7.3601	7.0236	6.7101	6.4176	6.1446	10
11	10.3677	9.7868	9.2526	8.7604	8.3064	7.8868	7.4987	7.1389	6.8052	6.4951	11
12	11.2552	10.5753	9.9539	9.3850	1.8632	8.3838	7.9427	7.5261	7.1607	6.8137	12
13	12.1338	11.3483	10.6349	9.9856	9.3935	8.8527	8.3576	7.9038	7.4869	7.1034	13
14	13.0038	12.1062	11.2960	10.5631	9.8006	9.5220	8.7454	8.2442	7.7861	7.3667	14
15	13.8651	12.8492	11.9379	11.1183	10.3796	9.7122	9.1079	8.5595	8.0607	7.6061	15
16	14.7180	13.5777	12.5610	11.6522	10.8377	10.1059	9.4466	8.8514	8.3125	7.8237	16
17	15.5624	14.2918	13.1660	12.1656	11.2740	10.4772	9.7632	9.1216	8.5436	8.0215	17
18	16.3984	14.2920	13.7534	12.6592	11.6895	10.8276	10.0591	9.3719	8.7556	8.2014	18
19	17.2261	15.6784	14.3237	13.1339	12.0853	11.1581	10.3356	9.3719	8.7556	8.2014	19
20	18.0457	16.3514	14.8774	13.5903	12.4622	11.4699	10.5940	9.8181	9.1285	8.5136	20
21	18.8571	17.0111	15.4149	14.0291	12.8211	11.7640	10.8355	10.0168	9.2922	8.6487	21
22	19.6605	17.6580	15.9368	14.4511	13.1630	12.0416	11.0616	10.2007	9.4424	8.7715	22
23	20.4559	18.2921	16.4435	14.8568	13.4885	12.3033	11.2722	10.3710	9.5802	8.8832	23
24	21.2435	18.9139	16.9355	15.2469	13.7986	12.5503	11.4693	10.5287	9.7066	8.9847	24
25	22.0233	19.5234	17.4131	15.6220	14.0939	12.7833	11.6536	10.6748	9.8226	9.0770	25

TABLE 2 (Contd.,)

Present value of Re.1 payable or receivable annually for N.years

Year	11%	12%	13%	14%	15%	16%	17%	18%	19%	20%	Year
1	0.9009	0.8929	0.8850	0.8772	0.8621	0.8621	0.8547	0.8475	0.8403	0.8333	1
2	1.7125	1.6901	1.6681	1.6467	1.6257	1.6052	1.5852	1.5656	1.5465	1.5278	2
3	2.4487	2.4018	2.3612	2.3216	2.2832	2.2459	2.2096	2.1743	2.1399	2.1065	3
4	3.1024	3.0373	2.9745	2.9137	2.8550	2.7982	2.7432	2.6901	2.6386	2.5887	4
5	3.6959	3.6048	3.5172	3.4331	3.3522	3.2743	3.1993	3.1272	3.0576	2.9906	5
6	4.2305	4.1114	3.9976	3.8878	3.7845	3.6847	3.5892	3.4976	3.4098	3.3255	6
7	4.7122	4.5638	4.4226	4.2883	4.1604	4.0386	3.9224	3.8115	3.7057	3.6046	7
8	5.1461	4.9676	4.7988	4.6389	4.4873	4.3486	4.2072	4.0776	3.9544	3.8372	8
9	5.5370	5.3282	5.1217	4.9464	4.7716	4.6065	4.4506	4.3030	4.1633	4.0310	9
10	5.8892	5.6502	5.4262	5.2161	5.0188	4.8332	4.[illegible]586	4.4941	4.3889	4.1925	10
11	6.2065	5.9377	5.6869	5.4527	5.2337	5.0286	4.8364	4.65[illegible]0	4.4865	4.3271	11
12	6.4924	6.1944	5.9176	5.6606	5.4206	5.1971	4.9884	4.7932	4.6105	4.4392	12
13	6.7499	6.4235	6.1218	5.8424	5.5831	5.3423	5.1183	4.9495	4.7147	4.5327	13
14	6.9819	6.6282	6.3025	6.0021	5.7245	5.4675	5.2293	5.0081	4.8023	4.6106	14
15	7.1909	6.8109	6.4624	6.1422	5.8474	5.5755	5.3242	5.0916	4.8759	4.6755	15
16	7.3792	6.9740	6.6039	6.2651	5.9542	5.6685	5.4053	5.1624	4.9377	4.7296	16
17	7.5488	7.1196	6.7291	6.3729	6.0472	5.7486	5.4746	5.2223	4.9897	4.7746	17
18	7.7016	7.2497	6.8399	6.4674	6.1280	5.8178	5.5339	5.2732	5.0333	4.8122	18
19	7.8293	7.3658	6.9380	6.5504	6.1982	5.8775	5.5845	5.3162	5.0700	4.8435	19
20	7.9633	7.4694	7.0248	6.6231	6.2593	5.9288	5.6278	5.3527	5.1009	4.8696	20
21	8.0751	7.5620	7.1016	6.6870	6.3125	5.9731	5.6648	5.3837	5.1268	4.8913	21
22	8.1757	7.6446	7.1695	6.7429	6.3587	6.0113	5.6964	5.4099	5.1486	4.9091	22
23	8.2664	7.7184	7.2297	6.7921	6.3988	6.0442	5.7234	5.4321	5.1668	4.9245	23
24	8.3481	7.7843	7.2829	6.8351	6.4338	6.0726	5.7465	5.4509	5.1822	4.9371	24
25	8.4217	7.8431	7.3300	6.8729	6.4641	6.0971	5.7662	5.4669	5.1951	4.9476	25

TABLE 2 (CONTD.)

Present value of Re.1 payable or receivable annually for N.years

Year	21%	22%	23%	24%	25%	26%	27%	28%	29%	30%	year
1	0.9009	0.8929	0.8850	0.8772	0.8696	0.7937	0.7874	0.7813	0.7752	0.7692	1
2	1.5095	1.4915	1.4740	1.4568	1.4400	1.4235	1.4074	1.3916	1.3761	1.3069	2
3	2.0739	0.0422	2.0114	1.9813	1.9520	1.9234	1.8956	1.8684	1.8420	1.8161	3
4	2.5404	2.4936	2.4483	2.4043	2.3616	2.3202	2.2800	2.2410	2.4830	2.1662	4
5	2.9260	2.8636	2.8035	2.7454	2.6893	2.6351	2.5827	2.5320	2.4830	2.4356	5
6	3.2446	3.1669	3.0923	3.0205	2.9514	2.8850	2.8210	7.2594	2.7000	2.6427	6
7	3.5079	3.4155	3.3270	3.2423	3.1611	3.0833	3.0087	2.9370	2.8682	2.8081	7
8	3.7256	3.6193	3.5179	3.4212	3.3289	3.2407	3.1564	3.0758	2.9982	2.9247	8
9	3.9054	3.7863	3.6731	3.5655	3.4631	3.3657	3.2728	3.1842	3.0997	3.0190	9
10	4.0541	3.9232	3.7993	3.6819	3.5705	3.4648	3.36443	3.2689	3.1781	3.0190	10
11	4.1769	4.0354	3.9013	3.7757	3.6564	3.5453	3.4365	3.3351	3.2388	3.1473	11
12.	4.2785	4.1274	3.9852	3.8514	3.7251	3.6060	3.4933	3.3868	3.2859	3.1903	12
13	4.3624	4.2028	4.0530	3.9124	3.7801	5.3423	5.1183	4.9095	4.7147	4.5327	13
14	4.4317	4.2646	4.1082	3.9616	3.8242	3.6949	3.5733	3.4587	3.3507	3.2487	14
15	4.4890	4.3152	4.1530	4.0013	3.8593	3.7291	3.6010	3.6010	3.4834	3.2682	15
16	4.5364	4.3567	4.1894	4.0333	3.8874	3.7509	3.6228	3.5026	3.3896	3.2832	16
17	4.5755	4.3908	4.2190	4.0591	4.9099	3.7705	3.6228	3.5177	3.4028	3.2948	17
18	4.6079	4.4187	4.2431	4.0799	3.9279	3.7861	3.6536	3.5294	3.4130	3.3037	18
19	4.6346	4.4415	4.2627	4.0967	3.9424	3.7985	3.6642	3.5386	3.4210	3.3105	19
20	4.6467	4.4603	4.2786	4.1103	3.9539	3.8083	3.6726	3.5458	3.4271	3.3158	20
21	4.6750	4.4756	4.2916	4.1212	3.9631	3.8161	3.6792	3.5514	3.4319	3.3198	21
22	4.6900	4.4882	4.3021	4.1300	3.9705	3.8223	3.6844	3.5558	2.4356	3.3230	22
23	4.0725	4.4985	4.3106	4.1371	3.9764	3.8273	3.6885	3.5592	3.4384	3.3274	23
24	4.7128	4.5070	4.3176	4.1428	3.9811	3.8312	3.6918	3.5619	3.4406	3.3274	24
25	4.7213	4.5139	4.3232	4.1474	3.9849	3.8342	3.6943	3.5640	3.4423	3.3286	25

SUGGESTED READING

1. Anthony, R.N. : Management Accounting Principles (R.Irwin)
2. Anthony, R.N. : Planning & Control System : A Framework for Analysis (R.Irwin)
3. Anthony, R.N. : Management Control Systems Cases and Reading (R.Irwin).
4. B.I.M. : Interfirm Comparison (B.I.M. London).
5. Banerjee, B. : Cost Accounting (World Press).
6. Bell, M.I. : Marketing Concepts and Strategy (Macmillan).
7. Beyer, Robert : Profitability Accounting for Planning and Control (Ronald Press).
8. Buel, Victor : Marketing Management in Action.
9. Chakraborty, H. : Advanced Accountancy (World Press)
10. Chakraborty, S.K. : Management by Objectivess-Integrated Approach (Macmillan).
11. Chatterjee, B.K. : Accounting & Finance for Managers (Jaico).
12. Chatterjee, B.k. : Marketing Management Concepts & Stretegies (Jaico).
13. Carbin, Arnold : Implementing the Marketing Concept (B.I.M.)
14. David K.R. etc : Sales Force Management (Ronald Press).
15. Dearden, J. : Computers in Business Management (Taraporewala)
16. Druker : Managing for Results.
17. Driuker : The Practice of Management.
18. Gopalkrishnan : Spare Parts Management (Jaico).
19. Hansen, H.L. : Marketing Text, Techniques and Cases (R.Irwin)
20. Helfert E.A. : Techniques of Financial Analysis (Jaico).
21. Horne, Van : Financial Management and Policy.
22. Horngren, C.T.: Cost Accounting : A Managerial Emphasis. (P.H)
23. Howard : Working Capital.
24. Hunt, etc. : Basic Business Finance (Irwin)

25. CIMA : Selling and Distribution Cost Analysis (Gee & Co.).
26. CIMA : Report on Marginal Costing (Gee & CO.).
27. CIMA : Profitable use of Capital in Industry (Gee & Co.).
28. CIMA : Investment Appraisal, Evaluating Risk and Uncertainty (Gee & Co.).
29. CIMA : Cost Reduction (Gee & Co.).
30. CIMA : Accounting under Changing Price Level (Gee & Co.).
31. CIMA : Presenting of Information to Management (Gee & CO.).
32. ICWA : The Break Even Concept and its Practical Dimensions (ICWA India).
33. ILO (Geneva) : How to Read a Balance Sheet (ILO).
34. King. W.R. : The Quantitative Analysis for Marketing Management.
35. Kotler, Philip : Marketing Management — Analysis, Planning & Control.
36. Levitt, Theodore : The Marketing Mode.
37. Matz, etc. : Cost Accounting.
38. Miles, I.R. : Techniques of Value Analysis and Engineering.
39. Murthy, V.S. (Edited) : Marketing Finance & Evaluation (Bombay University).
40. Murthy, V.S. : Management Finance (Vakils, Feffer & Simons).
41. Murthy, V.S. : Reading in Marketing Planning & Operations Research (Bombay University).
42. Murdick & Ross : Information Systems for Modern Management (Prentice Hall).
43. Prodhan B. : The Board and Financial Management (Business Books)
44. Rose : Management Audit (Pitman).
45. Sasieni, etc. : operations Research : Methods & Problems.
46. Schaffler & Trentin : Marketing Information System.
47. Shukla & Grewal : Advanced Accountancy (S.Chand & Co.)
48. Sizer John : Perspectives in Management Accounting (CIMA - Heinemann).

49. Soudy : Economics of Distribution.
50. Standton & Buskirk : Management of the Sales Force (Irwin).
51. Thomas : Readings in Cost Accounting, Budgeting and Control (Taraporewala).
52. Tonning, W.A. : How to Measure and Evaluate Salesmen's Performance.
53. Wheldon's Cost Accounting and Costing Methods (Macdonald Evans).
54. Wilson, R.M.S. : Management Controls and Marketing Planning (Heinemann).
55. Williamson R.J. : Marketing For Accountants and Managers (CI-MA — Allied Publishes).
56. Wright : Discounted Cash Flow.